Writing with Scissors

Writing with Scissors

American Scrapbooks from the Civil War to the Harlem Renaissance

ELLEN GRUBER GARVEY

OXFORD
UNIVERSITY PRESS

OXFORD
UNIVERSITY PRESS

Oxford University Press is a department of the
University of Oxford. It furthers the University's objective
of excellence in research, scholarship, and education
by publishing worldwide.

Oxford   New York

Auckland   Cape Town   Dar es Salaam   Hong Kong   Karachi
Kuala Lumpur   Madrid   Melbourne   Mexico City   Nairobi
New Delhi   Shanghai   Taipei   Toronto

With offices in

Argentina   Austria   Brazil   Chile   Czech Republic   France   Greece
Guatemala   Hungary   Italy   Japan   Poland   Portugal   Singapore
South Korea   Switzerland   Thailand   Turkey   Ukraine   Vietnam

Oxford is a registered trade mark of Oxford University Press
in the UK and certain other countries.

Published in the United States of America by
Oxford University Press
198 Madison Avenue, New York, NY 10016

Garvey, Ellen Gruber.
Writing with scissors : American scrapbooks from the Civil War to the
Harlem renaissance / Ellen Gruber Garvey.
   p.   cm.
Includes index.

ISBN 978-0-19-539034-6 (hardback)
ISBN 978-0-19-992769-2 (paperback)

1. Scrapbooking—United States—History.
2. Cut-out craft—United States—History.
3. United States—Social life and customs.
4. United States—History—Sources.   I. Title.
TT870.G34 2012   745.5938—dc23   2012005221

1 3 5 7 9 8 6 4 2

Printed in the United States of America
on acid-free paper

CONTENTS

ACKNOWLEDGMENTS

This book has been so long in moving from scrappy beginnings to completion that nearly everyone I know has helped me in some way. I am especially grateful to many who have generously contributed to it, through critiques, challenges, and wanting to hear more. The book's faults are my own, but its virtues are the product of many hands and brains.

In the final stages of the project, Barbara Hochman and Susan K. Harris read through the manuscript and were always ready to comment on revisions whether through ongoing meetings or transglobal emails.

Smart and perceptive readers who commented on individual chapters provided a generous balance of criticism and support: Jane Anderson, Megan Benton, Robin Bernstein, Leah Dilworth, Roger Gilbert, Lisa Gitelman, Edi Giunta, Janet Golden, Kathy Jones, Elizabeth Long, Carla Peterson, Rochelle Ruthchild, Karen Sánchez-Eppler, Alison Scott, Alexandra Wettlaufer, Wayne Wiegand, Sarah Wilburn, Heather Andrea Williams, Sandy Zagarell, and Laura Zimmerman. Sarah Swartz's good advice gave me courage to do what was needed. I am grateful to all for their help.

Without funding and, crucially, *time* provided by the following institutions, this book would not exist. A National Endowment for the Humanities fellowship at the Massachusetts Historical Society allowed me to begin to see scrapbooks' role in people's Civil War newspaper reading, and to discover the work of Henry Ingersoll Bowditch and his relatives, and Caroline Healey Dall, among others. Peter Drummey's vast knowledge of MHS's collections was indispensable. Conrad Wright and Melissa Pino created a sense of connection between fellows with disparate interests. The attentiveness and collegiality of MHS's library, collections, and other staff made research a pleasure. Anne Bentley, Jennifer Sennott Caldelari, Rakashi Chand, Mary Fabiszewski, William Fowler, Megan Friedel, Brenda M. Lawson, Ondine E. Le Blanc, Kim Nusco, Aimée Primeaux, and Donald Yacovone all aided immeasurably in the experience of trying to make sense of the many puzzling items encountered.

A year at the National Humanities Center in North Carolina provided time, extraordinarily supportive facilities, collegial conversation, and the encouraging hum of other scholars working nearby, as well as the chance to explore scrapbooks at the University of North Carolina and Duke University. I am grateful to the Research Triangle Foundation, which endowed the Josephus Daniels Fellowship in honor of the University of North Carolina, which I held. The NHC staff were generous with their time and care. Josiah Drewry, Jean Houston, and Eliza Robertson tirelessly hunted down obscure books and articles. Thanks to Joshua Bond, Sue Boyd, Marie Brubaker, Karen Carroll, Joel Elliott, James Getkin, Sarah Payne, Pat Schreiber, Don Solomon, Marianne Wason, and Lois P. Whittington for so many instances of kind and attentive assistance and friendly company. Thanks to Geoffrey Harpham and Kent Mulliken for keeping the NHC going.

A We the People fellowship from the National Endowment for the Humanities was essential in allowing me to complete the book. I thank the anonymous reviewers and the staff of that vital institution for their faith in this project.

An appointment as a visiting scholar at New York University offered access to needed resources. A short-term fellowship at the American Antiquarian Society provided the chance to rummage in its unparalleled collections under the knowledgeable guidance and with the collegial conversation of Georgia Barnhill, Diann Benti, Ellen Dunlap, Paul Erickson, John Hench, Lauren B. Hewes, John M. Keenum, Thomas Knoles, Marie E. Lamoureux, Caroline Sloat, Laura E. Wasowicz, and S. J. Wolfe.

Released time from New Jersey City University for parts of this project reduced my teaching load for several semesters. Special thanks to my English Department colleagues for their patience in working out schedules so that I could accept fellowships, with particular gratitude to Hilary Englert and Irma Maini, chairs. I am especially indebted and grateful to Joanne Bruno, vice president for academic affairs, for ensuring that I could take the fellowships I was granted, and for doing so much to facilitate the completion of this book. I thank as well Dean Barbara Feldman.

Early on, an NEH summer seminar at the Boston Athenaeum under the direction of Richard Wendorf stimulated thought, conversations, and new understanding of the relation of the verbal and the visual content of scrapbooks. Participating in the Recycle Seminar at Duke University's John Hope Franklin Center contributed another layer of stimulating discussions. I am particularly grateful to Christina Chia at the Franklin Center for her continuing assistance. I wish to express my appreciation to the Warner Fund at the University Seminars at Columbia University for their help in publication. Material in this work was presented to the University Seminars Women and Society, and American Studies. Participating, too, offered years of fruitful exchange and support.

Collegial exchange of ideas is one of the great pleasures of scholarship. Parts of this book began as papers or presentations. Invitations to speak or write supplied both salutary deadlines and audiences whose sharp and thoughtful questions and encouraging comments enriched the book immeasurably. In addition to panel presentations at the American Literature Association, the American Studies Association, the International Conference on the History of Records and Archives, the Modern Language Association, the Society for the History of Authorship, Reading and Publishing, and the Society for the Study of American Women Writers, I am particularly grateful to these individuals and colloquia for invitations to present work: Peter Stallybrass, at the History of Material Texts Seminar, University of Pennsylvania; Daniela Bleichmar and Deborah Harkness of the History of the Book Roundtable, University of Southern California, at the Huntington Museum and Library; Priscilla Wald of the Americanist Speaker Series, Duke University; Glenn Handler, of the American Studies seminar at Columbia University; Julia Ballerini and Page Delano, Women and Society Seminar, Columbia University; Meredith McGill and Marja Dalbello of the Book History Seminar, Rutgers University, New Brunswick; Claire Parfait, for both the seminar of Le livre et l'édition dans le monde anglophone, Paris 7 University and the Authors, Publishers, Translators, and Issues of International Copyright in the Nineteenth Century conference, CRIDAF, Université Paris 13; Leah Price and Ann Blair of the Harvard Seminar in the History of the Book; the invitation to deliver the Brownell Lecture on the History of the Book at the University of Iowa's Iowa Center for the Book; Barbara Hochman, for both the Once and Future Book: Reconsidering Books and Reading in an Electronic Age international symposium and the Literature, Book History and the Anxiety of Disciplinarity workshop, Ben Gurion University; and Patricia Crain, of the Workshop in Archival Practice, New York University.

The nature of this project meant that I was less often looking for a specific item, and more often for types and genres of material. I am indebted to archivists and librarians around the country who alerted me to materials I would not have otherwise found and then brought out hidden treasures. I want to thank the staffs of all those libraries, especially Neda Salem and David Kessler at the Bancroft Library of the University of California at Berkeley; Stephen Nonack of the Boston Athenaeum; Dale Rosengarten, Special Collections, Addlestone Library, College of Charleston, South Carolina; Jean Ashton and Susan Hamson at Columbia University's Rare Book and Manuscript Division; Janice Ruth, Clark Evans, Eleanor H. McConnell, and Rosemary Fry Plakas at the Library of Congress; L. Rebecca Johnson Melvin of Special Collections University of Delaware; Elizabeth B. Dunn and Diana Michelle Belden of the Rare Book, Manuscript, and Special Collections Library, Duke University; Joellen ElBashir at the Moorland-Spingarn Research Center, Howard University; Cathy Cherbosque and Susi Krasnoo at the Huntington Library, San Marino, California; Jim Green and Cornelia S. King of the Library Company of Philadelphia; Matthew Turi and Mike Millner of the Wilson Library Special Collections, University of North Carolina at Chapel Hill; Kathy Jans-Duffy at the Seneca Falls Historical Society; Nicholas Ricketts at the Strong Museum in Rochester, New York; and the staff at the following institutions: African American Historical Society, Boston; Special Collections at Cheyney

University, Pennsylvania; Archives and Special Collections, University of Nebraska-Lincoln libraries; Schlesinger Library at Radcliffe; Sophia Smith Collection; the Houghton Library at Harvard; and many more. Librarians and archivists are the silent heroes of this project; scrapbooks are democratic archives, and we are indebted to the librarians and archivists who took them seriously.

Friends and colleagues who have given me the benefit of their learning, counsel, and encouragement and enriched my life in many ways include Janice Radway, Joan Shelley Rubin, Barbara Sicherman, Sandy Zagarell, and John and Joy Kasson. Others not previously named whose web of ongoing conversation this book ties into include Anna Mae Duane, Linda Grasso, Ezra Greenspan, Kim Hall, June Howard, Kathleen Hulser, Laura Korobkin, Lisa Merrill, Michael Penn, Erin Smith, Priscilla Wald, Sarah Willburn, and Paul Wright.

Through exchanges on our shared interest in scrapbooks, I have learned from Katherine Ott, Sarah Robins, Helen Sheumaker, Nichole Tonkovitch, and Susan Tucker. Colleagues who joined the long tradition of clipping from their reading to send me notes and references from their own reading or who passed along information in other forms, answered queries, educated on the materials I'd found, and guided me away from wrong paths include Hosie Baskin, Joshua Brown, Mary Chapman, Helen Deese, Paul Erickson, Eric Gardner, Jacqueline Goldsby, Bob Gross, Jaime Harker, Melissa Homestead, Leon Jackson, Roger Lane, Tan Lin, Reginald Pitts, Karen Schiff, Nomi Sofer, Amy Thomas, and Ronald and Mary Saracino Zboray.

Lydia Buechler, Frances Goldin, Steve Messina, and Jeanne Pfaelzer were generous with advice on publishing. At Oxford University Press, I am grateful for the attention this book has received from Brendan O'Neill and Lora Friedenthal.

I have benefited from the support of so many good friends who have offered encouragement, meals, and good company on the journey. I am thankful to have in my life Ilana Abramovitch, Joel and Susan Agee, Sally Bellerose, Ethan Bumas, Cathy Cockrell, Jacqueline Ellis, Donna Farina, Sue Finkelstein, Audrey Fisch, Julie Freestone, Vicki Gabriner, Janet Gallagher, Myra Goldberg, Sarah Gruber, Mina Hamilton, Sally Heckel, Ellie Kellman, Paul Lauter, Ellen Lippmann, Barbara Lipski, Charles Lynch, Catherine Raissiguier, Ellie Siegel, Renata Singer, Nancy Stiefel and Arthur Strimling, all of whom have contributed to this book, whether they know it or not.

Finally, I want to thank my partner, Joyce Ravitz, for listening, and for joy.

Writing with Scissors

Introduction

Book, Paper, Scissors: An Introduction to Nineteenth-Century Scrapbooks

Around 1870, Frances A. Smith began a scrapbook of newspaper clippings of remedies and recipes that any farmwoman might want. The information she pasted down pours forth in a largely unsorted torrent: cows next to curing scaly rashes in children, next to lightning rods and an admired poem, and then recommendations from Mr. John Hill of Hernico County, Virginia, of very reliable remedies for Foot-rot and Scab, in sheep. When I first read this scrapbook in a Nebraska archive, I assumed that Smith was a farmwoman, saving useful information for her work raising her children and animals. Instead, I discovered she was an unmarried Mount Holyoke graduate teaching school in the East when she started this scrapbook, and only later did she marry, move west, and become Willa Cather's "Aunt Franc." Her scrapbook embodied her aspirations. It saved up articles she thought she might need in her future homesteading life, and it made them a good deal more portable than the stacks of newspapers she had combed to find them. Writing her scrapbook with scissors let her send provisions ahead to her future self by bringing the community of helpful commentators from Eastern newspapers into an imagined future where she would need to know about sheep diseases, provide herself with poems she might otherwise not see again. It allowed her to dignify her clippings with the prestige of a bound book.[1]

Frances Smith Cather, like the other readers I discuss in this book, saw a constant stream of valuable information that had cost her almost nothing appear before her. Here we can see the seeds of our own twenty-first-century struggles with information overload. Like present-day users of the web, blogs, Facebook, and Twitter, these readers complained that there was so much to read that they were constantly distracted. Nineteenth-century readers felt inundated by printed matter, as cheap newspapers proliferated and took on increasing importance. As one newspaper explained in 1883, newspapers "contain so many fine sentiments, beautiful descriptions, touching incidents, items of importance, and matters of permanent interest culled from all departments of life," that it was hard to preserve all these valuable items. Newspapers constituted a new category of media: cheap, disposable, and yet somehow tantalizingly valuable, if only their value could be separated from their ephemerality. How to keep up with all that information, assess it, and find it again when needed? Just as present-day readers manage digital abundance with favorites lists, bookmarks, blogrolls, RSS feeds, and content aggregators, nineteenth-century readers channeled the flood of information with scrapbooks.[2]

In the second half of the nineteenth century, goods and messages traveled at unprecedented speed and volume across the growing country, spreading information in ways that made news central to economic and political life. National news entered into conversation and fueled ordinary social interaction. During the Civil War, people realized how much they wanted to hear news quickly.

Two momentous developments of the nineteenth century—the changes in African American life, from slavery to post-Reconstruction struggles, and ferment around women's rights—appeared in a daily press whose owners were neither African American nor women. But both women's rights activists and African Americans clipped from those newspapers. They collected, concentrated, and critiqued accounts from a press that they did not own, to tell their own stories in books they wrote with scissors.

Newspaper clipping scrapbooks allowed readers to save, manage, and reprocess information. Thousands of people made such scrapbooks: statesmen such as Abraham Lincoln, Frederick Douglass, and Charles Sumner; writers such as Mark Twain, Horatio Alger, Winnifred Eaton (Onoto Watanna), Lydia Maria Child, and Jack London; and actors such as Sarah Bernhardt, Anna Dickinson, Edwin Forrest, and Elizabeth Robins.

Writing with Scissors: American Scrapbooks from the Civil War to the Harlem Renaissance probes not only the scrapbooks of public figures but also how people in positions of relative powerlessness used their scrapbooks to make a place for themselves and their communities by finding, sifting, analyzing, and recirculating writing that mattered to them. Such scrapbooks open a window into the lives and thoughts of people who did not respond to their world with their own writing. As they saved printed matter and arranged it in ways that expressed their own ideas, they created value from their reading for themselves and their communities. Such private but widespread reworking of the mass-produced press in scrapbooks shows how national and world events entered into people's understanding and feelings—how Americans on both sides of the Civil War, for example, used the newspaper to make emotional sense of the war, and to shape their new relationships to the nation. Scrapbook makers' work mirrored the practices of newspaper editors, who continually clipped and recirculated material, so that a single article in a local paper potentially reached millions of readers throughout the country. In an era when originality was not always valued, the same item could circulate around the press, into the home circle via the scrapbook, and sometimes even out into the press again.

In a sense, newspaper clipping scrapbooks were simply filing systems. But because the clippings were fixed in place, they have left us a record of how people read and grappled with what they read. Their approaches show, too, the power and limitations of recirculating materials (Figure Intro.1).

About an hour later Ben and Silas entered the cabin, where they found Jack and his mother sitting side by side near the fireplace, he holding her dear old hands in his big ones, while her motherly face beamed with perfect happiness.

"This is my Jack," she said proudly, by way of introduction, to Silas.

"Yer my own brother, Silas Carrick," he cried, grasping Silas' hand; "after all yer've done fur my mother I couldn't never call yer aught else. Besides, I'm in need of an own brother. I hain't got none," he said, with a supreme contempt that utterly ignored the relationship of Peter Tompkins.

As Silas Carrick returned the pressure of Jack's hand and looked into the clear blue eyes, that revealed a kindly nature, he felt satisfied that the mother would never lack for love and truest attention from her Jack.

"A feller never gits too old ter need mother," he said; "an' I kain't begin ter speak my obligations ter Providence fur bein' so good in bringin' mother safe ter me. I want ter just git Peter Tompkins out o' my head, an' think only o' good things an' good folks, as'll help me ter be the better man I'm aimin' ter make o' myself. I was awful down spirited like, but now my Thanksgivin's runnin' over!"

"An' so be mine!" cried Jack's mother. "The Lord has restored me ter complete happiness, after all my trouble, with my Jack on this blessed Thanksgivin'."—A. H. Gibson, in New York Observer.

AN EASTER CAROL.

Easter Day, Easter Day,
Sing, O children, while you may,
As the angels sing who love you,
As the birds sing high above you,
  On this heavenly day.
For the birds know spring is nearer,
And the angels, heaven is dearer,
While the singing children say,
"Jesus lives, and lives alway."

Easter Day, Easter Day,
Do not linger where He lay
From the loving and the scorning,
Till this glorious, golden morning,
  Hidden awhile away.
That the darkness may not hide us,
Nor the long, green sods divide us,
When we're tired of work and play,
From this Jesus, risen to-day.

Easter Day, Easter Day,
Ah! the dawn was cold and gray,
But the King in beauty waking,
All His sad old earth is breaking
  Into hope of May.
And the children sing forever,
Knowing death nor life can sever
Love from love—they sing and say,
"Jesus lives and lives alway."

...s for Using Books.

...er hold a book near a fire.
...ever drop a book upon the floor.
Never turn leaves with the thumb.
Never lean or rest upon an open book.
Never turn down the corners of leaves.
Never touch a book with damp or soiled hands.
Always keep your place with a thin book-mark.
Always place a large book upon a table before opening it.
Always turn leaves from the top with the middle or forefinger.
Never pull a book from a shelf by the binding at the top, but by the back.
Never touch a book with a damp cloth nor with a sponge in any form.
Never place another book or anything else upon the leaves of an open book.
Never rub dust from books, but brush it off with a soft, dry cloth or duster.
Never close a book with a pencil, a pad of paper, or anything else between the leaves.
Never open a book farther than to bring both sides of the cover into the same plane.
Always open a large book from the middle, and never from the ends or cover.
To avoid injuring the leaves of books, never put a pencil mark in a library book.
Always keep books out of the reach of small children, and in a clean dry place.
Always keep any neatly-bound borrowed book covered with paper while in your possession.
Never attempt to dry a book, accidentally wet, by a fire, but wipe off the moisture with a soft, dry cloth.
Never write upon a paper laid upon the leaves of an open book, as the pencil or pen point will either scratch or cut the book leaves.
Never lend a borrowed book, but return it as soon as you are through with it, so that the owner may not be deprived of its use.

Never cut the leaves of a book or magazine with a sharp knife, as the edge is sure to run into the print, nor with the finger, but with a paper-cutter or ordinary table knife.
Never hold a small book with the thumb pressed into the binding at the lower back, but hold it with the thumb and little finger upon the leaves and three fingers upon back.

THE LITTLE FLOWER.

BY GERALD MASSEY.

A little flower so lonely grew,
  So lonely was it left,
That heaven looked like an eye of blue
  Down in its rocky cleft.

What could the little flower do
  In such a darksome place,
But try to reach that eye of blue,
  And climb to kiss heaven's face?

And there's no life so lone and low
  But strength may still be given,
From narrowest lot on earth to grow
  The straighter up to heaven.

Figure Intro.1 Page from Baxter scrapbook, a typical newspaper clipping scrapbook of stories, poetry, and advice containing a list of rules for care of books. (Author's collection)

Nineteenth-Century News and Newspapers

The late nineteenth century was a time of tremendous changes. Enslaved African Americans became free and gained some political power, but they were attacked and disenfranchised by the end of the century. Women entered into public life, speaking in public, organizing for causes such as married women's right to legal ownership of their own property, and campaigning for the right to vote (not obtained until 1920). Great waves of immigrants arrived, and immigrants and native-born people left friends and families behind and moved westward, displacing native peoples. The growth of free public schooling led to increased literacy. Scientific discoveries and technology changed the look and sound of the country—the U.S. Patent Office issued thick volumes recording the many new inventions—and telegraphs and railroads linked the nation. All these developments made their way into newspapers with growing readerships, who often clipped items for their scrapbooks.

Newspapers and magazines multiplied overwhelmingly. Newspaper prices dropped as new printing and paper manufacturing technologies made publication cheaper, and newspapers moved to profiting from advertising sales rather than relying solely on revenue from selling copies. The first one-cent paper appeared in the United States in 1833, and other cheap papers followed. With low prices came high circulation: aggregate circulation of the nation's dailies was close to a million in 1860.[3]

During the Civil War, the telegraph made newspapers the fastest way to learn of events of the war, while newspapers connected home and field through the imagined community of newspaper readers—readers who felt connected to one another and to the nation through their awareness of others reading the same newspaper at the same time. The imagined community of readers convened in the flesh to hear war news read aloud to crowds, from newspapers posted on the streets. Newspaper reading became a habit, as readers eagerly sought news of their friends and family on the battlefield, as in Thomas Nast's 1864 engraving "The Press on the Field" (Figure Intro.2). Sketch artists at the front sent back drawings that newspapers engraved and printed, along with maps. Although men continued to read newspapers in barber shops and saloons, even by the 1830s people were more likely to own their own copy of the paper. More and more, newspaper reading became part of domestic life, and editors acknowledged that women were among their readers. Many newspaper readers began making scrapbooks during the war, saving battle accounts, political news, poetry that moved them, and evidence that their own side was winning.[4]

Newspaper reading and the quantities of printed matter grew even more dramatically after the war. Americans had greater access to cheap printed matter, and with higher literacy, more people were reading it and acquiring more pages of it. Cities often supported a dozen or more dailies, and the largest of them had half a million readers each by 1900. Even impoverished readers

Figure Intro.2 "The Press on the Field," with vignettes of "Newspapers at Home" and "The Newspapers in Camp." *Harper's Weekly*, 30 April 1864, 280-281.

received papers second- or thirdhand. Cheap weeklies and monthlies, too, flourished in the form of mail-order papers, farm papers, and story papers. In the second half of the nineteenth century, the reading of a large percentage of Americans was likely to be made up of periodicals that rapidly passed through their hands—or that stayed around: "We have so many old newspapers that we cannot afford house-room for them all," Julia Colman complained even in 1873, and the overflow grew.[5]

Newspapers contained more than battle and political news. They were full of the fragmented or "morselized" information that became particularly popular in the press of the second half of the nineteenth century. Papers provided troves of tidbits and factoids—household hints, information about word origins, geographic one-liners, and scientific or historic or agricultural items. Columns of miscellany asserted the preciousness of facts and raw information; the many scrapbook makers who saved such tidbits evinced their trust that these fragments of knowledge were important, and faith that their value would become evident in time. Some miscellany columns even carried headings such as "for the scrapbook" (Figure Intro.3). Some publications addressed a segmented or specialized readership. *Puck* magazine's 1883 futuristic fantasy of the apartment where everything is delivered (Figure Intro.4) envisions a segmented readership and listenership, with each member of an affluent family receiving his or her preferred reading matter—from *Boys' Terror* to the religious

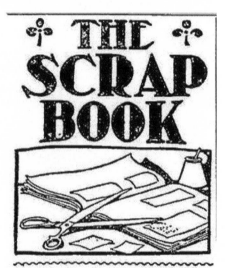

Figure Intro.3 Newspaper column heads suggesting that items in a miscellany column be clipped for the scrapbook. From the *San Jose Evening News*, 26 June 1908, 6; and the *Savannah Tribune*, an African American paper, 12 Aug 1912, 7.

IN THE PARLOR.

Figure Intro.4 The futuristic household, with media tailored to each member, 1883. (Frederick B. Opper, "The French Flat of the Near Future: Everything on the Premises," *Puck*, 17 Oct 1883, 100)

papers—individually, through slots in the walls, and prefiguring the radio by listening to their separate choices of music through telephone lines: a proto-internet. The papers spool directly into wastebaskets.[6]

All that fragmented, proliferating, disposable reading was symptomatic of the accelerating pace of life, an 1892 *Harper's Monthly* column complained: "The magazine, in a generation that must run as it reads, takes the place of the book. Must we all go to making scrap-books in order to preserve the good things that fly on the leaves of the winged press?" On an institutional scale, approaches for preserving those good things and coping with the rising tide of print included library vertical files and cataloging and classification schemes such as Melvil Dewey's decimal system for slicing topics into categories and subcategories, or the later Library of Congress Subject Headings for standardizing subject categories, allowing a work to be categorized in multiple ways. Beginning in the 1880s, commercial clipping bureaus scanned a city's or a nation's papers on behalf of clients, clipping items on topics they had been commissioned to find. The envelopes full of clippings they sent out sometimes made their way into scrapbooks, but they also heralded a shift to a more widespread understanding that newspapers held fragmented information that could be remade in other configurations—a concept that

scrapbooks had demonstrated—and that is crucial to our present-day understanding of information.[7]

Harper's complaint about a mobile, fast-moving generation of skimmers and
scanners may sound familiar. Today's readers, too, scramble to cope with a super-
abundance of print riches, now turned digital and flashing at us from our many
screens. Scrapbooks are the direct ancestors of our digital information
management. In the nineteenth century—at home and in workplaces and institutions—readers adapted to the proliferation of print by cutting it up and saving it,
reorganizing it, putting their own stamp on it, and sometimes recirculating it.
Stacks of newspapers were unwieldy and obsolete; the modern household kept
scrapbooks.

Who Made Clipping Scrapbooks?

Tens of thousands, and possibly hundreds of thousands, of Americans made
scrapbooks. Men and women from all classes and backgrounds, and with surprisingly diverse educations, did so for professional, domestic, educational,
and political use and for many more reasons. Newspaper clipping scrapbooks
were often adjuncts to professional careers. Authors clipped records of their
work and made scrapbooks intended for reference, keeping accounts of publications. Physicians' scrapbooks documented their own medical careers and
assembled case records and news articles related to their medical interests.
Actors were particularly avid scrapbook makers. The reviews and playbills
they saved supplied evidence that long-vanished performances had taken
place, and they sometimes used their books as a job-hunting aid to show to
theater managers. Theater fans might paste down the same pile of playbills
and reviews to preserve the memory of attending those performances.
Politicians and ministers used them both coming and going: they stored up
material for speeches, though few joined Charles Sumner in brandishing his
scrapbook on the Senate floor as backing for his arguments. After having
addressed a crowd, speakers such as Abraham Lincoln sometimes relied on
newspaper stenographers for transcriptions of their talks, and pasted them
(or had them pasted) into books.[8]

Some nineteenth-century writers insisted on gendering scrapbooks. These
commentators claimed that men's scrapbooks were models of order, in which
statesmen and ministers gathered materials for speeches and sermons. They
derided women's scrapbooks as miscellanies of trivial poetry and household
hints. However, women and men deserve equal blame or credit for nearly all
types of clipped collections. Statesmen such as Thomas Jefferson and Charles
Sumner clipped helpful hints or poems or jokes; women activists such as Caroline
Healey Dall and Elizabeth Boynton Harbert collected materials for their
speeches.[9]

Although scrapbooks helped readers cope with plenitude, they also anticipated shortage. Teachers clipped and pasted their own anthologies for pedagogical use so that they would have poems and other works at hand in their
schoolrooms. They passed their practice along to their students, who collected
clippings from home and made scrapbooks as part of their classwork, learning to
sort and categorize. Students were praised for creating valuable works from
waste paper.[10]

Because it used common, sometimes free materials, scrapbook making was
available to people of all classes. A scrapbook maker might keep up the activity
for a lifetime, or return to it on occasions—such as a war—that heightened
their relationship to the newspaper. The scrapbook was understood as a metaphor for the knowledge, reading, and taste stored up over a lifetime: "Could we
have all the scrapbooks of one lifetime extending from youth to age, we should
have a literary history of that life," wrote one commentator. Pictures therefore
often represented scrapbook makers as children, while the scrapbook *user* might
be a wise gray head (Figures Intro.5, Intro.6, and Intro.7). The scrapbook stood
as an analog of a life itself, so that General William Tecumseh Sherman's
immense scrapbook of documents and clippings related to his affairs was
reported to have been filled to the last page a few weeks before his death.
Extending the trope, Elkanah Walter Gurley, the author of a book on making
scrapbooks, elaborately updates Ben Franklin's conceit of himself as a book full
of errata, to declare,

> Our life is a living Scrap-book. Clipped from the scroll of Time and pasted
> by the hand of Fate, every day brings its contributions, and the leaves

Figure Intro.5   Boy and girl making scrapbooks, *Harper's Young People*, 27 Dec 1887, 156.

Figure Intro.6 Advertisement for Chase's Glue, showing children making scrapbooks, 1880s.

accumulate until the book is filled.... We are all Scrap-books, and happy is he who has his Pages systematized, whose clippings have been culled from sources of truth and purity and who has them firmly Pasted into his Book.[11]

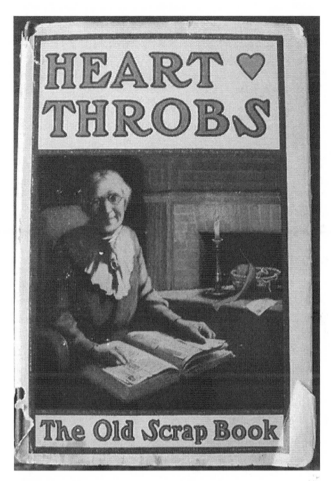

Figure Intro.7 "The Old Scrap-Book," *Heart Throbs in Prose and Verse: The Old Scrap Book* Joseph Mitchell Chappel, ed. (New York: Grosset and Dunlap, 1905).

Many scrapbook makers—particularly rural ones—created anthologies for their own use. This book, *Writing with Scissors*, got its start when a used bookstore owner blew the dust from a hefty, leather-trimmed collection of Puritan sermons. "Seen anything like this?" she asked me. Baxter, *Saints Rest*, the spine proclaimed. Inside, the pages of Richard Baxter's sermons were covered by stories from the 1880s rural weeklies called farm papers, possibly from Massachusetts. I had asked her about 1880s scrapbooks of colorful advertising trade cards. But this scrapbook was a revelation. The compiler had obliterated a book of sermons to create a booklike anthology, leading off with a story I knew well, Mary Wilkins Freeman's "The Revolt of Mother." It's usually read today as a feminist fable of a woman taking over male space for herself and her family. Judging by what the compiler had grouped it with, however, I saw that she had read it as endorsing a very different ideology: women's obligation to turn the home into a harmonious site of good works and thus stabilize the family and improve moral character. She had obliterated sermons, taking over male space with her own ideas of what was important. I was hooked.[12]

Since then, I have paged through hundreds of scrapbooks in the reading rooms of well-appointed libraries and the storerooms of more hard-pressed libraries and historical societies, clicked through digitized pages, and rolled through pages on microfilm. Each scrapbook holds its maker's past and embodies a life of reading and saving. Every scrapbook is its own world, compelling and impossibly frustrating. A few lines from James Tate's poem "Horseshoe" capture the experience of puzzling over these documents:

> I can't read the small print in the scrapbook:
> does this say, *Relinquishing all bats, feeling faint*
> *on the balcony?* There is so much to be corrected here,
> so many scribbles and grumbles, blind premonitions.
> How does one interpret, on this late branch, the unexpected?[13]

And much is unexpected in every scrapbook. What fascinates me is the story lying under the paper and paste. The disheveled clippings, cut from newspapers with different typefaces and column widths; the mix of poetry, articles, and the popular miscellaneous fun facts columns. Each scrapbook seems both opaque and tantalizing on first reading; magnetic and impossible. Similar questions occur in examining each scrapbook. Who are these recurring names? What topics do the columns treat most often? Was it the scrapbook maker's intention to collect that topic, or is it an accident that the article is in this group?

Gradually, their stories emerge, though often incompletely. Eventually I discovered the identity of the African American man who placed clippings about lynchings next to clippings about his own ascent in the civil service hierarchy and his attendance at musicales; elsewhere I figured out that a young girl pasted down clippings her now-dead mother had collected years earlier; and I understood why Susan B. Anthony led off her scrapbook with an article opposing women's speaking in public pasted next to her own teaching credentials. I saw why a white Southern woman pasted her household-hints clippings over the used ledger of her family business and its record of slave owning, and why Elizabeth Boynton Harbert used a Mark Twain self-pasting scrapbook. I tell their stories in this book.

Scrapbook Development

Like present-day scrapbooks, nineteenth-century newspaper clipping scrapbooks are personal and emotionally expressive, and they carry information about family relationships. The use of the word *scrapbook* for both is not a meaningless coincidence. But the path from nineteenth-century clipping scrapbooks to today's photo-filled, family-centered scrapbooks leads through several lines of ancestry.[14]

Scrapbook has been a flexible term, used alongside *album* and *portfolio* and *commonplace book*. Especially early in the nineteenth century, and commonly in England, *scrapbooks* referred to portfolios of drawings, or collections of prints or silhouettes, and books which could circulate among friends or in which visitors to a household inscribed a few lines or a verse or drawing, later known as autograph albums or friendship albums. Jointly created friendship albums could mark a relationship between a family and its circle. For example, Amy Matilda Cassey, a well-off African American abolitionist in Philadelphia, kept an album between 1833 and 1856 filled with the drawings, poems, and essays common to the genre. But with a contributor list that reads like a joint Who's Who of nineteenth-century activists and the Philadelphia African American elite, including Frederick Douglass, William Lloyd Garrison, Lucy Stone, and Robert Purvis, the album not only documents these connections but allows the contributors to share and reinforce abolitionist sentiments. Like present-day scrapbooks that are displayed to family, friends, and fellow scrapbookers, this compilation was also a performance: its writers could address subsequent contributors and visitors who would also read the book, in a type of manuscript publication. Visual presentation was important; Cassey's contributors carefully show off their penmanship and even calligraphy, as well as their taste in selecting and writing. Such albums might also have drawings or other matter pasted into them. Like them, newspaper clipping scrapbooks were sometimes created by multiple contributors. Like present-day scrapbook creators, friendship album makers used blank books bought for the purpose, sometimes with elaborate covers framing their efforts.[15]

Commonplace books were another scrapbook antecedent. They gained popularity during the Renaissance and continue in various forms into the present. Readers use them to create a record of their reading by copying out passages from other works. Such a book might be shared by two or more people, and passages in it often recirculated back into the compiler's own writing, with or without credit. Some commonplace books contain lengthy passages that extend over several pages, but once cheap print was available, preserving long articles or other works by cutting and pasting them appealed to more compilers, though some books contain both copied and clipped items.[16]

Many scrapbooks are diaries of sorts—a form of life writing that may or may not be chronological but records and preserves elements of life experience and memory cues. Nineteenth-century scrapbook makers sometimes wrote diaries as well, with these two genres segregated into separate volumes. Other diarists, however, stuffed their journals with press clippings, sometimes pasted in and sometimes loose between the leaves. Most such journals are described simply as diaries—like Mary Boykin Chesnut's *Civil War Diary*, where the original volumes contain newspaper clippings of poems and news items she alluded to in her writing.[17]

Other nineteenth-century diarists reflected the growing importance of the public press in their lives. Edward Neufville Tailer, Jr., for example, a New York merchant and banker, kept a diary for sixty-nine years, beginning at age eighteen in 1848. As current events and politics took more of his attention, he began to paste clippings beside his handwritten entries. As historian David Henkin notes, Tailer first clipped references to himself or friends in the paper, as illustration or documentation, but by the late 1860s the newspaper clippings were central to his diaries, usually without evident relation to Tailer's personal life, and written commentary is squeezed to the margins. His book constructed his "daily life in relation to the public sphere, organized around Tailer's regular reading of the daily newspaper." Tailer was part of a trend. The timing of his transition from writing with a pen to writing with scissors coincides with the burgeoning of scrapbook making during the Civil War.[18]

The commercial and consumer public world dominated a type of scrapbook that children and young adults wrote with glue in the 1880s, using colorful advertising cards. They covered pages with mass-produced print: free advertising cards, calling cards, religious motto cards. These scrapbook makers practiced connecting their desires and longings with printed advertising images and expressing their individuality through their arrangements of the cards—and their feelings about the advertised goods, elevating them in elaborately bound albums (Figures Intro.8, Intro.9, and Intro.10). In the memorabilia books that became popular in the following decades, mass-produced print such as advertising cards and product wrappers, foreign currency, college pennants, ticket stubs and programs, and postage stamps mingle with individually marked items such as invitations, dance cards, report cards, telegrams, drawings, and correspondence; and all join three-dimensional objects beyond printed matter: leaves, flowers, hair, fabric, and cigarette butts. Photographs, first confined to specially made albums with slots for the stiff portraits mounted on boards dictating the arrangements, entered scrapbooks as inexpensive *carte-de-visite*-sized studio portraits. Snapshots became available and dominated memorabilia scrapbooks by the end of the 1800s. (Newspapers did not publish photographs until the late 1890s.) Items documented the compilers' social activities and helped to define and mark their place in the developing youth culture.[19]

Though they express individuality, memorabilia scrapbooks often mark entry into group identities and experiences, as with attendance at school or college, and they show people expressing their identities—as theater fans, college students, young married women, mothers, or soldiers. Memorabilia scrapbooks articulated these identities via pages laden with drawings and souvenirs. The

Figure Intro.8 Scrapbooks of advertising trade cards and calling cards, 1880s (Private collection).

absence of such typical items as invitations might denote exclusion, as in the scrapbook of an African American student at Amherst College in the early 1890s.[20]

But for all their visual abundance, these memorabilia books may express only a partial view of their makers' identities. The scrapbook of the Staten Island photographer Alice Austen, for example, who went on to live with her partner Gertrude

Figure Intro.9 Elaborate cover of advertising card scrapbook, 1880s. (Private Collection)

Tate for five decades, has surprising omissions. Although she began the scrapbook when she had for years been taking and developing sophisticated photos of her family and friends and taking notes on her use of a demanding, difficult technology, her scrapbook takes no notice of this absorbing interest. Her photographs from this period show her and her friends cross-dressing and playfully mocking courtship customs. But the scrapbook focuses on her theater attendance, boat races, the college activities of young men she knew, and participation in dances and tennis—chronicling the conventional pursuits of an upper-class heterosexual young woman of the 1880s and 1890s (albeit an athletic one). Austen's scrapbook suggests how bounded by convention memorabilia scrapbooks were even early in their development, and how we must crack the codes of any scrapbook and any kind of scrapbook to begin to understand them.[21]

*

What can we make of the widescale shift in the meaning of the term *scrapbook*? Instead of designating the scrapbook volumes made predominantly of newspaper clippings by both men and women in the 1800s, the term is almost exclusively applied in the twenty-first century to elaborate visual albums documenting family

Figure Intro.10 Albums with elaborate covers were often valued possessions. Photo circa 1880s. (Author's collection).

and personal life—mostly made by women. When I've told people that I am working on a book about nineteenth-century American scrapbooks, the assumption is that these scrapbooks look much like the currently popular, purposely manufactured elaborate scrapbooks filled with family mementoes and decorated with purchased ornamental materials sold in scrapbook-making stores and crafts stores.

The scrapbooks popular today merge photograph albums with memorabilia scrapbooks. According to Jessica Helfand, the current wave of scrapbooking began in 1980, set off by an exhibit of Marielen Christiansen's fifty scrapbooks in Salt Lake City. Christiansen and her husband soon wrote a scrapbooking how-to book and opened a scrapbooking supply store, which grew into the multimillion-dollar business Keeping Memories Alive. Scrapbooking is now a multibillion-dollar industry of dedicated scrapbooking stores, departments in crafts stores, goods, and activities. As a practice with its roots in the Mormon community, fervently absorbed with genealogy, this wave of scrapbooks unsurprisingly turns toward the family for its subject matter.[22]

Primarily engaged in documenting family and domestic life, scrapbooking has developed into a hobby supplied by specialized stores and departments in craft stores. Although some scrapbookers have moved their projects to the web, for others the physicality of paper, scissors, and glue are crucial marks of permanence in a digitized world. Open a twenty-first-century scrapbook, and you will likely see colorful arrangements of family photos pasted on shaped or artfully torn paper accompanied by small amounts of text in carefully chosen typefaces or handwritten in colored or glitter ink, with commercially available stickers and rub-on decorations scattered around the page.

There are scant visual similarities between newspaper clipping scrapbooks and the scrapbooks supplied by Making Memories™, Scrapbooking Supplies R Us, and Scrapfest, and their contents are wildly different. But their makers' commitment to saving and archiving offers us another way of understanding them together. Many nineteenth-century scrapbook makers sought to create lasting works to pass along to others by creating venues to display them, or bequeathing them to others. Twenty-first-century scrapbook makers demonstrate their dedication to creating long-lasting works by using archival-quality papers said to endure for centuries. The term *archival* invokes a repository of authoritative history and cultural memory, as though to confer authority on any scrapbook collection. In her discussion of how cultural knowledge and memory are produced, Diana Taylor points to the rift between the authority of the archive of supposedly enduring materials, and the "ephemeral *repertoire* of embodied practice/knowledge." Despite seeming nonconcrete and ephemeral, Taylor explains, repertoire is enduring. It is an enactment of "embodied memory: gestures, orality, movement, dancing, singing." The meaning of such enactments can remain stable even as the details change.[23]

Although the current scrapbook movement zealously seeks to create an archive, most commonly to celebrate family activities, we might better define its work as repertoire: the embodied practices or gestures of cutting, arranging, and pasting materials, and displaying the resulting books to others. Compilers have used similar gestures from one century to the other, but to different ends. The late-twentieth-century proliferation of "scrapbooking" as a verb signals that the practice is at least as important as the product. When scrapbookers congregate in classes, conventions, or cruises devoted to scrapbooking and exchanging ideas about it, they participate in what Taylor identifies as the repertoire's mode of reproducing knowledge: being there and being part of the transmission. Like nineteenth-century scrapbook makers, the present-day scrapbookers engage in what I call *performing archivalness*, acts and gestures of preservation, they express the will to save, organize, and transmit knowledge through a homemade archive.

The repertoire of the actions of cutting and pasting for remaking print, too, survive and have moved into new arenas. Today, the "cut and paste" terminology used by computer programs and applications reflects the history of scrapbook making: the icons at the top of our computer screens refer to the formerly literal practice of cutting and pasting as part of writing. Before I wrote with a computer, like many writers I laid out sections of writing on a table and cut them apart and rearranged them—the actions now referred to by computer icons of scissors and clipboard. Putting old sentences and passages into new relationships is a crucial part of writing. Commenting on file cards (the new media of his time), Walter Benjamin asserted in 1923 that a book is an outdated means of scholarly communication between two boxes of file cards: one scholar records research onto cards and makes a book out of them, and another goes through that book and makes his or her own set of cards, and then another book. Benjamin joked that the writer ought to just sell the cards, but of course we read for the organization that the book imposes—the order and interpretation of those rearranged sentences.

The order of those rearrangements, the calculated cutting and pasting inside nineteenth-century scrapbooks, is often difficult and sometimes impossible to follow. Nonetheless, scrapbooks have something to tell us—about what their makers meant to save, and about our own ways of managing information.[24]

Nineteenth-Century Information Management and Ours

Traces of scrapbooks survive in our digital world beyond the repertoire of gestures of archivalness and of cutting and pasting. Scrapbooks, newspaper collections, clipping services, library cataloging systems, filing systems, and even pigeonhole desks embody overlapping modes of thinking about information, how to concentrate it, and how to find it again. They are the foundations of more recent filtering of information via digital methods such as Google, LexisNexis, and blogging. They all understand that pieces of information—whether in the form of articles, books, or snippets—are detachable, movable, and classifiable under multiple headings. Although the clipping scrapbook seems solidly grounded in the materiality of paper and paste, it leads toward the understanding that items can be detached from their original sources while keeping connected to them via identifiable format and typeface, even if the name and date of publication have been snipped away. Items could be drastically recontextualized and moved into new meanings, while additional copies could be categorized in other directions.

In the twenty-first century, we are so accustomed to the cut-and-paste terminology of our digital devices that these terms are nearly extinct metaphors. Instead of reading a paper newspaper with shears or penknife in hand to clip articles of interest, we read online news sources saved and organized by digitized place marking and cut-and-paste functions. Instead of pasting an article into a book to preserve, display in the home, or pass around to friends, we "paste" it into an email to circulate to dozens or thousands of willing or unwilling recipients, or attach it with a figurative paperclip to other documents, or paste it into a website, with or without credit.

Scrapbooks were a crucial technology for writing with scissors, commenting on media, and recirculating both original articles and the compilers' own understanding of them. Like blogs, Facebook, and recirculated emails, they fuse reading and writing and make something new. The kinds of scrapbooks encountered in *Writing with Scissors,* made over a century ago, underlie our present-day ways of thinking about information, news, and its relationship to our lives. Like Frances Smith, the schoolteacher, sending valuable information on ahead to Frances Smith Cather, the farmwoman she imagined becoming, we continue to disassemble and reassemble our reading material, compiling it to use it ourselves and pass it along to our future selves or to others.

Contents of the Book

Writing with Scissors illustrates how people used scrapbooks to manage printed matter and tell their own stories with it, from the standpoint of such groups as African American amateur historians and women's rights activists, individual writers and scrapbook innovators like Mark Twain, and Union supporters and Confederates living through the Civil War. It links scrapbook making to the many ways editors and readers recirculated writing. When people made scrapbooks, they demonstrated a desire to save fleeting bits of information that would otherwise be lost. They created their own archives. But many scrapbooks themselves have been lost and do not appear in archives and repositories. *Writing with Scissors* concludes by examining the later developments that have led to our present digitized information environment.

The first chapter, "Reuse, Recycle, Recirculate: Scrapbooks Remake Value," takes up the history of how readers have kept track of their reading, starting with bookmarks and commonplace books. Scrapbook making grew as cheap and even free books to paste over, became widely available. Readers displaced old book information with new clippings, asserting their individual hierarchies of reading matter: the stories they liked mattered more than sermons or information about new patents. Scrapbooks were part of a larger practice of isolating items from their original publications to recirculate within the nineteenth-century press. Editors stripped items of their attribution, or added a new authorial attribution. Authors such as Ella Wheeler Wilcox countered by devising methods to keep names attached to their works.

Mark Twain was one such author. Chapter 2, "Mark Twain's Scrapbook Innovations," finds that his ambivalent relation to recirculation was tightly bound to the scrapbook he invented, which invited its buyers to write a book with Mark Twain's name on it, wielding their own scissors. The relationship of authorship to writing with scissors is complicated. Twain used the circuits of reprinting and recirculation to promote his scrapbook, while he undertook various frustrating attempts to protect his intellectual property from reprinting, including battling Will M. Clemens, a "maggot" who fed on his work.

The increasing popularity of scrapbook making—and the corresponding market for Mark Twain's 1877 scrapbook—had its seeds in the large number of Northerners and Southerners who made scrapbooks during the Civil War to grapple with and articulate their new understandings of nationhood, by saving poetry and battle news. Chapter 3, "Civil War Scrapbooks: Newspaper and Nation," illustrates that scrapbooks expressed national grief and rage in a private, domestic format. The contrast between the scrapbooks of a Northern abolitionist man who collected newspaper poetry to mourn his son, killed in battle, and a Southern Confederate woman, whose scrapbook is a kind of ideal newspaper where Confederate victories continued and grateful slaves abounded, tells much about the differing ideas of nationhood and the meaning of the war across the divide. Scrapbooks became their own battlefields of propaganda for saving accounts of triumphs and comparing them with emerging realities.

Realities were changing rapidly for African Americans during and after the war. Chapter 4, "Alternative Histories in African American Scrapbooks," demonstrates how African Americans wrote histories unavailable in books by making scrapbooks of clippings from both the black and the white press. Scrapbook histories were weapons, and communal knowledge. In massive compilations—dozens or even hundreds of volumes, in some cases—black people asserted ownership of news and culture and passed along critical, oppositional reading of newspapers. Whether or not they were adept with a pen, they wrote books with scissors, chronicling black life through the Harlem Renaissance.

Abolitionists, African Americans, and women's rights activists all documented their activities in scrapbooks. Chapter 5, "Strategic Scrapbooks: Activist Women's Clipping and Self-Creation," shows that scrapbooks kept by Susan B. Anthony, Elizabeth Cady Stanton, Alice Dunbar Nelson, and less-well-known suffragists such as Lillie Devereux Blake, Caroline Healey Dall, and Elizabeth Boynton Harbert, constitute a complex conversation about women's participation in the public realm. Scrapbooks both documented that participation and experimented with ways to present it to varied audiences; they were a training ground for impression management. Like other speakers, writers, and actors, women who wrote and spoke in public kept clipping books to document their talks and track their publications. Even the fact itself that suffragists looked to the press for personal history marks an extraordinary assertion of selfhood for women and a claim to act in the public arena. They passed along their understanding that the press was not a simple record, but a set of voices and conversations to be read critically.

Although scrapbook making was a cheap, accessible practice that allowed people to create fixed arrangements of materials that mattered to them, Chapter 6, "Scrapbook as Archive, Scrapbooks in Archives," illustrates that preservation in the larger bricks-and-mortar archive has been less democratically distributed. As institutions often preferred to "document the well documented," the materials that people sought to save in the egalitarian archive of the scrapbook often vanished or lost connection to their makers.

Some scrapbooks themselves did survive, but the idea of saving and storing newspaper items took on new forms. Chapter 7, "The Afterlife of the Nineteenth-Century Scrapbook: Managing Data and Information," demonstrates how scrapbooks led the way in materializing an understanding that information was detachable, movable, sortable, and not wedded to the context in which it had been published. Other technologies developed in the late nineteenth century for accessing newspaper articles again, and then for sorting and mining them to turn them into data to move information faster. Robert Budd, an African American entrepreneur in New York, created a newspaper storage establishment. His work highlights the difference between thinking of newspapers as material objects and as movable data. In the 1890s, clipping bureaus took over and industrialized the work of saving and sorting the press that individual scrapbook makers had previously done. Scrapbooks receded as an ideal means for keeping the massive quantities of clippings that the bureaus produced; clipping savers turned toward more flexible modes of sorting and filing by multiple subject headings that developed at the same time.

1

Reuse, Recycle, Recirculate

Scrapbooks Remake Value

When Mark Twain, Susan B. Anthony, Charles Sumner, Frederick Douglass, and thousands of less prominent scrapbook makers read piles of newspapers with scissors in hand and pasted down the resulting clippings in a new format, they participated in a long history of activities for managing reading matter. They acted much like newspaper editors, who could write substantial portions of their newspapers with scissors. Editors converted clippings into text, stripping them of their material qualities—paper, layout—to move them back into circulation in new contexts. Scrapbook makers, by contrast, embraced the materiality of their cut-up papers, as they often obliterated the contents of substantial printed books to make a home for their decidedly tangible clippings.

Early Technologies for Managing Manuscript and Print: Bookmarks, Bookwheels, and Commonplace Books

The quantities of printed matter that nineteenth-century readers felt overwhelmed by may seem petty to us now. We can see how relative the sense of being overwhelmed is, however, if we explore the line of scrapbooks, clipping services, and web management devices in line with the varied technologies that let readers manage a confusing plenitude of texts and create new value from them. Because the sense that texts are overwhelmingly abundant is so shifting and relative, the lowly nondigital bookmark is one ancestor of both scrapbooks and electronic tools to manage digital profusion. Bookmarks not only allowed the reader to find the same place again in a book but made it easier to group or compare passages in different parts of the same book, or in different books—like opening multiple onscreen windows at once. Such technology assisted active modes of reading, and the move between reading and writing. Medieval bookmarks made of a bead or other anchor with a bundle of ribbons or threads running out from it, marking many pages in the same book at once, made it easier to compare passages. The most elaborate and expensive approaches to accessing several passages at a time were the Renaissance bookwheel and other revolving lecterns, specialized apparatus for holding many open books. The seated reader turned the device to move between desired passages, holding them all open for reference, presumably while distilling them into a new form by writing something else from them. The bookwheel assumed that a limited number of books would be wanted at one time; the three-dimensional bookmark assumes that the reader will recall what book the desired passage was in.[1]

The *commonplace book,* which straddled reading and writing, gained popularity during the Renaissance and continues in various forms into the present. In it, readers write out appealing or notable passages from other works. Commonplace book creators sometimes sort items into categories, and they might mine them to quote in their own writing, as Renaissance pedagogy urged. The commonplace book serves some of the functions of both the bookmark and the bookwheel. Instead of simply marking a place, it makes a new book of other people's writing. A trail of references may mark the way back, but more likely it leaves the reader of the commonplace book with something new: a collection of passages that lead nowhere but have been remade into freestanding "quotes" and sayings recontextualized for new use. Crucially, the reader becomes an author. Some commonplace book compilers even publish their compilations in their entirety. Others reprocess the passages in other ways, as did Ralph Waldo Emerson and Henry David Thoreau, who jointly kept a commonplace book that they mined for their own writing. The practice continued to be a widespread pedagogical activity, encouraged in children and others, In her memoirs, Kate Sanborn, a nineteenth-century author, lecturer, and anthologist, cites a verse on the subject she learned as a child:

> In reading authors, when you find
> Bright passages that strike your mind,
> And which, perhaps you may have reason
> To think on in another season;
> Be not contented with the sight,
> But jot them down in black and white;
> Such respect is wisely shown
> As makes another's thought your own.

She memorized the poem (another way of making another's thought one's own). And while memorizing it and copying it, Sanborn deleted the author's name, very effectively making it her own, as many readers did in abstracting passages and copying them into their books.[2]

The commonplace book implied leisure and patience, or possibly a supervising teacher requiring students to fill pages. Additional devices for managing textual abundance adapted and extended commonplace book basics. *John Bartlett's Familiar Quotations*, first issued in 1855, was an extended, public commonplace book, offering snippets and extracts. It constituted a database of passages, initially intended to jog the reader's memory for already familiar passages. Such compilations soon substituted for reading the whole, providing apt lines to pop into speeches and articles.[3]

In 1833, the Rev. John Todd, frustrated with the individual commonplace book's limitations, complained that "making extracts with the pen is so tedious that the very name of a commonplace book is associated with drudgery and wearisome ness." Todd adapted a system described by John Locke to tie reading to an alphabetized catalog, so that invisible threads run out from the index to bookshelves. The reader could buy Todd's *Index Rerum* in the form of an alphabetized blank book, with the letter at the top of each page subdivided by vowels (Ba, Be, Bi, etc.). The user entered a word on the page matching the first letter and first vowel following, noting an item pertaining to "commonplace book," for example, on page Co. Todd worried that valuable material was getting away from its readers, lost in mists of memory; at the same time he worried that readers wasted time on the quickly passing "world of Reviews and Magazines and papers," the contents of which were not worth remembering and so, he said, eroded the memory. His system therefore privileged the permanent book. With its origin in Biblical concordances as much as Locke's ideas about note taking, the *Index Rerum* foreshadows the digital keyword search. But it was a technological road not taken: the ephemeral periodical won out. Most surviving copies of John Todd's work were abandoned after a short time, often repurposed as commonplace books or, by the 1850s, scrapbooks.[4]

The Coming of the Scrapbook

By the 1850s, many Americans were making scrapbooks. The scrapbook both democratized and industrialized the commonplace book. With it, saving passages was no longer fused to the ability to transcribe them. Nineteenth-century literacy was widespread among American-born whites, and restricted among blacks. But literacy was often still characterized by a split between knowledge of reading and of writing. One could be an avid and extensive reader, but not a skilled writer, either in the sense of composing or facility in handling a pen.[5]

Scrapbooks allowed all types of readers to "write" a book with scissors. Children were even encouraged to store up barely understood writings in their scrapbooks to enjoy when they could read them better. Walt Whitman, a scrapbook maker himself, relied on this idea of the scrapbook as a storehouse of reading matter to grow into when he handed a poem he liked to a child, saying, "Here bubby, is a scrap or two for your scrap book. . . . It's a bit for you to understand by and by." Not only could an adult reader "write" a book with scissors, but a child could write with half-understood words.[6]

More people could save parts of their reading with scrapbooks than with commonplace books, and scrapbooks incited those readers to save larger blocks of material. The capacity to include a long article and perhaps underline relevant passages instead of copying only the most desired parts let scrapbook readers revisit something of the original context and use, instead of only an isolated line or two. That larger swath of included context thus became even more material that the scrapbook recontextualized. Like Thoreau and Emerson's commonplace book, or *Bartlett's Familiar Quotations*, scrapbooks freed passages for recirculation. More than commonplace book compilers, scrapbook makers, who no longer worked with a pen in hand, often dropped information about the article's source.

Yet even when scrapbook compilers snipped off source information, the clipping scrapbook inevitably saved a sample and record of the newspaper medium in which compilers encountered their reading. Their books don't preserve only copied words, but pieces of newspaper. Inside the scrapbook's layers of paper and glue, the press itself is an element in the stories that scrapbook makers tell. Scrapbook compilers saved the mediated experience: the memory and evidence of *where* and in what form they had read an item. It mattered that the poem had been on the same newspaper page as the news of a disastrous or victorious battle; the juxtaposition, no longer visible once it was clipped, entered in the maker's associations with it and his or her desire to save it. If compilers pasted down multiple articles about the same battle, they might make knowledge of the event fuller or denser. The repetition also marked a re-encounter, seeing the event again and again, each time through the lens of a different newspaper. So when one reader made a roughly chronological scrapbook of newspaper poetry and included the same poem at least twice, only a few pages apart, it is possible that she forgot she'd already pasted the poem in, but pasting in the poem twice may have marked encountering it in different newspapers, on different days, in different surroundings, allowing her to mark that re-encounter as well as save the poem.

The mass media flickers between information and noninformation as it replaces old news with current news and discards the past, Niklas Luhmann argues. The past is cast into the shadowy realm of no-longer-news, no-longer-useful information, while a new event moves into the spotlight. Today's newspaper is always on the top of the pile; the new story replaces the old on the website. This flicker appears most dramatically in scrapbooks meant to record momentous events. The clippings, which have flickered off into no-longer-news, are more visible as a medium, as newspaper rather than news. In scrapbooks that preserved stories on battles of the Civil War, or Emancipation, or the Johnstown Flood, or the chronicle of a lynching, for example, the apparatus of newspaperly urgency—datelines, internal information about date and time, breaking news about the developing story, soon superseded by other news—sticks out, because once the event has receded in time, these trappings of timeliness become obtrusive reminders that this is a residual piece of paper, no longer news. Such scrapbooks highlight the experience of reading the successive days of unfolding news and record the experience of encountering that news. If media in the present is always presenting the newness of information, when a newspaper clipping is saved it becomes visible as media. It has turned into a record of—and perhaps nostalgia for—having once thought of the event as new.[7]

As media extends to new modes, newspapers still retain iconic power, such that many newspaper readers who by 2008 were doing most of their news reading online nonetheless bought newspapers announcing Barack Obama's election to save the paper record of the historic victory. Owning that front page both pointed toward posterity and gave it a place in the lineage of other newspaper front pages announcing election victories (including one that is all about media: the 1948 photo of the victorious Truman holding up the mistaken "Dewey Defeats Truman" headline). Nineteenth-century scrapbooks reveal an earlier version of this mediated relationship to experience. Scrapbooks merge the *practice* of saving with the *record* of saving.

Exchanges and Scissors Swingers

The newspaper clippings that eventually filled scrapbooks were on their own journeys through the press, filling and refilling columns. Reprinting and free recirculation were facts of life in nineteenth-century U.S. publishing. As one "Song of the Editor" asserts, editors who plied their shears were not "cabbaging" or stealing, but lawfully snipping and filling their columns with the proceeds.

> Clip! Clip! Clip!
> No "cabbaging" shears his hand doth hold
> But those with which the current gold
>   By lawful right he'll clip—
> The [printer's] devil is gone, but he will not fail
> Of a prompt return with the morning mail,
>   A basketful of "exchanges"—
> And then the editor opens and skims—
> Accidents—deaths—discoveries—whims—
>   As over the world he ranges.
>
> Paste! Paste! Paste!
> With a camel's hair brush and broken cup,
> He gathers scattered fragments up,
>   And sticks them on in haste.[8]

Newspapers and magazines snatched up and reprinted one another's articles, poetry, and fiction, not always crediting the source, sometimes dropping the author's name, and sometimes altering the work, in a tumult of clipping, claiming, and publishing under new mastheads that Meredith McGill has rather decorously termed a "culture of reprinting." On large papers, a special "exchange editor" went through other papers for material, while on smaller publications "paste-pot-and-scissors work" was part of the general editor's tasks.[9]

Newspapers swapped subscriptions with one another in "exchanges" and allowed free reprinting, with credit. The material gathered this way was also referred to as their "exchanges," as were the papers they exchanged with, so that special columns were sometimes dedicated to work "from our exchanges." *Exchange* might suggest a simple one-for-one passing back and forth of papers, but as with some of the word's other uses, such as the telephone exchange and the stock exchange, the term also comprises circuits of connection and diffusion. The Post Office recognized the value of exchanges as a method for spreading news and information around the country, and allowed newspapers to send their exchange papers free. A newspaper might have more than a thousand other papers on its exchange lists.[10]

Exchanges among publications allowed newspapers in one locality to pick up and run news from another and helped to create a local press that covered the nation—and indeed ranged "over the world"—without specific correspondents in every locality, or using them to fill in when correspondents' dispatches did not arrive. As another bit of editorial doggerel explained,

> The editor sits at his desk. . . .
> Exchanges are lying about—
> While waiting dispatches delayed,
> He clips and he clips and he clips
> And that's how a paper is made.[11]

This recirculation of material was a mechanism unifying the country, journalists and commentators often remarked. The exchange system spread news, poetry, fiction, essays, opinions, and occasionally advertising notices throughout the country via a decentralized network. As one journalist asserted, "A man who reads the daily exchanges of the country may see an idea travel from the Atlantic slope to the Pacific and from the Pacific to the Atlantic as visibly as a train of freight cars runs over the Vanderbilt system." Like the Vanderbilt railroad system, the exchange system both carried materials—paper and ink—and was a system of communication. Such recirculation helped make local literature national. Even work by obscure writers might be diffused widely. From the local reader's point of view, the presence of an item—say, a poem—in the local paper gave the piece a local flavor, especially if information on its distant origins was omitted. Thus readers of a Baptist magazine could read Wordsworth as a Baptist poet, as Joan Shelley Rubin suggests. Some of the same poems circulated in both Union and Confederate presses, with Northern and Southern readers equally confident that the soldier they wept over had been fighting on their own side.[12]

What was the value of a newspaper constructed this way? Many editors thought exchanges resulted in superior products. The exchange system produced local newspapers by yoking together scattered producers who shared labor and resources by sending their products to one another for free use. The tools of reuse—scissors or shears, and pastepot or gluepot—were shorthand terms for the practice, and editors were even sometimes called "scissors swingers" or "brothers of the pen and shears." "The scissors, well used, can give the product of five hundred brains in one newspaper, and one brain plus five hundred is a great deal better than when it stands alone on its own originality, no matter how great that originality may be," the editor of the *Hartford Post* wrote in 1886. Newspapers were already collaborative enterprises, only to be improved by additional collaborators. If the collaborators were unpaid, so much the better. "A keen eye, a sharp pair of blades, and a credit attachment ought to furnish about one-third of the matter for a readable newspaper," he concluded. Another newspaper explained that the exchange editor's "practiced eye gleans anything that may be of interest to the readers....Judiciously done, 'the exchange man' can reflect public opinion upon any given subject." The article (self-servingly written by the exchange editor) proclaims that reading the exchanges makes him "better, wiser, and of more use to his paper." Cartoonists, who were largely outside the circuits of reuse because graphics could not be readily copied from one paper to another, could be harsher in their assessments, as is evident in "Involution of the News Editor," (Figure 1.1), where the editor becomes nothing but scissors, and "A Night Editor," in a cartoon on how women are pressed into doing the most tedious part of their husbands' work (Figure 1.2).[13]

THE INVOLUTION OF THE NEWS EDITOR.

Figure 1.1 "Involution of the News Editor," *Life*, 25 Oct 1883, 210.

A NIGHT EDITOR,

Figure 1.2 A scissors-wielding "Night Editor," detail from the cartoon "A Warning to Maidens," showing women with their husbands' dullest tasks foisted on them. *Life*, 25 Mar 1884.

Scissorizing and Credit

With a familiar clatter
I've clipped the best matter
That's come to this office for years.
So when you have read it
Please give me the credit
I'm the editorial shears.
                        —"The Editorial Three"[14]

The personified tools of editing seemed to lead a life of their own. Editorial scissors were a member of the indispensable "Editorial Three," of pencil, scissors, and paste, this poem goes on to explain. Newspapers had no reason to hide their use of scissors and paste, as the headings for the *Chicago Inter Ocean*'s exchange column "Scissors and Paste" make clear (Figures 1.3 and 1.4). The nineteenth-century humor magazine *Life* featured the tools as well, posing its cherub mascot "Winged Life" presiding over the exchange column with the playful heading "Aut Scissors, aut Nullus," revising the more conventional rejection of mediocrity, "aut Caesar, aut nullus" (either Caesar or nobody; Figure 1.5). The acceptance and even celebration of such reprinting reflects a premium on familiar,

Figure 1.3 Exchange editor with the scissors of his trade. *Chicago Inter Ocean* column heading, "Scissors and Paste: Wheat and Chaff Gleaned from Our Esteemed Contemporaries," 13 Oct 1895.

Figure 1.4 Animated paste and scissors from *Chicago Inter Ocean* column heading, "Scissors and Paste: Wheat and Chaff Gleaned from Our Esteemed Contemporaries," 30 June 1895, 23 col. A.

well-accepted material as a source of wisdom and enjoyment. Originality seemed overrated.[15]

Newspaper editors and publishers benefited not only from exchanges allowing them to stock their columns with material that was fresh to their readers, at no cost, but as well if other papers picked up their work and followed the custom of crediting the newspaper it came from, enhancing its stature. So in her 1886 novel *Taken by Siege*, Jeannette Gilder, the editor of the *Critic* and a veteran of other

Figure 1.5 Life magazine's cherub mascot, "Winged Life," clips from exchanges, 14 Nov 1907.

editorial positions, tells of a young journalist whose "local stories began to be largely copied by the State papers, and *The Freelance* got a reputation that it had never had before." Magazines such as *The Century* even primed the pump of reprinting by sending out "special sheets of extracts you can use handily," adapting the newspapers' desire for material to reprint to generate publicity for a monthly magazine. Editors were not alone in benefiting from exchanges; the exchange mechanism's potential for proliferation enticed others who had information to spread. A missionary writer suggested hopefully that if even one column "of interesting religious matter could be introduced into each of [the nation's many] papers, it would be equivalent to the annual distribution of more than sixteen hundred million tract pages." But casting a column upon the waters was no guarantee of seeing it reprinted a thousandfold. The exchange process was a selective one, because editors engaged in a gatekeeping or winnowing process (despite the *Chicago Inter Ocean*'s offer of both wheat *and* chaff). This role is vividly illustrated in a drawing in *Baldwin's Monthly,* featuring the editor as a sifter, dividing wheat from chaff, as well as a clipper (Figure 1.6), and in the titles of publications such as *Texas Siftings*.[16]

If the writer's name as well as the newspaper's was attached to the recirculated items, exchanges could therefore be understood as a spontaneous, decentralized index to the popularity of a writer's work. So in Lillie Devereux Blake's 1874 novel *Fettered for Life*, Frank Haywood, a reporter for the *Trumpeter*, is succeeding when his reports on his travels in the South "meet with the highest praise from all quarters, and are copied all over the country." And if the writer's name remained with the work, the exchange system could generate publicity for an author or even a product. In Fanny Fern's 1854 *Ruth Hall* the indication that Ruth is achieving acclaim as a writer is in the number of her pieces that are copied into exchanges: "A good sign for you Mrs. Hall; a good test of your popularity," her publisher tells her. And Ruth's spiteful brother, the editor of another periodical, instructs his staff not to "scissorize" and reprint his sister's work, so as not to give her further publicity.[17]

Figure 1.6 Editor as sifter, *Baldwin's Monthly*, Oct. 1874, 2.

Exchanges both reflected popularity and generated publicity from that popularity. Book publishers also noted an author's popularity in newspaper exchanges as a sign that the writer's reputation was substantial enough to carry a collection of the pieces into a book. Fern's fictionalized account of reputation built by scissorizing is corroborated by her publisher, James Cephas Derby, who reported discovering her: "As a publisher I had occasion to look over the newspaper exchanges quite frequently." Struck by seeing Fanny Fern's sketches in many papers, he correctly concluded that "gathered together and published in book form [they] could not fail to meet with a popular demand." Many readers evidently wanted to see the columns they might have already read in newspapers in the more dignified book form, which could be given as a gift as well as savored again.[18]

But credit for recirculated work did not reliably circulate back to the author. Newspapers had an institutional stake in promoting their own names and by extension one another's names, rather than highlighting the names of the possessors of those five hundred brains the *Hartford Post* editor praised for making a strong newspaper. Authors complained that editors were more likely to include the originating paper's title than the author's name. Savvy action by authors could keep their names attached, but anonymity exerted its own pull on recirculated writing.

Scrapbooks in the Circuits of Exchange

Although published items might well meet with editorial shears and pastepot and reappear in another newspaper, and exchange editors might keep an article or poem circulating for years or even decades, an individual physical copy of an item was likely to be re-formed via one of many modes of recycling common to nineteenth-century newsprint, all of which ignored its printed content and reduced it to paper: wrapping fish or other goods; insulating clothing, shoes, bedding, and walls; cutting into dress patterns and quilt backings; folding into hats for printers and newsboys; lining trunks, drawers, shelves, and baskets; stocking the kindling and outhouse pile; shredding to make papier-mâché goods; pulping to produce new paper; and for bookbinders, lining the spines of books—including scrapbooks.[19]

Scrapbooks, however, reused and recontextualized the physical copy of an item as printed matter, giving it a new purpose. Saving clippings overcame the daily press's ephemerality and disposability with a claim that newspaper items might be worth the kind of intensive reading associated with the Bible. The iconic, intensively read newspaper item is the single clipping of advice or poetry treasured in a wallet; its worn and tattered state inspires readers to beg editors to reprint the item—a familiar trope even in present-day Dear Abby columns. Enshrined in the solidity of a scrapbook, the single clipping becomes one of many, all worthy of rereading. "Read and re-read the best of [your scrapbooks]; study them and memorize their useful and pleasant thoughts, and you will never regret the time occupied in making your SCRAP-BOOKS," E. W. Gurley wrote in his 1880 scrapbook-making guide. He explained that exchange editors' labor in sifting and recirculating items could guide the scrapbook maker in choosing what would be worth rereading: "As a general thing, original articles are not the best. Those items, stories, and poems which have gone the rounds of the press until they have had the corners knocked off, have proved their worth by their circulation; it is 'the survival of the fittest.'" Like exchanges, scrapbooks endorsed an ideal of reuse and recirculation, of making the old continually new, in preference to originality. They rotated in the same circuit with exchanges, since much of what readers clipped might have already recirculated.[20]

Scrapbooks served as a waystation, part of a cycle of recovery from ephemeral newspapers sliding toward physical deterioration and destruction. Just as the appearance of a writer's work in the newspaper exchanges demonstrated his or her popularity, the scrapbook was understood as evidence of readers' approval. Commentators contrasted the emotional intensity attributed to the acclaim embodied in the scrapbook with both shallow popularity and overbearing high-cultural authority: "If the scrap-books of the land could to-day be drawn forth from their receptacles, we should find that Alice Cary has a place as a poet in the hearts of the people, which no mere critic in his grandeur has ever allowed," says one writer in a typical version of this move. She was accurate: the poetry of Alice and Phoebe Cary, sisters who wrote mainly on rural life, appears in nearly every poetry or general clipping scrapbook seen for this study. Similarly, one magazine defended the honor of hardworking "literary drudges," addressing the reader in this way: "The contents of your scrapbooks are made up, for the greater part, of the clever productions of literary drudges, while the effusions of pompous men of fame are found lining your trunks or enclosing your purchases from the dry goods shops." The figure of those literary drudges, like the five hundred brains so helpful in the Hartford newspaper office, contests the value of originality and literary genius. Both stand up for the value of reuse. Appreciation for short story writers, too, was demonstrated by their inclusion in scrapbooks. Scrapbooks thus constituted a dispersed system of value, which commentary often explicitly set against the more centralized power of prestigious book and magazine publication.[21]

Both newspaper exchanges and the contents of scrapbooks were understood as an index to the popular heart. They registered popularity, and they undercut the premium on originality endorsed by Romanticism—the idea that writing was produced by individual genius. After all, by the time works had "had the corners knocked off" they had likely lost their bylines as well, or even had new attributions attached to them. This was all very well from the newspapers' point of view, but if the author's name did not appear on the work snipped for newspaper or scrapbook, it did not build the author's fame.

Authorial Credit and the Circuits of Recirculation

Authors potentially garnered significant benefits from the exchange and reprint system by the late nineteenth century. Ideally, from the writer's point of view, publications paid for the right to be the first off the presses with a story or poem, and to thus acquire bragging rights. The purchasing publication not only featured the author's name with the item but could include the name in advertising a new issue or the year's offerings. Reprints in the papers that exchanged with the first publisher would ideally credit and publicize both author and publication, and thus bring authors higher fees for first publication rights.[22]

If (but only if) the author's name remained attached, writers reaped publicity that could raise their pay for article publication and attract publishers for book projects and draw audiences and fees for lectures. Authors riding the circuits of circulation were something like present-day rock musicians not signed with a record company, whose songs can be downloaded free and so who earn little from their recordings but find that the publicity generated by free downloading boosts their earnings from live appearances and sales of merchandise such as t-shirts, thus further increasing their fan base and consequently earnings from their tours. "A writer's work is his literary stock-in-trade which a reputation enhances in value," R. C. MacDonald explained in 1898. "This reputation is obtained, to a great extent, through the press, which, by copying and giving proper credit, makes the writer's work and name familiar to a large circle of readers." It often didn't work that way, however. MacDonald complained that when his magazine verse was copied without credit in a widely circulated Sunday paper, it was picked up and distributed even more widely without credit, in the self-perpetuating "chain of copying" that gave him no return.[23]

Launching his career as a lecturer, the humorist Bill Nye, who sometimes lectured alongside Mark Twain, praised exchange editors with their "sharp scented and alert...pair of scissors" for using already published work—like his—rather than "cheap original" manuscript but protested bitterly against those who snipped off the author's credit for work initially published with it. They were like thieves stealing a man's only shirt from the clothesline while he is "in bed and therefore helpless," he complained. As long as the roving editorial scissors were alert and sharp-scented, and the author was helpless and naked in bed, their anonymous works built the newspapers' (but not the authors') reputations. Publishers omitted authors' names out of carelessness or indifference, and sometimes deliberately, to keep the focus on the publication rather than the writer. Authors who wished to keep the correct name attached to a piece through the reprinting circuit and in and out of scrapbooks had to plan and persevere.[24]

If they strategized, authors could fuel their fame even with what began as anonymous reprinting. Ella Wheeler Wilcox built her popularity as a poet when she realized she could harness recirculation. She was paid for her early poems and essays of the mid-1860s, but they appeared anonymously, a situation "unsatisfactory to my ambitious nature. I carefully copied them, and sent them to country newspapers throughout the west, requesting the editors to credit them to the proper eastern periodical. This was sometimes done, but the editor more frequently gave them as original contributions to his paper." Her name, in either case, went into circulation with the poem. (Her choice of the word "copied" here significantly aligns her with editors, who referred to their reprinting of works as "copying" them and might flag an item within their newspapers "please copy.")[25]

Samuel Clemens experimented with a number of methods to attach his name to his work as he launched his career in the 1860s. The literary scholar Loren

Glass suggests that he first adopted "Mark Twain" as a nom de plume essentially to give his work a brand name and keep recirculated work from disappearing into anonymity. But even his catchy pseudonym would not have been enough incentive to editors with their cabbaging shears to leave it intact, as the fate of other pseudonymous humorists shows. Clemens made it impossible to sever the works from the byline by writing in first person about a character named Mark Twain, who is frequently addressed by name. In an early item from his Nevada days, when his brother was secretary of the Nevada Territory and he had been using the pseudonym for a year, for example, he jokes about the large number of office seekers who want him to use his supposed influence. One of the men greets him,

> Why darn it, Mark, how well you're looking! Thunder! It's been an age since I saw you. Turn around and let's look at you good. 'Gad, it's the same old Mark! Well, how've you been—and what have you been doing with yourself lately? Why don't you never come down and see a fellow? Every time I come to town, the old woman's sure to get after me for not bringing you out, as soon as I get back. Why she takes them articles of yourn, and slathers 'em into her old scrap-book, along with deaths and marriages, and receipts for the itch, and the small-pox, and hell knows what all, and if it warn't that you talk too slow to ever make love, dang my cats if I wouldn't be jealous of you. But what's the use fooling away time here?—let's go and gobble a cocktail.

The conniving flatterers in this 1864 "Letter from Carson City: Concerning Notaries" flesh out the persona who can be addressed and referred to as "Mark" as a slow talker and convivial drinker. His writerly bona fides are dangled before the reader in disarmingly disreputable form via the greeter's wife's scrapbook, which collects Mark's articles along with a hodgepodge of recipes and household hints. Twain spoofs the idea that an author's presence in a scrapbook validates his or her reputation. That "Mark" first appeared as a character in the 1863 article where Twain first used his pen name is hardly a coincidence; rather, it suggests Twain's decision to keep a tight hold on his authorial credit. The chumminess other characters exhibit toward "Mark" invites those quoting him to do the same and also invites the reader into this intimate relationship.[26]

Authorship and the Anonymity Function

When anonymous and pseudonymous publication dominated, much writing seemed to emanate from the newspaper itself. In an influential essay, "What Is an Author?" Michel Foucault defines named authorship, "the author function," by the end of the eighteenth century as having several characteristics, some of which apply to the nineteenth century. Authorship has legal status allowing texts to be owned and copy-righted; it allows authors to protect their interests in a work, and to be sued and punished for what they write. By the late nineteenth century, named authorship had come to be expected in works of literature, while scientific authors generally effaced themselves in the name of objectivity; other works eventually emerged in U.S. copy-right law as unauthored and not ownable (news, for example). As Foucault explains, the act of writing does not instantaneously or automatically make someone an author, but rather the author function arises socially, as works are interpreted and classified—grouping texts under a name, establishing a relationship between some texts, and differentiating them from others. Being an author is distinct from writing a work. So, for example, the works of Carolyn Keene, the "author" of the Nancy Drew mysteries, were written by many biological beings, but are all authored by Keene. Authorship functions something like a brand. As Mark Twain became better known, it reflected glory on newspapers to have one of his stories—readers recognized the brand—and so even the reprinted pieces where he did not appear as a character retained his name as author. Foucault's model explains why readers would find a name desirable and seek to name an author for an anonymously published work, in order to group it with other works by the possible author.[27]

But Foucault's definition of the author function does not provide a full explana-tion of how periodical readers and writers experienced authorship as newspapers recirculated materials, and readers copied and clipped them, in the nineteenth-cen-tury. As cut-and-pasted works were sheared of authorship or context and nudged back into circulation in their new form, they partook of what I call the "anonymity function." In the circuit of free recirculation, in a time when readers had come to expect named authorship, anonymity is not just the absence of a name, but a function itself.

Anonymity developed its own momentum and qualities as it mediated bet-ween writer and reader. Under anonymity, recirculated poems and stories bearing only the attribution of the newspaper from which they were copied seem to ema-nate from the entire field of the newspaper: its editors, writers, and the imagined other readers who make up the community of the newspaper. Anonymous author-ship defaults to the publication and thereby builds up the publication. It is classi-fied there and both partakes of and contributes to its authority and personality—the sense that the publication, no matter how disparate its contents, embodies a point of view that can be represented by figures such as *Life's* Winged Life cherub of Figure 1.5, or the editors in Figures 1.2, 1.3, and 1.6, or more subtly through tone and attitude. When a story appeared without author attribution in a rural weekly, credited "from *Harper's Monthly*," the rural readers in that setting would understand it as representing a distinctive *Harper's* point of view, not one of many varied items *Harper's* editors selected, and not the work of a specific author. Anonymous newspaper items also become part of the larger run of printed matter that conventionally has no author—forms, calendars, tickets, city directories, streetcar cards, advertisements, or Patent Office reports. Though issued by the largely partisan press of the nineteenth century, newspaper items could thus seem neutral, authoritative fact.[28]

At the same time, anonymity was understood as a stand-in for another identity. If an author's name had been attached to the work initially, it might be shed along the reprint trail. Anonymous publication increased velocity midcentury as items with and without their authors' names spun faster through the proliferating, rapidly circulating papers and exchanges. But because anonymity in poetry, stories, and advice was experienced as a lack by the middle to late nineteenth century, readers and editors attached new attributions to works. Those attributions might be as explicit as a name, or as shadowy as "a soldier dying in the hospital at Port Royal," but they had imaginative force and staying power.

The anonymity function—an invitation to project identities onto anonymous productions—was harnessed to reprinting and put to energetic use during the Civil War. It allowed sentiments issuing from one site to appear to be widespread rather than official or particular. So, for example, support for governmental policy could be put into the voice of the people. John Murray Forbes, an advisor to Lincoln's government and president of the New England Loyal Publication Society, a nongovernmental group organized in support of the Union, clipped or reprinted published articles favoring "vigorous prosecution of the war" and sent them out to make it easy for editors to reprint them. The prominent men of the society initially planned to sign the letters advocating republication but abandoned the plan in favor of sending them "anonymously with a printed or written line, saying, for instance, that a 'fellow-countryman calls your attention to the inclosed important article as valuable for circulation.'" They thus engaged in what present-day bloggers call sock puppetry, taking on a false identity to create the sense that many people endorse a position, as for example speaking from an invented persona to disguise the fact that an ecstatic restaurant review on a foodie website emanates from the restaurant's owner, or that praise for a reporter's work and attacks on his critics come from the reporter himself. The Loyal Publication Society's claim that the articles were passed along by an anonymous man in the street seemed more persuasive even than putting the authority of illustrious men behind it; the item could be spoken in the voice of many newspapers with diverse political affiliations, rather than by the federal government. Forbes's business role as a railroad builder and financier no doubt sensitized him to the power of recirculation, launching ideas to travel as "a train of freight cars run over the Vanderbilt system." The Loyal Publication Society sent hundreds of printed slips all over the country to nine hundred newspapers, reaching more than one million readers. Although the society may not have gone so far as to concoct a full identity for "a fellow-countryman," its choice to conceal the members' own identities allowed editors to fill the vacuum with their own imagined ideas of an ordinary reader sending the item. This filling-in process shaped the workings of anonymity in the press, as readers, clippers, and editors demonstrated their abhorrence of the authorship vacuum.[29]

Anonymity didn't always need deliberate manipulation of men such as Forbes to draw forth the face of an imagined author. Readers, too, brought their desires to fill the vacuum of anonymity. Civil War readers brought painfully powerful needs to their newspaper reading—needs that created the authors they wanted. One Civil War poem, Mary Woolsey Howland's "Mortally Wounded" (1863), offers a case study of how the anonymity function worked in relation to newspaper reprinting and scrapbook saving. I explore it in detail here because the poem's trail through broadside, newspapers, magazines, stories, and scrapbooks illuminates how reprinting functioned not just for author and publisher but in the readers' experience as well: recirculation's impact on reception.

Newspapers published during the Civil War included stories about the war, poetry, and letters from local regiments. Civilians at home seemed especially eager to hear stories of soldiers maintaining the values of what Henry Ingersoll Bowditch, a Northern abolitionist, called "religious trust and confidence that under God all events would ultimately be for our best good." They wanted to know that soldiers had "died well," even though not surrounded by loving family. Soldiers shared this ideal, the historian Drew Faust has found, to the extent of writing letters to their dead comrades' families that followed a virtual checklist of attributes of a "good death," including testimony of a belief in God and their own salvation. Poems in the voice of a dying soldier established a role for the reader on the home front as a sympathetic listener, sharing the soldier's feelings, and they created an imagined circuit of emotional response, at least from the home front point of view.[30]

Howland's poem was propelled through the circuit of reprinting and scrapbook saving because its anonymity invited reattribution. Her 1863 poem demonstrates the gathering aura of authority to speak in the voice of a soldier acquired through circulation and layers of attribution. "Mortally Wounded" picked up new titles, among them variants of this headnote: "The following lines were found under the pillow of a soldier lying dead at Port Royal." In the course of its travels, it acquired diverse attributions to soldiers.[31]

The poem is in the voice of someone ready to die, and it speaks for all the dying with a conventionally proper Protestant spirit of resignation to God's will. It appears in full in Figure 1.7 to make it easier to see the changes it underwent as it recirculated.

> I LAY me down to sleep,
> With little thought or care
> Whether my waking find
> Me here—or THERE!

Mary Woolsey Howland grew up in an affluent family well connected in publishing and literary circles. She married a wealthy Episcopalian clergyman and lived in Astoria, New York, with her five young children during the war. The Woolsey Howland family first printed "Mortally Wounded" as an anonymous

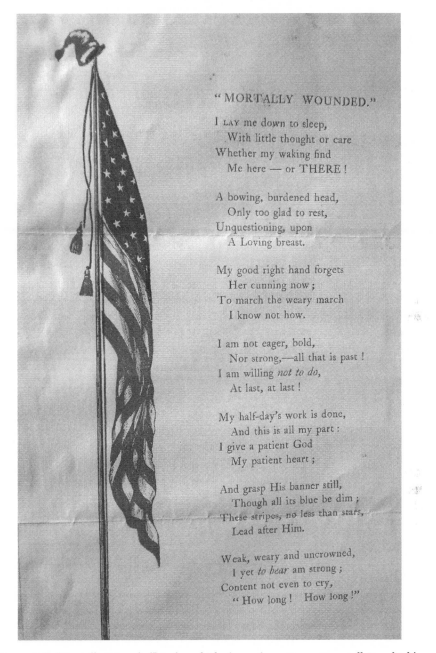

Figure 1.7 "Mortally Wounded" in broadside form, from Henry Ingersoll Bowditch's "Waifs" scrapbook. (Massachusetts Historical Society)

broadside, where it is flanked by a U.S. flag topped by a liberty cap. The poem was probably given to soldiers in this form. Mary Howland's sisters and cousins made up a formidable distribution network: Mary's sisters Georgeanna Woolsey and Jane Stuart Woolsey, who worked as nurses and hospital administrators, and another sister, Eliza Woolsey Howland, and their cousin Sarah Chauncey Woolsey both nurses and helpers in Union hospitals, all participated in spreading her poetry, as did Henry Hopkins, a hospital chaplain and family friend. This poem soon appeared in newspapers—possibly arriving there through her family connections, as had a previous anonymous Howland poem. The anonymity of her poem's initial private publication was an ordinary product of Victorian propriety and Howland's role as a domestic woman. But the anonymity function created an effect that was the same as if she had cross-dressed or sent it out under the assumed name of a soldier.[32]

"Mortally Wounded" traveled far on fraudulent identity papers and was extensively reprinted, acquiring introductions establishing two distinct lineages. One attributed it to "S. S____, a Massachusetts Sergeant," but more often it carried the heading, "The following lines were found under the pillow of a soldier who was lying dead in a hospital near Port Royal, South Carolina." Howland's anonymous broadside, which her relatives scattered about the hospitals, might well have made its way beneath a dying soldier's pillow. But most of the reprints insist that a soldier endorsed the sentiments by actually having produced them. Read with that assumption, the poem's speaker upholds sentiments of self-sacrifice and puts his body behind them: he really must have died, otherwise the space under the pillow would not have been searchable. That searchable space softly and tastefully denotes his death. The powerful implication that the dying soldier had actually *inscribed* the words and left them under his pillow tenaciously adhered to the poem. Dropping the final verse of the poem, as most reprinters did, aided the poem's reconfiguration. Instead of waiting patiently to die or survive longer, and asking "how long, how long?" the speaker becomes a soldier marching in God's army with the stripes of the U.S. flag analogized to Christ's wounds. Shortening it gave it firmer closure within the military context.

Reprinters elaborated the deathbed scene created by deleting the final verse and adding the "found under the pillow" attribution. The lines "carry intrinsic evidence of their genuineness under the circumstances....Unconsciously, the writer, in his artlessness, has reached the highest triumph of art," one writer gushed. Another, writing twenty-five years after the war, jumped in to turn the scene into a tribute to the U.S. flag: "One soldier who had been brave in battle, who had received his death-wound, and whose life was slowly ebbing away, gazed upon [the flag], and then, with faltering hand, wrote these heart-felt lines." Despite widespread affirmation of belief in the genuineness of the poem as dying words, the poem's literary qualities distanced it from the plausible speech of a dying person, and thus from the voyeuristic implications of intruding on an actual deathbed. That was too sacred for intrusion, Mary Woolsey Howland's mother complained, in rejecting a request from eager fundraisers to gather *actual* dying words of soldiers for a collection.[33]

Almost a year after the close of the war, an African American paper, *The Christian Recorder*, picked up the poem from an 1865 reprinting in the compendium the *Living Age* and went on to endow the soldier with solidity and specificity in its introduction: "We have never, we believe, seen verses more true and touching than those which we give below. . . . That nameless soldier had a cultured mind and a noble spirit, and on his poor pallet in the Southern Hospital went out a light that might have cheered and illumined many." For this Protestant paper, the soldier's authorship and "his" death are crucial to the poem's value. Although Howland herself had died by the time of this reprinting, the *Christian Recorder* would hardly have praised a woman's death at home in the same terms; it was crucial that the sentiments be those of a soldier. Howland's anonymity obscured those threads that would tie her war poems to other pious poems to classify them as the entirely appropriate and even predictable sentiments of a minister's wife. The relation of Howland's poems to one another was known to her home circle, and eventually to some postbellum anthologies, but not to those who read her poems on slips of paper or in newspapers.[34]

The anonymity function offered readers and editors a vote on the most appealing or useful version of authorship, and even which stanzas to use. The elision that shifts a poem from "inspired by" to "found with" or "written by" is pressured by the need to hear the voice of the dead, to believe that they are at peace with their death and agree that the sacrifice was worth it. The ethical problem of speaking for dead soldiers who could not refute such claims seems not to have disturbed those who circulated poems and attached attributions to them. Newspaper recirculation created and reinforced the belief that the poem was written by a soldier, and this certification by authoritative sources gave it credentials that paradoxically reinforced its place in the domestic world.[35]

Recirculation and anonymity allowed the poem to be repeatedly inserted into the discourse of war and mourning, both literally and figuratively. Henry Ingersoll Bowditch, whose scrapbooks mourning his son killed in the Civil War are discussed in Chapter 3, found the poem so meaningful that he pasted three copies of it into his poetry scrapbook, classifying it under the headings "Religious hope and consolation," "Campaign incidents and life," and "Elegiac." Its profuse reprinting and staying power resulted in his having the broadside, a newspaper copy, and another hand-copied for him fourteen years after the war. Recirculation and reprinting not only spread the poem far and wide but layered and amplified its meaning for its readers. The poem's supposed connection to a soldier's death in the hospital made it the occasion within stories and anecdotes for firmly placing other pious soldiers' deaths in the religious framework of salvation, and modeling the saving and hand-to-hand sharing of news-paper mourning poetry. In an 1866 story in the Methodist monthly the *Ladies' Repository*, for example, a young woman who has lost her beloved in the war despairs at the postwar situation, as she reads the newspaper, and expresses her feelings in a phrase that sets up the poem's "patient heart" as a response: "It seemed too hard to bear—harder because being a woman, I might not give indignant voice to my most indignant heart." She believes the sacrifices of war were not worth it. When she finds her Aunt Deborah Parsons, who was a nurse in a Union hospital, weeping over "a little slip of newspaper" with "Mortally Wounded" on it, she reads the clipping—thus reprinting the shortened version in the story. "'Poor boy,' said aunt Debby wiping her eyes, as I unconsciously read the lines aloud, 'that's just the way many a one has died.... That was the way with Jamie; nobody knew just when he went.'"[36]

Reading Howland's poem—in the form of a treasured clipping—becomes the occasion for Aunt Debby to tell the story of Jamie, a pious soldier she nursed. The clipping allows Debby to express her grief and talk about her experience. Reprinting it in the story sends it back into circulation and makes it available for more of the clipping it models for the magazine's readers. The story both uses, and shows how to use, the recirculated poem to connect domestic life to the dying soldier, relieve feelings through sympathetic weeping together, and channel postwar despair into religious faith that suffering will be rewarded. Hand-to-hand domestic recircula-tion dramatized within the story brings the poem full circle from its origins in domestic religious life, while the story's publication in a Protestant monthly silently returns it to its origins in the parsonage—with Aunt Deborah Parsons's surname alluding to the poem's ministerial work.

Although later modes of public, asynchronous writing collaboration such as wikis often notify earlier contributors when later writers make changes, and at least in theory resolve conflicts in a single document, the newspapers' and scrap-books' dispersed modes of distributing information and literature meant that even attempts to correct information, such as an anthology that published accu-rate attribution, could go unseen, or be deliberately ignored in favor of the preferred version of authorship. The vacuum of anonymous publication sucked authoring possibilities into it. It allowed shadowy, specific, or multiple attribu-tions to be applied to a poem. The author function creates and names an entity with legal responsibility for a piece of writing; the anonymity function—an unnamed author combined with recirculation—protects a work's openness to reattribution. It thus protects the capacity of the work to be understood, in mul-tiple settings, as coming from diverse sources, and it thereby protects the varied understandings and interpretations that flow from those attributions. Readers and even editors seemed to understand every contradictory attribution as con-tributing a new layer of information. The lines could be found under a pillow as though produced by a dying soldier, and somehow also be by Mrs. Robert Howland, as one 1896 anthology had it.[37]

Newspapers reprinted the text of items and sent them around the exchanges, but clipping savers like Aunt Debby and Bowditch and other scrapbook compilers clipped the physical iteration out of the newspaper. Scrapbooks were therefore more than just another node on the recirculation circuit. Some scrapbook compilers took visible, identifiable advantage of the repetition of a poem in multiple newspapers to clip it several times. For other scrapbook makers, the impact of exchanges and reprinting was direct but less visible.

Creating New Value

Clipping and saving the contents of periodicals in scrapbooks is a form of active reading that shifts the line between reading and writing. Readers become the agents who make or remake the meaning and significance of their saved items. The fact that recontextualizing newspaper items into a scrapbook changes their value was a transformation that struck nineteenth-century readers with great force. The transformation from trash to treasure, the instability of value, and the potential of the disregarded and marginal to reveal astonishing worth are themes that appear repeatedly in nineteenth-century popular writing, in works that illuminate the cultural assumptions of their period—such as the story of Dick Whittington's cat. The story, published in many American nineteenth-century story collections and school readers, appealed to the sense that riches lurked in the commonplace. The rat-catching cat, common in London, is packed off on a trading voyage to a rat-infested land with no cats. Dick wins a fortune for his now-valuable recontextualized cat. Other stories apply this move to clippings.[38]

In one short story in the popular press, a clipping in a newspaper critic's scrapbook unmasks a murderer by exposing a long-hidden connection between the killer and his victim. The recontextualized clipping, juxtaposed with knowledge of a crime, reveals covert motives. In another story, a newspaper editor keeps scrapbooks on the evil deeds of all the men in his town. The editor's scrapbooks serve as a hidden record and conscience. The articles are simply dormant in the newspaper, but the scrapbook activates them and gives them value by juxtaposing them with other clippings that reveal hidden meanings.

Obviously, such stories flattered newspaper workers, and were thus more likely to emerge from the slush pile to be published. More crucially, they assert that what seems to be junk can, in a new context, be the source of power.[39]

Scrapbook makers sometimes invoked the term *gleaning* to describe their work, and columns of miscellaneous matter in the periodicals were headed "Gleanings." (One scrapbook I have seen even has a print of Jean François Millet's painting "The Gleaners" on its cover.) Gleaning implies gathering the small bits, the leftovers, the dropped grapes or the grain left in the corners of the field—the surplus and excess—and making a meal of them. The gleaner does not own the land and did not produce the crop or livestock but steps in when it is ready, takes what is available, and puts it to her or his own uses.[40]

In Agnes Varda's film on twentieth-century gleaning, *The Gleaners and I,* which follows people who take up the left-behind stuff of fields, markets, and street corners to put it back into circulation as nourishment or art, materials are waste and treasure simultaneously according to the person and the context. One artist, for example, displays a map, which he earnestly explains gives the schedule of where and when to look for valuables on the street. Varda points out that it is a trash-collection schedule. If seen correctly, the material in the corners of the fields, in the margins of discarded print, is precious. This transformational potential—treasure lurking in news clippings—is expressed repeatedly in nineteenth-century commentary, where newspapers are full of riches, but worthless in piles; the riches can be concentrated and compiled into scrapbooks, where we can see their worth because the material in them is findable again as they become the repository of the wisdom of the past.[41]

Agricultural gleaning has important reciprocal elements: the gleaners' bounty depends on the planter's willingness not to squeeze every possible bit of profit from the land; following the biblical injunction to leave food for the gleaners, the landowner does not pursue every last scrap of grain or produce but leaves some unclaimed. Just as authors cannot nail meaning to a fixed spot, neither can they or their publishers control the circulation and ordering or reordering of meaning. Even when copyright locks down the right to reproduce a text, readers have the option of moving an old text to a new context, creating a new tier of private circulation: clipping texts out of newspapers, pasting them into scrapbooks (or today onto web pages), and circulating this new compiled version. Gleaners can still create multiple meanings and readings from the text—and can even bake bread from gleaned grain and sell it under the gleaner's label.[42]

Scrapbook makers gleaned the press and then built and solidified community through their activities of gathering and reusing. Like present-day fan groups writing and sharing fan fiction and analyses based on TV series, scrapbook makers applied sophisticated approaches to popular media and remade it into a new form as they enriched their sense of connection through that work. At least one group of nineteenth-century African American scrapbook makers knew one another and invited others to see the works they created. Representations of scrapbook makers as a community collaborating in their scrapbook making are most closely associated with families and children. The farm family in particular, in its isolated home, is envisioned

> gathered around the fireside of a winter's evening overhauling a bundle
> of papers....Each one may have his or her own book. The father may

have the general topic of the "The Farm," the mother "The Home." One of the boys likes horses and cattle, and he is on the lookout for everything in that line; one of his sisters is poetical, another romantic, and "poetry" and "stories" will fall to them, and so on through all the topics.[43]

Scrapbook making is imagined as an occasion for domestic sociability, a way of uniting the interests of the farm and farmhouse through the medium of the pastepot. E. W. Gurley here holds out the ideal that by sifting through and gleaning the detritus of the cheap press, the marginalized rural family can glean, classify, and recontextualize marginalized material and thereby create value from it. As a group gathers to pull apart mainstream culture and remake it for their own uses, they create their own cultural nexus, a knot of threads leading into and out of the family or community, and they make themselves more culturally central.

Imposing the Scrapbook Maker's Will

The scrapbook's ability to transform trash to riches and power, or at least to authority, to make clippings valuable through recontextualizing and repurposing, slid along two axes. The first was the shift in audience—transporting the clippings either to other people, for whom the clippings would be a rich novelty, or to a future self, who would need the gleaned information and items and could put them to uses unavailable to the earlier self holding the pastepot. Creating value through a shift in audience implied that the scrapbook maker's selection from the newspaper at the time of pasting were worth preserving and passing along. Through the coercion of choosing and rearranging items—and obliterating the pasted side of the clipping—the scrapbook maker enforced his or her will on the reader. The second was moving materials from the flickering ephemerality of an old newspaper into the permanence of a book: giving it the earmarks of value.

As they scissored in and scissored out, amassing and excluding, scrapbook makers imposed their will on what they read. They created a version of the newspaper that preserves only what they considered worth preserving, and organized that material within their own structure of arrangements and juxtaposition. Twenty-first-century scholars may be profoundly grateful to a scrapbook maker who saved clippings from newspapers of which no other copies exist; nonetheless, those choices also excluded materials that we now can't see—left behind in the trash or obliterated by paste. The scrapbook's coercive reordering of media, its way of materializing its maker's assertion that what he or she selects from the newspaper is more important and valuable than the rest, is highlighted in an 1878 story, "Frederick Dean's Will," in which a man keeps a scrapbook of financial clippings. His adopted daughter jokes with him, "Who but you would ever have thought of a scrapbook of financials?" and teases him to include "a love story, or a bit of poetry"—items she considers scrapbook essentials.[44]

After Dean's death, when his will cannot be found and his evil brother throws her out, she picks up his now sentimentally valuable scrapbook. Seeking communion with her adoptive father by reading the "financials" he read, she finds his missing will within its pages, leaving his estate to her. Like other scrapbooks, her father's collection both allows her to see through its maker's eyes and constrains her to read what he valued. Although the idea that riches lurk in the scrapbook runs through the nineteenth-century cultural understanding of scrapbooks, few scrapbook makers hold the power to reward their readers with an estate. Frederick Dean's "will," in the sense of intention or hope, survives in his scrapbook as his desire that his daughter read his favored reading matter. He materially rewards her for doing so. His legacy circumvents the structures of biological kinship both through law and through the intellectual and spiritual connection that impels his adopted daughter to try on her father's reading interests by reading his scrapbook. The will of other scrapbook makers likewise survives in their scrapbook's selections and arrangements of stories, articles, poems, and pictures.

At its most basic, almost any scrapbook was intended for its maker's future rereading, or even for reading a saved item for the first time, like the child who received a scrap of poetry from Walt Whitman. The future and ideal selves that scrapbooks address might be living in very different circumstances from those of the scrapbook maker, as was true for Frances Amanda Smith Cather.[45]

Many scrapbook makers seem to have felt great confidence that their future selves would always remember their reasons for saving material as they read their scrapbooks, that the grief expressed in collecting poems about dead children would always be fresh, or that the scrapbook itself would cue recollections if they needed to explain it to someone else. They rarely include explanatory text or obvious connecting threads between items, which were perhaps so overwhelmingly evident to the scrapbook maker that they seemed superfluous. Perhaps the scrapbook maker assumed he would be the only reader, or would be present to hover at the reader's elbow, saying, *I chose this because... ; this obituary is of my old schoolmate; this poem is by my mother's favorite poet.* Scrapbook makers who refused to lend their scrapbooks exerted another method of controlling how people read the clippings they had amassed and given value to. Lending it out meant ceding control. E.W. Gurley's 1880 guide to making scrapbooks noted that, of his thirty scrapbooks, his volume "Fun" was "usually seized by my reading friends, and is a favorite volume with book borrowers, would-be borrowers. For I would as soon loan my clock, or my cow, as my scrapbooks." Scrapbooks made the value readers saw and created in their clippings manifest by ensconcing them within the covers of books.[46]

Scrapbooks and Cultural Transmission

Scrapbooks were often suggested as an ideal gift for an invalid child or adult alone in sickbed and in need of amusement, but too ill to make her own—picture scrapbooks for children, stories and poetry for adults. Whether or not the recipients enjoyed their gifts, putting together a scrapbook of wastepaper to pass along to someone who is imagined to benefit from it had a seductive appeal. Like giving old clothes to the poor, it let the giver feel beneficent with no expense. It allowed the maker—in Frederick Dean's top-down move—to pass down his or her version of the newspaper, and thus the giver's taste, at very little cost. The middle-class children's magazine *St. Nicholas* urged children to form a "Ministering Children's League" to do good deeds, which included making scrapbooks for poor, invalid children. It was attractive to church groups, who organized socials for young people to make scrapbooks for shut-ins preferably clipping the religious press, and so again passing along the will of the creators, further shaped by the adults supplying the papers. The young people, moreover, were inculcated with the sense that their choices of what to pass along were worthwhile, and that their cultural detritus was valuable. In the 1930s, the *Chicago Defender* used this idea to get material from a northern black newspaper into the hands of Southern black children, as Chapter 4 discusses.[47]

Making scrapbooks was both work and a leisure activity; making scrapbooks also occupied children who might otherwise require the adult labor of supervision. Like gatherings to finish quilts (another popular nineteenth-century form that used scissors to create new value from scraps and discards), scrapbook socials imbued the scrapbook with associations of memory—the creator's memory of the origins of the materials, and the memory of social interaction in "overhauling a bundle of papers" to create the book.

The trope of passive, grateful receipt of scrapbook beneficence appears repeatedly in fiction, where a kindly summer visitor sparks a poor crippled boy's finer sensibilities with the gift of a scrapbook of material from magazines in Elizabeth Stuart Phelps's "The Madonna of the Tubs," for example. The trope was shopworn enough by 1888 that Louisa May Alcott renovated it in a children's story, "Little Pyramus and Thisbe," in which poor crippled Johnny takes on the donor role by making scrapbooks for neighbors of the street corner where he sits. The papers and scraps that blow around him create what he calls his circulating library: the wind circulates the papers around him, and he pastes them into scrapbooks made of brown paper or more newspaper, which "afterwards made the rounds of neighbors until they were worn out." The arrival of the young daughter of an Italian artist in the house next door inspires him to dig through the wall next to him with his scissors, into her garden, to offer her his scrapbooks as gifts, while she gives him oranges. The exchange escalates, until he is taken into her family to be educated as an artist. His esteem for his collected pictures and the mutuality of the exchange permits a different relationship from the largess of wastepaper circulating from the rich to the poor, or the healthy to the well, in the usual version of the exhortation to make scrapbooks for the poor or ill. The poor, ill child's making and circulating scrapbooks that enforce his will as a reader marks him as a doer and cultural authority, able to put his mark on paper as an artist.[48]

Repurposing Books as Scrapbooks:
Useless or Useful?

When one early-nineteenth-century commonplace book keeper carefully transcribes a passage from Jane Porter's novel *Thaddeus of Warsaw*, and a scrapbook maker about the same time pastes over a copy of that same novel with gems of poetry and useful facts clipped from newspapers, we may be seeing different generational preferences at work. The older generation, with its commonplace book, honors the slow-moving novel, while the up-to-the-minute early adaptor of scrapbook making discards the 1803 historical novel in favor of *au courant* materials of the 1830s. The scrapbook maker valued the small format of this edition of *Thaddeus* for making a pocket-sized compendium capacious enough to include an article attacking the dangers of novel reading and another short snippet praising newspaper reading (Figure 1.8). The medium created boundaries for the collection. Each item's *newspaperness*, its appearance in a newspaper as well as its content, defined it as something accessible to clipping.[49]

Rather than buy blank books or albums, many scrapbook compilers reused and pasted over books. The volumes they obliterated ranged from outdated school textbooks and government reports to used business, farm, and plantation ledgers, and to novels, sermon collections, and Bibles. They prized the visual and tactile qualities of the bound book as well as its prestige. So a clipping pasted into a scrapbook that obliterates a book of Richard Baxter's Puritan sermons shows the esteem for books felt by someone who had in a sense destroyed a book. It is a list of twenty-four rules for the physical care of books: "Never hold a book near a fire. Never drop a book upon the floor....Never turn down corners of leaves....Never write upon a paper laid upon the leaves of an open book, as the pencil or pen point will either scratch or cut the book leaves," etc.[50] (see Figure Intro.1).

The possibility of repurposing printed books takes advantage of the authority of printed books, even while questioning it. The suggestion is to keep an evaluative, critical, and acquisitive eye toward books: Are they worth keeping in their present state, or would they be more useful pasted over with newspaper clippings? It seems as outrageous as cannibalism, as though we asked, Is this person more interesting as a dinner companion, or as a steak? The answer evaded a morality that considers books sacrosanct. What, then, made a book's binding and paper seem more worthwhile than its contents?

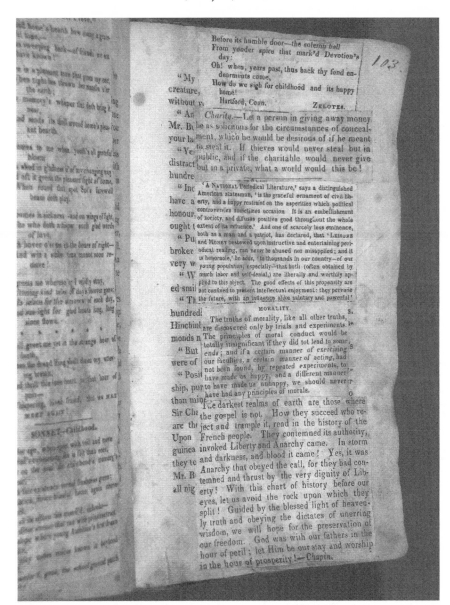

Figure 1.8 Two pages from *Thaddeus of Warsaw* scrapbook: Article praising periodicals and article attacking novel reading. (Author's collection)

Government-issued Patent Office reports, including agricultural reports, headed the list of books repurposed as scrapbooks. Margaret Lynn, who grew up in the Missouri Valley in the 1870s and 1880s, recalled that her brothers and sister fashioned scrapbooks from agricultural and horticultural reports, a heavy box of which her family received every year, presumably to distribute to neigh-

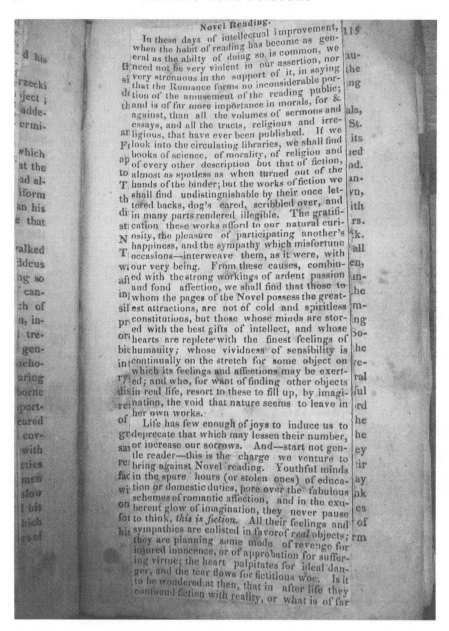

Figure 1.8 Continued

bors. These tedious reports were not blank but instead empty of any meaning for Lynn; making them into scrapbooks redeemed them.

From our point of view the books were quite unreadable and almost piti-
fully useless. A book that couldn't be read was an abject thing. It didn't

seem possible that so many books should be published with absolutely nothing in them. They were full of pictures, and that was promising, for naturally one expects the presence of pictures to indicate literature of the lighter sort. But such pictures as they were when you came to look at them! Common bugs in all stages of unbeautiful growth; worms only less ugly than in life; hens, mere hens, standing up to have their pictures taken.... It was really surprising that men could think it worth while to waste print on such matter as this—they must have wanted tremendously to make a book.[51]

She and her siblings, too, "wanted tremendously to make a book." Lynn felt a passionate connection to literature, a craving for the company of "folks in books." (She later became an English professor.) But the literature she encountered seemed unconnected to the life around her. The poets she read spoke of flowers she had never seen, and she asked, "Who had ever heard of the Missouri in a novel or a poem?" Such complaints often lead to calls for literature grounded in daily experience. Instead, her scrapbooks gave her a more tangible alternative for melding the seemingly incompatible elements of farm life and poetry. The poems she admired in the local press were no more local in subject matter, but she could use them to obliterate the unbeautiful hens and worms. Her scrapbook physically replicated literature's ability to carry her away from common bugs. Hers was one among thousands (Figure 1.9).

Those useless books particularly favored for remaking as scrapbooks had their own history. Congress began issuing the Patent Office's yearly reports and its agricultural reports in 1849, and distributing them free to constituents, especially during campaigns. Congress supported the appropriations on the theory that voters would be pleased to have a fat volume full of useful or not-so-useful information, heavily illustrated, even if the illustrations were of unbeautiful hens and bugs. By 1873 the annual printing of the Patent Office's agricultural reports ran to 260,000 copies of a ponderous volume of more than five hundred pages. Characteristically without named authors, government reports embodied institutional authorship. They were thus another manifestation of the kind of anonymous, morselized, self-effaced information characteristic of the newspaper columns that often displaced their pages with newer information. The contents of the reports lost out to the power of newness, at least at the moment of pasting. The claim of presenting up-to-date information on farming or inventions incited readers to soon regard the information as outmoded. Following the logic of the media's flicker of information rapidly turning to noninformation, clippers replaced it with other media.[52]

Their heft and availability made the Patent Office's agricultural reports particularly enticing for pasting over. E. W. Gurley's 1880 advice book on making scrapbooks recommends using these volumes of four hundred pages or so because they were the right size to hold two columns per page, and "better

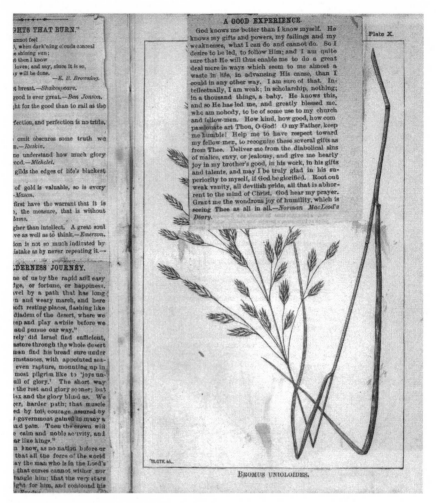

Figure 1.9 Agricultural report repurposed as scrapbook. (Author's collection)

adapted to the [home] library than larger and more cumbrous books prepared expressly for scrapbooks." The reports "can be found in nearly every farm house, and are seldom read." The panopticon of the Web lets us spy on Gurley as hustler: in 1896 he wrote to the agency publishing the *North Carolina Agricultural Report* to cadge more copies: "I read and preserve all your publications and find them good and instructive. . . . Keep the bulletins coming to me. [I h]ave them all on file. I can't run the ranch without them." "Preserve" was clearly an ambiguous term. Other advisors on making scrapbooks luxuriated in the freely distributed abundance as well: "There are 500, 600, and 700 pages in each book. These books can be obtained . . . a few at a time, and cost nothing. (I have now thirteen copies ready for use when I need them)," one writer boasted. The editor of the California magazine *Overland Monthly* describes in 1896 finding the scrapbook he kept as a young man, and wrote, "It is an old 'Agricultural Report,' and emits a damp, aged odor." He assumes his readers will understand his offhand compression, without stopping to explain that he made his scrapbook by pasting clippings into an old book. Their abundant pages incited others to join in with their own power to choose information and impose their own will on a book.[53]

Other government and official documents attracted the pastepot as well: Joseph W. H. Cathcart, an African American janitor who worked in a Philadelphia office building where city directories, government reports including legislative reports, and banking reports must have been discarded, used them and covered over the kinds of financial materials Frederick Dean valued, to make his dense assemblage of clippings on the rapid shifts in African American legal standing and life during and just after the Civil War. His use of the well-bound, uniform books gave his works a solid authority on his bookshelves, which drew comment from reporters. (The density of his pasting often makes it difficult to discern what underlying book he supplanted.).

Used ledger books, once the transactions they recorded were complete or the business was dissolved, were also often pressed into service. Susan B. Anthony thanked the businessmen of Rochester for giving her ample, spacious used ledgers to paste up her history as a speaker and suffrage campaigner. The ledgers' imposing size, 11 by 17 inches, gave her retrospective work more scope for juxtaposition and proclaimed the importance of the history they contain. Reusing books allowed a scrapbook maker to perpetually renew his or her library, even if an obsolete law tome's print was replaced with plans for house building, or the outdated geography book with religious verse, or the no-longer-tolerable book of Puritan sermons with sentimental stories. Such reuse signals greater regard for newer material and often at least implies a critique of the original book.[54]

Clippings Talk to Books

Just as newspaper items in scrapbooks carry with them a surplus of information beyond what they may have been selected for, books repurposed as scrapbooks are still both the books they once were and the scrapbooks they have become. The dialogue between the two texts can be complex, as in the case of the book of Baxter's Puritan sermons displaced by stories and verse endorsing the value of home. The scrapbook maker plies the shears at the crossroads of media.

Gurley called scrapbooks "secret histories," for good reason. They may reveal at least as much through what they choose to obliterate as in what they

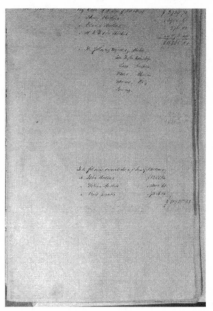

Figure 1.10 Facing pages from Horlbeck family scrapbook, 1854 ledger page enumerating enslaved people facing a page covered by baseball clippings from around 1915. (Southern Historical Collection, Library of the University of North Carolina at Chapel Hill)

paste down, and they can suggest more about family ties and fractures in the language of erasure. So for all the white South's tradition of veneration and nostalgia for its antebellum history and its saving of victorious Confederate war news and Confederate memorabilia in scrapbooks, I have seen at least two scrapbooks that cover over this history rather than feature it. In the early twentieth century, a white South Carolina child pasted a collection of 1910s and 1920s baseball articles and World War I cartoons over what started out as an 1830s plantation ledger that enumerates slaves. The pastings stop short of obscuring all the listings of enslaved people's names, but they interrupt the ledger's use as a historical document. The affluent white child plays alongside the origins of the family's wealth, directing the reader's attention away from spidery handwritten tables of "Negroes" listing "1. Old Louis, 60, $500; 2. Simon Peter, 40, $1200; 3. Bella, 38, $500," to bright magazine ads for a film of *Tom Sawyer*, and cheery sports news. In handing the book over to the child to use in play, did older household members choose to cover over the plantation past? (Figure 1.10) Another white Southerner writing with scissors and pastepot, Sallie Robertson of Caswell, North Carolina, who had lost her brother in the Civil War was in her forties in the 1870s when she made her scrapbook from a family ledger. She seems to have deliberately obscured her family's recent slaveholding history more assiduously than its involvement in tobacco, as she piled recipes and advice, often attributed to exchanges with Northern newspapers, more thoroughly over the pages keeping track of slaves.[55]

Pasters need not explain a stance or articulate a position; all they have to do is slap clippings over earlier writing to create a record that expresses at least indifference, and possibly outright hostility, to what lies underneath. For the 1880s owner and pastebrush wielder of Baxter's *Saints Rest*, originally a gift from L. G. Swett to her sister E.P.G. in 1843, the ties that linked the book to the sisters were insufficient reason to preserve the contents of the book; its sermons likewise lacked interest. It was more worthwhile as an armature for stories of women and girls reknitting families and improving their lives by providing nicer homes—a new religion of domesticity, now well housed in a book with the sermon writer's imprimatur. The generational saga is sketched with an eraser.[56]

Puck magazine's 1883 futuristic fantasy of the affluent apartment where everything is delivered (Figure Intro.4) imagines a future of individualized, segmented periodical reading, with papers disposed of as soon as read. Actual households and individuals saved their newspapers and did their own segmenting. They followed their individual curiosity and interests, or cut and pasted as a family enterprise, as Gurley suggested. Far from unspooling newspaper directly into wastebaskets as the cartoon family does, they pasted fresh material and writing that had already circulated through the press into permanent repositories: substantial books that had once been valued for some other content. They borrowed the authority that came with the heft and substantial binding of such books, and even its residual authorship. Or they bought fresh new blank books—which, in the case of Mark Twain's Self Pasting Scrap-Book, already had an author's name attached.

Mark Twain's Scrapbook Innovations

In the years after Samuel Clemens invented the name "Mark Twain," he became popular as a humorous writer and lecturer, traveling the country on grueling lecture tours. In 1865 his "Jim Smiley and His Jumping Frog" (later titled "The Celebrated Jumping Frog of Calaveras County") raised him from a local Western favorite to a writer the whole country wanted to read and sought out by name, and whom any newspaper would want to publish. His publications increased his popularity as a lecturer, while his comic lectures fed the appetite for his written work.

Samuel Clemens was well aware, early on, of the benefits and disadvantages of recirculation. Adding the character *Mark Twain* to his works made sure that his pen name stayed attached to his works as they rode the Vanderbilt railroad of recirculation. He brought the same strategizing to naming the scrapbook he invented, and he took advantage of the newspapers' habit of recirculation to promote it.

Mark Twain's Patented Self Pasting Scrap Book

Once the name Mark Twain became valuable, its presence in newspaper columns helped advertise his books. Although republication in newspapers and magazines without pay was customary and brought writers some benefits, books were another matter. If reprinting and being "scissorized" into other papers was a sign of a writer's popularity, one payoff (as Fanny Fern learned) was book publication. But nineteenth-century writers were often in the galling position of receiving nothing when book publishers made money from republishing their work in anthologies, or even publishing entire collections of their work that had previously appeared in newspapers or magazines. Periodical publication usually placed works in the public domain (it was rare for newspapers or magazines to undertake the cumbersome process of copyrighting individual works within their publications, as was legally required to secure copyright at that time). Though sometimes called "piracy," such reprinting was legal. Earnings for Twain's books were often diverted into the pockets of others when the books were legally reprinted without his permission, with no profit to him.

In contrast to reprints interfering with Twain's profiting from his writing, hitching his name to a consumer product from which he profited gave him con-flict-free benefits from the newspaper circuit of free reprinting; unlike his recircu-lated writings, the scrapbook posed no danger of satiating the reader with the sampled work. The circuits of exchange and recirculation benefited his scrapbook-manufacturing enterprise both directly, by keeping free publicity for the scrap-book moving through papers and magazines, and indirectly, because the quantities of clippings in circulation generated the need to file and accommodate them. Scrapbooks were suggested in most discussions as the best type of repository. After 1877, newspapers often proffered Mark Twain's Patented Self Pasting Scrap Book as an especially good choice of scrapbook. The Mark Twain scrapbook was thus an engine rechanneling the benefit stream of recirculation, at least to one writer. It invited every purchaser to create his or her own pirated book.

Samuel Clemens was a man of faith in innovation and quick wealth. He dab-bled in invention, devising an "adjustable and detachable strap for vests, panta-loons or other garments requiring straps," and a history game, and he invested disastrously in other people's inventions. A former printer, he was seduced by the Kaolatype, an unsuccessful process for casting with clay rather than engraving the plates used for book illustration and for binding decorations; and by James Paige's automatic typesetting contraption, on which Clemens famously lost at least $180,000, bankrupting himself in the process. His scrapbook, however, made money when, beginning in 1877, the New York stationery company of his friend Daniel Slote manufactured it in many sizes and styles, selling it from 40 cents to $5.00.[1]

Clemens first described his scrapbook to his brother and occasional business helper, Orion, in a letter that was vigilant about its status as a legal document recording the creation of his idea, urgently calling attention to the postmark's standing as evidence. From the first, he complicated the terms for understanding what he told his brother was his "great humanizing and civilizing invention." He frames its utility from the point of view of a consumer who wants to keep a scrap-book, as Clemens did. Yet he describes the blank book in the language of a printer: its adhesive strips should be a "length of say 20 ems, small pica"; then becomes a user again: the blank between the strips should be "about as broad as your finger." It is to be both a portable convenient invention, and a printed book, like other books he has written. And in fact the label inside the scrapbooks identifies the scrapbooks as "published" rather than manufactured or printed, by Slote's statio-nery firm. By 1902 the scrapbooks even included a dated title page. The scrapbook pages were covered with gummed strips, which the user moistened like older postage stamps (Figure 2.1).[2]

Slote and Mark Twain jumped on this ambiguity in marketing the books. Their comical ad featured a letter from Twain to Slote, proposing the scrapbook, which explained that his scrapbook would "economize the profanity of this country" by preventing irritation when the glue could not be found or was dried out, and it was

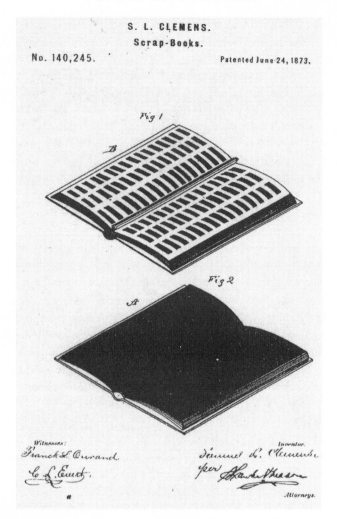

Figure 2.1 Drawing from the patent application for Mark Twain's Self-Pasting Scrap-Book, showing gummed strips.

therefore a "sound moral work." Mark Twain's name and the letter's cleverness caught editors' attention. Newspapers refashioned the ad to include it in columns of miscellaneous paragraph items and nascent literary gossip sections, reprinting it for free. The intimate tone of the letter allowed them to quote it as though it were a personal communication with them: "Mark writes..."[3] (Figure 2.2).

Newspaper writers and critics understood that a comical ad from Mark Twain invited them to collaborate in promoting the book by saying something witty in response to this novelty. The *Danbury News* picked up Twain's line about profanity, reporting that the scrapbook was "a valuable book for purifying the domestic atmosphere, and... contains nothing that the most fastidious person could object

DIFFICULTIES OF THE OLD STYLE SCRAP BOOK.

MARK TWAIN'S DESCRIPTION OF HIS INVENTION:

HARTFORD, Monday Evening.

MY DEAR SLOTE :—I have invented and patented a new Scrap Book, not-to make money out of it, but to economise the profanity of this country. You know that when the average man wants to put something in his scrap book he can't find his paste—then he swears; or if he finds it, it is dried so hard that it is only fit to eat—then he swears; if he uses mucilage it mingles with the ink, and next year he can't read his scrap—the result is barrels and barrels of profanity. This can all be saved and devoted to other irritating things, where it will do more real and lasting good, simply by substituting my self-pasting Scrap Book for the old-fashioned one.

If Messrs. Slote, Woodman & Co. wish to publish this Scrap Book of mine, I shall be willing. You see by the above paragraph that it is a sound moral work, and this will commend it to editors and clergymen, and in fact to all right feeling people. If you want testimonials I can get them, and of the best sort, and from the best people. One of the most refined and cultivated young ladies in Hartford (daughter of a clergyman) told me herself, with grateful tears standing in her eyes, that since she began using my Scrap Book she has not sworn a single oath.

Truly yours,   MARK TWAIN.

ADVANTAGES OF THE NEW STYLE SCRAP BOOK.

Figure 2.2 Mark Twain promotional letter advertisement with "before" and "after" pictures on the effects of using his scrapbook.

to, and is, to be frank and manly, the best thing of any age—mucilage particularly." The *Norristown Herald* announced, "No library is complete without a copy of the Bible, Shakespeare, and Mark Twain's Scrap-Book." Slote's ad then used these endorsements as blurbs in ads; the ad appeared, among other places, in the Chicago literary periodical *The Dial* at least twenty times over seven years, usually in its book advertising section—sometimes under the heading "one of the humorist's best works." With blurbs that resembled the quotes from book reviews appearing in other book advertisements, the scrapbook ad blended in with other book ads. Surrounding it as well by ads for literary workers' implements such as pens and pencils, *The Dial* ad asserts the permeability of reading and writing, and it normalizes the idea that one can "write" a scrapbook, either as Twain did or as the compiler who buys the volume will do.[4]

Magazinists "managed to get considerable fun out of it," Robert Underwood Johnson, a *Scribner's Monthly* editor reported, and such fun resulted in periodicals granting column inches to the scrapbook. Johnson reviewed the scrapbook with mock solemnity, as though it were Mark Twain's autobiography, exuberantly playing on the book's blank page after page of parallel gummed strips: readers "peer through the palings of his father's fence ... and behold him in the sportive innocence of childhood, throwing his grandmother's gridiron at the cat." The strips become "pontoon bridges" on the Mississippi, the "railroad [tracks] on which Mr. Clemens went to California ..., [an illustration] of the ladder on which Mr. Clemens rose to fame," and, irresistibly, a reflection of the author's increased ability to stick to things. The fact of the notice's recirculation even became something the press could self-reflexively comment on. Boston's *Literary World* asserted that the scrapbook had "received more original humorous notices from the press, perhaps, than any work ever issued."[5]

Newspapers and magazines were attracted to recirculating the ad because it raised their own status as well. The scrapbook's sales promotion asserted that periodical items were worthy of preserving in a new invention by an up-and-coming author and celebrity. Its blank pages could endorse their own product. Thus *Harper's Weekly* hailed it as "a book in which can be carefully preserved the many fine engravings from the drawings of Thomas Nast and other eminent artists, with which the pages of *Harper's Weekly* are filled."[6]

The idea that Mark Twain's Scrap Book was a book he had written spread beyond the waggish reviews. Like his written books, it bore his name. A bogus interview with Twain places him in a newspaper office with a self-referential scrapbook by way of authenticating detail: "'Oh, I drop in here once in a while,' he said, 'to look over the papers for notices of myself and my articles, which I always keep in a scrap book—a Mark Twain self-gumming scrap book,' he added, with a faint smile." One edition of the scrapbook promoted the connection between his authorship and the book with a cover illustration of a frog holding a Mark Twain scrapbook, a reminder of that celebrated jumper (Figure 2.3). The confusion over whose book it is—a book authored by Twain, or clipped by him? an empty book

Figure 2.3 Mark Twain's Scrap Book cover connects his "Celebrated Jumping Frog of Calavaras County" with the scrapbook. The frog holds a copy of the scrapbook. (Image courtesy of Kevin MacDonnell)

whose authorship travels with the scissors that clipped it?—is reflected when present-day librarians and archivists catalog clipping collections pasted into Mark Twain books. More than one library catalog gives the misleading impression that it owns scrapbooks compiled by Mark Twain; many catalog the scrapbooks, listing him as author, without clarification.[7]

Perhaps it was this "authored" quality of the book and not just its cost that made Margaret Lynn of Missouri, who with her siblings made scrapbooks out of useless agricultural reports, feel inhibited by the gift of a Mark Twain scrapbook. Rather than just being a more convenient version of the agricultural reports, it obligated her to "choose carefully and economically the matter that was to be perpetuated in its orderly pages." It "almost put the making of scrapbooks on a new plane, and forbade the use of inferior material," she wrote.[8]

Buyers who had already bought a Mark Twain's Scrap Book extended the range of his authorship in the sense of his brand name. Twain's name on the scrapbook thus united the author function, in Foucault's sense of someone with responsibility and credit for the document (as the library catalogs show), with the literal brand name. Twain's brand name started to replace the generic term "scrapbook," just as *aspirin* replaced salicylic acid, and *linoleum* became the only name for certain floor coverings. A week after President James Garfield's 1881 shooting, the *Chicago Inter Ocean* related that a White House clerk responded to the wounded president's "desire to have reports of the calamity and press comments preserved" by clipping the newspapers on the shooting and illness: "The different accounts are cut up and pasted in a Mark Twain Scrap-Book." Its presence in advertising pages and literary puff pieces gave the book greater dignity; this was not simply a copy of the agricultural reports readily available from Congress in a theft from its original purposes, but a special book that the White House had invested money in, choosing from many available styles to make a solid historical record. Although Twain was a humorist, his name paradoxically endowed scrapping with greater gravitas.[9]

Advertisements that included its price and various levels of luxuriousness ensured that readers knew the cost; when they encountered it in other contexts, readers understood without saying that it might be a lavish purchase. The utility of the shorthand that a brand name like Mark Twain's Scrap Book offers is played out in Mary Abbott Rand's 1881 children's story, "The Christmas Grab-Bag." Joy Yeaton, a "good, rich girl," proposes to her family that they escape their gift-giving rut and have a grab bag, shaking up the allotment of already-purchased gifts and redirecting them to unintended recipients within the household. Each rerouted gift reveals an unexpected side of its receiver. Instead of being handed one of the hair ribbons intended for the servants, Norah, the Irish lower-level servant, draws "Mark Twain's 'Scrap-book,'" originally intended for Joy's staid older sister Eliza.[10]

"When the use of the volume was explained to her," Norah expresses great pleasure and reveals a dormant need for the book: "haven't I ben kapin' ivery blessed bit of po'try that I could find in any owld paper. Many's the song they've sung to me." She dives into the kitchen and brings out a "roll of paper scraps" which include "such gems as Longfellow's 'Rainy Day,' Lucy Larcom's 'Hannah at the Window Binding Shoes,' Miss Kimball's sweet little 'Crickets,' and others."[11]

Any scrapbook can bridge comic and solemn works, and yet Mark Twain's Scrap Book seems to have a special capacity to bridge a comic character and somber poetry in this story. The gift of Mark Twain's Scrap Book allows the comic dialect-speaking Norah to reveal herself as a secret reader with a taste for poetry of loss, sadness, and endurance, on a plane with the family's and Rand's tastes. Because the author's name on the scrapbook becomes joint ownership—the scrapbook will always be Mark Twain's Scrap Book even as it is bestowed on Norah—it elevates and makes more visible Norah's use of it. It authorizes—both in the sense of *permit* and *put the name of an author to*—her choice of reading matter. Norah, who has taken advantage of the cheap availability of poetic "gems" in the newspaper, can now sumptuously house them. The shorthand "Mark Twain's Scrap-Book" for the book's special possibilities was so useful that reviewers of Rand's short-story collection singled out this incident in their summaries.[12]

Even as mainstream literary representations flattened immigrant servants into simple comic characters without complex thoughts or responses, middle-class employers worried about what was hidden behind the unprobed façade: Were servants entertaining dissolute company in the kitchen or attic bedroom, or handing out the employer's goods to family and friends, with whom they conspired in incomprehensible tongues? If employers acknowledged that immigrant servants had needs and feelings, how threatening would those feelings be? But the gift of Mark Twain's Scrap Book neutralizes the threat of interiority as the capacity for thought and feeling passes through Eliza, "an ideal minister's wife, of the passive form," to Norah, whose loneliness and deprivation are suddenly apparent to the family via her taste in reading. Mark Twain's Scrap Book Americanizes her, or makes her Americanness visible as it classifies her choice of clippings, all by American poets, under the ownership of an American author. And now that she can paste her clippings into this disciplined, regimenting scrapbook, everyone can know she has been in the kitchen intoning "My life is cold, and dark, and dreary," empathizing with Hannah's loss of her lover, or appreciating the cricket's "melancholy cheer." Mrs. Yeaton responds with tears of sympathy: her "eyes somehow had become dim.... She had not dreamed that poor Norah enjoyed poetry." She recognizes shared humanity in someone to whom she intended to give the trivial present of a hair ribbon. (The story does not pursue Norah's newly revealed qualities but parallels them with other dislocations of expected identity and revelation of desire. Eliza breaks loose from the constraints of her role as minister's wife, not by writing poetry in the voice of a soldier, but with self-adornment, enjoying the opal earrings intended for her gadabout sister, while Joy receives the clasp knife meant for her brother and reveals a gender-bending taste for whittling.)

The humorist's name on the outside authorized the scrapbook's contents. It could also be used to mask or cover, by associating a distinctly un-Twainian clipping collection with his persona, and tricking readers into reading it with more credence. Thus librarians used a Mark Twain's Scrap Book to discipline children's reading. In the 1880s, when cultural and moral watchdogs asserted that exciting dime novels with sensational, crime-centered plots would lead children to a lawless life, the staff at a Rhode Island library claimed they had successfully stopped boys from reading dime novels behind the covers of library books. The librarians collected newspaper cuttings of "accounts of the crimes committed by boys instigated by reading dime-novels" and pasted them into "a Mark Twain scrap-book." Boys caught with dime novels were handed this collection with Mark Twain's name on it, and told to read it. The plan went as the librarians hoped, they reported, and boys gave up their sensational fiction to accept "something better in exchange." The librarians underscored their scrapbook's disciplinary purpose through the claim that the boys had successfully internalized its message: "We have had no occasion to use the book for several months." In a neat parallelism, just as the boys hid their dime novels behind library books, the librarians hid their disciplinary texts behind Mark Twain's name. Despite Twain's own anarchic play with literature, his flouting of the boundaries of literary propriety, and his more complex views of the relationship of reading to action, his scrapbook literally provides cover for a reductive idea of reading—inadvertently bearing out the advertising claim that his scrapbook is a moral work. Using his name as bait entices children who had enjoyed Twain's writing to read the scolding contents of the library scrapbook and makes it seem that Twain endorses the claim that reading dime novels "instigates" crime. Just as from the reader's point of view the authorship of anonymous articles defaults to the newspaper, the unsigned news articles the librarians clipped would seem to come from the man whose name was on the book's label. Although the children who were subjected to a barrage of moralistic writing likely hid their dime novels more successfully or read them outside the library, when librarians shared the story with one another at a professional meeting, Mark Twain's name seemed to also endorse the disciplinary success of this approach to policing children's reading.[13]

In Rand's grab-bag story, the use of Twain's brand name marked the story's events as up to date; for the librarians talking with other librarians, concerned with classification and information storage, the brand proclaimed their expertise in new technologies of saving and deploying texts. In both, the Mark Twain scrapbook made the work of saving clippings more visible.

Authorial Companionship, or the Loneliness of the Scrapbook Paster

The printed form with its blanks incites writing, while it limits the shape that writing can take. In filling out a printed form, we are not alone, facing the alarming or liberating blank page that could go in any direction, but rather see the tracings of a map to walk our pen along; it guides (or coerces) our actions. A form makes the act of writing interactive and more social; a companion (or official) has been there before us, marking the way. Both Mark Twain's Scrap Book and the repurposed book are printed forms in this sense. Both incite readers to cut and paste and shape actions. The Patent Office report or agricultural report, once it is repurposed as a scrapbook, embodies a script for making a particular type of scrapbook from it. It scripts pasting into columns, suggests the desirability of covering over all the existing type, and urges the paster to join his or her clippings with the world of print. The territorial fight for space embodied in erasing someone else's words by replacing them with yet other voices of one's own choosing is more active and interactive than pasting on a simple blank page.[14]

Mark Twain's Scrap Book scripts actions even more restrictively than the repurposed book. Although it is literally blank, its glued strips make it almost impossible to paste items down other than in columns. Since unused glued strips might become damp and stick to the wrong side of a clipping, it scripts filling in each page before moving on to the next. Since writing on the strips is difficult or impossible, the glued strips restrain the compiler from adding handwritten comments to the pages, unless they are on the clippings themselves or in the sharply constricted margins.[15]

The illustrated advertisements for Mark Twain's scrapbook showed family members working at their scrapbook together, as in the harmonious "After" in Figure 2.2, but the gummed pages meant that the pursuit no longer entailed the work of preparing glue, covering the table with protective paper, and getting out or cleaning the brush, activities that made it more efficient for several people to work together on their scrapbooks. With the gluepot, family scrapbook making could control the children's reading. When Julia Colman in her 1873 article "Among the Scrap-Books" visits the May family engaged in scrapbook making, she notes that even though "making scrap-books may seem a feeble instrumentality for controlling this great difficulty—the improper reading of the children," it can push children in the right direction. When they make scrapbooks as a family, with a parent's watchful surveillance of the process, they are safe from the dangers of a child "breaking away" or "having his purity tampered with by viler books." Mrs. May occupies a central position, handing out slips to be pasted, "like a hospitable house-mother, carving and serving up newspapers." The May children convene around the gluepot. Mark Twain's Scrap Book, however, frees the clipper from the gluepot and thereby makes ad hoc, decentralized pasting easier. Scrapbook upkeep could be done alone, while traveling, or in a short session. Without a gluepot to gather around, it no longer needed to be sociable or more subject to supervision. A child could "break away" and attach clippings in unmonitored solitude.[16]

Yet Mark Twain's trademarked presence could make that solitude less solitary. As we have seen, librarians could harness the authority of Twain's "authorship" of his scrapbook to discipline children's reading. Twain's presence also jumps over the worrisome responsibility of filling the blank page alone through his scrapbook's companionable offer of shared authorship with his lively, convivial public character. In this, he drew on another element of brand names: the characters that personified brands, putting a human face on the distant corporation. The smiling Quaker Oats Quaker, for example, trademarked in 1877 (the year Mark Twain's Scrap Book came on the market), provided a face for the distant corporation with whom the customer had no face-to-face interaction. Shopping shifted from the generic; the shopper didn't buy just a scoop of oats from a barrel, but a package of Quaker Oats, easily identified through its smiling Quaker; not chocolate, but Walter Baker Chocolate, with its Dutch maid figure. The character became a friendly presence in the home. Packaged, branded goods carried a surplus of companionship and good feeling that cycled back into association to the brand, so that buyers were invited into a fictional world of interaction with the smiling Quaker or the Dutch maid. Children's magazines and adult writing invited their readers to flesh out such characters through play, experience them as companions, and cultivate an imagined relationship with them. Advertisers slowly took up the enterprise of developing narratives and personalities for their characters.

At the same time, in their reading, readers sought a confiding intimacy from authors; they expected to "get at the author," as Barbara Hochman has shown, when they read a story or novel. Mark Twain obliged in his writing, with a conversational, yarn-spinning narrative voice, developed into a face-to face relationship with readers through his lecture tours. He embedded these qualities in the authorial brand he constantly produced through his fiction, in which he figured as author and sometimes as character. Twain thereby not only made his fictional worlds available for play and interaction in his writing but made himself available as a character and companion, in his fiction and through use of "his" scrapbook. Even if pasting articles into a scrapbook could now be more briskly businesslike and less leisurely or social, Twain's "company"—in the sense of his companionship as well as his business entity—kept it from being solitary. An MT scrapbook was not an empty scrapbook. It was already "Mark Twain's Scrap Book," as in Figure 2.4. An advertising booklet for the scrapbook featured Mark Twain's face

Figure 2.4 Cover, Mark Twain's Scrap Book emphasizes Twain's ownership or authorship.

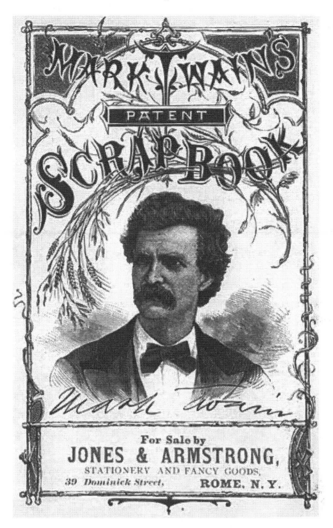

Figure 2.5 Advertising booklet cover featuring Mark Twain's image. (Harry Ransom Center, University of Texas, Austin)

on its cover (Figure 2.5). The user is invited to join in the jocular qualities of Mark Twain's Scrap Book, as with a scrapbook cover stamp in which the cherub kicks over a gluepot while holding aloft Mark Twain's Scrap Book, celebrating the novel qualities of using this scrapbook in a burlesque of elevated style, and a similar concept on the label on the inside cover of an 1892 version (Figures 2.6 and 2.7).[17] The scissors-wielding cherub who casts a net to draw in clippings on another of Twain's scrapbook covers visually echoes the humor magazine *Life*'s mascot of Figure 1.5 (Figure 2.8).

Patented Clemens, Trade Mark Twain

Mark Twain's trademark on his Self-Pasting Scrap Book both connected his personality with the book and protected it legally. Twain was professionally interested and politically engaged in the issue of protecting what is now called intellectual property. He availed himself—or tried to—of the three separate legal modes for doing so: copyright, patent, and trademark law. Copyright protects unique expression of ideas and thus scientific or useful and literary productions, and the right to reproduce a work. But nineteenth-century U.S. copyright had large gaps in its protective shield, gaps that allowed publishers in this country to freely reprint copyrighted materials from outside the United States, and vice versa, and they allowed free reproduction of any works already been published without individual copyright—as was usually true of items published in newspapers. These thereby entered the public domain.[18]

Twain's position on protecting his writing shifted over time. On the international front, he was initially content with the absence of international copyright protection, since it allowed him as a consumer to buy pirated British books cheaply. But once he became better known through his publications and through his lecturing career, as his oeuvre grew and he grew concerned about the financial future of his daughters, he sought to tighten his own (and other authors') legal posses-

Figure 2.6 Mark Twain's Scrap Book cover: Cherub kicking over the gluepot. (Harry Ransom Center, University of Texas, Austin)

Figure 2.7 Cherub pointing to the mess of the gluepot while holding Mark Twain's Scrap Book. (Image courtesy of Sandy Babb)

Figure 2.8 Cherub on the cover of a Mark Twain's Scrap Book casts a net to draw in clippings. (Image courtesy of Between the Covers)

sion of works. He campaigned for what Siva Vaidhyanathan calls "thick" protection: international agreements and copyright extending for the author's life plus fifty or sixty years. Twain traveled to Canada and England to be present on the day of publication and thus secure each country's copyright protection.[19]

Twain's experience patenting and marketing the scrapbook taught him that scrapbooks were in at least one respect superior to his written books. He could protect scrapbooks more securely against being copied or reproduced without his permission. Even before the scrapbook was produced, it was protected by patent law. Although copyright protects the right to reproduce a work, patent bestows "the right to *exclude* others from making, using, offering for sale, selling or importing the invention." He did not have the same power over his written books, and at least one collection was essentially reprinted without his permission.[20]

Patent law appealed to him enough that he praised the Patent Office as a way-station, guarantor, and generator of originality. In *A Connecticut Yankee in King Arthur's Court* (1889), it is one of the first modern institutions Hank Morgan establishes to "improve" his medieval world, for he "knew that a country without a patent office and good patent laws was just a crab, and couldn't travel any way but sideways or backwards." The copyright office enjoys no such celebration in his writings. On the other hand, copyright protects unique expression of ideas, and the right to reproduce them, so although Twain's scrapbook was a book, as a 1901 legal history using Twain to highlight the distinction noted, "It was a simple, practical contrivance for accomplishing a useful result, and as such could be patented, but not copyrighted"[21] (Figure 2.9).

The scrapbooks also brought him into contact with trademark law, which seemed like a promising strategy for protecting his intellectual property. Clemens trademarked the name "Mark Twain" as a mark of ownership of his literary property and sought to extend trademark law to protect his writing. He argued in an 1883 lawsuit against a publisher that had reprinted a collection of his stories without his permission that Belford, Clarke & Co. violated his trademarked pen name by using it on the collection. His own collection consisted of uncopyrighted works previously published in newspapers. Belford, Clarke simply picked up and substantially reprinted the whole compilation, even copying the title and cover. Twain lost the suit when the judge ruled that "the use of a nom de plume or assumed name by an author" did not extend special protection: "Trade marks only protect vendible merchandise, and can not be applied to or protect literary property." His trademarked name of Mark Twain could successfully protect his blank scrapbook as "vendible merchandise," but he could not extend its protection to his words in a story or novel.[22]

Twain's earnings from the scrapbook no doubt also raised his opinion of trademark law. Claims of how much he made from the scrapbook vary greatly, with newspapers wildly proposing that a million had been sold, bringing him extravagantly high profits, more than from any of his books. The actual record of revenues is murkier. Although Twain eventually accused Daniel Slote of stealing scrapbook money from him, what is certain is that the popular scrapbook attracted

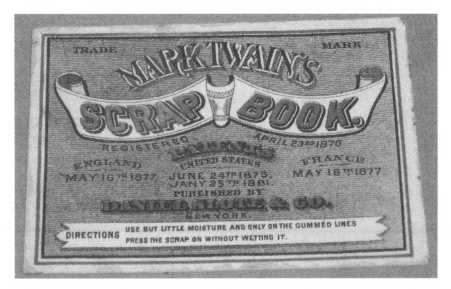

Figure 2.9 Trademark label, Mark Twain's Scrap Book, certifies that it is patented as well as published.

much notice in the press, sold well, and the probably modest-but-steady earnings from it ran in a more straightforward line into Mark Twain's pockets than did his earnings from his written books.[23]

Twain did not achieve the firmer hold on his intellectual property he sought through applying legal techniques from the scrapbook to his other books, but he did apply techniques from his scrapbooks to his own writing.

The Scrapbooks of Emmeline Grangerford and Other Authors

By July 1876 Twain had not only patented his scrapbook but also created the most famous fictional scrapbook in American literature, Emmeline Grangerford's. In the Grangerford episode in *The Adventures of Huckleberry Finn*, Huck lands at the home of the feuding backwoods aristocrats the Grangerfords. He relays his wide-eyed appreciation of the genteel parlor with its death-obsessed decor. He tells us that the late daughter Emmeline "kept a scrap-book when she was alive, and used to paste obituaries and accidents and cases of patient suffering in it out of the *Presbyterian Observer*, and write poetry after them out of her own head." One sample of this is her comically mawkish "Ode to Stephen Dowling Bots, dec'd." Her poems wrap death in convention and improbability sufficiently to free them from the taint of intruding on deathbeds. Although Emmeline is Twain's satiric object, her easy movement between clipping and writing points to the scrapbook's ability to straddle reading, editing, and writing. (And Huck does admire her work.)[24]

Like the scrapbooks that Twain and many other authors kept, Emmeline's preserves a record of her publications. Scrapbooks allowed writers to conveniently track their works published in newspapers and magazines, serving as a proto-photocopying machine. Author's scrapbooks have allowed present-day researchers access to records of what writers produced, sometimes constituting the only surviving copies, or evidence linking an author to pseudonymously authored material. The scrapbook of Winnifred Eaton (writing as Onoto Watanna), for example, helped researchers recover many previously unknown stories, including some in periodicals of which there are no other surviving copies. Horatio Alger's scrapbooks of work from the 1850s similarly link him to his various pseudonyms, as well as uncollected stories. Keeping such collections allowed beginning writers to read over earlier work to learn from its faults, while it let them later put the work to new purposes, Twain's prolific friend Brander Matthews suggested.[25]

Writers frequently used scrapbooks of their own works as waystations for works intended for republication. The scrapbook of the Boston women's rights activist Caroline Healey Dall, for example, contains her handwritten corrections on published articles to be used in reprinting. Twain collected his articles in scrapbooks to work with them as drafts for books. So before setting off for the Middle East on the *Quaker City* in 1867, he bought a scrapbook and asked his sister, Pamela Clemens Moffett, to paste in the articles he wrote from the trip (published mainly in the *Alta California*). In the days before carbon paper or copying machines, to obtain copies Twain would have had to laboriously press a copy on special paper and ink to keep with him before sending his handwritten pieces to the *Alta California*, and would have had to expensively mail such a copy home for safekeeping. Instead, he took advantage of the newspaper's cheapness and wide distribution as shared document storage—the equivalent of what might be called today cloud storage—for his articles. Anyone with access to the U.S. mails could subscribe to and access the *Alta California*; Pamela Moffett in St. Louis could thus use it as an accessible document where she could read Twain's drafts, clip, and paste them into the scrapbook. The scrapbook thus mediated between Twain's drafts in circulating his work out of the newspaper and into book form. When he returned from the trip, he had a scrapbook of printed articles as drafts to develop into *The Innocents Abroad*. The printed columns were easier to annotate and revise than manuscript, closer to the typewritten pages he later pioneered in using[26] (Figure 2.10).

Although scrapbooks were an intermediate form that allowed ordinary readers to turn clippings into books literally and physically, authors pushed the merger of reading and publishing still further, as they used the cut-and-paste technology of the scrapbook to revise clippings into a reproducible, published book—in the sense of editorial cutting and pasting familiar to us now via our word processing icons.

Special Correspondence of
Washing·
HER
few
ors v
celel
than
tlon:
stat(
and
cour
velo
mechanical constructi(
numbered on the fing

Figure 2.10 Los Angeles Times cartoon of Mark Twain using his own scrapbook. (*Los Angeles Times*, 2 Apr 1893, 24)

"Professional" Authorship and Scrapbooks

Emmeline Grangerford's scrapbook has become emblematic of a style of amateur writing that Twain mocked. Yet her mode of reusing and recirculating clippings was crucial to types of authorship engaged in by newspaper writers, anthologists, and literary writers. The idea of the author as individual genius held sway in the popular imagination and was central to arguments for expanding U.S. copyright protection, but a large proportion of the printed matter produced in the nineteenth and twentieth centuries resulted from corporate and composite forms of authorship. Many of these forms relied on reuse. Authorship was a practical task that entailed reshaping and recirculating existing writing, and scrapbooks show this work.

In pasting "obituaries and accidents and cases of patient suffering in it out of the *Presbyterian Observer*" as the basis from which to "write poetry after them out of her own head," Emmeline followed the lead of professional writers whose clipping, storing, and use of newspaper items won praise for substantiating the realism of their work. The British author Charles Reade reportedly drew on his extensive newspaper scrapbooks for the "facts on which his stories are founded" as well as "their actual incidents," and brought them out to prove that the "ultra-sensational" events he wrote about really happened. Wilkie Collins's plots were similarly attributed to newspaper clippings he saved in scrapbooks. He even was said to owe one novel's origin "to a newspaper clipping sent him from America by an enthusiastic admirer." He thus offered readers another way to write with scissors, by forwarding choice morsels to favorite writers. Even named and popular authors were thus understood to collaborate with known and unknown sources in a type of crowd-sourced authorship. Deshler Welch, a theater critic and editor, encouraged readers of *The Writer*, "a monthly magazine of interest to all literary workers," to follow the example of a newspaper critic whose extensive collection of scrapbooks allowed him to have "at hand the stories of notable crimes that could be weaved in[to] suddenly desired matter appertaining to some current sensation, or would suggest a plot for a detective story." Welch gives newspaper clipping a final ringing endorsement through Louisa May Alcott, as he recalls Alcott telling him, "The habit of reading with a pair of scissors in my hand has stood me in good stead for much of my literary work." Deshler does not specify what kinds of stories she sought, but perhaps she shared her creation Jo March's interests in *Little Women*: seeking material for her writing for sensational story papers, Jo "searched newspapers for accidents, incidents, and crimes... and introduced herself to folly, sin, and misery, as well as her limited opportunities allowed." Despite her narrator's aspersions on the type of sensational stories Alcott and her creation Jo both wrote, clipping the newspaper supplies the realism of authenticated detail.[27]

Lillie Devereux Blake, a suffragist who made her living for a time as a prolific writer of short stories and novels for high and low publications such as *Leslie's Illustrated Weekly*, *Harper's*, the Irish *New York Leader*, and the Beadle and Adams dime novel series, reused a small datebook as a scrapbook she headed "Articles about Woman's Position and Interesting Items." The "interesting items" included stories of "everyday heroism" and of brutality, evidently intended to be used as source material, either for fiction or for talks. Like Blake, Alcott, Reade, and Collins, Twain considered newspaper accounts as potential sources to write from. He had his secretary paste accounts of the 1873 installment of London's Tichborne Trial of a butcher claiming to be the heir to an English estate, which fascinated him, into six scrapbooks, though he later wrote that the story was too improbable to be useful to a "fiction artist."[28]

Twain's scrapbooks were an essential adjunct to his writing. They were the basis for *Roughing It* (1872), as well as *The Innocents Abroad*. Twain's biographer reports that under deadline pressure, producing a subscription book—which had to be fat, so that buyers saw it as a good value when sales agents knocked on their doors—"Sam [Clemens] swept up his scrapbooks and letters on the land of coconut trees, volcanoes, and hula... girls, and hurled them into the maw." Though this method sounds like a rather haphazard effort to fill pages, it also hints at the inclusive capaciousness in Twain's work that William Dean Howells praised as both lifelike in its associative structure and scrapbooklike:

> Anyone may compose a scrapbook, and offer it to the public with nothing like Mark Twain's good-fortune. Everything seems to depend upon the nature of the scraps, after all; his scraps might have been consecutively arranged in a studied order, and still have immensely pleased; but there is

no doubt that people like things that have at least the appearance of not having been drilled into line. Life itself has that sort of appearance as it goes on....An instinct of something chaotic, ironic, empiric in the order of experience seems to have been the inspiration of our humorist's art.[29]

Unless Twain is indicting himself, Emmeline Grangerford, "born" five years after *Roughing It* appeared, is surely not faulted for gleaning material from the newspapers but rather for not gleaning a broader variety. She opportunistically combs the obituary supply for occasions for conventional, nonspecific tributes, rather than as rich sources of detail and sensation to enliven her work. We might understand Twain's mockery of Emmeline as part of an argument about *what* in the newspaper is worthy of clipping, and with what sensibility: Reade's eye for sensational material, Twain's for comic incongruities and pretensions, Blake's attention to injustice to women, and Alcott's broad interests versus Emmeline's taste for death, death, and more death? "Everything seemed to depend on the nature of the scraps," Howells noted, but the work that emerged from these scraps depended on the eye, hand, and individual genius of the author.

Ordinary readers collected material and entered it into Mark Twain's Scrap Book, thus creating a book that jocularly shared authorship through his authorial brand name and borrowed the authority of his literary reputation, as they kept the book to themselves or shared it with friends or family. But as Twain's name became capital, it grew attractive to entrepreneurs. Belford and Clarke essentially reprinted his anthology and scooped up the profits. The seamier side of clipping and recirculating without the reshaping and rewriting that Twain, Reade, Collins, Blake, Alcott, and even Emmeline Grangerford undertook appears in the work of slapdash anthologists like Belford and Clarke, and what might best be called literary reprocessors.

"A Mere Maggot": The Enterprising Will Clemens

One literary reprocessor shadowed Twain and took hearty advantage of the coincidence of their surnames to launch his own publishing career. The fact that the name Samuel Clemens was as well known as "Mark Twain" allowed entrée to William Montgomery Clemens, an avid, energetic cutter and paster who developed a tone of familiarly hobnobbing with famous people and offered that intimacy to his readers. Will M. Clemens not only clipped and reprinted work Mark Twain had written for the press but bought up letters Twain had written and reprinted those along with writings about him. Although Will appears to have been no relation at all, reviews and advertisements for his lectures repeatedly describe him as Samuel Clemens's cousin, nephew, and even brother—who therefore possessed special knowledge of his celebrated "relative," about whom he could presumably offer the reader even greater insight and intimacy. Mark Twain however, called him a "troublesome cuss," said he "can't write books—he is a mere maggot who tries to feed on people while they are still alive," told his secretary that he was "a charlatan and a cheat," noted privately that he was "born a fraud and will remain one," and sought legal remedies against his work.[30]

Will M. Clemens reused many writers' work wholesale and piecemeal. He issued collections of anecdotes by and about prominent men and collections of fragments and sweepings that rode on the fame of writers, such as *Famous Funny Fellows: Brief Biographical Sketches of American Humorists. A Ken of Kipling* merged anecdotes and unauthorized reprints. One reviewer called it "the most uninspired volume about a great literary artist that it is possible to conceive," complaining that "it is compiled from a newspaper scrap-book by [Will Clemens] who would be equally industrious on any subject likely to hold the public interest for more than a week.... There is nothing in the book but a compilation of facts already in the public possession" and even these are sometimes garbled. (Kipling named it in two lawsuits, complaining that it attributed work to him that he didn't write, and later that it had been included as part of a compilation violating a visual trademark he had attempted to attach to his work.) The *Mark Twain Story Book* was a similar production. Twain attempted to chase Will Clemens away from another invasive publishing project in 1900 by claiming that "the laws of the several civilized countries...protect a nom de plume, it being a trade mark, by verdict of a court: it cannot be introduced into a chapter-heading or a book title without the owner's consent." By this time Twain had already lost his 1883 lawsuit attempting to assert that his pen name enjoyed special protection as a trademark, but the claim must have still seemed promising as a scare tactic.[31]

Will Clemens's publications reprocess newspaper clippings into books, which he then profited from, while they potentially undercut the earnings of their authors. He pioneered novel forms of unpaid republication, for example using newer technologies of photographic reproduction to ride the 1890s craze for artistic advertising posters with his magazine *The Poster*, flush with copies of the posters. Here again, he could take a piece whole and resell it, incurring only the expense of reproduction. He even went after Mark Twain's spoken words, publishing transcripts of his paid lectures. Twain's ability to earn money from the grueling work of lecture tours depended on the audience's belief that they would hear the author perform fresh, unpublished material. Will Clemens's publication of the transcripts made them vulnerable to being republished in the town where he was about to deliver the talk. Newspaper critics would complain of staleness if they heard a lecture they had already read, and nineteenth-century audiences were not shy about expressing displeasure, so Twain had reason to worry. Like early spam mailers on the internet, who claimed that they were simply adding advertising to the email mix just as it was present in newspapers and magazines, Will Clemens insisted on his right to use such work, responding to Twain's objections to the biography he proposed to write that "in no instance have I or would I copy a line of your copyrighted work. But your public spoken utterances become public property once they are spoken and there is no law against writing truthful facts about a man's life."[32]

The biography being objected to, Will M. Clemens's *Mark Twain: His Life and Work* (1892), was the first biography of Twain. Will wrote it with scissors, cutting, pasting, and reworking published articles about Mark Twain without credit. The glue Will Clemens joins them with is an unctuous insinuation of intimacy, both through the public assumption that they were related, which Will Clemens nurtured, and by referring to him as the familiar "Mark." More intriguing is his publication of Twain's brief letters to him, out of which he got remarkable mileage, reprinting them in at least three places. These reprints are all the more noteworthy considering that the letters reject Will's requests for help.

Will Clemens began writing to Twain seeking a connection with him when he was eighteen, and he persisted for decades. Each letter is written on the letterhead of a different business Will was involved with—"Foreign Stamp Dealer," "Editor, *Chicago Literary Life*," "Will M. Clemens, Criminal, Civil, and Political Investigation," among others. His letters shift from the wildly familiar—addressing the author first as "That Uncle of Mine," or "Dear Mark"—to a somewhat more restrained, formal, but still invasive tone. Others plead for attention and offer his services as a private secretary, explaining to the forty-six-year-old Twain "you are getting on in years, your work is more laborious, and your working hours perhaps more disagreeable and lonesome." Twain politely refused his help, responding to a request for information on his life: "Your letter received. Lord bless your heart! I would like ever so much to comply with your request, but I am thrashing away at my new book, & am afraid that I should not find time to write my own epitaph in case I was suddenly called for." Will Clemens published the refusals as evidence of their close relationship, presumably oblivious to the barbed southernism, "bless your heart," a slap at someone for overstepping. In a second letter Will reprinted, Twain dismisses another request by enclosing an already published profile—he had obtained printed copies for responding to such requests—and then Will published this rejection, too, as evidence of personal contact. Will manufactured and conveyed a sense of fellowship by trimming the frame away as he cut and pasted, positioning whatever a reporter discovered about Twain as though Mark Twain told it directly to Will Clemens. A chapter devoted to "Mark Twain at Home," for example, insinuates that Will had actually been invited into Twain's house, rather than cobbling together information from others; he invites the reader in with him:

> Seated in his richly furnished library...he will tell an anecdote or discuss a literary or social question with a calm directness and earnestness, revealing to you an entirely new side of his character, that has nothing in common with that which he is wont to display to the public who throng to his lectures.[33]

Will Clemens's career depended on recirculation. Unlike editors whose recirculation of a writer's work helped build the writers' reputations, and who paid writers for first use of materials that then entered the exchanges, Will's relationship to the authors whose work he reused in books was essentially parasitical; Twain had reason for calling him a maggot. He slid between editing and writing jobs for numerous publications and found another way to reprocess clippings in 1888, by starting a newspaper clipping bureau in San Francisco. A tradition in his family, which he surely promulgated, claimed that his "uncle" Mark Twain had helped him start the bureau to boost lagging sales of his scrapbooks by making sure people had clippings to paste into them.[34]

But even if someone like Will M. Clemens did not rush in to follow a writer and glean from his fields and claim a relationship to him, for late nineteenth-century authors celebrity and the means of obtaining it were full of traps. Writing that circulated freely through the press after first publication brought fame and perhaps readers' interest in hearing work performed in a lecture, or reading more of the author's work in book form, or could ensure that work was in greater demand, thereby raising the rates magazines and newspapers paid for first publication of stories. It could also sate the readership's interest, and work could end up under someone else's byline.

Recirculation Gone Wild: "Punch, Brothers! Punch with Care!"

Renaming himself Mark Twain and tucking his pen name into the text itself in the form of a character named Mark Twain had allowed Samuel Clemens to benefit from the circuits of newspaper recirculation. Creating humorous advertising for his scrapbook garnered him free publicity, which then traveled those circuits as well. To advertise the scrapbook, he and Slote also produced a free sample of his writing that is itself about a wildly reproducing bit of writing.

Dan Slote's stationery company published a slender collection of Mark Twain's stories, *Punch, Brothers, Punch and Other Sketches*, in 1878. The book straddles advertisement and book. One edition's back cover has the image of an open scrapbook, filled with a letter from Mark Twain, and endorsements, as though pasted into the scrapbook. The final page carries a list of the styles available. Some copies of the story collection were given away as premiums with the scrapbook, and some carried ads for other products too.[35]

The book's title story is a remarkably apt choice for its task: It tells how a bit of doggerel goes viral—like the ad Twain wrote for his scrapbook. The narrator, Mark, reads this verse in the newspaper and can't get it out of his head:

> Conductor, when you receive a fare,
> Punch in the presence of the passenjare!

A blue trip slip for an eight-cent fare,
A buff trip slip for a six-cent fare,
A pink trip slip for a three-cent fare,
Punch in the presence of the passenjare!
CHORUS: Punch, brothers! punch with care!
Punch in the presence of the passenjare!

Mark, once infected, must pass it along to others.

Fittingly, the story's sticky verse had its origins in an item that made the rounds of the exchanges. In 1875, *The New York Tribune* published a stanza of what it called "horse-car poetry"—a verse made up from the rules for punching tickets on the horse-drawn streetcar. It was an early instance of found poetry, or what its author, Isaac H. Bromley, soon called "ready-made poetry."[36]

Found poetry in general engages with the unauthoredness of most of the writing we read. In present-day usage, the term applies to taking utilitarian writing that is meant to be transparent and not call attention to its language, and tweaking it so that it makes us pause and notice its construction, wording, sound, and pacing. Annie Dillard, who has written twentieth-century poems from materials such as book indexes, notes that framing a found text as a poem, "doubles its context. The original meaning remains intact, but now it swings between two poles." It defamiliarizes the most ordinary, unnoticeable kinds of writing and jolts them onto a different plane, bringing another set of expectations and readerly tools to them.[37]

The technique was a favorite of surrealists, a verbal equivalent of collage. Bromley's phrase "ready-made poetry" even seems to anticipate Marcel Duchamp's "ready-made" sculptures of urinals and bicycle wheels. But just as Victorian scrapbooks often resemble modernist collage yet proceed from very different assumptions and ideas, the nineteenth-century popular version of found poetry played with the possibility that metrically regular, rhymed verse lurked in utilitarian phrases. To adopt Dillard's formulation: Bromley's verse multiplied the context of rules to the possibility of finding poetry in the subject of horsecars and the onomatopoetic replication of the rhythmic jog trot of the ride. In a later article on how he came to write his initial *Tribune* verse, Bromley reported reading to himself the conductor's rules on a streetcar card, noticing that "it looks like poetry, for each line begins with a capital letter, and that in many cases is the only distinguishing mark of a poem. Then too, it scans well; it rhymes, it trips, it runs with a skippity-skip, and you can sing it." He exclaims to his friends, "It's poetry, by George!" He and his friends tinkered with it to regularize the meter; they added a repeated line to give it a concluding whomp.

Bromley's little gem soon left the horsecar tracks to travel extensively on the "Vanderbilt [railroad] system" of newspaper exchanges, though originally "published with no suspicions of its nearly unlimited possibilities of popularity." Its dissemination was driven by the possibility of inventing local versions using regional dialect, translating it, parodying it, adding verses, taking up the subject of the horsecar for other poetry, or setting it to music. The collaborative author-ship of found poetry—the poet's collaboration with the original prose, as well as Bromley's collaboration with his friends in tweaking the verses—develops into wiki-like shared authorship via recirculation, with readers and editors passing adjustments and variants along. The "epizooitic" of horsecar poetry, as *Harper's Monthly* calls it (implicitly blaming its spread on those jog-trotting horses), refers to inventing "doggerel aimed at the street railroad."[38]

In this telling, the poem replicates through the usual print channels: editors clipped and picked it up from one another's papers, elaborated it, and passed it along. The idea of "ready-made poetry" rapidly fell away, but the genre of "horse-car poetry" blossomed "wherever the newspaper with a humorous column exists." Twain's version of it, however, takes it in a new direction, focusing on the catchiness of the verse, not the newspapers' reworkings. Adopting but not claiming credit for the horsecar-card instructions already formed into a regular-ized verse, he wrote a first-person account of a man who reads it in the news-paper and can't get it out of his head. The verse literally infects its hearers; it takes over the narrator's thoughts and saps his ability to work, eat, or sleep, and imposes itself on top of his reading. The only cure for the infection is further recirculation.[39]

After two days of madly repeating the jingle, "Mark" recites it to a minister friend, who finds that its meter takes him over and gets into his sermon at the funeral of a dear friend, where his parishioners nod their heads in time to the rhythm dominating his talk. An aunt of the deceased arrives too late for the service, and their discussion of the man's deathbed and sacred final moments is overrun by the "remorseless jingle." The minister gets rid of the infestation by passing it on to students at a nearby college. The story ends with the impos-sible warning to the reader not to read the rhymes in the just-concluded story.

The story is a classic account of the transmission of what has since been called a *meme*, an idea, style, or usage that spreads from person to person. In Twain's story, however, the verse is like a physical object: it can be given *away* so that the giver no longer has it and seems immune to reinfection. Its circulation shares the ink-and-paper qualities of a scrapbook item, not of the content or concept that travels through the press.

As soon as Twain's story appeared as "A Literary Nightmare" in the *Atlantic Monthly* in 1876, it was reprinted and referred to in the press. Reprints and refer-ences kept his name firmly attached to the story and even added it to the heading. By 1876 he was prominent enough that his celebrity was an attraction of the story and fuel for reprinting it. Once Twain's story was in circulation, further articles about horsecar poetry focus less on the proliferation of new verses about horse-cars and more on Twain's account of the item's irresistible oral circulation and repetition. So Twain's biographer reports:

Its publication in the *Atlantic* had the effect of waking up horse-car poetry all over the world. Howells, going to dine at Ernest Longfellow's the day following its appearance, heard his host and Tom Appleton urging each other to "Punch with care." The Longfellow ladies had it by heart. Boston was devastated by it. At home, Howells's children recited it to him in chorus. The streets were full of it; in Harvard it became an epidemic.[40]

The verse took on a life of its own, even following Twain's lead of juxtaposition with a funeral sermon by audaciously intruding into the sacred precincts of an actual deathbed. When the actress Charlotte Cushman was dying, her nephew offered her milk punch, at which she smiled, replied, "Punch, brothers! punch with care," and "then fell into a sleep from which she never wakened." Mingling the comic and the pathetic, a revered classical actress who had performed many solemn and elevated death scenes uttering drastically inappropriate last words was jarringly distasteful enough that the story was not widely circulated.[41]

Although Mark Twain never claimed authorship of the *verse*, and the story's narrator explicitly says he found it in a newspaper, nonetheless as Twain's story was quoted and recirculated the press increasingly credited him with the poem. As the workings of the anonymity function in Mary Woolsey Howland's poem demonstrated, anonymity is unstable. The magnet of Twain's name attracted his authorship to the verse; Will M. Clemens joined in to promote the misattribution. He first reprinted a chunk of "A Literary Nightmare" in his 1892 *Mark Twain: His Life and Work*, where he claimed that the earlier fad for creating and translating horsecar poetry was a response to the Twain story, and not the other way around. Twenty-five years after initial publication of Twain's story, Will was still getting mileage out of it with a long article mangling its history in a San Francisco magazine in 1901. In 1922 he republished Twain's story in a magazine he ran.[42]

If the magnet of Twain's name could draw reprinting and publicity, then hitching the advertising for his book-without-words to a story about a poem without an author, which unrelentingly causes every hearer to repeat it, seemed a winning strategy. Printing the story about recirculation gone wild in a book distributed for free would generate sales for another work, a scrapbook, which would leave readers eager for more material from newspapers—presumably including Twain's work— to affix to their scrapbook pages. Through their inexorable recirculation through the press, both Bromley's own version of horsecar poetry and Twain's story about it generated clippings suitable for compiling into a scrapbook.

Mark Twain was ahead of his time in recognizing the power of media's flotsam and jetsam to take over one's thoughts. In the decade following, advertisers devised many catchy slogans to do what the conductors' instructions had done without forethought, binding catchy slogans more tightly to articles for sale and a slogan's recirculation. They took the power of cutting, pasting, and recirculating that Twain had been so ambivalent about when it swept up his writing, but that had so successfully promoted his scrapbook, and joined it to the ear worm of jingles and catchphrases, to create even more potent selling engines.[43]

The Language of Scrapbooks

Mark Twain kept scrapbooks for various purposes, mocked scrapbook keepers in his writing, and invented a new type of scrapbook; he also altered and innovated the language for talking and writing about scrapbooks. The *Oxford English Dictionary* identifies him as one of the first writers to use "scrap book" as a verb, in 1879. In other words, he conceived of scrapbook compiling as a discrete activity, which not only needed the convenience of gummed pages instead of a gluepot but required a speedier mode of expression than the cumbersome "cutting items out and pasting them into a scrapbook," or "working with scissors and glue." That grand commonplace book, the *Oxford English Dictionary*, which shuffles literature and sorts it into quotations supporting its definitions, takes three of its four supporting citations for the verb "to scrap book" from Mark Twain:

> 1879 'MARK TWAIN' Let. 12 Nov. (1917) I. 369 Put the enclosed scraps in the drawer and I will scrap-book them. 1881—Tramp abroad xlvi, I scrap-booked these reports during several months. 1883 North Star 25 Oct. 3/2 We trust that our wage-earning readers especially will scrap-book these Letters, for after-study. c1898 'MARK TWAIN' Autobiogr. (1924) I. 139 He usually postponed the scrap-booking until Sunday.[44]

This usage didn't catch hold until the 1980s, when the gerund *scrapbooking* as an ongoing activity, and *scrapbooker* as someone who regularly performs it, appears. The word *scrapbook*, in my reading of much nineteenth-century material on the practice, was rarely used as a verb, even in works about scrapbooks. The shorthand verb was more usually "to scrap," inspiring puns on fighting, or jokes that a scrapbook is a record of prize fighting. The pun hints that making scrapbooks can be an aggressive or contentious act. Scrapbook compilers wrest items from their old context and force them to tell a new story.

Through the language of juxtaposition, scrappers reframed newspaper clippings to analyze and critique their accounts, or to insist on more satisfying versions of events. As the next chapter shows, scrapbook compilers constructed their own nationalisms on both sides of the Civil War, through their scrapbooks.

3

Civil War Scrapbooks

Newspaper and Nation

The Civil War was a mediated war, experienced through the press both at home and on the battlefield. The war set off a frenzy of newspaper reading in the United States, given urgency by the new telegraphed battlefield reports in the newspapers. The "imperious" newspaper called to readers, Oliver Wendell Holmes, Sr. wrote, summoning people to buy it "at unusual hours...by the divine right of its telegraphic dispatches" (Figure 3.1). Americans who had not previously habitually read a daily paper, or who had been content with a single one, soon scanned morning, afternoon, and evening papers to keep abreast of the progress of the war, particularly of places where family, friends, and acquaintances were positioned. As newspapers assumed new prominence in the lives of Americans during the Civil War, many people—North and South, male and female—preserved the unfolding war by unfolding their newspapers and clipping and pasting articles into scrapbooks. Their many scrapbooks show us northerners and southerners imagining nationhood and articulating their makers' connection to the United States or Confederate nation. Scrapbooks both preserved history and allowed individuals to perform or enact the preservation of history. Accounts in memoirs, fiction, and articles substantiate scrapbook making's cultural significance.[1]

Families with members near the battle zones were absorbed in news reading. The mother of two daughters who had gone to Washington as nurses, for example, wrote to them, "I have just been devouring the *Times*—that part of it at least, and that only, which tells of the war movements—everything else is passed over with a very slighting glance." Once she read her newspapers, she circulated them to other relatives and they were then were added to bundles for soldiers. Other families did the same to keep soldiers connected to home and confirm that they were continuing to participate together in a shared text public, a sense of national affiliation constructed through reading the same newspapers.[2]

Northerners understood the newspaper as part of a powerful network binding the nation, as in Thomas Nast's *Harper's Weekly* cartoon "The Press in the Field" (shown in Figure Intro.2), where sketch artists and reporters preside over battles and gatherings of contrabands (enslaved people who escaped across the lines to the

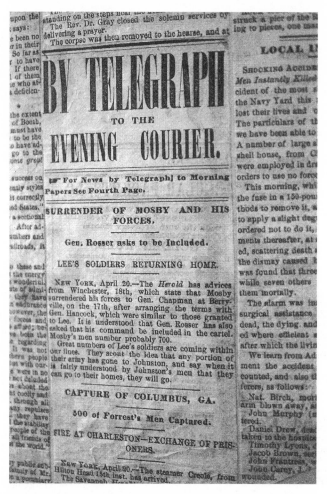

Figure 3.1 Newspapers prominently featured the special status of telegraphic dispatches, in type larger than the headline. (Charles French, Civil War Scrapbooks, Massachusetts Historical Society)

Union camps) and newsboys bring the news to the domestic hearth, while couriers bring a bundle of papers back to camp, for soldiers to read (Figure 3.2). Soldiers were eager to read about the events they had just taken part in themselves. Following the Battle of Bull Run, some even paid three dollars a copy, for back issues covering that battle, to at least one newsboy who carried news to Union soldiers in the field.[3]

Newspaper Scrapbooks in Civil War Literature

Events reported in the newspaper were refracted in the culture; they became the subject of literature, and poems referred to specific newspaper reports. Poets, novelists, and memoirists took note of the growing importance of

Figure 3.2 "The Newspapers in Camp," detail of "The Press in the Field." *Harper's Weekly*, 30 April 1864.

the newspaper and recorded Americans' dense engagement with it, as in Herman Melville's "Donelson," from his *Battle-Pieces* (1867), which incorporates headlines and includes crowds reading newspapers. In fiction about the Civil War, the newspaper becomes a tissue connecting characters at home and on the battlefield, supplying an assurance of veracity.[4]

The newspaper becomes something like a character in *A Household Story of the American Conflict: The Brother Soldiers and Forward with the Flag* (1867), Mary Robinson's multivolume novel for children, intended for Sunday School libraries. The newspaper mediates the various Northern characters' relationship to the war—acting as the go-between, and presenting it in another layer of media. The Warren children gather eagerly to hear news reports of heroism at the front read aloud. All members of the family are equally avid to discuss the war, and the three young children regard a session of newspaper tales from the front as particularly delectable at story time. They model eager listening and engaged response for Robinson's readers.[5]

As various Warren relatives head out for the army or hospital work, the thread of the newspaper stitches the family close, pulling together news of its members in distant places and uniting its emotions. Mr. Warren's newspaper reading—and his reading aloud, into the narrative—takes primacy over other activities, and even the sons' letters home from the front repeatedly quote from the newspaper. One reviewer found Robinson's wholesale quotations from periodicals excessive, but Robinson defended herself, since the story's claim to accurate depiction of life during the war depended on including the experience of knowing the war through the newspaper. Reading the newspaper aloud in the novel points to the urgency of news, but the family's newspaper reading also stages its *remoteness* from contact with war. The Warrens consume the war in the form of print, which provides entertainment—good stories and moral tales, suitable for Sunday School texts.

One son, Frank, heightens and preserves the mediated experience of war and nation comprehended through newsprint by making a scrapbook from all this newspaper reading. His scrapbook is more than an additional device for inserting newspaper clippings into the narrative, though it is that (every item becomes part of the novel as other characters offer Frank material for his scrapbook or as they ask Frank to read stories of exemplary courage from it). But his family and visitors affirm the significance of Frank's scrapbook, thus reinforcing the value of saving a record of the momentous events that the newspaper embodies, and of their own individual experience of encountering the war as well as solidifying their experience of the nation through the newspaper.

Robinson retrospectively recorded Northerners' use of the press. Edward Everett Hale's popular story "The Man Without a Country," however, flattered the feelings of Northern newspaper readers at the height of the war and further illuminates Civil War scrapbook making. Hale produced the story as part of his "standing agreement" with the editor of the *Atlantic Monthly* to write articles to "keep up people's courage." It offered its Northern readers the sense that their position was entirely enviable. The story analogizes Confederates, cut off from the United States, to Philip Nolan, the story's subject, who is desperate to reconnect to it. Court-martialed for participating in Aaron Burr's attempt to form a separate republic, Nolan wishes to "never hear of the United States again!" and shocks the presiding officer into conferring a unique sentence: he is never to hear or read the name of the United States again. For Hale, a newspaper owner's son, newspapers are a site of national identity, and Nolan's nationalism is defined by his longing for the United States through the banned printed word. Nolan (No Land) is sentenced to sail in U.S. Navy vessels, passed from ship to ship, barred from hearing any news of his country or its people.[6]

He suffers intensely. Nolan shows no desire for news of family members; rather he seeks information about the nation itself.

> He had almost all the foreign papers that came into the ship, sooner or later; only somebody must go over them first and cut out any advertisement or stray paragraph that alluded to America. This was a little cruel sometimes, when the back of what was cut out might be...innocent....Right in the midst of one of Napoleon's battles,...poor Nolan would find a great hole, because on the back of the page of that paper there had been an advertisement of a packet for New York, or a scrap from the President's message.

The United States, in other words, is growing in importance as well as size; nearly everything in the news of the world touches on it, even if only through the accident of being printed on the same sheet.

The news Nolan sees is scissored out. He attempts to reconstitute a world by scissoring in: he makes a scrapbook of observations of nature, drawings, and "bits of plants and ribbons... and carved scraps of bone and wood." This "very curious" scrapbook, which could signal developing an identity connected to the natural world, transcending nationality, is instead primitive and incoherent. His true reconstitutive project is revealed on his deathbed, when a shipmate visits him in his aptly named "stateroom" and finds it a "shrine," an elaborately remade world of handmade patriotic paraphernalia—all improvised signs of his longing for the "real" versions of connection to the United States that he has been denied.

Nolan recognizes his isolation from the nationalism that is constructed through reading together with others. He cannot participate in an imagined public sphere, a text public, through which citizens bring their awareness of others reading the same publications at the same time into a sense of belonging to a community or nation of others whom they may never meet, and who define themselves in relationship to that textually constructed sense of nation. Nolan can construct only a hidden, makeshift, incomplete shrine to national feeling in his stateroom. As Nolan pants with envy of the ordinary condition of the story's readers, Hale elicits his readers' appreciation of the status quo—in this case, their ability to speak of their country, their unobstructed reading of a whole newspaper that has not had holes clipped out of it, and their being able to clip their own choice of articles from it, all as rewards for loyalty to their country.[7]

With this support and cheerleading, the ideal Northern reader of "The Man Without a Country" could recognize his or her good fortune in being free to wave the Stars and Stripes and celebrate a seamless connection to the country's past. Northern readers were aware of others reading the *Atlantic Monthly* and the many newspapers that immediately reprinted or summarized Hale's story. Their awareness extended to the misguided Confederates, who had severed themselves from their connection to the country's history as well as its present. Newspaper reading was closely tied with cherishing and saving that connection to nation.

Newspapers and Scrapbooks vs. Domestic Life

Robinson's and Hale's stories mark a period when people were conscious of living through an epochal time and recorded their experience, North and South, through scrapbooks, as well as diaries and letters. They found that clipping and saving printed information on the fast-moving events of the day was often more efficient than writing it out, as Ella Gertrude Clanton Thomas, a Confederate woman who kept a diary and a scrapbook, noted. She found that her clipping collecting displaced her journal writing, in parallel to the larger events of the war displacing her accustomed domestic life: "A great many important events which occur in our country's history I would allude to more fully in my Journal if it was not so much easier a plan to paste the printed account."

Although she intended the scrapbooks and journal for her children's future perusal, she was uneasy with how much her writing and collecting took her thoughts away from their proper domestic grounding: "Again political events have absorbed so much of my Journal to the exclusion of domestic matters that one might readily suppose that I was not the happy mother of four darling children." The original volume of Mary Boykin Chesnut's more famous Confederate diary, too, contained news clippings as well as frequent references to newspaper reading. Thomas's fear that following political events—especially in the newspaper— undercut or belied her domestic, maternal role was not confined to the South but reflected a more general American cultural assumption that newspaper reading was inappropriate for women and that women simply were not newspaper readers. Although women all over the country in fact read newspapers, visual representations of newspaper reading almost invariably show men of the family in control of the paper, while images of women holding newspapers largely hold them up for ridicule (as will be evident in Chapter 5, where women's newspaper reading is discussed further).[8]

Although Thomas Nast's representation of domestic reading in "The Press at Home" vignette in "The Press in the Field" conventionally sets the paterfamilias

Figure 3.3 Lilly Martin Spencer, "War Spirit at Home" (1866). The newspaper-reading mother is a self-portrait of Spencer. (Newark Museum)

in possession of the paper as the family's designated reader (Figure Intro.2), wartime evidently offered a rest from the expectation that women did not read newspapers. Representations of women taking up this activity, however, were usually conflicted. Lilly Martin Spencer, a Northern woman artist, foregrounds women's newspaper reading in "War Spirit at Home" with some ambivalence: her painting features a woman whose engrossment in the news of the Northern victory at Vicksburg in the *New York Times* causes her to nearly drop her baby and to ignore her older children romping around the room in celebration of the news she has evidently read to them (Figure 3.3). Like the arms of a scale, her hands literally balance baby and newspaper. Thomas experiences a similar tension in balancing her avid interest in the newspaper with performing her proper absorption in her children.[9]

As Thomas discovered a side of herself powerfully engaged with political and national events, she attempted to reconcile the contradiction with her domestic maternal role within the scrapbook by interpreting her collection of newspaper clippings as an element of her children's education. News reading thus fed her duty as a Confederate mother, which included building the Confederate nation and inculcating its nationalism in her children through saving "our country's history" in scrapbooks.

Scrapbooks Reflect National Divisions

Civil War scrapbooks express and cement their makers' sense of connection to their separately defined sides. The differences between Northern and Southern scrapbooks dramatically foreground sectional, political, and ideological divisions, as they created and recreated in the home the sectional meanings of nation. Confederates, fighting the Yankees in the War Between the States, made scrapbooks that expressed their sense of belonging to a new nation (or "State"), their fury at the "tyranny" of Lincoln and the Northern states and at the constant insults and affronts visited on them by the Union, and their belief that loyal enslaved people would support the Confederacy. Unionists, fighting the Secessionists in the War of Rebellion, used their scrapbooks to celebrate their connection to the earlier history of the United States and its poetry and songs, framed their efforts as steadfast loyalty, and often connected the war to the abolitionist cause. Each side's scrapbooks marked grief and loss, claiming its own side's slain soldiers as martyrs in a holy and ennobling fight. Each side celebrated the outpouring of poetry and songs the war engendered as a phenomenon unique to its own side, an exalted expression of heightened patriotism, and therefore a sign of its moral superiority. Scrapbook compilers brought the war news, maps, letters from camp, lists of the dead, accounts of heroism, and poetry that filled the newspapers into their scrapbooks to express loyalty to one side of the conflict. Even after the war, people continued to place Civil War clippings in their scrapbooks, marking the place of the war in their own lives and their family's, and extending their sense of connection to that epoch making through the newspapers.

No single element of Civil War scrapbook making was an innovation, but the scale on which cutting and pasting was practiced was new. Thousands engaged in it, and collections were sometimes massive. Elkanah Walter Gurley, a Northern white Civil War veteran, in *Scrap-books and How to Make Them* (1880), recalls having been set on the scrapbook-keeping path when, as a small-town editor receiving exchanges at the end of the Civil War, he received material that he couldn't use in his paper but that was "too good to be lost." The papers left him "struck by the vast amount of information, on all points and of every grade of quality, which flowed in a continuous stream before" him. His pile of clippings overflowed into flour barrels, was almost thrown out, and was partially eaten by mice before he pasted it into scrapbooks to keep it safe. The urgent sense of living through momentous times led him to consider it a collection, rather than clippings held in reserve for recirculation in the newspaper, and it evidently inspired the shift to pasting. Gurley had been an editor and teacher before serving in the Union army from 1862 to 1865. The war whetted his appetite for stockpiling newspaper clippings. His interest in making clippings useful subsequently extended into a large collection of scrapbooks, and then into writing a book on how to make them. In that book, he notes, "Anyone can now see how valuable would be a collection of the best newspaper items published from 1860 to 1865." He assumes that his 1880s readers who need a guide to scrapbook making, who missed the moment for gathering and pasting Civil War materials, now looking back, understand that they were inside "history"—the subject of a topical volume he suggests making—and regret not gathering and pasting the materials.[10]

Just as Gurley's clipping collecting may have been shaped by being away fighting the war and unable to collect the clippings he would have wanted, other scrapbook makers who saw the war as a discrete subject to take up soon after it began left scrapbooks that are marked in the most basic ways by their own loyalties. Time and enlistment marked the scrapbook of Charles Pickering Bowditch, from an abolitionist family in Boston. He began his scrapbook when he was seventeen in 1859 and anticipated the Civil War scrapbook vogue by first collecting material on the Austro-Italian war, taking special note of the fact that the items were telegraphic dispatches brought by steamship (he later became vice president of the American Telephone and Telegraph Company). He soon shifted to follow the more swiftly arriving battle news of the Civil War, but his collection paused abruptly at the point when he enlisted in the Union Army.[11]

Wartime scrapbook making was a way for people to display loyalty to the cause by showing their avid interest in it. Soliciting help to fill gaps made clipping collecting into a social enterprise and allowed scrapbook makers to backdate their involvement. Ellen Tucker Emerson wrote to her father Ralph Waldo Emerson in 1861 that her sister Edith, age twenty, "wishes me to say that if the early papers of the war remain she means to cut out for her scrapbook the best part of them so, not to destroy them." Edith found enough earlier clippings to make a scrapbook reaching back to 1860.[12]

Others stopped partway through the war because they became dubious about the journalistic enterprise itself. David Curtis, for example, reported:

> At the beginning of the Civil War, fired with boyish enthusiasm, I deter-
> mined to keep a complete collection of all the war news as it should be
> published from day to day. That would give me, I reasoned, a complete
> history at a comparatively small cost, and having, at that time, the idea
> that newspapers were published for the purpose of printing the truth, it
> seemed clear that my history would be accurate. I do not study that his-
> tory now. Strange as it may seem, I never completed it.[13]

Although Curtis suggested that he didn't consult these scrapbooks because he lost faith in the newspapers' truthfulness, he also raised the possibility that the act of making them was more important to him than using them. Because the scrapbooks were tied up with the experience of reading the newspapers, the heated moment of participating in history by reading about events that profoundly impinged on his life—even if he was not in the battles them-selves—and binding them into a homemade history was what counted. The volumes embodied a fantasy that these scrapbooks would be both significant and useful in the future. But the fantasy was made both enticing and impos-sible by conceptualizing the task as compiling "a complete collection of all the war news." With that self-directed mandate, it hardly seems "strange" that he did not complete it. The vastness of the newspaper record meant that the actuality would always fall short; looking at it would be a reminder of its inadequacy.

Although Civil War scrapbooks makers like Curtis were ostensibly creating a record or archive, they were also doing what I call "performing archivalness" or record making: engaging in the clipping and saving activities that displayed the intensity of their emotional engagement in the moment with this reading.

The Material Life of Civil War Scrapbooks

The very different material conditions of access to printed matter in the North and the South shaped each section's scrapbook making, while ideology marked the scrapbooks' divergent purposes and uses. Northerners were awash in swift-running streams of newspapers that they dipped into for their ample scrapbooks; Southerners suffered an increasing drought, both of newspapers and of materials from which to make scrapbooks.

The South: Paper and Chronology

Paper shortages in the South cut into newspaper production and caused them to be printed on odd lots of paper (including wallpaper), while the locally manufactured ink was sometimes faint. Newspapers were not casually tossed aside after reading, but passed along. Aside from the scarcity of matter to paste into the scrapbook, volumes to use for the books themselves were scarce. Ella Thomas complains in 1863, "during this summer I have been much interested in pasting a scrap book. I have two filled and cannot buy another in Augusta altho I have material enough to fill several more." A year later she was still clipping newspapers, but had no book to paste them in: "I have cut out for the scrap books (which I cannot buy) an account of all the important events which have taken place."[14]

A massive scrapbook made by a member of the Moses J. Solomons household in Savannah, Georgia, filled 483 pages of a large ledger book between 1861 and 1863. Reusing ledgers and other books for scrapbooks was common, North and South. Solomons, however, seems to have run out of space in the scrapbook, so that later clippings paste over and obliterate earlier ones, testifying to the urgency of the act of pasting itself in performing archivalness. An 1862 item in this scrapbook reporting on "Books and Letters Found in the Federal Camps" via a visit to a deserted Union camp at Shiloh expresses resentment of the Union's abundant access to paper for propagandizing:

> All the letters and envelopes, as well those used by the soldiers as those received from home, were embellished with some motto or device, the object of which is to inculcate devotion to the Union and hatred of the South. I brought away a number of letters, envelopes, and sheets of paper, not one of which is without the ever-present Federal flag.

Another Confederate scrapbook maker, who pasted over a North Carolina physician's account book from two decades earlier, saved a plea from newspapers for the materials for making paper. "Rags! Rags! Rags!" made the rounds of Southern newspapers whose editors felt the pinch of the paper shortage:

> Anything that paper makes,
> Every editor now takes,
> And will pay you for your rags,
> And your good-for-nothing bags,
> Bring them in, and bring them soon,
> Morning, evening, and at noon.

Paper was sought for other uses too: Southern newspaper readers were urged to use sheets of newspaper at home to supplement their cotton bedding, so they could send the household's blankets to the soldiers fighting in colder climates.

Paper shortages in the wartime South heightened the desirability of clipping the paper, not just from the usual need to rescue desired items from the oblivion of disorderly piles of paper. Rather, Southerners also had to catch items before the newspaper was reused, added to the bedding, or pulped.[15]

Newspaper material in Confederate scrapbooks is generally restricted to clippings from Southern papers. The Northern blockade of the South largely kept Northern papers out of the hands of Southern scrapbook makers. Commercial reading rooms in Southern cities offered access, for a fee, to Southern papers, and to Northern papers received under flag of truce, but reading room papers were not meant for clipping. One result of the scarcity of newspapers was that the version of a Confederate nation that Solomons and other Southerners created in their scrapbooks could not be a straightforward history made from a chronological culling of the press. With supplies and transportation disrupted, households might not have received newspapers in a steady, chronological stream. With newsprint scarce and precious, scrapbook makers would have waited their turn, after all others in an extended circle were through with the paper, before cutting it up. Much might also be missing by the time they received a copy of a paper.[16]

The Solomons scrapbook maker clipped from multiple newspapers between 1861 and 1863. Although it has not been possible to ascertain precisely who in the family made the scrapbook, and it may have been supplied by more than one person, the book's attention to women's work for the Confederacy—from fundraising to spying—suggests that it might have been made by a woman, possibly the third wife of Moses, Henrietta Emanuel Solomons, born in Georgetown, South Carolina, and aged twenty-four at the start of the war. Because others who have used this scrapbook have done so, I will refer to the maker as an individual, Solomons, and use feminine pronouns.[17]

Receiving newspapers from earlier dates inspired more clipping and pasting of favorite events, or poems printed months or years previously. The result was that Southern Civil War scrapbooks are characteristically recursive, moving back and forward in time, rather than chronological. Solomons repeatedly pasted material on General P. G. T. Beauregard's victories at Fort Sumter and the first battle of Bull Run, reverting to these early Confederate victories after they had been superseded by defeats. Perhaps she knew people in those battles and sought information about them; perhaps she admired General Beauregard and became a fan, following dispatches about him. Like present-day military re-enactors, she replayed favorite battles. The chronology of her book is further complicated because when she ran out of space in the book, she pasted additional, though not always newer, items over the old, choosing to preserve some items while obscuring others.

This book preserves clippings of interest to historians, but the scrapbook that Solomons wrote with scissors and pasted into the family's bulky business ledger is not a coherent history itself. Rather, it is her ideal newspaper, a recursive history of the war and the situation of the South. Solomons clipped from the papers angry tirades against Lincoln; heartening celebrations of Beauregard's and other Confederate victories; poems and articles commending women for their work for the Confederacy through knitting, fundraising, cross-dressed spying, and spying in feminine clothes; accounts copied into Southern papers from the British press on the strength of the Confederacy; reports that the contents of dead Yankees' pockets reveal their unwillingness to keep fighting; and soothing accounts of loyal slaves. Poems mourning noble dying soldiers are usually distanced from specifics, in line with conventions for elegiac verse. Her scrapbook is abstracted from the time stream of the press or chronological history, and instead it forms a reservoir of emotions, so that she can repeatedly dip into them. Its repetition of accounts from different points of view highlights, too, the mediated quality of her experience of the war and acknowledges that her clippings are not a transparent reflection of events.[18]

Although a chronologically or topically organized scrapbook still allows the reader to leaf backward and forward, and thus revisit material out of sequence, this and other Southern scrapbooks often make it difficult to view events *in* sequence. In the Solomons scrapbook, history does not sit still in a chronologically organized past but is something to which one can repeatedly return, to revive the immediacy of a moment when the South was winning. This is one of many Confederate scrapbooks that lay the emotional groundwork for the postwar lost-cause ideology.[19]

Other Southern Civil War scrapbooks similarly spiral through time, avoiding or unable to achieve a straightforward trajectory. A dedicated Confederate woman in Charleston, Elizabeth Mary Lesesne Blamyer Wigfall, in her scrapbook ranging from 1847 until after the war, collected a poem emblematic of Southern scrapbook recursiveness. The 1859 poem, popular during the Civil War, was often known by its opening couplet, "Backward turn backward, O Time in your flight/ Make me a child again, just for to-night." Written by Elizabeth Akers (Allen), of Maine, "Rock Me to Sleep," in the voice of a woman wishing to be a child again, cared for by her dead mother, ends with a plea to be clasped in her mother's embrace to die. With the gender of the speaker switched, it was one of several poems understood to be about soldiers missing their mothers, which were popular both North and South. The reiterated longing it expresses to turn time backward, away from "tears," is emblematic of the general wartime desire to retreat to a time before widespread destruction and death. Southern scrapbooks like Wigfall's mirror the desire it expresses to reverse the direction of time. Such scrapbooks allow their readers to page through in sequence, but readers find themselves moving back into earlier items as they go. Wigfall's scrapbook carries another mode of refusal of the new order in including an item on the suicide of Edward Ruffin, who fired the first shot at Fort Sumter, and who said at the end of the war that he couldn't live under the U.S. government. Recursive Southern scrapbooks materialize their refusal of the new order.[20]

The North: Paper and Histories

Unlike their Southern counterparts, Northern scrapbooks responded to a flood of newspapers and reveled in their access to print, paper, and a functioning postal service. Unlike Philip Nolan, Northern readers could work with the genuine article, and not resort to rocks and ribbons. Region and access shaped the materials available to an anonymous Northern scrapbook maker, for example, who saved large engravings of battle scenes and political cartoons related to the war from *Harper's Weekly*. Such visual information was easy to get in the North, but generally unavailable in the less technologically developed South, where most news illustrations were rudimentary. So Frederick Cabot, a Boston abolitionist, took advantage of access to Northern and Southern newspaper sources to paste three or four newspaper items per day onto folded sheets for the duration of the war. His nationalist expression pointedly included the rebellious states in the nation. The uniform sheets, accumulated in large piles, are so tightly folded as to suggest that they may not have been opened again after initial reading and possible private circulation, or even after pasting; like David Curtis who thought he was making a useful history of the war, Cabot may not have "studied" that history once he created it. The items are various—maps of battle sites, lists of the killed or wounded without dates or attributions—as though performing archivalness, the act of clipping and pasting without any intent to reread or use, was central. His massive clipping collection conveys the sense that his following this news of battles, his pinning the maps to paper with sealing wax as he did, would help secure those distant places just as the Union Army was working to secure them on the ground. The maps he clipped from the pictorial weeklies offered visual and tactile command of disputed territory.[21]

Northern cutting and pasting often embodied scrapbook makers' personal desire to make sense of the war they were living through, and to save a record of their mediated relationship to it. For many, scrapbook making embodied a feeling of duty to save the nation's history. Northerners used their broader access to newspapers and paper to make scrapbooks that asserted the continuity of their Civil War scrapbooks with other histories of the United States. They culled the press to create massive, formal looking multivolume histories in their scrapbooks. Charles French, a hardware and later drug merchant of Boston, for example, pasted eleven large ledger volumes, four columns across, following the news of the Civil War, densely covering the pages with clippings that proceed from the election of Lincoln and move with methodical intensity through the war and after. An occasional handwritten note fills in for missing articles by summarizing them. One of his scrapbooks appears in Figure 3.1. Similarly, Dr. John George Metcalf, a Massachusetts state legislator and member of the American Antiquarian Society, collected material from 1861 to 1865 for his scrapbook to which he gave the formal title "The Irrepressible Conflict." It was a joint effort: soldiers from his town sent him letters and ephemera in the course of the war. Such collecting relied on a functioning postal service that let him receive the contributions. Northerners from other states, too, set out to mark the role of their states and localities in the conflict and to be sure that their version survived as a usable record. Mrs. G. S. Orth, for example, the wife of an Indiana Republican politician, "commenced carefully selecting the best editorials, letters, etc. from the current newspaper literature of the day," with a special focus on reports from soldiers in the newspapers.[22]

Passion for the subject sometimes overrode a sharply defined record. Joseph W. H. Cathcart (1823 or 1827–1895), an African American in Philadelphia, made more than a hundred scrapbooks mainly on black life, organized by topic (further discussed in Chapter 4). The categories he organized his scrapbooks into included the Rebellion covered in three huge scrapbooks, but he also pasted Civil War material in his scrapbooks designated as covering slavery, and some material on black soldiers in his scrapbooks on the Freedmen's Bureau. His scrapbooks thus define the Civil War as inextricable from slavery and show African Americans taking up arms as freedmen. The scrapbook spines announce an intent to classify, but what, really, during the Civil War, could be outside of the category of slavery? One 448-page volume, "Slavery," begins in 1863 with forty pages of Congressional proceedings, largely dealing with the war, the Confederacy and how its adherents are treated, and the status of black people. He pasted in his "Slavery" scrapbook a debate on a resolution to expel a member of the House who supported the Confederacy and columns discussing whether the word "white" should be added in front of "male" for District of Columbia voters. Other items include a report that Mr. Wilson of Iowa introduced a bill to amend the Constitution to declare slavery incompatible with a free government, and articles on the gathering of black regiments and the activities of the Freedmen's Bureau. Material dealing with the Confederacy finds a place in the "Slavery" scrapbook, since he understood the Civil War to be fought over slavery, and the Confederacy to be engaged in defending it.[23]

The widespread feeling that newspapers held special yet fleeting information about the war was reflected in the commercial realm as well. In 1861, Frank Moore began editing his Northern *Rebellion Record: A Diary of American Events with Documents, Narratives, Illustrative Incidents, Poetry, etc.* His digest of Northern and Southern newspaper material and other documents that would elucidate "the questions at issue, or the spirit and temper of the people, whether loyal or otherwise" was issued weekly and monthly, eventually winding up in 1867 with twelve bulky volumes. It was an ongoing, published scrapbook, writing a history with scissors on the fly, while encompassing many of the genres of material that appeared in the press. Its assertion that newspapers were central to creating a historic record, and indeed its existence, both paralleled homemade scrapbooks and inspired emulation. Though Moore's preface to the first volume asserted that his wide collecting, with "entire impartiality," would include many secessionist documents, his intent was by no means impartial; the documents were meant to be useful to analyze the "most extraordinary and unjustifiable conspiracy and rebellion" after the "nation is restored…to a peaceful and prosperous Union." Claiming the war as a set of "American events" framed the work's nationalistic purpose, while asserting that secessionist documents could be understood as part of American history. Reviews of Moore's work both celebrated its capaciousness and complain about its inevitable gaps: not enough maps, while a copy of the Confederate Constitution is lacking and would be most useful, says *The North American Review.* The gaps even in this substantial record inspired others to fill in by compiling their own rebellion records.[24]

Partisanship: Sectional Reading

The antebellum press was already highly sectional as well as partisan. Southern papers before the war had banned abolitionist material, an exclusion given legal teeth by Southern state laws forbidding use of the mails to distribute content likely to cause unrest. Readers understood that newspapers were closely affiliated with political parties; journalistic aspirations to objectivity arose later. Readers knew how to work with the press's partisanship, so when Abraham Lincoln made a scrapbook of reports containing his debates with Stephen Douglas, he clipped the shorthand transcriptions of his own words from the Republican papers, and took the transcriptions of Douglas's from the Democratic press, assuming that each party's press would accurately report its own man's words, but not the opponent's. Northern censorship during the war filtered "unauthorized" telegraphic war news, resulting in temporary reports of Union victory in battles where the Union was actually defeated, and it sometimes banned from the mails newspapers that published reports critical of government officials or military actions. Southern newspapers observed voluntary censorship of unfavorable war news. Many magazines were less overtly partisan before the war, but during it they, along with newspapers, voluntarily and by coercion, were enlisted in Edward Everett Hale's project of "keep[ing] up people's courage" and comforting their own side, through carefully choosing and pruning what they published.[25]

Voluntary censorship and circulation of disinformation could be extreme. The final Confederate issue of the Vicksburg, Mississippi, *Daily Citizen*—printed on wallpaper because of paper shortages—announced imminent victory for Robert E. Lee's forces July 2, 1863, just before Vicksburg was captured by the Union.[26]

Each side's interest in reading the other side's press appears in different modes of reading across the lines. Unlike David Curtis, who stopped making his scrapbooks after losing faith "that newspapers were published for the purpose of printing the truth," partisans made scrapbooks as a tool for monitoring and uncovering deceptive reports. In William Mumford Baker's 1866 novel *Inside: A Chronicle of Secession,* on the lives of Union sympathizers living in a Confederate town during the war, both sides are avid for newspapers, and Northern papers circulate furtively among the Union sympathizers, who reasonably fear being lynched if their leanings are known. Neither side wants to believe news of its side's reverses. In the scrapbook of war news that Ferguson, a Union man, compiles, the physical condition of the papers, too, marks the dwindling resources of the

INSIDE.—A CHRONICLE OF SECESSION.

Mr. FERGUSON AND HIS RECORD.

Figure 3.4 Thomas Nast's drawing of Ferguson's massive scrapbook as a kind of book of judgment for comparing accounts, from *Inside: A Chronicle of Secession* (1866).

Confederacy: newspapers are "from a yard across down, toward the later dates, to sheets of eight inches, and of all the colors of the rainbow, according as wrapping paper was being resorted to under stress of the blockade" (Figure 3.4). Ferguson is interested precisely in the *inaccuracy* of the news, and he delights in classifying and analyzing the rumors he sees constantly circulating in the Confederate press into seven categories: the North is on the edge of bankruptcy, European countries are about to recognize the Confederacy, etc. Saving such items and comparing the fanfare each assertion is given when it appears allows him to notice the nearly imperceptible way it is dropped. Although newspaper editors evidently depended on the flicker of the daily replacement of daily newspapers to promulgate an endless supply of new claims, providing hope rather than facts, Ferguson retrieves the assertions from oblivion and pastes them into a record meant for critical media analysis. He articulates his critique through the language of juxtaposition. "Yesterday's news is forgotten because to-day's news is so much more glorious; then, yesterday's rumor was false, it seems, but that of to-day is certainly true," Ferguson explains to a friend.

> It is but to dash off the lie best suited to the hour in a few rapid lines, send it to the next paper, and in a few days it is read and believed over the whole South. If you had studied this collection as I have, Sir, you would find that just when all the appearances are at their darkest for Secession, then, and exactly then, the largest and most splendid lie is whizzing overhead.[27]

Similarly, Daniel Hundley, a Confederate officer and prisoner of the Union forces in Sandusky, Ohio, read the Northern newspapers he had access to with relentless skepticism. He bought a scrapbook in 1864 and "propose[d] to fill it with the newspaper history of the times, which if I can preserve it until the war is ended, will be of incalculable service to me" in showing the contradictions he had found among stories. He escaped from prison, presumably leaving his scrapbook behind. As both the fictional Ferguson and the historical Hundley understood it, scrapbooks recorded the daily press and enabled a critical reexamination of it. They propose to cut across the media flicker, its quality of *dailyness*, the fact that "today's paper" is always presumed to be the more accurate version; "yesterday's paper" is not to be consulted, and its propagandizing becomes invisible.[28]

Evidence of projects to uncover such traces of propagandizing was dangerous. Even though the scrapbooks were made from local newspaper articles, wrenching articles into new juxtapositions betrayed their subversive reading. The texts were freely available, but reading them with a critical eye and inscribing that critique for others to see via cutting, pasting, and the language of juxtaposition produced forbidden knowledge. Materials that were published as straightforward accounts, and that at least some readers believed were sincere claims of events, became parodic in the hands of more skeptical remixers. Ferguson in *Chronicle of Secession*

Figure 3.5 Ferguson locks his scrapbook and the U.S. flag away; from *Inside: A Chronicle of Secession* (1866).

must lock his scrapbook away in his safe along with the U.S. flag to avoid lynching (Figure 3.5). After the war, scrapbook makers continued to use their scrapbooks as tools to critique the press, using the language of juxtaposition to compare articles and using the scrapbook's ability to preserve to undermine the newspaper's incessant replaceability.

Scrapbooks documented allegiance more directly as well and entered into Confederate prosecution of Unionists for treason. After Lincoln's election, a white New Orleans editor who kept his antislavery sentiments out of the newspaper he published was nonetheless arrested and his home rifled. His indictment included charges concerning his "scrap-book full of Anti-Slavery extracts." A scrapbook was also evidence of treasonous attitudes in the account of a minister brought before a Mississippi tribunal and charged for treason in Confederate territory shortly after Mississippi voted to secede. His opposition to secession was known, he writes. His accusers offered the contents of his bookshelf and scrapbook as evidence of his position, asking rhetorically, "Have you any abolition works in your library, and a poem in your scrap-book, entitled 'The Fugitive Slave,' with this couplet as a refrain, 'The hounds are baying on my track; / Christian, will you send me back?'" His ownership of abolitionist works and the deliberate act of cutting out and saving such a couplet confirms that a connecting line runs from the subversive poem to his eyes and loyalties. His accusers assumed straightforward affinity in his reading; they did not allow for the possibility that he might be reading abolitionist works critically or making a compilation of material with which he disagreed. In this case, they were right and the idea of a close association between the clipper's loyalties and the material saved in a scrapbook is reinforced later in the account, when the narrator, escaping from the Confederates, is himself treed by hounds and recalls the couplet. He had not only clipped the poem and memorized it but entered into its actions himself.[29]

Within the Northern and Southern Civil War papers, and in articles collected in scrapbooks, the press became a many-layered sign of nationalism. Where New York papers had once offhandedly noted that an item was copied from the *Richmond Dispatch*, and the *Macon Telegraph* had once easily reprinted exchange items from the *Philadelphia Inquirer*, the blockade and mutual suspicion reframed exchanging and reprinting as spying or debunking propaganda. Items attributed to the other side's newspapers were sometimes said to have been found on the body of a dead enemy soldier, or discovered in a captured town. A Northern paper, for example, printed "Scraps from the latest Southern papers: The very last copy of the Newborn (N.C.) *Progress* published by its secessionist editor," before the town was captured, contained lines regretting that Unionist "traitors" had not been hung when the Confederates had them. A Boston woman collected the article in her scrapbook, where it became both evidence of Southern furious, murderous intent and reassurance that such designs were safely contained, now that the North had captured the town as well as the newspaper's inflamed editor.[30]

The act of collecting and pasting newspaper clippings during the Civil War was a complex mode of emotional expression. It encompassed both *retaining* and *containing* materials—treasuring them and pinning them down securely, as though owning them and putting the items under one's thumb gave power over them. Like the popular scrapbooks of colorful advertising cards of the 1880s, where young people saved representations of desirable products, framing them in social settings, Civil War scrapbooks expressed hopes, desires, and dreams by encompassing representations of desired situations or states of being. In contrast to Ferguson's scrapbook in *Inside: A Chronicle of Secession*, bent on critiquing the media and lining up evidence of its lies, scrapbooks like that of Solomons, which treasure accounts of victory— sometimes inaccurately, while overriding chronology to recur to some favorite battle repeatedly—created an idealized newspaper or counterfactual history.

Confederate Nation Building and the Solomons Scrapbook

The Confederate press helped to fuel anger at the Union, confidence in a secessionist victory, and pride in the Confederacy. In their homes, Confederate scrapbook makers created their own sense of participating in a new nation and separating from the old by saving verse celebrating the Confederacy and defaming Lincoln and the Union.

Solomons began her scrapbook in 1861 with "The Devil's Visit to Old Abe," venting Southern anger at Lincoln and the Yankees, whom the poem says the South shall soon punish and sweep to their doom. Rage at Northern tyranny and attacks on Lincoln are hallmarks of the book. Solomons notably supports her patriotic Confederate sentiments with poems and articles that use black voices to attack Lincoln and the Federal forces, cheer on the Confederacy, and endorse slavery. Solomons used newspapers selectively to construct a comforting version of the discomfiting war by accumulating accounts representing enslaved black people, who had the profoundest reasons to oppose the Confederacy, as loyal to their white masters or the Confederacy in general, and helping or asking to help in the war effort. Southern newspapers drew on the minstrel tradition of enunciating white sentiments in blackface, but they marked racial difference textually, with dialect alone, rather than burnt-cork faces. Unlike minstrel shows, which took place in a theater or other demarcated time and venue, however, the newspapers Solomons collected placed these representations in the same register with news accounts, an understanding Solomons reproduced in her scrapbook juxtapositions.

Written representation by the newspapers and that Solomons collected of enslaved people as loyal Confederates mirrors the foundational American political issue of political representation. In the antebellum South, the "three-fifths compromise" of electoral representation written into the Constitution allowed the Southern states to count three-fifths of every enslaved person in the census tally of population for forming congressional districts and voting in the electoral college, while whites essentially took over their votes, since slaves could not vote. The South thus used the presence of enslaved people to enhance both the political and representational power of antebellum Southern whites, while refusing black people a genuine voice. Literary representation, as seen in the Southern press and endorsed by the scrapbooks of Solomons and other Southerners, continued this representational displacement via written ventriloquism, putting words into the mouths of fictitious black characters to affirm the legitimacy of the Southern system, allowing Southerners to believe that blacks supported the Confederacy.

In one such poem, titled "Yankee Doodle, to the Georgia Volunteers," in the Solomons scrapbook, "Uncle Tom says, 'Master, we/Can whip dem *saitful* [deceitful] debils'"; he asks to "jine de boys" in fighting the Yankees, and gleefully narrates the Confederate victories at Bethel Church and Manassas (Bull Run). The poem offers the added bonus of being singable to "Yankee Doodle," thus recapturing a patriotic American tune for Confederate use. In "A Southern Scene from Life," the "little Missis" tells her Mammy that Lincoln means to free her, but Mammy explains that the difference between her coal black face and the child's "red and white…soft and fine" skin "with yeller ringlets" self-evidently results in Mammy's slavery and the little girl's liberty and wealth. She concludes that:

> "I'de rudder my old Missus save
> An nus [nurse] Young Missus too

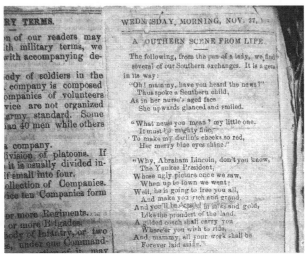

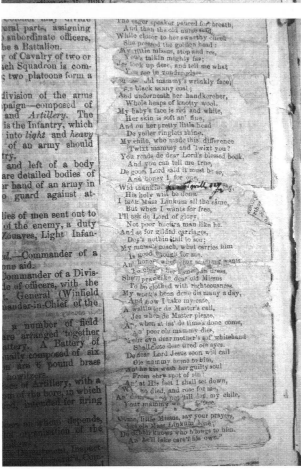

Figure 3.6 "A Southern Scene from Life," with worn section. (Davidson County, North Carolina, physician's account book, Duke University. Special Collections Library)

Dan go to Yankee lan and starve
As foolish niggers do."

She will instead wait for freedom in heaven, she says, and ends the dialogue with insulting comments about Lincoln. At least one reprinting of this popular poem insisted that it was rooted in reality. The *Macon Telegraph* introduced it as "the versification of a conversation that actually took place.... There is truth and feeling in it—indispensable essentials of poetry, expressed in smooth and natural verse." An anonymous scrapbook maker who repurposed a North Carolina physician's ledger book savored this same poem and evidently carried it around before pasting it, so that it was heavily frayed and partially torn, with handwritten corrections added to make up for a tear. The newspaper's heading on this version notes that it has been "in several of our Southern exchanges"[31] (Figure 3.6).

Accounts of black slaves loyal to their white masters or the Confederacy in general were evidently important to Solomons as evidence of the solid foundation of the Confederate nation. The accounts are threaded throughout the three-year accumulation of the book. In addition to other poems similar to "A Southern Scene from Life," such as "Philanthropy Rebuked," in which an enslaved woman refuses a Yankee's offer of freedom, Solomons saved a vertigo-inducing item reporting on the "Speech of a Patriotic Negro" at a black supper in Texas to raise funds for Confederate soldiers. The undated item reports the speaker asserting, in comic dialect, "We must dribe de bobolitionists from ole Kintuck, dat forrin land whar dis nigger was born, an ole Virginny, whar dis nigger's fader and mudder was fotched up." This account thus finds black people both participating, as the Solomons family did, in fundraising efforts for the Confederates, while adding black voices to anger at Northern abolitionists, using the decades-old burlesque language of "bobolition" broadsides and blackface performances, which mocked its speakers while acclaiming their ostensible sentiments. Such works thus claim black endorsement for Confederate sympathies while reassuringly framing such endorsement as issuing from people too foolish and ineffectual to be threatening.[32]

In other newspaper items she collected, loyal slaves wish to fight beside their masters or actually do so; others knit for the soldiers. Enslaved blacks captured by the Union express themselves "very anxious to get back to their masters." One account features a Confederate captain's faithful servant Mat, who not only buries his fallen master and returns to the plantation to "deliver all the messages and valuables with which his master had entrusted him" but cannot live without his master and first declines, and "despite the best medical attention and the kindest nursing he died February 4, 1863." The designation of a death date a month after the Emancipation Proclamation reinforces Solomons's sense that good, loyal blacks would rather die than be free, or could and should find freedom only in death.[33]

The Emancipation Proclamation marks the beginning of another thread in this scrapbook. Solomons continued to collect and paste stories of loyal blacks wanting to return to their masters or killing Union officers to protect white Southern homes, but by fall 1862, when drafts of the Proclamation were circulating, this new strain was launched with an anonymous bombastic poem, "For Abraham Lincoln. On Reading the Emancipation Proclamation." The poem worries that Lincoln "wou'st unband/the negro from his easy chain" and arm him to "see with joy 'gainst us arrayed/the bludgeon and the assassin's blade." Lincoln is still attacked as a devil in this poem, but black figures are no longer part of the chorus denouncing him; rather, with emancipation on the horizon, they are armed, but not to help the Confederacy. Rather they turn into "brutal fiends, whose reeking knives/Would spare nor sex, nor youth, nor age." The result would be that "wholesale murder clot our land." Solomons envisions the murder resulting from arming blacks as terrifyingly different from the bloodshed the war was already immersed in.[34]

Other items she preserved from the same time shift uneasily between envisioning slaves as loyal, faithful servants or as "brutal fiends." An October 9, 1862, clipping reports that boats with Federal forces came upriver to the "residence of Reuben King, Esq (a sterling old man of 84 years) [and] robbed him of all his negroes." One boat went on to another plantation, where "only one *white* man landed, he was followed by a gang of armed negroes who seized Mr. McDonald in the presence of his wife and dragged him on board their boat." Later, a white "gentleman . . . saw many negroes armed with sabres and guns enter the negro quarters and begin to search the houses." Armed black men are seen not as soldiers but only as a gang. Solomons collected a second, elaborated telling of the same event printed a month later, which she pasted twenty pages further on in the scrapbook, presumably when that paper came into her hands. In this version, at King's plantation, "the Abolitionists . . . forced some 50 negroes to accompany them, in spite of their piteous cries and lamentations, to free, clothe, and educate, as they stated" and ordered shot those who refused to go. At the McDonald plantation, "these *philanthropic, noble* friends of the black man . . . sent *armed negroes* ahead to bear the brunt and receive our bullets, should any soldier be present. *How Yankee! How brave!*" (Emphasis in the original.) The second account foregrounds and intensifies the responses of the enslaved people at King's: no longer simply passive property, they become loyal servants piteously lamenting their forced removal from their masters. The scene at McDonald's shifts from fury and fear of the gang of armed black men to framing the scene to assert that only the whites have agency: the black men's courage in spearheading the assault is interpreted as Yankee cowardice—using black men as shields.[35]

The newspapers that Solomons read vacillated in how they presented the threat of armed ex-slaves. She continued to accumulate stories of loyal slaves, and thus reinforce and insist on her belief that blacks and whites share a common community of loyalty to the South, and therefore to the plantation slavery system and to the Confederacy. However, more stories that run against the "loyal servant" strain appear as the scrapbook proceeds. One page before the final page contains an item reporting that Isaac, an enslaved man, "outraged and brutally murdered a young lady" and sank her body in a creek. Men of Cockrun, Mississippi, pursued Isaac to

Memphis, where General Sherman refused to give him up and called the men "murderers themselves, and further accused the whole Southern Confederacy of murder, bloodshed, and rapine." The black men who figure in earlier stories as loyal defenders of white families and their possessions can no longer be relied upon to guard white owners against the Yankees, but instead turn on the whites. The story hints at the white terrorist tactic of accusing black men of rape and lynching them, which would gather force after Reconstruction. It shows the increasingly conflicted beliefs Solomons held about what slaves might actually think and feel, and what they might do if the Confederacy lost and the Emancipation Proclamation became effective. And yet the massive scrapbook could provide the weight of reassuring evidence; when Solomons sees or hears of slaves escaping to join the Union army, the cumulative bulk of the collected articles on loyal slaves bolsters her belief that such accounts are aberrations. Her scrapbook constructs the emotional ground of Lost Cause ideology: the belief in a benevolent plantation past of reciprocal caring between slaves and slaveholders, and the idea that the Civil War was a just and noble war, fought over states' rights, rather than slavery.[36]

The nation building that Solomons engaged in her scrapbook was inflected by her identity as a Jew. Solomons, as a member of a Jewish storekeeping family, was aware of Jews' precarious position as relatively recent immigrants and cosmopolitans with ties to the North. Her construction of her family's and her own national identity as Confederates may have been all the more vehement for the family's tenuous hold on their status as Confederate citizens. The scrapbook records a protest against an 1862 attack on the Jewish community of Thomasville, Georgia, where Jewish merchants and peddlers were accused of speculation and disloyalty to the Confederacy and ordered expelled from the town. Family was an important articulation point between individual and nation for other scrapbook makers as well.[37]

War and the "Family"

The scrapbook of Richard Yeadon Dwight, of Charleston, who had served in Holcomb's Legion of South Carolina, turned the Confederacy into family, while the Boston abolitionist Henry Ingersoll Bowditch's scrapbook made his own family emblematic of the Union cause. Both were coincidentally physicians. By examining these books together, we can see how responses to war were mediated through the newspapers and circulated back into individual scrapbooks. Northern and Southern scrapbooks alike framed an understanding of the war and its meaning and thereby made claims about the nation. The contrasting accounts and the metaphors they used expressed and shaped differences in thinking about the war. Civil War scrapbooks served as repositories or reservoirs of national feeling as they embodied arguments about the purpose of the war, and what victory or defeat would mean.[38]

Henry Bowditch lost his oldest son, Nathaniel, in the war in 1863. He created a group of memorial scrapbooks for Nat, and then for other Massachusetts officers, and extended his work to a memorial cabinet that held the scrapbooks and the memorabilia he associated with Nat, such as the bloody glove Nat was wearing when he was killed. Henry understood slavery as the cause of the war and thus of Nat's death. The memorial cabinet contained memorabilia of Henry's abolitionist work in the 1840s, when Nat was a young child: small clubs carried by the Boston Anti-Man Hunting League to which Henry belonged, and scrapbooks on Henry's work on a petition campaign around the case of George Latimer, an escaped slave recaptured in Boston. Henry's own work as an abolitionist seemed to him to be seamlessly connected to Nat's life as a soldier, and so both were memorialized in his scrapbooks. The cabinet also contained material on Henry's father (described there as "Nat's grandfather") who had died in 1838, and brother who had died in 1861, both of whom were also named Nathaniel. Henry's entire family was inextricable from and emblematic of the Union.[39]

For Richard Dwight, the Confederacy and the South became his family. The trope of the Confederacy as family appears in various forms in a scrapbook he made after the war, pasting over a blank book of receipts for wartime deliveries of beef to Richmond hospitals. His treatment of the Fort Pillow massacre uses this framing. The massacre was a notorious unleashing of fury at armed ex-slaves, in which Confederate troops attacking Fort Pillow in Tennessee in 1864 killed black soldiers who were wounded or had surrendered. The Northern press condemned the attack as an example of the "brutality and cruelty of the rebels"; Northern response appears in Joseph Cathcart's "Slavery" scrapbook, where an editorial deplores the Fort Pillow massacre of black soldiers by Confederates as "a policy deliberately decided upon," refuting the idea that it transpired in the heat of battle. Holcomb's Legion was not involved at Fort Pillow, but for Dwight the massacre was prompted by unforgivable assaults on the Southern, white family. Dwight saved a poem justifying the massacre, James R. Randall's bloodthirsty "At Fort Pillow." It begins as though responding to those who might have heard of the brutalities against the black soldiers and think that killing the wounded is ungallant, "You shudder as you think upon / The carnage of the grim report." It asserts that there is more to the story that prompted such actions: "There are deeds you may not know, / That scourge the pulses into strife; / Dark memories of deathless woe / Pointing the bayonet and knife." Although the black soldiers are mentioned only once, as those the speaker *doesn't* condescend to "smite," the words "dark" and "black" recur as a displaced reminder that the presence of armed black soldiers was at stake for the Confederacy at Fort Pillow.[40]

The poem is overloaded with justifications for the Confederate actions: the enemy camped in a cemetery so that the speaker's mother's grave "Is crushed, with splintered marble heaps, / To stall the horse of some dragoon," and then a white woman was raped, "the only woman of our race." The speaker depicts a vividly bloody battlefield scene unusual in Civil War poetry, as though given permission by the Southern readers' assumed approval of the killing of rebellious ex-slaves.

Stating that "dabbled clots of brain and gore" is justified because the poet's blood is overheated by "The thought of desecrated graves / And some lone sister's desperate cry!" The piled-on justification for the killings makes them personal and familial: bloody sabers avenge the speaker's dead mother and "lone sister" and remake the Confederate nation as a white family (Figures 3.7 and 3.8).

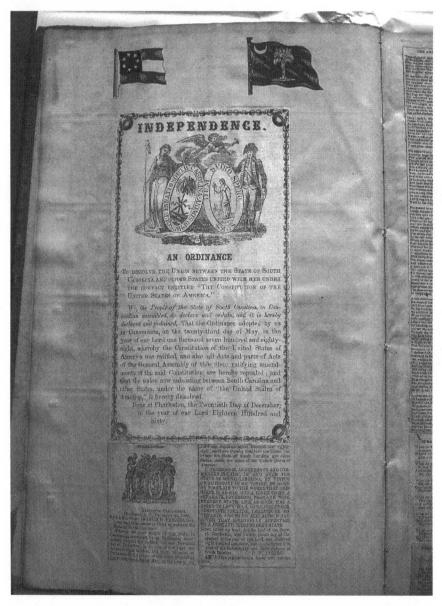

Figure 3.7 Confederate Richard Yeadon Dwight's scrapbook, made after the war, opens with South Carolina's declaration of secession. (South Carolina Historical Society)

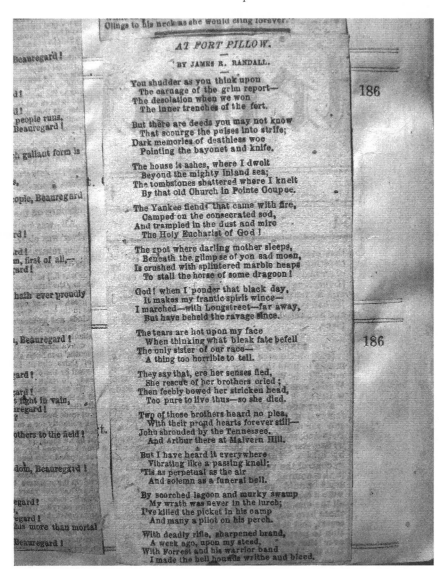

Figure 3.8 "At Fort Pillow" (partial), from Richard Yeadon Dwight's Confederate scrapbook. (South Carolina Historical Society)

Dwight continues this theme of the Confederate family with a clipping on the "noble hospitality" offered by the "peerless daughters of South Carolina," who, as railroad cars of the wounded go through, hold out cups of milk to cheer the men. Nursing turns more literal than metaphoric as daughters give milk to the soldiers, circulating infantile white nourishment, making the soldiers "a child again, just for to-night," like the soldiers singing "Rock Me to Sleep." For Dwight, pasting his book after the war, stories of loyal servants do not have the appeal they did for Solomons, and no black hands or bodies are brought into this exchange.[41]

Another of James R. Randall's poems that Dwight saved was popular enough to appear in other scrapbooks as well. "The Lone Sentry" adds a fatherly General Stonewall Jackson to the family. Seeing his men's exhaustion, Jackson keeps watch over the camp so they can all sleep. After his death, he continues to watch over the camps in spirit. Dwight's postwar scrapbook of clippings saved during the war shifts back and forth from moments marking defeat to reminders of the spirit with which the Confederates began. Like Solomons, he shows the Lost Cause ideology in formation as he reminds himself of the nobility of the cause and keeps it alive.[42]

"The Nation's Heart": Scrapbooks of Mourning Poetry

Theorists of war have noted the powerful, visceral excitement of *entrainment*, synchronized moving together in rhythm, as in marching. The scrapbooks of Civil War poetry point to the related satisfaction of *feeling* together with others; the poems widely circulated in the newspapers gave concrete evidence that others shared these feelings. In general, as we have seen, scrapbooks were understood as accurate—if hard to tally—evidence of a poem's popularity. Inclusion in many scrapbooks showed that even a critically disparaged poet "has a place as a poet in the hearts of the people." Saving Civil War poems in scrapbooks, even in some that seem too densely filled to be read, was a sign of feeling oneness with what Henry Ingersoll Bowditch called "the nation's heart," and it allowed the collector/reader to experience that feeling again. Collecting poetry in scrapbooks was a way of creating nation by affirming shared emotional bonds.[43]

Nineteenth-century daily papers contained poetry; during the Civil War, much of it was related to the war or brought into a relationship to the war via its title or notes. Frank Moore's *Rebellion Record* published a poetry section in every issue, entitled "Poetry, Rumors, Incidents, etc.," culling the Northern and Southern press for their productions, though by no means catching all. Many Civil War scrapbook makers mixed poetry with other matter in newspaperlike fashion; others, such as Joseph W. H. Cathcart, who included Civil War–related poetry in his other scrapbooks as well, created a volume called "Poetry and Rebellion," containing "about a thousand war songs." Nathaniel Paine, a Worcester banker and member of the American Antiquarian Society who had an eye toward historical preservation, made an ambitious anthologylike scrapbook of Civil War poetry, on specially printed paper, called "Poetry of the Rebellion," with materials largely confined to 1861 and 1862. He gave up on pasting after the first volume and left a pile of clipped, unpasted poems. In scrapbooks exclusively holding Civil War poetry, Cathcart, Paine, and many others made their own anthologies of newspaper poetry unlikely ever to appear in books.[44]

The same urgency that newspaper readers felt about saving the news engaged their relationship to newspaper poetry. It comprised a record of emotions. In the North, "The hearts of all our people were 'tuned'... 'up by successive events' to higher and higher enthusiasm, or suddenly brought rudely down, by disastrous reverses, to the lowest depths of despair—These various moods of the popular heart are shadowed out in the poetry, that sprang up everywhere," Henry Ingersoll Bowditch wrote in Boston in the introduction to his scrapbook titled "Waifs: Chiefly Poetic, Gathered During the Rebellion," made up of poetry he saved, beginning at the time of his son's death. The "Waifs" scrapbook was one of the items in the memorial cabinet he made for his son.[45]

North and South shared many attitudes toward mourning poetry and practices of using them. A published collection of Confederate poems also called them "waifs" and hailed the Confederate newspaper poems in almost the same terms as Bowditch did Union poems: William G. Shepperson, who edited *War Songs of the South* in 1862, admired the newspaper poems as "a spontaneous outburst of popular feeling.... Through the Poet's Corner in the newspaper, they have sped their flight from and to the heart and mind of the people." Newspapers copied one another's poems, and magazines such as the *Southern Literary Messenger* reprinted them, too, as "the many excellent little poems the war has called forth," reinforcing their cultural value.[46]

Poetry scrapbooks were already an established tradition before the war, growing out of commonplace books into which readers copied out favorite poems. Newspapers routinely published poetry, both original and reprinted from magazines and other newspapers, and both obviously topical and without evident connection to the news. Memorial tributes to individuals and poetry expressing grief for unnamed dead people made up an enduring portion of newspaper poetry before and after the Civil War, and they were often saved in clipping scrapbooks. People who knew the deceased were likely to save a poem, of course, but collecting such poetry was also part of nineteenth-century culture, shaping and strengthening community ties. Collecting Civil War memorial poetry tied individual grief to a sense of national significance.[47]

Scrapbooks of mourning poetry may not directly reflect the biographical facts of a compiler's life. Anne Greenough Gray Whitney, of Boston, for example, kept a commonplace book, later turned scrapbook, where she began transcribing and collecting newspaper poems and stories about maternal death starting in 1826 when she was twenty-six, years before her own mother's death in 1829. Whitney's eagerness to place the book into her daughters' hands before they could read it—it is inscribed first to one infant daughter, and then to another who survived the first—suggests that for her it expressed something fundamental about the mother-daughter bond, and that anticipatory grief was inextricable from love. The stories and poems written out before Whitney lost her mother, and before her own daughters were born, become directions to her own children on how to feel when their mother dies. The book is a more general inculcation into their culture's widespread ideas and ideals, such as the duty to care for the sick, the belief in an afterlife, and proper ways to think about the dead. (At it happened, her children lost their father, not their mother, when they were young, and Anne Whitney lived on another thirty years.)[48]

Although some scholars have assumed that nineteenth-century American mourning practices were part of women's domain, with women as the designated mourners, both men and women wrote and collected mourning poetry and partic-ipated in its private as well as commercial circulation. In 1841, for example, Pickering Dodge, a Salem, Massachusetts, merchant, transcribed 186 pages of poetry for an album entitled "For the Infant Dead," as a fifteenth-anniversary present for his wife. Their two-year-old son George had died the year before. The book is a "monument" to the child. He explains to his wife that he has "employed some of my leisure hours during the past winter in transcribing for you a collec-tion of pieces, prepared in many instances by parents suffering under the severe dispensation of bereavement." Even as poems and a sermon in the book affirm the superiority of heaven to life, both individual works and the book itself return repeatedly to grief. The poems are not so much about children as about the expe-rience of loss; not about the boy, but about losing the boy.[49]

Notably, to create his gift Dodge withdrew from his family into his own mascu-line space—his study or library—to work through his grief, as he painstakingly copied the poems onto carefully organized blank sheets he then sent to a binder, creating a beautifully bound manuscript volume from printed materials as a monument. "Mingled feelings of gratification and regret" accompanied his with-drawal to work on it. His labor on it away from his family was intended to bind the family; it was meant for the other children in the family and to become part of the family's story of itself.[50]

Dodge's move into masculine space to copy his book from periodicals and printed books is not incidental, but central to investing the collection with the authority that gives it continued power in the family as a discrete object. It was not something to be added to and commented on by the next generation, as was Whitney's commonplace-book-turned-scrapbook. Such a withdrawal is the stan-dard move of the anthologist, who retreats "to the library's sacrosanct masculine quiet...finally emerging, compilation in hand, to supervise the literary experience of the family parlor," Kristin Silva Gruesz notes. In the nineteenth-century affluent American household, domestic space has often been thought of as feminine. However, work like Dodge's reminds us that the era's ideology of separate spheres for men and women limited women's range away from the home but opened the home to men, for whom it was a refuge, and who held authority over sentimental discourse.[51]

So when Bowditch made his "Waifs" album of poetry in memory of his twenty-three-year-old son, he was participating in an established tradition. Bowditch, like Dodge, worked deliberately and carefully, pasting onto sheets of paper and writing a table of contents and headnotes, creating a self-contained work that he then sent to a binder and that does not invite others to add to it. Working decades after Dodge, he pasted rather than copied. His "Waifs" poetry scrapbook constitutes a complex meditation on and mediation of his own reading. The conventional poetry of war spoke to him and touched his heart—and, he believed, "not alone mine but...the nation's heart." Reading it and saving it during the war became another way of participating in the common, group experience of war, feeling in common with others, although he did not paste down his clippings for over a decade, dating his introduction March 17, 1875, the "12th anniversary of Nat's fatal wound."

Personal, sentimental exchange as a means of asserting continuing ties to the dead and linking the community via the inscription of poems was an ongoing practice, as Mary Louise Kete describes in her work on a memory book created in a small Vermont community during a period that overlaps the war. Like the memory book makers, Bowditch documented and preserved a community's agreement about the importance of mourning, and of keeping ties to those mourned. But Civil War poetry circulated through newspaper exchanges, and the substantially public element of Bowditch's scrapbook project shifts it from hand-to-hand circulation. Unlike Pickering Dodge's transcriptions, which dropped source information, creating a more anthologylike appearance, as do many poetry scrapbooks, Bowditch's collection often preserves its connection to the circuits of newspaper circulation, and thereby to the broad readerly community through which the poems traveled. When information about what paper a poem came from was missing, he often added it by hand, and some clippings specify their original source before reprinting via newspaper exchanges. The connections Bowditch's poetry collection participates in are not one-to-one and personal; rather the circuit through the newspapers allows it to speak for the collective "nation's heart."[52]

Bowditch discusses his response to the time- and occasion-bound quality of the poetry he collected. Although in the 1870s the poems were still important enough to him for him to make the scrapbook, he is also suspicious of the operation of sentiment; the poems, he acknowledges, touched him because of the emotional state he was in at the time, and reading them later brings back memories of that state, and through that, memories of Nat. He seems surprised, perhaps even embarrassed, by the poetry that moved him ten and twelve years before.

> I present these waifs of poetry etc., which I gathered during the Rebellion, not as specimens of the divine art of poesy, though some of them are worthy of all praise, but simply to illustrate the tendency of the times.... These various moods of the popular heart are shadowed out in the poetry, that sprang up everywhere.... In all seasons of great joy [and] in great sorrow, the heart finds relief in poetry. Many write at those periods who never [would] ... at other times. It is true the poetry is often very poor, maybe absurd. I had almost said ridiculous, but one cannot ridicule a great woe and we feel a pity for the sufferer.

Bowditch earlier participated in widespread practices of sentimental reading: on a trip to Scotland in the 1830s, he obtained a lock of hair saved by a relative of the subject of a favorite Robert Burns poem and carried it in his pocket for twenty-five years. He was nonetheless uneasy enough with sentiment to shift between distancing himself from the work (the poems "illustrate the tendency of the times") and presenting himself as a representative specimen of someone who was moved. Most scrapbooks are without commentary; perhaps the maker assumes that the scrapbook maker is the ultimate reader or will always be at the elbow of another reader to explain the choices. But Bowditch classified his poems into categories, occasionally adding an explanatory note. Accordingly, the first of the sections into which he has divided the poems is

> expressive of Religious trust and confidence that under God, all events would ultimately be for our best good. They seem to me, all of them, beautiful, though some of them do not allude to passing events, and were written before the war began, they, nevertheless, appear to me appro-priate for all times, and therefore I caught them as they floated by during the Rebellion. Each and all, every time I read them, bring back the reli-gious aspirations of my* heart, which, I think, were never stronger than at times, during the war.
> *not alone mine but in the nation's heart.

His asterisked addition, linking his own sentiments to the nation's, both enhances the significance of his emotions and points to his sense of emotional unity with others, which was part of his experience of wartime. His use of the word *nation* rather than *union* affirms that the nation encompasses the secessionist states. He retroactively extends his sense of a community of feeling to Southerners, acknowl-edging that they might have felt the same emotions.

Some of the poems were produced by people who in ordinary circumstances would not have been impelled to write, and they even seem to spring "naturally" from people, as Bowditch saw it. That so many people produced them as well as read them spoke to the depth and density of the emotions:

During the war often when horrible tidings came to us from Ball's Bluff in Bull Run—that twice fatal spot for our armies—the whole nation seemed prostrated over newly-made graves. Funeral marches and elegies broke out naturally from the hearts of all—to be replaced by songs of triumph and of exultant joy, when victory crowned our armies.

Bowditch's "Waifs" categories move among grief, pain, triumph, and mockery. The fourth section sends the soldiers out, and the fifth brings home live volunteers, but it is only after the achievement of "a glorious peace!" that the sections commemorating deaths appear. With his final section, embodying a scholarly distancing, Bowditch steps into a new role; instead of commemorating and preserving his emotional response to the works, he turns documentarian and saves popular broadsides to which he claims no emotional connection.

Bowditch's collection marks the particularities of his situation as well as his personal taste. He largely omitted poems exhorting men to enlist, in part because the main outpouring of these came in the first year of the war, before he began collecting. He excluded as well poems about the home front, and the popular Civil War poems about soldiers missing their mothers (Elizabeth Akers Allen's "Rock Me to Sleep" is absent, though a parody of "mother" poems is sequestered into his selection of broadsides). He knew some of the poets he included, like his abolitionist comrade John Greenleaf Whittier, and his medical school classmate Oliver Wendell Holmes, Sr. Other poets' names themselves had special meaning for him.

The fifth section, "The Joys of the Returning Volunteer," is one of only two he doesn't comment on. His inclusion of such a section, in a book whose genesis is in his son's death and failure to return, seems a remarkable effort. The section notably excludes mention of sons returning specifically to parents. Its first poem is "Returned," by Kate Putnam (Kate Putnam Osgood). She shared her name with Nat's fiancée, whom Henry came to think of as another daughter. Kate Putnam (Katherine Day Putnam) died in 1873, after Bowditch collected the poem, but before he completed his book. In "Returned," the speaker comes to passionately love her absent sweetheart while he serves in the army, is imprisoned, and returns at the end. Another poem by this poet, "Driving Home the Cows," a wish fulfillment poem in which a father who has lost all three of his sons in the war is surprised by the arrival of the youngest, not dead but only missing an arm, would seem to also belong in this section. But Bowditch mutes the pain of that fantasy by placing it in section 2, "Loyal." Unlike most parents of Civil War soldiers, whose sons' bodies remained on or close to the battlefield and who might have indulged this fantasy, Henry traveled south to bring Nat's body back to Massachusetts.[53]

He saved "Mortally Wounded," Mary Woolsey Howland's anonymously published, widely recirculated poem in the voice of a dying soldier that begins "Now I lay me down to sleep," three times, the only repetition in his scrapbook. (Its recirculation is discussed in Chapter 1.) The poem affirms religious faith, which for him is mingled with faith in the Union cause. It also expresses his belief that it speaks for men in camp and that it is a suitable elegy for Nat. One of the sections "Mortally Wounded" was pasted into was

> Sixth: Elegiac, or mourning for the dead, slain in battle or by disease in camp. The whole nation seemed to find comfort in song [poetry], good, bad or indifferent. The deep underlying thought of heartfelt sorrow seemed to sanctify even the least worthy. As I read these poems again, after the lapse of ten years, I am glad that I saved them from the fleeting tide of time, and I am ready to place them one and all here in memory of the noble dead. Among them will be found not a few dedicated to the memory of the 2nd father of his country—Abraham Lincoln.

Bowditch thus linked mourning for his son with mourning for Lincoln.

For those who collected "Mortally Wounded" and distributed it after the war, as modeled in the *Ladies' Repository* story where Aunt Debby, who has nursed dying soldiers clips it, shares it, and weeps over it as an authentic expression of soldiers' reality, it could by association bestow a "serene and holy" death on their loved ones. Recirculation of "Mortally Wounded" both spiritualized and universalized the war, so that all could participate on equal footing, whether on the battlefield or at home or in church. The poem consoles the living by speaking through the soldier's persona; the attributions to soldiers and commentary on those soldiers cumulatively asserted the authenticity of that soldier's voice and passed along (all) soldiers' consent to this idea of the meaning of their deaths. Collecting "Mortally Wounded" was consonant with Bowditch's concern that his son should have followed his friend William Lowell Putnam's lead in "serene and holy" exemplary dying. He comments on Putnam, "I rejoice to think that when Nat received his fatal wound and felt himself near his end, his deportment reminded Col. Curtis of the noble resignation evinced by Lieut. Putnam." Bowditch's hunger to hear voices of soldiers in camp, like his son's, appears elsewhere in the scrapbook. Although Nat Bowditch wrote an abundance of letters home, which Henry transcribed into a separate book—in an act of inhabiting Nat's body to reproduce what he wrote—Henry's scrapbook shows the bereaved father still seeking the voice of the soldier. He saved five poems by "Private Miles O'Reilly," whose works in the voice of an infantryman were widely published in the newspapers—perhaps unsurprisingly, since they were written by a newspaper writer turned officer and eventually general, Charles Halpine. Again, the claim to authenticity was crucial to their popularity, and yet the Irish dialect of the poems frames their ideas and sentiments as comic.[54]

The conventional poetry of the Civil War can often seem distressingly and willfully naïve in its refusal to acknowledge the horrors of war, its sentimentality, and its idealistic sentiments, whether those sentiments are of Northern national unity and attacks on slavery such as the most famous and enduring Civil War poems, Julia Ward Howe's "Battle Hymn of the Republic," or of Southern freedom from tyranny. When we read the poems as they were placed in scrapbooks made by individual readers, we can begin to understand these poems' power for their readers.[55]

Most present-day literary critics reject the high-flown sentiments of popular Civil War poetry. Instead they prefer to focus on three poets whose writing resonates with post–World War I sensibilities, which focus on war's futility and waste: Herman Melville, Walt Whitman, and Emily Dickinson, more recently claimed as a Civil War poet. Yet Melville, Whitman, and Dickinson were not poets that Civil War scrapbook makers sought with their scissors. Melville's and most of Whitman's and Dickinson's Civil War poems did not appear in the newspapers at the time, but in books after the war. In collecting their poems and pasting them into scrapbooks, the scrapbook makers looked for justification of the war and for consolation for their grief in losing loved ones.

Melville records the sense of intense communion of readers who nearly merge with the newspaper displayed on a bulletin board, and the loss of the boundary between public and private, in "Donelson," where

> Flitting faces took the hue
> Of that washed bulletin-board in view,
> And seemed to bear the public grief
> As private, and uncertain of relief....

Civil War scrapbook makers not only sought to save the sense of living through momentous times but preserved a record of grasping those events through reading specific newspaper articles. Henry Bowditch's poetry scrapbook suggests that readers also sought to preserve the emotional *experience* of reading particular poems in the immediacy of the news-saturated surroundings of the newspaper setting. Scrapbooks didn't simply preserve clippings to review; they served as a souvenir of sorts of the intense relationship with the newspaper. The act of making an individual, personal selection from the mass-produced press asserted both individual tastes and needs and the connection with the rest of the nation and its reading and emotions through the newspaper (Figure 3.9).[56]

Border-Crossing Poetry and North-South Reconciliation

In the Civil War, as Bowditch and Solomons could have told us, the identity and affiliations of newspapers that published an article or poem mattered a great deal. Most of the poems in Bowditch's "Waifs" scrapbook with visible attribution are from the *Boston Evening Transcript*, an abolitionist Union-supporting daily, and a few are from the *Boston Daily Advertiser*, edited by Edward Everett Hale's father and later his brother, though Bowditch read other papers. Not surprisingly, none

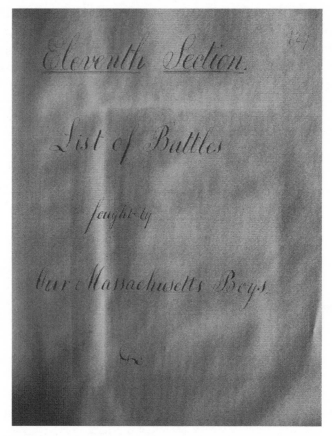

Figure 3.9 A section title from Bowditch's "Waifs" scrapbook marks his inclusion of newspaper reports as part of the experience of reading the poems that moved him after his son's death. (Massachusetts Historical Society)

are from the *Boston Courier*, which he considered a copperhead paper, sympathizing with the South; nor were any of the items he clipped reprinted from the *Courier*.[57]

Whether a poem appeared in a Northern or Southern newspaper was even more crucial. During the war, Southern newspapers sometimes reprinted poems from the Northern press with the attribution intact, but they were unlikely to do so knowingly if the poem concerned the war. Although Northern and Southern Civil War scrapbooks created very different versions of nation, common ground appears in several war poems that crossed the lines to appear in Northern and Southern newspapers and scrapbooks and laid the groundwork for shared understandings of the war.

"Somebody's Darling," by Marie La Coste, first published anonymously, was one of several poems notable for appearing in both Northern and Southern newspapers during the war. In 1864, this poem about a soldier dying alone in the hospital sprawled across both sides of the conflict, appearing in the Raleigh, North Carolina, *Weekly Standard*; the Richmond, Virginia, *Daily Dispatch* in the South; in William Lloyd Garrison's devotedly abolitionist *Liberator* in the North; the Unionist *Walla Walla Statesman* in the West; and elsewhere. In each, it appeared without the author's name or any comment about the poet. It thus allowed readers to assume that, like other war-related poems appearing in the columns of their paper, it represented their own side, and that the unnamed "Somebody's darling, so young and brave" borne alone "Into a ward of the whitewashed walls / Where the dead and the dying lay" had been fighting in their army. Anyone could step into the role of the absent "somebody" of the poem, no longer present to kiss the "the snow of that fair young brow." Collected in scrapbooks on both sides of the conflict as well, it appears unattributed in Bowditch's "Waifs" in Section 6: Elegiac, and it was also pasted, unattributed, into the Solomons scrapbook (Figures 3.10 and 3.11). When war-related poems appeared in the newspapers during the Civil War, their roots in timeliness and news events were easily understood; even when the poem was not tied to a specific battle or event, readers needed no prompting to connect the poem with the war, as with Elizabeth Akers Allen's 1859 poem "Rock Me to Sleep," which was understood as a war poem.[58]

After the Civil War, texts such as nationally distributed magazines and school reading textbooks took up the task of shaping emotions that the nation could share. Shortly after the war, a Southern anthology published "Somebody's Darling" with attribution to Marie La Coste, pointedly noting that she wrote it in Savannah, and thus claiming it for the South. Taking the new information about its origin from that anthology, several Northern periodicals marked a mood of national conciliation by reprinting this already-familiar poem, which its readers had assumed from previous newspaper appearances was Northern. *Littell's Living Age*, a Boston-based weekly digest of other periodicals, reprinted it from Bowditch's favorite, the *Boston Transcript*, in 1867, copying *The Transcript*'s note, "The following exquisite little poem was written by Miss Marie Lacoste, of Savannah, Georgia, and originally published, we think, in the *Southern Churchman*. It will commend itself by its touching pathos to all readers. The incident it commemorates was unfortunately all too common in both armies."[59]

If during the war "Somebody's Darling" had commemorated the death of an unknown soldier on the reader's own side and spoke of sectional loss, after the war it became emblematic of shared national suffering. The poem became a verbal tomb of an unknown soldier, specifically a white youth—pale, blond, blue-eyed, and snowy-browed—where the mourning North and South comfortably gather, in one of many reiterations exemplifying the postwar reconciliation of North and South that increasingly excluded black people from the conception of the remade nation. When the poem appeared in the Northern press after the war in its newly revealed Southern identity, it expressed this new set of shared emotions. Its place in a daily newspaper rooted it in a new historical moment, gathering a new set of readers around it.

Another poem that crossed borders after the war focused on the symmetry of loss, graves, and tears on both sides, without privileging blond snowy brows. "The

Blue and the Gray," an 1867 poem by Francis Miles Finch, a Northern judge, offered a way for both black and white clippers to celebrate reconciliation. It appears in one of Joseph W. H. Cathcart's scrapbooks in Philadelphia, collected from two different copies of the *Sunday Dispatch*. For a white South Carolina boy born in 1861 and working on his scrapbook in 1874, collecting "The Blue and the Gray" perhaps offered a way to understand the war and continue a connection to his dead mother.[60]

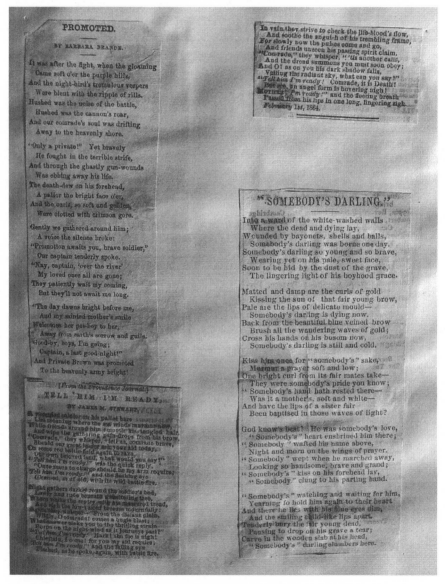

Figure 3.10 "Somebody's Darling," from Bowditch's "Waifs" scrapbook. (Massachusetts Historical Society)

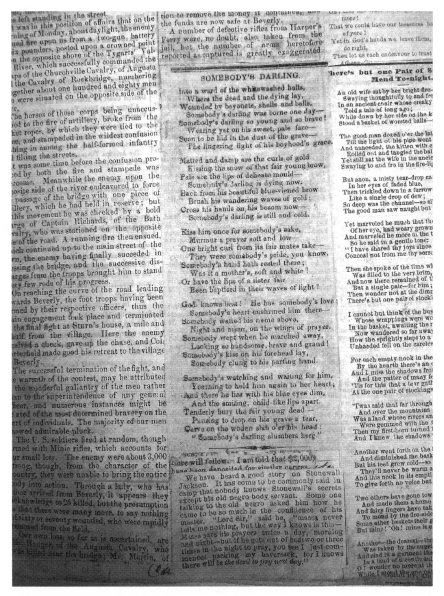

Figure 3.11 "Somebody's Darling," from Solomons scrapbook. (Duke University Special Collections)

Adults sought to pass the ideology and emotions of reconciliation along to future generations. As Oliver Wendell Holmes Sr. wrote to James Russell Lowell in 1881, "When the school-children learn your verses they are good for another half-century." Postwar editors crafted texts to sell to schools across sectional differences. "The Blue and the Gray" made its way into the textbook anthology McGuffey's Fifth, by 1879, where it carried a note that had been in the *Atlantic*

Monthly, informing children that it commemorated the "noble action" of a group of Mississippi women, who "strewed flowers impartially" on graves of Confederate and Federal troops. Lacoste's poem "Somebody's Darling," too, was soon picked up by school readers and recitation books such as *McGuffey's Fourth Reader* (first without author attribution in 1866) and was in at least seven other readers by 1896. Often, the author's name but no information on her Confederate affiliation was given, thus presenting the war as a nonsectional experience and allowing broader textbook sales.[61]

The Postbellum Scrapbook and the Reconstructing Nation

Grief for the overwhelming losses of the war crossed sectional borders. Border-crossing poetry such as "Somebody's Darling" helped articulate that common experience, even as it defined the right kind of soldier for whom to share grief. But Civil War grief was also highly differentiated. Nearly all Northern Civil War scrapbooks end with or devote considerable space to material on Abraham Lincoln's 1865 assassination, less than a week after Robert E. Lee's surrender. Whether those scrapbooks primarily saved eulogies, poetic tributes, and black-bordered programs from memorial ceremonies or material on the hunt for John Wilkes Booth, Lincoln's death became a horrified, grief-soaked end marker and occasion for mourning all the dead of the war, as well as the nation's leader. Southern scrapbooks, however, rarely acknowledge Lincoln's death. Southern scrapbooks that encompassed the end of the war move directly to postbellum mourning of the Lost Cause, sometimes marking Lee's surrender or his death five years later. Southern scrapbooks' habit of doubling back on themselves means as well that in their pages the war seems never to end.

Not only the contents of individual scrapbooks but the concept of the Southern scrapbook took on the work of asserting a new place for the white South in the U.S. nation. The Confederate scrapbook became an iconic object, representing resourceful and determined work by Southern whites who lacked the means of the North. Southern poetry anthologists made the association by referring to their works as collecting "scraps" or as "gleanings," while a review in a Southern publication inverted the usual critical standards by praising another anthology as "little more than a printed scrap-book." At least one published scrapbook became part of the project of building sympathy for the South in the North, serving as an ambassador for the South. Titling Lizzie Cary Daniel's anthology a *Confederate Scrap-Book* permits inclusion of tributes to gallant generals. Its recipes, too, show off the South's pluck in making do with tree bark to dye cotton or wool, as a sign of Confederate privation. The concept of the Southern scrapbook, as well as the contents of individual scrapbooks, was turned to reshaping the idea of a nation that included both North and South and accepted the white Southern version of events. Daniel's book was published in 1893 to help raise funds for a monument to Confederate soldiers and sailors and to restore Jefferson Davis's home as a museum. The title page presents it as "Copied from a Scrap-book kept by a young girl during and immediately after the war," but although the idea of such a scrapbook appealed, the contents were evidently not satisfactory, and so it was filled out "with additions from war copies of the 'Southern Literary Messenger' and [London] 'Illustrated News' loaned by friends, and other selections as accredited." She dedicates the volume to her father, "Col. John B. Gary, himself a faithful soldier and patriot"—not a term that would have gone down easily for Northerners just after the war. Yet the group that published the volume considered it likely to engage Northern sympathies and influence Northern conceptions of Civil War history. They donated copies to Northern institutions where it could help establish a new understanding of the South. The book was appealingly presented as child's work, and its publication as a spontaneous decision, despite the additions and editing that turned it into a more formal anthology.[62]

After the war, children not only recited poems associated with the war in their classrooms but engaged with the war through complexly layered scrapbook making. One Northern multigenerational scrapbook displays the multiplying emotions a scrapbook might embody. At age fifteen in 1883, Elizabeth Farnham May of Roxbury, Massachusetts, pasted her collection of Civil War era poetry "Scraps collected by mama" into a Mark Twain Self Pasting Scrap Book. Elizabeth's mother, Elizabeth T. Farnham May, had died five years earlier; her father, Judge John Wilder May, died the month she began the scrapbook. Although she included many Civil War poems, her scrapbook looks very different from those made during the war because she used an 1877 Mark Twain scrapbook. Its poems are therefore marshaled into the neat columns produced by the pre-glued strips—not clippings herded and jammed together, as in Confederate scrapbooks marked by paper shortages, or the dense conglomeration of profusion shaped by the desire to save the intensity of Northern newspaper reading. The daughter's scrapbook combines 1860s newspaper tributes to dead infants and a humorous item mocking lawyerly language with Civil War poetry that yearns for the return of the dead. The "scraps collected by mama" and pasted up by the daughter included Bret Harte's "A Second Review of the Grand Army" and Kate Putnam's "Driving Home the Cows," both from 1865. Harte's poem envisions all the Union dead rising from their graves and marching through the capital, with a statue of Washington come to life, honoring them. In Putnam's popular poem, a father is surprised by the return of the youngest son, believed dead, "For Southern prisons will sometimes yawn. / And yield their dead unto life again"—an image that might well have appealed to an orphaned child.[63]

Elizabeth May's mother lost her first child in 1859, and until at least 1869 she collected poems mourning babies as well as these Civil War poems about loss and fantasized reunion. The elder May's loss of an infant daughter and whatever losses of friends and relatives she might have suffered in the war shaped her taste for collecting these poems. When her daughter layered them into this scrapbook in 1883, they marked the younger Elizabeth's loss of her mother and her father. She found Civil War clippings so full of emotion that they could be repurposed to speak of other griefs. Perhaps she found that triangulating her grief through imagining what her mother might have felt made her grief more endurable. The work embodies nostalgia for a time the younger Elizabeth did not live through, when her parents were alive. Pasting down her mother's clippings during a period when the popular press was endorsing reunion narratives featuring North-South reconciliation, she instead invested her feelings in the emotional field of the war.

When two or more generations contributed to a scrapbook in the South, they, too, created emotionally complex documents. At least one suggests disagreement about the meaning of the war. The wife of a U.S. congressman turned Confederate, Juliana Paisley Gilmer of Greensboro, North Carolina, first kept a diary and then in 1862 switched to a scrapbook that seems dominated by private grief. Both are in the same style of blank composition book, previously used for accounts in the case of the scrapbook, and both lack the bombastic excitement that the Solomons scrapbook reflected early in the war. Rather, Gilmer noted in her diary:

> The present gloomy state of the country cast a shadow on the future....I fear I am destined to see much distress in our land....A year ago our country was powerful prosperous and happy and now what a sad change, we see brother arrayed against brother and those who were our friends meeting to kill and destroy each other.

Her choice of clippings for her scrapbook was similarly melancholy. Rather than mourn the adults who have met to "kill and destroy one another," she focused her grief on dead children. She collected 1862 tributes to Willie, a dead two-year-old, possibly a nephew or cousin. She makes another poem speak of him, by changing the age of its subject from fifteen to two with her pencil. Twenty years earlier Gilmer had lost a six-year-old son named William, her own father's namesake, and she had lost a grown daughter in 1858. She linked mourning for children and mourning that might be for soldiers with Phoebe Cary's poem "Happy Women," which joins the pain of women who will "never smile" to hear the step of an expected loved one at the door with "mothers left to weep, / Their babies lying in the dust."[64]

Gilmer's ambivalence about the South's "sad change" evinced in her diary expresses itself, too, in omitting from her scrapbook the many Southern newspaper poems glorifying and mourning men killed in battle. Her wartime collecting of infant elegies instead suggests another expression of the desire reiterated in other scrapbooks, especially Southern scrapbooks, to turn time backward, to a time before losses. Here, it undergoes a complex transmutation: instead of the speaker in Elizabeth Akers Allen's "Rock Me to Sleep" becoming a child again, the young men killed in the war are returned to infancy and mourned as infants while

Gilmer returns to her own young adulthood, mourning her own infant William. In collecting public, newspaper poetry to return to many layers of grief, she is like nineteenth-century bereaved parents who ordered postmortem daguerreotypes and photographs of their dead children. Writing of nineteenth-century U.S. childhood, Karen Sánchez-Eppler has analyzed this as mourning not the child but the loss itself, "an open wound [that] provides a site where internal pain remains internal yet becomes externally visible." Unlike these images of the mourned children, homemade anthologies such as Juliana Gilmer's and Pickering Dodge's pull poems from the public store and insist on their applicability: loss pools together and can be dipped into by all.[65]

After Gilmer died in 1865, an anonymous hand took over her scrapbook and insisted on another vision. This second compiler shifted the book to endorse the emerging Lost Cause ideology that was engaged in producing nostalgia for Confederate glory. The new scrapbook maker used Fanny Downing's 1866 "Confederate Gray" to turn time backward along a Confederate national timeline and express retrospective zeal for "the visions bright / I saw" at the beginning of the war. "I saw a nation spring to breath, / I saw a people proud and grand / Do battle to the very death / For freedom and their native land. / I saw a cause pure of all harm, / Thrice noble, and without one stain." Downing's speaker puts away his old gray uniform and looks forward to joining Stonewall Jackson in heaven. The second compiler's revived (or unsubdued) enthusiasm for the war was at odds with Gilmer's sense that the war had brought "a sad change." Among the poems in this second portion of the scrapbook is one attributed to an exchange "from a Northern Paper: God Help the South," expressing sympathy for the South in the familiar vocabulary of Confederate discourse: "God help the South, dear sunny land, / By tyrants crushed and riven, / Betrayed, insulted, conquered, taxed—By negroes ruled and driven." The scrapbook ends with laments on the 1870 death of Robert E. Lee.[66]

Nothing in the scrapbook comments on its double authorship, or on the shift from one mode of commemorating the war to the second. The retrospective collaboration hints that the second paster means to correct Gilmer's mournful reflection with the angrier, more martial, and nostalgic vision that became a keynote of the white South in following decades.

Paper Graves

Civil War scrapbooks were largely made of newspapers, but they were not bound to the newspaper's relentless forward movement through time. As we have seen, Southern scrapbooks in particular allowed and even invited a return to earlier moments; they helped compilers ignore chronology and paste yet another article on a battle that brought good news to their side, and they invited readers to leaf forward and back, and "turn backward time" in its flight.

Bowditch commemorated the end of the war in his "Waifs" scrapbook with a section on the 1865 Return of the Standards or regimental flags, as the tokens of the missing soldiers: "How many eyes filled with tears as troop after troop marched up, and we saw, in spirit only, the shades of dead comrades, walking, or on horseback, by the sides of their surviving comrades! Our cheers of greeting for living were choked by sobs for the beloved dead."

Bowditch carefully refuses the fanciful idea of seeing again the shades of dead comrades, conscientiously noting that such a sight is "in spirit only." He did not collect Bret Harte's "A Second Review of the Grand Army," though others, among them Elizabeth Farnham May, did. Harte's poem begins with the poet reading a news report of a gathering of the living soldiers, the Grand Review of the reassembled Union armies in Washington; he imagines the dead marching in a second, larger review. The speaker sees "a phantom army come": "The men whose wasted figures fill / The patriot graves of the nation."

Harte reanimates the slain and praises their valor. By contrast, Walt Whitman's "Ashes of Soldiers" from the 1872 *Leaves of Grass* simultaneously summons the dead to march and with repeated words of negation makes them dead again. Whitman calls the dead to "silently gather," but "sound no note" and details the sounds trumpeters and drummers are *not* to make. Civil War scrapbooks perform something of the same action of simultaneously summoning up and reburying. The issues and emotions left unsettled after the Civil War continued to churn through the scrapbooks. As E. W. Gurley, the editor and Union soldier who began his avid interest in clipping the newspaper with Civil War items, proclaimed, when you have finished a scrapbook, "It is not a grave in which you have buried all these good and beautiful thoughts, but a living treasure always open to your hand."[67]

That treasure was made up of newspaper clippings. The Civil War brought a great increase in newspaper reading. A wider swath of Americans learned to think of events as news, to expect to find material relevant to their lives in the newspapers, and to look to the newspaper to connect with their fellow citizens. In the years following, newspapers became even more ubiquitous, and contained valuable material ever at risk of being lost. Newspaper readers developed a greater need to make scrapbooks to contain, organize, and preserve their newspaper reading, while consolidating their sense of family, region, and nation.

4

Alternative Histories in African American Scrapbooks

In 1854 Frederick Douglass urged the readers of his newspaper to clip out an article called "Black Heroes": "Colored men! Save this extract. Cut it out and put it in your Scrap-book." The item told of armed African Americans soldiers in the Revolutionary War and listed the names of eighteenth-century "black men who had fought and bled for their country" as proof of black people's stake in the nation. In exhorting "colored men!" to cut out the extract, put it in their scrapbooks, "and use it at the proper time," Douglass suggested that the clipping itself could be ammunition for a cause, and that deploying it was the act of a soldier. He thus identified a crucial potential in nineteenth-century scrapbooks made of newspaper clippings: scrapbooks could be a weapon.[1]

All scrapbook makers create meaning out of disparate materials. From the varied materials they collected, African American scrapbook makers of the late nineteenth and early twentieth century deliberately created alternative records, or what one black journalist of the 1880s called "unwritten histories." Such histories were meant to fill gaps in mainstream accounts and assert African American importance in the nation's history. African American readers did this by recontextualizing clippings scissored from both the black and the white press in their scrapbooks. As they did so, they critiqued the white press, sometimes with pen and pencil notes, and sometimes entirely through the subtle language of juxtaposition.[2]

The "unwritten histories," or gatherings of previously scattered bits of information, carried out four related projects. They amassed and preserved evidence that black people had not simply witnessed all parts of American history but had been active agents of it and were capable, patriotic citizens. Second, the scrapbooks asserted race pride, showing the struggles and advancement of blacks as a group, documenting the achievements of black individuals, and highlighting black people's racial affiliation, if that wasn't evident in the article. They thus presented what later came to be called strong black role models. Third, they compiled evidence of oppression and mistreatment of black people, often using the testimony of the antagonistic white press to strengthen their case. They thereby read against the grain of the white press and used the white press against itself, like an attorney questioning a hostile witness. Finally, as documents shared within black communities, scrapbooks offered those communities a historical record. The path they built allowed access to records that were blockaded in segregated libraries and newspaper files.

This chapter draws on the work of more than a dozen nineteenth- and early-twentieth-century African American men and women who made scrapbooks, with special attention to three African American men who created ambitious, monumental scrapbook collections that exemplify these four projects. They worked from a sense that valuable materials would be lost if they did not save them, and that these valuable morsels of information needed to be drawn out from the mostly white press and recontextualized. The oldest, Joseph W. H. Cathcart (1823 or 1827–1895), a Philadelphia janitor, created his collection of more than one hundred massive pasted volumes starting in the 1850s. His friend William H. Dorsey (1837–1923) of Philadelphia made nearly four hundred scrapbooks between the 1870s and about 1903, many of them on African American topics, and collected books and artwork related to black history that he displayed in a museum in his home. Dorsey was part of a network of black historians and bibliophiles. In a later generation, L. S. Alexander Gumby (1885–1961), a gay black collector and salon host of the Harlem Renaissance, created more than a hundred elaborate scrapbooks, mainly in the 1920s. He was part of a circle of collectors that included Arthur Schomburg, whose collection formed the core of the New York Public Library's Schomburg Center for Research in Black Culture, a key archive for African American history. Other African American scrapbook makers—from Washington, D.C.; Durham and Raleigh, North Carolina; Boston; Atlanta; St. Louis; Kansas; and California, among other places—created smaller compilations. In creating black history from disparate materials, some included personal memorabilia but insistently framed personal documents, too, within a larger historical context of black experience. It is possible that women also made such extensive collections. The fact that these three men's collections survived may have been because their collecting was aided by involvement in all-male networks of bibliophiles, in Dorsey and Gumby's case, and Cathcart's location in an office building, where he had greater access to materials to work with.[3]

More prominent African Americans of Cathcart, Dorsey, and Gumby's times used scrapbooks to document their own activities and the movements they were involved with: Sojourner Truth's scrapbooks have disappeared, but Frederick Douglass made scrapbooks in the late 1880s and early 1890s—earlier ones may have been destroyed with many of his other papers in an 1872 fire. Mary Church Terrell, a civil rights activist, journalist, and leader in the black club women's movement, used her substantial collection of clippings on lynching and other issues important to the black community in her speaking and writing. Newspaper editor and publisher T. Thomas Fortune (or possibly his wife) kept a scrapbook on his activities. His friend, an early pan-Africanist, black nationalist editor, and journalist, John Edward Bruce, known as Bruce Grit, saved his articles and correspondence in scrapbooks. Political leaders such as the Reconstruction-era Senator Hiram Rhoades Revels documented portions of his life and career in a scrapbook, and Pap Singleton, the leader of the Exoduster movement to Kansas, also kept scrapbooks. Black performers and other celebrities, among them the boxer Jack Johnson, kept scrapbooks of clippings about themselves, as actors and musicians often did. Pauline Hopkins made scrapbooks of her theatrical appearances, which Lois Brown drew on in writing Hopkins's biography. The writer and educator Anna Julia Cooper made scrapbooks later in life, mainly of her own writings. Alice Dunbar-Nelson's scrapbook of her work on women's suffrage and its journey into an archive are discussed in later chapters. But for the study of scrapbooks and what they allowed the black community to do, the works of the collectors highlighted in this chapter are most revealing.

Like whites, black readers saw much material appearing and disappearing in the press that it seemed important to save. For African American clippers, however, it was vital to follow what the white press was saying about black people, both for its news value, straightforwardly preserving information, and to critique the white press's casual assumptions. When the white press wrote about black people at all, especially from the 1880s on, blacks were likely to appear as criminals, or as stereotyped characters in comic dialect stories. From slavery times onward, the African American relationship to the public sphere embodied in the white-owned newspaper was necessarily a critical and often oppositional one. Black readers in the post-Reconstruction era critiqued the hostile white press in their writings and their scrapbooks and laid out its biases for other readers to see and discuss. Scrutinized closely, mined, sorted, saved to make a record, and recirculated either hand to hand in the black community or back into print in the black press, newspaper clippings could be powerful. Black readers thus creatively remade the white newspaper as something that fed their own interests.

The White Press and the Black Scrapbook

African Americans who made scrapbooks out of press clippings from the daily newspaper had a more complex relationship to their sources than did whites. Nonimmigrant white people in general could assume that newspaper writing about whites' actions and endeavors would start from the assumption of their ordinariness: that crimes committed by whites were the product of individual motives, not of racial pathology, that the achievements of whites were accorded respect on their individual merits, without being questioned or mocked because of the subject's race. But African Americans reading the white press encountered a minefield.

The post-Reconstruction era imposed a familiar and dismal set of restrictions on black people. The "black laws" restricted black job mobility and movement. Segregation prevailed north and south, and whites maintained a campaign of extralegal violence against blacks, such as through lynchings. Still, it was a time of new opportunities, such as increasing black readership, with the rate of black literacy reported in the U.S. census rising from 19 percent in 1870 to 43 percent in 1890. This postbellum time of tumult and change, of new opportunities but of powerful enemies that were more diffuse than the slaveholding South had been, made it easier and more necessary for black people, especially those in the North, to obtain news of what was happening in other black communities. A small black press grew steadily in importance and gained national circulation, but black weeklies or monthlies (almost never dailies) were undercapitalized, had difficulty obtaining steady subscribers, met with other obstacles, and thus rarely lasted. The public sphere of print was essentially the white press, and black writers and the black press, along with black literary societies, encouraged African American readers to read, respond to, and use that press.[4]

So it is not surprising to find as early as 1864 the African Methodist Episcopal Church's Philadelphia-based weekly *Christian Recorder* promoting newspaper reading and scrapbook making to fit young African Americans for their new place in the world. A dialogue presents Fanny and Annie, two sisters whose children fare differently in school. Fanny's children read and learn from newspapers and are far ahead of their cousins who do not. They possess advanced practical knowledge, so Fanny's son retrieves a lost bucket from Annie's well, having learned how from the newspaper. Fanny explains that not only do her children read the newspaper but she has taught them "to make a scrap-book together, in which they save all the useful, interesting little items that would otherwise be lost or forgotten." The article's anonymous author follows up this idea, exhorting, "Will not every mother take to heart this lesson, and encourage her children to read with care the family paper, and instruct them how to preserve in a readable shape the useful items they may find in it?" This article in a black paper presents scrapbooks as the logical next step from newspaper reading, allowing newspaper readers to save the general knowledge they have read, and to pass it along. Even from an early age, black children will be following Frederick Douglass's urging to save significant material in scrapbooks to "use it at the proper time," even if in this case the "proper time" is when the bucket has fallen into the family well, leaving the family without water for dinner. Implicitly, more important occasions are to follow.[5]

"The reading men and women get a living a great deal easier than others," Fanny tells her sister, situating post-Emancipation literacy in the new context of self-sufficiency, moving past the antebellum need to prove that black people are intelligent, or to conduct abolition work. She urges her sister to take a family paper and a religious paper—these were usually weeklies, such as the *Christian Recorder*, with items of useful, morally instructive, and entertaining information for children and adults—as well as the political paper her household already gets, so that her children will be "more intelligent men and women when they grow up, and be far better fitted to take care of themselves in the world." Although the article says nothing about service to the race, or using one's literacy to teach others, in this period, when many literate African Americans were teaching the Southern freed-people to read, the *Christian Recorder*'s northern black readers would surely have assumed that such actions were part of becoming those better-fitted men and women.[6]

The omission of this call to serve the race or any mention of the family's race is less surprising when we discover that the *Christian Recorder* reprinted the article from the white religious press. It had appeared in at least two white-run publications before the *Recorder* picked it up without credit—a common newspaper practice, as we have seen. When read in those white publications, it is a predictable pitch to subscribe to religious papers, praising such papers as sources of knowledge and advice. We have already seen how anonymity coupled with recirculation creates the anonymity function and could make work seem to issue from the publication itself. When the article speaks in the voice of *The Christian Recorder*, Annie and Fanny seem African American, and Fanny seems to address some of the aspirations of striving black people, as she advocates both newspaper reading and scrapbook making. Just as the poem "Mortally Wounded" had a different meaning read as a poem by a dying soldier instead of as a poem by a minister's wife at home, the same article could be read very differently when appearing in the black or the white press.[7]

The changes in interpretation this article itself undergoes, depending on what periodical it appears in, are emblematic of how cutting and pasting into a new context alters meaning as a text moves between the newspaper and scrapbook or some other form of print, and between the white newspaper and the African American scrapbook. Just as black publications such as the *Christian Recorder* recontextualized articles from the white press, so African Americans who scissored items out of the white press gave them new significance in their own collections.

African Americans often conferred this new significance via the critical mode of reading them. For example, when African Americans collected insulting articles from the white press they exemplified the strategy for dealing with offensive material that Marielle Rosello has called "declining the stereotype"—that is, both refusing the stereotype and analyzing it—much like "declining" it in the sense of the grammatical declension of a noun: learning all the forms the stereotype might take and analyzing how it fits into the overall language. Because it was at least initially public and accessible to both black and white readers, printed matter was available to be analyzed.[8]

Access to Print

An essential quality of the public sphere of print is the anonymous, faceless encounters it offers to readers. W. E. B. Du Bois famously explained this quality of the printed word in reference to reading recognized literary greats in 1903:

I sit with Shakespeare and he winces not. Across the color line I move arm in arm with Balzac and Dumas, where smiling men and welcoming women glide in gilded halls. . . . I summon Aristotle and Aurelius and what soul I will, and they come all graciously with no scorn nor condescension.

Newspapers offer the same quality of access, even if to scruffier interiors than gilded halls. Access to the white press brought black people into an information commons they might otherwise have been barred from. The fact that readers were faceless and invisible to the publisher enabled access to information that whites in other settings, such as schools or public lectures, sought to deny to black people. The power of facelessness in reading newspapers was more dramatically evident before Emancipation, when literacy and access to newspapers offered the possibility of silently and invisibly joining a community of readers by jumping over distance and boundaries, fording a virtual river, to learn of the existence of others opposed to slavery.[9]

In the most famous example of this dynamic, Frederick Douglass sets out this power of newspapers: as an enslaved youth, he hears whites blame slaves running away or attacking their masters on incitement by abolitionists, and he is eager to know who such people are and what the word *abolition* means. He can't ask anyone, and the dictionary only leads him in circles, defining abolition as "the act of abolishing." Finally, in a copy of the *Baltimore American* he has gotten hold of, he learns "the incendiary information denied me by the dictionary."[10]

A pro-slavery newspaper, hostile to Douglass's interests, which assumes no enslaved people are among its readers, provides him with the information those around him do not want to hear. The newspaper connects him to abolitionists in the North, because the Southern papers reprinted abolitionist writings to excoriate them. So when his mistress later reacts with rage at seeing him with a newspaper, he characterizes her fury as directed at someone "discovered in a plot by some dangerous spy." African Americans continued to use the white newspaper as a valuable resource that had to be treated with a critical eye throughout the century. At the same time, white newspaper editors often disregarded or refused to acknowledge that they had black readers. "Spying" continued to be an apt metaphor for black newspaper reading.[11]

"Unwritten History": Newspapers and Scrapbooks

Writing in 1886 in her women's column in the black weekly the *New York Freeman*, the African American journalist Gertrude Bustill Mossell joined together two suggestions for creating an "unwritten history." She regretted that it was now too late to clip from newspapers to make a complete collection of the speeches and writings and comments about Frederick Douglass: "How it would show the honor and reverence he had gained through a long life—the changes of public sentiment.... What an interesting unwritten history it would be!" She urged her readers to begin creating actual volumes from which "some able writer in the future may write a volume of interest and value to us as a people. Every thought of us as a people has value." Her conception of "unwritten history" included material printed in the paper but not in book form; even if her readers weren't "able writers" they could compile the materials for a "history."[12]

Mossell's plea to black readers to create scrapbooks of "unwritten history" begins by focusing on the oral tradition. She suggests that young people gather and write down the stories of elderly black people: "the aged ones who bore the burden and heat of slavery and prejudice; the ones who were pioneer laborers in the work of opening the school, church, and railroad facilities to us" and "are fast passing away." She contrasts what black listeners and future black readers will gain from such accounts with the trivializing treatment white writers accord them: "Another race is gathering the curiosities of their dialect, or idiosyncrasies for its own amusement, but this vast treasure house of future life and thought we leave idle, or let drift from our grasp." Instead, "beautiful lessons,... [and] much valuable information might be gained from them."

When Mossell wrote this, her fellow Philadelphian William Henry Dorsey had already amassed a substantial scrapbook on Douglass. And although he did not interview anyone himself, he had also set out to document the lives of elderly black people, through forty years of collecting "biographical and obituary" clippings—including at least one article about Mossell—and by collecting nearly two hundred articles on black centenarians.

William Dorsey's "Colored Centenarians"

William Dorsey was the son of Thomas Dorsey, who had escaped from slavery in Maryland to become a prosperous caterer and thus a member of Philadelphia's black elite. Dorsey graduated from the Institute for Colored Youth, which later became Cheyney University, and was an artist, a founding member of Philadelphia's American Negro Historical Society, and an avid collector of books and artwork as well as newspaper clippings, all following his interest in African American history and life. He supported his interests through his inheritance from his father, who had invested in rental property; with patronage jobs as the mayor's messenger for eight and half years; and as a turnkey in charge of prisoners in Philadelphia's Central Police Station, starting in 1882. He sorted his clippings into separate scrapbooks on such topics as black migration, colored churches of Philadelphia, crimes, the 1871 murder of black educator Octavius Catto while defending the right to vote, segregation and integration of public schools, reminiscences of abolition societies, black pugilists, and many topics not directly related to African American life, such as at least twenty-eight books on Native Americans, fourteen on Pacific Islands, one tracking Robert Ingersoll, and another on William Gladstone. Most of his clippings are from the white press, though he also saved entire issues of black newspapers.[13]

Each scrapbook of William Dorsey's huge compilation is representative in its own way of his decades of reading, clipping, sorting, and pasting. The small, fifty-page scrapbook that he named "Colored Centenarians" exemplifies his project of creating an alternative history by cutting items out of one newspaper context—where each centenarian is an isolated curiosity—and pasting them into the new context of his scrapbook. Here they speak of African American people's active involvement in every phase of the nation's history. "Colored Centenarians," too, demonstrates Dorsey's orientation to his community. This scrapbook leads off with a four-line obituary clipping that stands alone on the page with a neatly drawn box around it. Dorsey wrote only sparingly in his scrapbooks, other than to supply dates and newspaper names, or sometimes to correct words or to argue; but this article, hand-dated "Press, November 10, 1866," drew a personal comment. The clipping reads:

> "Old Katy Jackson," a colored woman over one hundred years of age, died at Pottstown last Saturday. She saw General Washington in the year 1790, when on his way to suppress the whisky insurrection.[14]

Dorsey noted, "The above was my Great Grandmother—on my mother's side—William Henry Dorsey" (Figure 4.1). Other than this mention, there is little family memorabilia in Dorsey's sprawling collection. The Katy Jackson clipping and its position at the head of this scrapbook speaks of Dorsey's choice not to surround this information about his great-grandmother with family history but to find a larger history for her, and to place her at the head of a long line of black centenarians. Dorsey saved the 1866 clipping for some time before making the scrapbook, evident from the fact that "Colored Centenarians" is pasted into an 1873 government report (Figure 4.2). Dorsey collected items for it from at least forty newspapers from 1860 to 1899. The book includes long features and interviews, as well as two-line notices (Figure 4.3).[15]

The lives of all the colored centenarian in Dorsey's scrapbook encapsulate the drastic changes in black life marked not only by the Civil War, and also the longer sweep of American national history. Even when white-authored obituaries and elegiac materials on Northern antebellum black Americans characteristically muted the facts of their subjects' enslavement, Dorsey's recontextualizing the clippings by bringing them together, and in company with the rarer black-authored materials, shifts their meaning. Many of Dorsey's subjects lived through the country's founding as a slave nation and then either individually gained freedom or were emancipated as part of the country's repudiation of slavery. Their

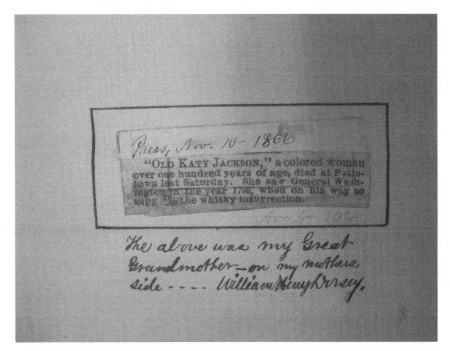

Figure 4.1 First page of William Henry Dorsey's "Colored Centenarians": Katy Jackson clipping. (Cheyney University Archives and Special Collections)

Figure 4.2 Cover, "Colored Centenarians." Dorsey superimposed over the title on the cover of this slim report on city finances his own handwritten label: "Colored Centenarians—Newspaper C...." (Cheyney University Archives and Special Collections)

lifetimes link the two national conditions—not just the "before and after" that any black person born before Emancipation experienced but a deeper "before" that included the nation's claim to have achieved freedom during the American Revolution while keeping them enslaved. The clippings amassed in Dorsey's scrapbook make African American significance in the national story inescapable.

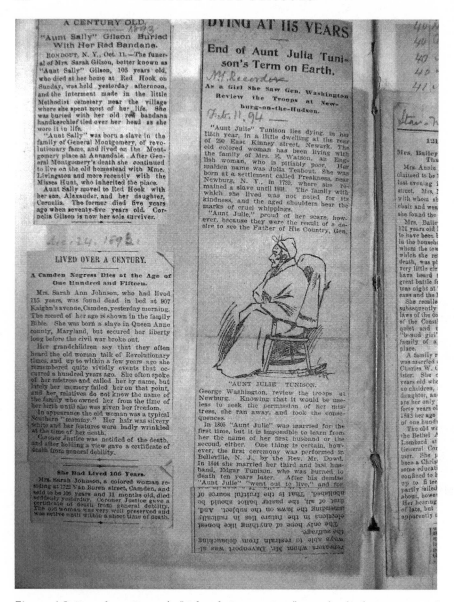

A CENTURY OLD.
1893

"Aunt Sally" Gilson Buried With Her Red Bandana.

RONDOUT, N. Y., Oct. 11.—The funeral of Mrs. Sarah Gilson, better known as "Aunt Sally" Gilson, 105 years old, who died at her home at Red Hook on Sunday, was held yesterday afternoon, and the interment made in the little Methodist cemetery near the village where she spent most of her life. She was buried with her old red bandana handkerchief tied over her head as she wore it in life.

"Aunt Sally" was born a slave in the family of General Montgomery, of revolutionary fame, and lived on the Montgomery place at Annandale. After General Montgomery's death she continued to live on the old homestead with Mme. Livingston and more recently with the Misses Hunt, who inherited the place.

Aunt Sally moved to Red Hook with her son, Alexander, and her daughter, Cornelia. The former died five years ago when seventy-five years old. Cornelia Gilson is now her sole survivor.

Dec. 14, 1892

LIVED OVER A CENTURY.

A Camden Negress Dies at the Age of One Hundred and Fifteen.

Mrs. Sarah Ann Johnson, who had lived 115 years, was found dead in bed at 907 Kaighn's avenue, Camden, yesterday morning. The record of her age is shown in the family Bible. She was born a slave in Queen Anne county, Maryland, but secured her liberty long before the civil war broke out.

Her grandchildren say that they often heard the old woman talk of Revolutionary times, and up to within a few years ago she remembered quite vividly events that occurred a hundred years ago. She often spoke of her mistress and called her by name, but lately her memory failed her on that point, and her relatives do not know the name of the family who owned her from the time of her birth until she was given her freedom. In appearance the old woman was a typical Southern "mammy." Her hair was silvery white and her features were badly wrinkled at the time of her death.

Coroner Justice was notified of the death, and after holding a view gave a certificate of death from general debility.

She Had Lived 106 Years.

Mrs. Sarah Johnson, a colored woman residing at 1722 Van Buren street, Camden, and said to be 106 years and 11 months old, died suddenly yesterday. Coroner Justice gave a certificate of death from general debility. The old woman was very well preserved and was active until within a short time of death.

DYING AT 115 YEARS

End of Aunt Julia Tunison's Term on Earth.

N. Recorder

As a Girl She Saw Gen. Washington Review the Troops at Newburg-on-the-Hudson.

Feb. 11. '94

"Aunt Julie" Tunison lies dying, in her 115th year, in a little dwelling at the rear of 290 East Kinney street, Newark. The old colored woman has been living with the family of Mrs. E. Watson, an English woman, who is pitiably poor. Her maiden name was Julia Teabout. She was born at a settlement called Preakness, near Newburg, N. Y., in 1780, where she remained a slave until 1801. The family with which she lived was not noted for its kindness, and the aged shoulders bear the marks of cruel whippings.

"Aunt Julie," proud of her scars, however, because they were the result of a desire to see the Father of His Country, Gen.

"AUNT JULIE" TUNISON.

George Washington, review the troops at Newburg. Knowing that it would be useless to seek the permission of her mistress, she ran away, and took the consequences.

In 1805 "Aunt Julie" was married for the first time, but it is impossible to learn from her the name of her first husband or the second, either. One thing is certain, however, the first ceremony was performed in Belleville, N. J., by the Rev. Mr. Dowd. In 1844 she married her third and last husband, Edgar Tunison, who was burned to death ten years later. After his demise "Aunt Julie" "went out to live," and for

Figure 4.3 Page from Dorsey's "Colored Centenarians" scrapbook showing mix of articles. Bottom of clipping is folded. (Cheyney University Archives and Special Collections)

Although the collected individual news items were sometimes the work of careless or patronizing white reporters, the scrapbook as a whole reached beyond hostile reporting to create an implicit narrative that embodies U.S. history in the lives of African Americans. It makes these elderly black people the *most* representative of the nation's history.[16]

Some of the subjects in Dorsey's scrapbook claim extraordinary life spans: 116, 125, 127, 135, even 170—as though granted an extra lifetime or two to make up for the years of enslavement. For Dorsey's purposes, it was not important whether the elderly people in his scrapbook, accurately assessed or exaggerated their age. Most former slaves were without birth records or other official documentation. This situation allowed them the paradoxical freedom to assert the standing of their own memory, perhaps drawing on community traditions and making themselves the representatives of those otherwise lost traditions. The majority were born into slavery, some to African-born parents; four were enslaved in Africa. Their recompense takes the form of living long enough to see freedom and outliving their former masters. Acknowledging their great age, too, accords them the virtue of perseverance, evident in the stories of how they lived. Their claim to great age makes a place for them in print—a claim to distinction and newsworthiness. Although an unnamed newspaper report mocked a man who swore he was 170, white newspapers rarely attacked the other claims but rather quoted people who buttressed them. After all, the subjects would not have achieved space in the newspaper if their claim to a biblical life span could be dismissed out of hand. Even people who could more readily have staked space in the newspaper reinforced their claims to it through age. Sojourner Truth's New Year's greeting to newspaper readers in 1880, for example, said she was one hundred years old. She had certainly lived a long life—ninety-six at her death in 1883, according to historians—but the assertion that she had passed the century mark became a crowning distinction, like an honorary degree.[17]

As the centenarians in these news items validated their claims to great age, they asserted the African American presence in the nation. Verifying their age through their relationship to U.S. history and having those recollections validated through newspaper publication intertwined them with that history. Some centenarians affirmed their age through documents, including free papers. Reporters accorded special status to testimony from whites vouching for a subject's great age, much as a certifying introduction from a white person was part of the formula of slave narratives; the family that once owned Laura Perryman of Woodville, Texas, gives her age as 108, for example. But more often the subjects' own statements carried the weight of the article. Some powerfully linked themselves with experiences that transcended regional history or boundaries and thus rooted their history in the land and heavens, as they recounted where they were during overarching natural phenomena such as the Dark Day of May 19, 1780, when New England was covered by forest fire smoke and fog; or gave their age on witnessing the sunspots of 1799 or the 1833 Leonid meteor shower (known as the night the stars fell). Many of the centenarians established their age through recalling national or local history in relation to their personal chronology. Edward Dunsmore "was a man long before the British burned Havre de

Grace in 1814 and he was a witness to that scene," an 1893 obituary notes. Charles Fitzgerald was a "bound boy, just 15 years of age, when they were beginning to erect the United States Bank building on Chestnut street," in 1795, in Philadelphia. Jane Turner, dead in 1881 at age 105, was a married woman when the British bombarded Lewes, Delaware, during the War of 1812 (Figure 4.4).[18]

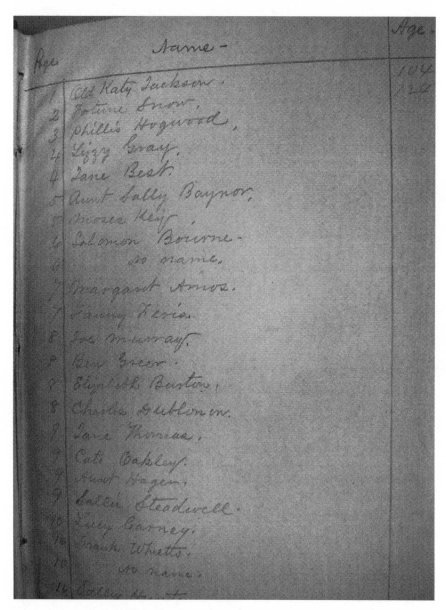

Figure 4.4 Partial table of contents of Dorsey's "Colored Centenarians" scrapbook. (Cheyney University Archives and Special Collections)

Defining American History

Centenarians were inherently newsworthy, but the 1876 centenary of the founding of the United States made stories from people whose memories traveled so far back particularly compelling to newspaper editors and reporters—so much so that interviews with centenarians with their questions on whether the subject had seen George Washington or used tobacco seemed formulaic enough to parody. Reporters sought out and published stories on people who had been present to hear the Liberty Bell toll at the signing of the Declaration of Independence, like Miss Rebecca Anderson at age 111 in 1878, or who remembered seeing the British burn Richmond, or who, like Minnie Jefferson of New York, was born on the Jefferson plantation and could remember the appearance of the "Father of his Country" "to this day."[19]

The role, or even the presence, of black Americans in the founding of the country was contested, especially because the centennial became an occasion for reknitting the white North and South after the Civil War. When Philadelphia proposed to celebrate the country's centennial with a great exposition, the city's black community lobbied for recognition of African Americans' role in the founding of the country. Robert Purvis, a black Philadelphia leader, advocated using July 4, 1876, as the date to remind the nation that "it was an incontestable fact that the blood of a negro was the first shed for liberty in the Revolution, and that blacks had taken an active part in the War of 1812 and in our late civil war for freedom." He and others met with limited success.[20]

Dorsey was clearly sympathetic to this effort. Yet his approach went far beyond commemorating Crispus Attucks to suggest the omnipresence of African American engagement in the founding of the nation and in its wars. His collection hints conversely that *every* elderly African American possessed a connection to the nation's history.[21]

The difference in status between white and black centenarians, and the history of blacks and whites, together make this massing of black elders in Dorsey's scrapbook tell a story that is not simply about touching the past. It spotlights the starkly contrasting experiences of white and black in relation to the founding of the country. Lizzie Gray's brief obituary, for example, notes that she was taken from Africa during the American Revolution and spent the war on a British ship. Though the reporter fails to remark on the contradiction of someone's slavery beginning in the freeing of the country, and being released from British captivity into slavery, Dorsey's language of juxtaposition provides that irony by setting stories of black people participating in the fight for the country's freedom next to stories like Gray's, and next to stories of people owned by the founding fathers— who are sometimes the same enslaved people fighting for the freedom of the country. Because the white newspapers published such accounts in isolation, they lacked either the sense of accumulated historical knowledge or the implicit irony that Dorsey's compilation supplies. His scrapbook allows readers to line up repeated assertions of black involvement in the founding of the country against the rhetoric of the country's freedom and the enslavement of these elders. The collected accounts of these black people who "Claimed to be Older Than the Country," as one headline framed it, or who had roots in the time of the founding of the country assert their primacy in the national historical narrative.[22]

Not only was the founding embedded in the slave past but some of the accounts in Dorsey's "Colored Centenarians" imply that the enslaved black people were the *superior* patriots. So Mary McDonald stood up for the needs of the nation against the Rees Howell family of Virginia, her masters. She recounts being a twelve year old when the Continental soldiers came through from Valley Forge: "My mistress told me not to give the soldiers anything to eat, but some of 'em came to the house and I gave it to 'em." She told her mistress "you got a plenty...and they haven't. I'm just a going to give 'em something to eat, says I, and I did too." She claimed a role in nurturing the country's birth—a role appreciated by the staff at the Philadelphia Home for Aged and Infirm Colored Persons, who had heard the story and referred to it. In her account of acting against the will of her mistress, she offers a very different version of black involvement in the early nation than Joice Heth, exhibited in 1835 and 1836 by P. T. Barnum as the 161-year-old nurse of George Washington. Heth's exhibition rooted the country in slavery as an acceptable practice, framing it as necessary to the birth and nurturing of the country, as Linda Frost notes. McDonald, instead, shows herself resisting white slave-owning authority to help create the country.[23]

Dorsey's "Colored Centenarians" scrapbook also pointed out substantial African American military involvement in the country's formation—a touchstone for patriotism and citizenship. Abolitionists had drawn on information about black military service to argue that black people were loyal, capable citizens with a stake in the country, and that the country had obligations to them. William Cooper Nell published his 1855 account of the long line of black men who had fought for the United States, *The Colored Patriots of the American Revolution*, arguing that service legitimated black people's claim for abolition and rights. Postbellum works continued to publicize black participation in the U.S. military.[24]

Dorsey's "Colored Centenarians" scrapbook positioned black people as enduring agents and actors in the country's defense, presenting black people acting with valor and skill in a wide variety of roles, doing the hard labor of founding the nation. Several men featured in the scrapbook, such as Fortune Snow, said they had fought in the Revolutionary War. James James, 135 years old in 1887, was one of the laborers at Fort Moultrie during the unsuccessful attack of the British fleet. Women's work fighting for the nation was celebrated as well: "Aunt Phillis" (last name not given), 105 in 1872, said she had been a spy during the Revolution and a special servant to George Washington. Others sacrificed during the Revolution but gained nothing from that sacrifice: Fanny Ferris, born in 1762, was captured by Cornwallis's army in Virginia during the "Revolutionary war for the achievement of liberty and independence" and kept until after the siege of Yorktown; released by the British, she went back to slavery in the Ferris household.

Dorsey's centenarians had not simply seen George Washington but chosen to work alongside him. Dorsey's amassing of evidence suggests that their work in creating the country gave them an ownership stake in it.[25]

Black Biography and "Racial Uplift"

Dorsey's "unwritten history" of elders reached into a broken past, pulling some of its fragments together and extending beyond the range of published compilations of black biography. Collections of black biographies grew in the 1880s and took off in the 1890s, as part of Booker T. Washington's race uplift movement, promoting "much-needed stories of black success, repositories of seemingly self-made achievement." Such titles as *Men of Mark: Eminent, Progressive and Rising* (1887) and *Progress of a Race: Or, the Remarkable Advancement of the Afro-American Negro from the Bondage of Slavery, Ignorance and Poverty, to the Freedom of Citizenship, Intelligence, Affluence, Honor and Trust* (1897) proclaimed the importance of black achievement and solidified it in columns of type. But even though these books defined achievement broadly by including ministers, writers, teachers, and businessmen, they did not accommodate the range of this single scrapbook's interest in presenting confectionary workers, iron forgemen, sailors, laundrywomen, fortunetellers, woodchoppers, barbers, and domestic workers as esteemed elders.[26]

Voting marked another type of exemplary status for Dorsey. It was the only achievement he commented on in the handwritten index he compiled for the "Colored Centenarians" scrapbook. Next to John Gibson's name is the note "voter age 113." The clipping tells that in 1891 Gibson was taken to the polls by carriage from his residence at the Philadelphia Home for Infirm and Aged Colored Persons and had to be lifted out to vote, but he "is in possession of all his faculties, and has voted the Republican ticket straight since war time." Longevity gave the weight of repetition to Gibson's dedication to voting and marks the seriousness of black citizenship. Philip Sheppard of Philadelphia, age 107 in 1877, had "voted in every Presidential election since the time of Thomas Jefferson and always took an interest in politics." Articles about attempts to bar black people from voting appear repeatedly in clippings in Dorsey's other scrapbooks, and in those of other scrapbook makers, such as Charles Turner, a civil servant in St. Louis active in Republican Party politics. In "Colored Centenarians," however, black voters triumph.[27]

Recontextualizing the White Press, Refuting the Plantation Myth

Dorsey's cutting and pasting wrenched his scrapbook's articles out of white newspapers, where readers might have understood them as another thread in the developing plantation mythology of contented slavery and mutual loyalty between the enslaved and slaveholders. The articles that celebrate the ties between ex-slaves and the whites who owned them, juxtaposed in Dorsey's book with accounts of long-lived African Americans whose children or spouses were sold away from them, and who fought in the nation's wars, implicitly critique and refute the newspapers' acceptance of the plantation myth.

The 1887 obituary for Ann Timmens, age 106, for example, describes her through her relationship to her Maryland slaveholders, for whom she continued working after Emancipation: "Dr. Githens...gave her an ordinary school education and made her the nurse of his children," until she was fourteen, when he "presented Ann [along] with a large number of other slaves to his daughter for a wedding present." The article follows the genealogy of the white family, and has the flavor of being supplied by the white family to the newspaper in the heyday of plantation fiction. It is yet another tale of loyal slaves, gracious masters, and reciprocal care, until the moment comes when that loyalty and care flow only one way: "When Mrs. Alexander died, Ann fell to the charge of that lady's daughter Mary," for whom she subsequently worked for thirty years. "About nine years ago, fast becoming by reason of advancing years, incapacitated for work, she was relegated to the care of [her own] niece, Franis Jane Lewis, who lives with her husband, a junk jobber." From there, perhaps because she was ill, she went to the almshouse. The newspaper article downplays this shift out of the standard plantation mythology of gracious white slaveholders, but in Dorsey's book it is apparent in the surroundings of hardworking black elders and black people caring for one another.[28]

The 1886 obituary of 107-year-old Fanny Ferris also reads as though it was dictated by the white former slaveholders. According to its account, Ferris, single and childless, was freed by her owner's will in 1840: "Although at liberty to go where she chose, she was so attached to the family that she asked for and was granted permission" to live with them. A little arithmetic discloses, however, that she was seventy-eight years old at the time. Accounts of how elderly people without pensions or property scraped by further repudiate stories of warm connection between slaveholders and enslaved people. These recontextualized articles exemplify white former owners' failure to honor the former slaves' years of labor and to provide for them. Minnie Jefferson, 109 in 1894, who was formerly owned by Thomas Jefferson and not freed until the Emancipation Proclamation, made her living for a time by being put on exhibit "as the oldest colored woman in America."[29]

Centenarians in Other African American Scrapbooks

Black centenarians interested other African American scrapbook makers as examples of the distance between the plantation myth's notions of paternalistic caring from the reality of elderly black people's lives. The miscellaneous scrapbook of Charles Turner of St. Louis contains accounts of at least two black centenarians. A white paper reports in separate articles on "'Elder' Sam" Pryor, 102, "sixty years a slave" in Tennessee, who now travels around preaching, and Capt. Andy

Montgomery, 103, also an ex-slave, who preaches to a congregation in Atlanta. During the burning of Atlanta, Andy Montgomery interceded with General Sherman to ask him not to burn his cabin and part of town, thus protecting his master's house as well. Turner pasted the article on Pryor following an article on a black movement agitating for pensions for elderly ex-slaves, sharpening the sense that neither man has been recompensed for his services to whites. Ex-slaves' loving protectiveness of owners and former owners was a ubiquitous thread in postwar plantation fiction. But support evidently ran one way: the articles say nothing about Montgomery and Pryor's sustenance in their extreme old age. Perhaps both men were aided by the black community they preached to. Turner recontextualized the material from its initial focus on black-white good feeling by juxtaposing it with an item on the movement for systematic, widescale economic compensation for ex-slaves.[30]

Reporters and the Centenarians

Gertrude Bustill Mossell's complaint that white writers wrote about ex-slaves for "the curiosities of their dialect, or idiosyncrasies for [whites'] own amusement," is borne out in many of the items in Dorsey's "Colored Centenarians" scrapbook. Some of the interviewers are crude or patronizing or only want to know answers to the generic questions about seeing George Washington, tobacco use, and the like. Others allow only glimpses of individual black lives to emerge.

Though most of Dorsey's articles about elderly African Americans remain respectful (if they are not too brief to convey much of their point of view), a jocular or patronizing tone appears more often from the late 1870s on. But in juxtaposing them, Dorsey made it easy to see the difference between patronizing articles and those that accorded the elders respectful attention. For example, when two articles about the same man appear near one another in Dorsey's "Colored Centenarians" scrapbook, the juxtaposition highlights the shortcomings of one account and shows what could be accomplished when a reporter paid attention to the life of an elderly black person. Richard Rice, of Philadelphia, who verified his age by recalling that he heard his owner speaking of the slave rebellion in Haiti when he was nearly a man, presumably in 1791, was born in slavery, emigrated to Haiti, and returned to the United States. He was visited by two reporters in 1880, one of them from the *Press* who failed to note his name but patronizingly recorded his speech phonetically to emphasize "the curiosities of... dialect," in precisely the move of which Mossell complained. The *Press* reporter concluded his interview writing, "the old gentleman muttered some unintelligible sentences concerning his fifteen years in Canada, during which the reporter left." He titled the piece "A Maryland Slave," suggesting that the sixty or seventy years Rice had lived as a free man were of no interest.[31]

However, a few months later, a reporter from the *Inquirer* (a white newspaper known to have black reporters) stayed to listen to the full story and recorded it respectfully in an article titled "The Oldest Citizen." The *Inquirer* thought it was worth giving 16 column inches to Rice's travels and travails. Born into slavery in Maryland, freed at age twenty-four, Rice worked in a distillery and joined in a project for black colonization of Haiti, where he stayed three years, suffering the death of his son and wife there and permanent separation from two daughters when he returned to the United States. His labor went into building two bridges in Columbia, Pennsylvania. Married again, with two children, he emigrated to Canada in 1857, where farming was difficult; he then returned after seventeen years to live with his wife, supported by his daughter and ailing son-in-law, and surrounded at age 106 by the products of their labor: the blankets she spun and wove from wool from the sheep they had raised in Canada. The second article is full of names, allowing a local reader many points of connection to Rice's Pennsylvania associates. Although the article is in a white paper and calls its subject "Richard," it depicts a remarkable life that makes sense on its own terms, not in relation to white slaveholders.[32]

The article is not a vision of triumph and "progress of a race," however. Each of Rice's moves brings hardship and loss. Even so, the article speaks of dignity and filial caring in terms that fairly glow with respect; despite the poverty of the daughter and her husband, "the large end of the last loaf has always been reserved for the old couple." The reporter, who may have been black (and may even have been Mossell herself), honors him. Dorsey not only gleans from the newspaper a thoughtful account of the complex life of a black man but for good measure lets it show up the inadequacy of the work of an earlier supercilious reporter who can hear only "some unintelligible sentences."[33]

Dorsey's pairing of these two accounts opens the question of what might have happened if other reports had fleshed out these extraordinary ordinary lives treated in such a cursory way. How did Lizzie Gray endure after she was stolen from her four children in Africa? What was her experience of the Middle Passage? How did she learn English? Did she ever again in all her long life have news of her homeland? How did she survive without it? The obituary writer, fascinated by Gray's exoticism, is more interested in notating her purported dialect than in probing deeper. The fragments are tantalizing but not satisfying: "She was educated in her youth under the influence of Mahommedan tenets, and although she united herself many years ago with the Methodist church, she ever said that Christ built He first church in Mecca, and He grave was da."[34]

Dorsey's "Colored Centenarians" shows vigorous old people who keep working into great age, despite disabilities, and it celebrates their continued industry. Black industriousness was another contentious subject in the post-Reconstruction era. White Northerners went along with the claims of former slaveholders that black people were lazy and wouldn't work unless forced, and they allowed Southerners to legislate restrictions on black people's choice of how and when to work, and to enforce black labor via those "black laws." The figure of the lazy black person blossomed in the plantation fiction and theater that featured black indolence. Dorsey's scrapbook spoke back to such stories with ample evidence. Richard Hoops, of Osage City, Missouri, who "may be the oldest man" living at 123 in 1893, had pulled tree stumps from a field until a few years earlier and continued to fish for catfish. "Professor" Henry Richardson walked the streets of Philadelphia's fifteenth ward, garnering whitewashing and carpet-shaking jobs until at age 102 in 1892 he was missed from his rounds one day. Mary McDowell or McDonald, age 119, at the Home for Infirm and Aged Colored People for twenty years, could not only see well enough to thread a needle, but she sewed a thirty-foot rag carpet for the home in three months and won a prize for her sewing. Phillis Hogwood, at the same home, just turning one hundred, spoke of a lifetime of hoeing corn, pulling flax, and racking hay and told a visitor, "I could almost drive oxen now if I could get them yoked up." An unnamed man who purchased his own freedom and that of his nine children and joined the Union Army at age sixty-five, continued to work as a barber in Springfield, Massachusetts, at age ninety-seven. The scrapbook overflows with such examples of black perseverance. But the scrapbook entries also show black people who are legitimately leisured: What inhuman calculus would expect someone a hundred years old to work? Writing with scissors, Dorsey used the white press against itself, critiquing it and filling in its gaps. Other black scrapbook makers pressed the limits of the white press as well.[35]

Ida B. Wells and Anti-Lynching Scrapbooks

Although we can see the Civil War scrapbooks discussed in Chapter 3 as a genre—time-limited works exhibiting shared concerns with death, mourning, and nation building—African American scrapbooks are a genre in a different sense. The similarities and connections that join them are the links among scrapbook makers and between scrapbook makers and issues in the black community and the press. Material on lynching is one common thread through some African American scrapbooks. In their approach to saving materials on lynching, compilers may have learned from and followed at home the example and techniques the African American anti-lynching crusader Ida B. Wells (later Barnett) used in her work. If Wells made scrapbooks herself, they did not survive two fires that destroyed many of her papers. But she continued a tradition, pioneered by abolitionists Angelina and Sarah Grimké and Theodore Weld in the 1840s, of using the antiblack white press as a data source, systematizing it, and turning it against itself.[36]

An African American reading newspapers from the 1880s through the 1910s would have had to be blindly optimistic to notice only stories of black uplift, achievement, and involvement in the nation's history. During this period, southern whites worked hard to undercut black advancement. Laws disenfranchising black men were passed in the South, and whites lynched black men and women in unprecedented numbers, convincing a generally uncritical and incurious white press that

lynching was necessary to stop black "depravity." Black scrapbook makers who
saved accounts of lynchings and attacks on black voting used the Civil War scrapbook makers' strategy of retaining and containing; compiling accounts of these
events was one way to make sense of them, and to experience a sense of control
over them, by pinning them down and literally putting them under one's thumb.

Wells's anti-lynching crusade was recorded in the black press from 1892, and
eventually to some degree in the white press. After she and her business partner
in a black Memphis newspaper were themselves threatened with lynching for
publishing an editorial about eight black men who had been lynched, she moved
her investigative reportage to the *New York Age*, where, under the pen name "Iola,"
she published articles about lynching that grew into two pamphlets. Her crusade
was highly visible in the black community, with clubwomen and others honoring
her for her work and raising money to publish her articles in pamphlet form.[37]

Wells's writing on lynching quoted from and drew on the white press for much
of her evidence that the common justifications for lynching were false. She realized that the white press's antagonism to black equality often made it a more
credible source when its reports backed African American positions—like a hostile witness in court. She therefore relied on articles from white newspapers as
documentary evidence. Her 1892 articles and pamphlet *Southern Horrors: Lynch
Law in All Its Phases* drew on the white press and on community knowledge for
examples proving her points; her 1894 *A Red Record: Tabulated Statistics and
Alleged Causes of Lynchings in the United States* assembled many additional damn-
ing accounts and compiled the evidence of the white press into statistics. "Rather
than describe the brutalities of the lynch mobs herself, for example, she often
quoted verbatim Southern newspapers' graphic and enthusiastic descriptions of
human burnings and tortures," Gail Bederman notes in her analysis of Wells's rhe-
torical strategy. With the approving context of the white newspaper cut away, the
articles' details starkly reveal the actions of the mobs.[38]

Black scrapbook makers learned from Wells that they could mine the white
newspaper to use it against itself, and they employed her approaches as well. (All
the accounts of lynching I have seen in African American scrapbooks date from
1892 or later.) As African American scrapbook makers placed records of lynchings
in their scrapbooks, they shifted from being readers helplessly absorbing this
information or flattened and dispirited by news of horrifying violence to being
activists compiling data, whether or not they used that information publicly. They
thereby probed more deeply into the workings of racial injustice. William Dorsey,
for example, tracked the formulaic progress of the usual lynching stories through
the press: the capture of the accused, a press announcement of where the accused
was being held (so that a mob might break into the jail to get him), followed by the
story that a mob had killed him. Dorsey highlighted the white press's involvement
by collecting one sequence that includes a white newspaper owner standing up at
the hearing of a black man accused of assaulting a white woman, and calling for
his lynching.[39]

Charles N. Hunter (1851?–1931), a school principal active in party politics in Raleigh, clipping the North Carolina white newspapers, created pages comparing the outcomes of similar accusations brought against whites and blacks—black people lynched, and whites freed or lightly punished—eloquently deploying the language of juxtaposition and recontextualization. He paired, for example, an account of a sixty-year-old black man lynched for attacking a young white girl in Texas with a story that occurred a month later, of a sixty-two-year-old white man accused of attacking a fourteen-year-old white girl. Lengthy testimony from a doctor in the case against the white man asserted that she must have had relations with many men before and so presumably couldn't have been raped.[40]

Dorsey sought out accounts of people resisting lynching. He follows the story of George Denning, attacked by a Ku Klux Klan mob in Kentucky, who shot back and killed a mob member; his lynching was prevented by the governor, who sent in troops. The governor pardoned him from his seven-year sentence for the killing. When Denning was attacked, his eye gouged out, and his house burned, he won a lawsuit against the perpetrators for $50,000. This was a highly unusual outcome to what started as the usual lynching story.[41]

Wells pointed out that lynchings were often retribution for black achievement. This understanding seems to undergird the scrapbooks of Charles Turner, the civil servant in St. Louis who was active in Republican Party politics. His scrapbooks juxtapose clippings on lynchings with articles on St. Louis politics and patronage, memorabilia of his attendance at cakewalks and musicales, and accounts of prize fights and street fights. Similarly, his materials on his own political work there, his rank in city political appointments as a sergeant at arms to the city council, and his participation in dinners and soirees on the one hand but on suppression of the black vote on the other are accounts of two ends of a spectrum of black political and civic participation. For Turner, clippings on black achievements and clippings on black lynchings and suppression were not incongruous. His collections also suggest that even amid festivities and achievements, a black man in the former slave state of Missouri must be constantly aware of dangers. Missouri was a border state that had fought on the Union side, however, and St. Louis was a transportation hub, where Turner could take advantage of ample access to newspapers often not available to black people in the deep South. Creating his broad assortment of clippings, in at least seven volumes, was his mode of understanding the larger political situation of black people, even from his relatively privileged position.[42]

The connection to Wells is straightforward in the work of an anonymous black Boston scrapbook maker, probably a member of a black women's club. One item in the scrapbook is the entire souvenir program of the 1895 First National Conference of the Colored Women of America in Boston, at which copies of *A Red Record* were sold; another is an issue of the black women's club magazine, *The Woman's Era*, a souvenir of the 1896 First Annual Convention of the National Federation of Afro-American Women at which Wells spoke. Amid her other materials on women's clubs and New England poets, she saved articles on lynchings or attacks. Just as

Dorsey saved articles on African Americans resisting lynch mobs, she saved an item on an anti-lynching meeting at the Bethel AME church in Chicago, where the audience refused the pastor's invitation to sing "My Country Tis of Thee" on the grounds that, as one man expressed it, "I don't want to sing that song until this country is what it claims to be, 'sweet land of liberty.'" The group then sang "John Brown" instead. Although the pastor counseled "Christian forbearance" in the face of outrages, speakers instead called on the group to "join in one voice of protest." At that same meeting, Wells's future husband, Ferdinand Barnett, asserted that the South might go too far in its lynchings and bring down black retribution.[43]

The alternative histories that African American scrapbook compilations made out of disparate materials on abuses against black people included published books and articles. Scrapbook compilations on lynching became way stations for information to be turned into other publications, in line with the practice of such writers as Mark Twain, Wilkie Collins, and Lillie Devereux Blake, as we have seen. Mary Church Terrell drew on white newspapers, compiled into a scrapbook, as evidence. When she finally succeeded in interesting a magazine editor in an article on lynching, she found writing it

> was one of the easiest tasks in that line I ever attempted. For several years I had been keeping a scrap book, and all I had to do was to turn to it and find concrete examples proving that the statements that innocent Negroes had never been lynched and that the Negro was practically the only rapist in the country were absolutely false.

The resulting article, published in 1904, repeatedly points to the fact that her support often came from white and Southern newspaper articles. Even "the *Evening Post*, a Democratic daily of Vicksburg, Mississippi," acknowledges the barbarity of lynching, with an eyewitness account of the dismemberment and murder of two men by a mob. The contradictory claims of newspapers become further ammunition in her analysis. The scrapbook was a stop along the way to gather and concentrate information that could be used "at a proper time."[44]

When black scrapbook makers recontextualized articles and other materials produced by the murderers and their allies, they turned them from souvenirs, celebrations, or signals meant to threaten black people into exposures of white depravity. Black publications did the same. An account by Shirley Graham (later Du Bois) of reading a magazine that notably mixed lynchings with resistance and uplift stories shows that black publications assumed their readers understood this strategy. As a child living in Colorado in 1910 or later, Graham brought a copy of the African American monthly *The Crisis* to school study hall. A white teacher who looked through it

> was horrified by the pictures which accompanied a lynching story. She could not understand how my father allowed such a "gruesome" thing to

fall into my hands. Since "The Crisis" arrived at our house regularly each month and was freely discussed at the table I defended it stoutly. But I went away depressed at my teacher's ignorance, more than by the account of the lynching.

Crisis readers understood that the point of showing and talking about the horror of lynching within a black family and community was not the gruesome sensationalism and complicity that the white paper originally publishing a picture might have intended; rather its purpose was to increase awareness and provoke opposition. Even before *The Crisis* began publication in 1910, and in households that did not receive it, building a record at home by saving examples in the scrapbook, and circulating that awareness within the black community, was a mode of struggle against white oppressors.[45]

Hostile whites came to recognize the subversive power of the scrapbook, as one account suggests. When Atlanta police raided the home of the mother of Olen Montgomery, one of the Scottsboro Boys (nine black youths accused of assaulting a white woman in 1931 in Alabama) her "scrap book containing records of the four-year struggle to save the Scottsboro boys and copies of the 'Labor Defender,' were carted off by the police." Unlike the situation of the abolitionists whose "scrap-book full of Anti-Slavery extracts" and an anti-slavery poem are evidence of their disloyalty to the Confederacy, Viola Montgomery's loyalty to her son needed no evidence. Instead, owning and organizing the public record of the case—in a scrapbook—was evidently itself akin to weapons possession.[46]

If black people did *not* save white newspaper accounts of injustice toward African Americans, they might lose the chance to refer to events in the public record. Black people, especially in the South, could not count on continued access to the newspaper as chronicle and record. Public libraries were segregated in Southern as well as some Northern cities into the 1960s. The day's history could vanish.

Nearly a century after Frederick Douglass pointed out that a clipping could be ammunition in the struggle for equal rights, a significant battle turned on access to a clipping in the white press. Before the civil rights victories of the 1960s, Southern white newspaper offices also barred black people from access to this part of the public record. Craft and planning were needed to keep the public record from conveniently disappearing, as a story from 1930 illustrates. When President Herbert Hoover nominated Appellate Judge John J. Parker to the U.S. Supreme Court, the National Association for the Advancement of Colored People mobilized a campaign against his confirmation. As candidate for governor of North Carolina in 1920, Parker had advocated continued disenfranchisement of black people. A decade later, in a more liberal time, this stance would damage him in the national arena, if made visible to a larger public. But on the floor of the Senate, "a brazen and unequivocal denial was made that Judge Parker had ever made such a statement, or that the *Greensboro Daily News* had ever published the … clipping quoting Judge Parker's anti-Negro speech." Parker's white friends in Greensboro were protecting their own. The next day, copies of the clipping appeared on the senators' desks. An African American NAACP worker

> wise in the ways of Dixie, ... had known that there would have been diffi-
> culty in examining ten-year-old files of the newspaper had he gone him-
> self to look up the clipping. He had, therefore, sent a young Negro who
> looked white to get the facts, instructing him to copy the clipping.

Rather than transcribe the article from the *Greensboro Daily News*, the young man, perhaps less experienced in the ways of Dixie or wishing to leave quickly, cut it out with his penknife. Though that made it possible for the NAACP to reproduce copies and place them in the hands of Hoover, every senator, and the media, it left the organization vulnerable to the charge of theft that was immediately brought against it. Without open access to the newspaper's repository—or a scrapbook saving such evidence—clandestine entrée was needed to produce evidence of the nominee's white-supremacist position; it would otherwise easily have been confined to the public who approved of it.[47]

This account also points to the superior evidentiary standing enjoyed by the (difficult to access) white press. It would not have been sufficient for the NAACP to find an account of Parker's speech in a 1920 black paper. The white press's presumed antipathy to black equality made it a more credible source when the nature of its reports backed African American positions.

In 1886, Gertrude Bustill Mossell lamented the records of African American history lost through the failure to clip newspapers. By 1930, there were still significant repercussions to *not* saving an article.

Retaining and Containing in the Scrapbook

Making scrapbooks both saved a record or archive of materials and performed archivalness: the act of cutting and pasting demonstrates the seriousness with which the clipper perceives the article and allows the clipper the experience of making a record. Like ostentatiously photographing or taking notes on some form of public misconduct, it documents and serves notice that the event is being documented. Though scrapbook making might be more private, the scrapbook maker's action is a performance that promises, "I will remember." Saving accounts of white atrocities toward black people thus not only created a record but offered the possibility of experiencing a kind of control over it. Such control was still needed by 1955.

The activist and writer Joyce Ladner, age twelve at the time of the murder of Emmett Till in Mississippi, reports that she and her older sister bought the newspaper every day and "pored over the clippings of the lynching we kept in our scrapbook, and cried. Emmett Till was about our age; we cried for him as we would have cried for one of our four brothers." Ladner's ritual of saving material in her scrapbook was a very different mode of emotional expression from making the movie star scrapbooks that midtwentieth-century white children busied themselves with. Ladner's account opens the question whether the nineteenth-century African American scrapbook makers, too, experienced their scrapbooks as sites for memorializing the dead, creating pages to visit their grief and fear.[48]

If an article on lynching that had appeared in the hostile white press was cut and pasted into a published analysis by an African American writer or into a black scrapbook, it took advantage of the white press's authority and also shifted perspective to demonstrate the profound error of the white press's attitude. The white press could be harnessed to antilynching work, but it could not be allowed to stand on its own. Its distortions and omissions had to be explained and critiqued, often through the language of juxtaposition. Revealing the distortions of the white press was an ongoing black project, undertaken via many approaches. Beyond the antilynching crusade, black scrapbook makers used their scrapbooks as one element in a larger critique of white media.

Declining the Stereotype: Talking Back to the White Press

In collecting derogatory material from the white press, African American scrapbook makers "declined the stereotype" by both refusing it and analyzing it. Their scrapbooks hold up offensive and degrading portrayals for comparison and scrutiny; they allow their makers to notice and to teach others about the biases of the newspapers. In this spirit, one scrapbook maker clipped a long article from the *San Francisco Examiner*, "Let the South Alone in Handling the Negro Question." In it, the paper's owner, William Randolph Hearst, argued that the white South should be allowed to set policy about black people, warranting his claim on his Southern parents' experience. The scrapbook maker sidelined in red ink Hearst's lines "I wish all the influences in the North could understand that the least they can do is to leave the South alone, keep their hands off, and not complicate the Southern problem...by dangerous meddling." In explaining his beliefs, Hearst's editorial gives readers reason to assume that his paper will side with Southern lynch mobs and disenfranchisers. He thus provides important information on how to interpret the *Examiner's* writing. Perhaps not surprisingly, having declined Hearst's stereotype, this scrapbook maker more often selected clippings from the liberal white *San Francisco Call,* along with black papers. Using juxtaposition as a mode of critique, this anonymous west coast scrapbook maker used the context set by this editorial, following it with a report that a "measure to disenfranchise the Negro" had passed in Maryland. Such attacks were one result of "leav[ing] the South alone."[49]

African Americans highlighted the distortions of the white press through publications and community gatherings, as well as scrapbooks. Even before the "Outlook" column in W. E. B. Du Bois's magazine *The Horizon* began reviewing white magazines for their coverage of black life in, 1907, one group of black clubwomen formed a committee in the 1890s to track the white press. This

nineteenth-century equivalent of talking back to the TV set is not only more satisfying as a group, but the presence of others fights the media's erasure of one's
own reality. It fights as well the absence of *any* representation of black people, a
longstanding problem. Together, talking back, people constitute the kind of
community that Nancy Fraser has called a counterpublic. Such counterpublics are
"bases for withdrawal and regroupment," and also "training grounds for agitational activities directed toward wider publics." This work took several forms. A
few readers attempted to engage the hostile white press directly, in letters to the
editor. Even if they were not published in the white press, many were reprinted in
the black press, thus modeling a mode of deeper critical reading and engagement
with the press for other readers to take up.[50]

The alternative histories that scrapbook makers created also allowed them to
spell out their critique of the white press. Juxtaposition is a fundamental mode of
expressing ideas in scrapbooks, as we saw in Dorsey's use of it to express his judgments in his "Colored Centenarians" scrapbook; other African American scrapbook
makers additionally wrote out their criticisms of the white press. African American
scrapbooks sometimes preserved those letters or articles written to the white press
but published in the black press. Or they identified the writers of anonymous or
pseudonymous items by African Americans in the white press, highlighting both
the knowledge that a black person had spoken out and the identity of that writer.[51]

The comments John Wesley Cromwell wrote in the margins of his scrapbook
talk back to the white-dominated press and supplement his work on the black
press by amplifying and changing the direction of stories. He edited two black
papers, the *People's Advocate* of Alexandria, Virginia, and then Washington, D.C.,
which he founded in 1876 and left in 1889; and the Washington *Record*, which he
began editing in 1901. His scrapbook is focused on the 1890s, bridging a period
between editing the two papers.[52]

An 1897 obituary he collected of a white man, Thomas Gorsuch, of Lancaster,
Pennsylvania, exemplifies how his scrapbook commentary reframes and trans-
forms a story from the white press (Figure 4.5). The obituary notes that Gorsuch
witnessed the death of his father, Col. Edward Gorsuch of Baltimore, in
Pennsylvania's 1851 Christiana fugitive slave riot. The article is sympathetic to
the slaveholder Edward Gorsuch, explaining that when he tried to recapture an
alleged runaway, the ex-slaves fought back. The thirty-eight escaped slaves were
tried for treason, though two of them were excused from trial on plea of ill health.
The article notes that the two lived to be ninety-one and ninety-four. Though the
published story focuses on Gorsuch's loss and the presumed duplicity of the prisoners, implying that the court should have been harsher, Cromwell's marginal
annotation amplifies the meaning of this event in *his* life:

> I have heard my father frequently refer to this trial to confirm his belief
> in the power of prayer. Elder, after a Bishop, Nazrey at a religious service
> prior to the trial prayed that those testifying against the accused might

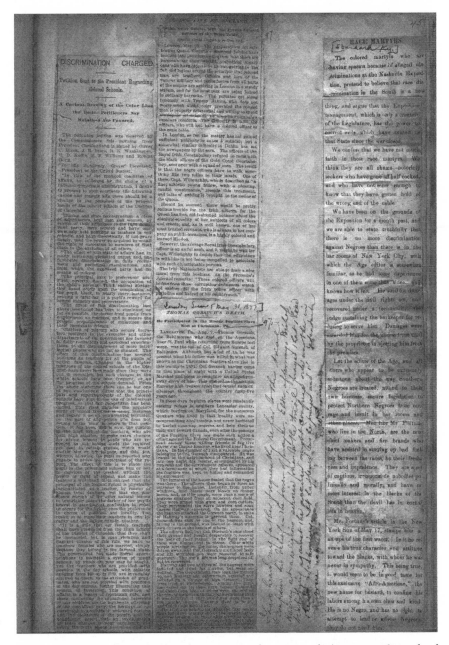

Figure 4.5 Cromwell scrapbook with annotation about Gorsuch. (Courtesy of Moorland Spingarn Collection, Howard University)

confuse one another in their testimonies. It happened as he prayed the
defendants were acquitted. JW Cromwell.[53]

The published clipping plays up postbellum white sentimentality about a son's
loss of his slaveholding father, but Cromwell's recontextualization and annotation
turn it into a story of the transmission of history and faith between an ex-slave
father and son. The published story suggests that trickster black prisoners feigned
illness and hoodwinked lenient whites to escape punishment. Cromwell makes it
a story of triumph through godly power. Cromwell's scrapbook does not simply
embellish the white press with his marginalia; rather his commentary resituates
news from hostile sources and forces it to tell another story.

As an editor and writer, Cromwell intervened in the white press by writing to
and about it. When the white Washington, D.C., *Times* published an article
claiming that the presence of hundreds of thousands of people of mixed blood in
the United States constituted a menace, Cromwell rebutted the article in an
unsigned editorial in his *Record*. He asserted that many of the capital's "whites"
were really of mixed race, and he wrote of a black bookstore clerk of Washington
who left for the far west, took up church work, and in 1898 returned to Washington
for the General Episcopal Convention, representing a white congregation as minister: "No one knew him to be colored where he labored, but his brother, a colored
barber here, has probably shaved the proprietor of 'The Times' many a time."
Cromwell saved this editorial on page 92 of his scrapbook, added his own name as
author in brackets, and then privately established both his knowledge of hidden
information and his tact in not revealing it by cross-referencing it with a later
entry. The obituary of a Washington, D.C., Catholic priest, Father Patrick Healy, a
former president of Georgetown University, on his scrapbook's page 112, carries
a hand-drawn emphatic finger pointing from the obituary to "See p. 92." His hand-
drawn brackets draw attention to the obituary's reference to Healy's brother, also
a Catholic priest, "the late Right Rev. James Augustine Healy." (James Healy died
August 5, 1900; Patrick Healy died January 10, 1910.)[54]

Cromwell's scrapbook becomes a repository revealing hidden information
about his own authorship of an editorial, and the more inflammatory information
about the black ancestry of a prominent man. His editorial, of unknown date,
fudges the facts enough not to give away James Healy's secret, since Healy was
Catholic rather than Episcopalian, and served in New England, not the far west.
But the scrapbook gives him the satisfaction of asserting his knowledge of the
real story and having insider's knowledge, superior to that of the white press.
Though as an editor and writer himself Cromwell wrote back to the white press
publicly through his own columns, he reserved material for the alternative history he created in his scrapbook. In his private (or privately circulated) scrapbook, he turned the white public press into secret evidence for his public assertion
that accomplished black people were hidden in plain sight behind white
identities.

Staking Out Space in the White Press

When an article about Dorsey's collection of African American books, artifacts, and scrapbooks appeared in the white press, a fellow collector and historian recognized that Dorsey had made an impact on the white world. Robert Adger wrote to him in 1896 to express

> pleasure and satisfaction...when I read the notice of your long and valued labors in the [Philadelphia] Times....I am proud that the very many readers of that paper should know that we have among us one so mindful as to preserve matter of so much historical interest in relation to our long oppressed and despised race. These showings are great helpers in solving race problems.[55]

Being written about respectfully in the white press was another way of writing back, and making black history visible. The scrapbook maker Joseph W. H. Cathcart excelled in this endeavor and appeared in the white press in numerous articles. Cathcart was, like Dorsey, a prodigious scrapbook maker. As a friend of both Cromwell and Dorsey, he may have inspired Cromwell's scrapbook making. Cathcart made more than 130 scrapbooks, not all of which survive. He began his clippings in the 1850s and pasted them up a few years later. The first clipping he collected, as he showed a reporter, was an advertisement for a runaway slave from 1856. His work included his Civil War scrapbooks (discussed in Chapter 3). He continued through the optimistic period of Reconstruction with news reports of congressional debates, and then into grimmer times, until his death in 1895. Cathcart wrote history with scissors, covering every page so densely with his clippings that the pages themselves are thick and heavy with his passion to save his findings.[56]

Twenty years older than Cromwell, Cathcart worked for decades as a janitor in a Philadelphia office building of miscellaneous companies—brokers, coal distributors, and an electric light company—where he also lived for part of this time. Born in the 1820s in Pennsylvania or New Jersey, Cathcart was a flamboyant character, sporting a large, unusually low-cut collar that left his upper chest exposed, and keeping his hair in plaits. His accessibility in an office building near the Philadelphia Stock Exchange may have drawn reporters. Feature articles about black people in the white press were rare, but articles about Cathcart treated his endeavor seriously. He must have helped the reporters notice that he was collecting their own ephemeral journalism and dignifying it in the permanent protection of bindings and bookshelves. One reporter praised the "great variety of subjects showing at once the broad range of the collector's tastes and the wide scope of the journalism of the past quarter of a century." His scrapbooks intervened in the white press by inspiring stories about them in that very press. The reports made their way around to other white papers, spreading word of his collection as far as St. Louis, New Haven, and Los Angeles and nationally, via the *Scientific American*, teaching the readers of those white publications that black people had a substantial history, and alerting black readers to his techniques as well.[57]

In repurposing old government reports and city directories to paste his clippings into, Cathcart gained handsome and dignified free volumes, which looked as orderly and businesslike on the shelves as sets of books and reports in surrounding offices. As he displaced one kind of official report with *his* report, his scissors and paste enunciated its commentary, usurping the gravitas of the obliterated material. The solidity and set-like orderliness of his massive scrapbooks materialized the significance of the African American history they contained and manifested their importance for his visitors. Visitors applauded this performance. One reporter noted that the scrapbooks filled a floor-to-ceiling bookcase, extending over a quarter the length of a fair-sized room. The sheer quantity of material entranced him: the collection was even larger than it looked, he calculated, since reprinted in book form, set in book-size type, rather than small newspaper type, it would fill several thousand smaller volumes (Figure 4.6).[58]

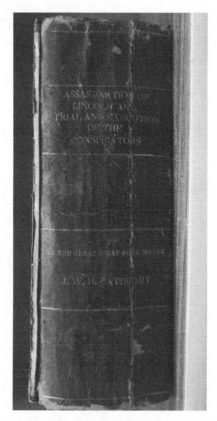

Figure 4.6 The spine of Joseph W. H. Cathcart's scrapbook on Lincoln's assassination. Cathcart had the reports and papers into which he pasted his clippings bound with his name on the spine. As here, he sometimes identified himself as "The Great Scrap-Book Maker." (Moorland Spingarn Collection, Howard University)

Through interviews explaining his scrapbooks, Cathcart taught others how to read the white newspaper. One reporter commented that his clipping selections were "judicious," casting his notes on Cathcart's volume on John Brown's raid in the form of a book review:

> The reader finds the telegraphic despatches, the speeches in Congress and at public meetings in different parts of the country, editorials on the raid and its consequences...with fugitive slave cases in Harrisburg, this city [Philadelphia] and elsewhere, showing the circumstances bearing upon the first effort of Abolitionism in arms.

The reporter understood that Cathcart's book did not narrowly focus on the raid and the trial but instead framed a narrative of cause and effect: anger at fugitive slave cases and inability to change the law led to armed revolt.[59]

Cathcart's sense of the meaning of history and what the Harpers Ferry raid was part of extended beyond what the reporter noticed. His scrapbook, stamped on the spine "John Brown's Insurrection at Harper's Ferry/JWH Cathcart," also comprises an account of a slave killing his purchaser, accounts of attempts to rescue fugitive slaves, the stopping of slave ships, and Touissant L'Ouverture's Haitian insurrection, grouping these instances of active resistance to slavery with John Brown's insurrection, with special attention to action taken by black people. Toward the end of this volume, Cathcart shifts to articles on secession and disunion, thereby linking them to the Harper's Ferry raid. The book ends with retribution: an 1886 item on the death of one of John Brown's captors.[60]

Reframing the White Press

L. S. Alexander Gumby, more than a generation younger than Cathcart and Dorsey, also saw saving clippings within a larger enterprise of preserving black culture and was part of a circle of African American collectors. A gay salon host of the Harlem Renaissance, who collected books and artwork, he created more than a hundred elaborate scrapbooks that honored clippings through elaborate presentation. His scrapbooks are marvels of frame making, full of pockets and envelopes for a reader to explore. Gumby remade the meaning of the material he collected from the white press, including items he clipped from antiquarian papers he bought. They honor their subjects. A section titled "The Runaway" in "Gumby's Scrapbook: The Negro in Bondage," contains an undated advertisement for a runaway slave, "Marcus, one of the House Servants at Mount Vernon." It explains that Marcus may try to pass himself off as one of the slaves Martha Washington intended to emancipate, though he was not one of them. Gumby made a precise paper frame for the clipping and covered it in cellophane. The frame highlights the document's authenticity—its aura, or charge—as it invites the readers of the scrapbook to feel the power of this document that

Figure 4.7 Page of L. S. Alexander Gumby's "The Negro in Bondage" scrapbook with the runaway ad for Marcus. The connection to George Washington is amplified with a Mount Vernon postcard. (From Gumby Scrapbook 89, Columbia University Rare Book Collection)

once could have caused Marcus's capture, while it testifies to Marcus's achievement.

He pasted clippings onto special heavy brown paper, made frames for them of leather-grained bookbinder's tape, and wrote identifications for them on cards engraved "Gumby's Scrap Book." He had some specially bound and stamped on the spine with titles in gold (such as "Gumby's Scrapbook: The Negro in Bondage"). Some volumes push assertion of his importance as a compiler past even the spine stamping and engraved cards. He sometimes included his own homoerotic Ex Libris bookplate, featuring three scantily clad men sporting with a book.

In the 1840s, abolitionists reframed runaway advertisements from the contemporary white southern press in another sense to mine them for information about mistreatment of slaves. Sarah and Angelina Grimké and Theodore Weld compiled them into a database from which to extrapolate evidence of beatings from the descriptions of scars given to identify the runaways, and they derived and broadcast knowledge of brutality at the highest levels of Southern society, drawing on the slaveowners' names on the ads. In isolating and framing the ad rather than combining it with other similar ads as a source of data, Gumby places Marcus on the two-dimensional equivalent of a pedestal almost a century after the ad was published, honoring his boldness and courage in running away. Abolitionists could use multiple advertisements effectively as data on the conditions of slaves because the ads were so ubiquitous in the Southern press; Gumby preserved and protected a single ad many years later. Marcus seems all the more heroic as a unique escapee, outside the context of thousands of others. Yet honored placement makes the heroism of this man's action visible as it was not, whether in the advertisement's initial publication or if processed into a larger abolitionist project. Moreover, its details link Marcus, like Dorsey's centenarians, to George Washington's family and establish that slaves in that household sought freedom (Figure 4.7).[61]

Sharing and Circulating Scrapbooks

Scrapbooks had a life and presence within black communities. Gertrude Bustill Mossell called them "unpublished histories," but private, hand-to-hand circulation is a form of publication too. William Dorsey opened his home to others so they could view his scrapbooks, books, and artwork that he had both collected and created himself in a three-room museum in his house. Visitors praised the taste and arrangement of his artworks and classified the scrapbooks with other rare items. "The Bystander," in Philadelphia's *Daily News*, a white newspaper, wrote:

> Pictures cover the walls except where they are hid by shelves, which are filled with books kept with scrupulous neatness and systematically arranged. These volumes comprise scrapbooks made from newspaper clippings having reference to the negro race; books written by or about

negroes, a collection of autographs of distinguished negroes, newspaper
biographies of eminent negroes and finally rare volumes such as the most
expert bibliographer would go in ecstasies over.

Another visitor saw Dorsey's collection as proof that Philadelphia needed a
black historical society and asked, "Would you believe me if I told you that his
studio has been visited by some of the greatest men, both black and white, of
the country?"[62]

Other visitors wrote about the museum as something available to their readers.
William Carl Bolivar, author of the long-running "Pencil Pusher Points" in the
black *Philadelphia Tribune*, reported in 1897, "On the eve of the 10th of this present month, I felt like breathing the air of Mr. William H. Dorsey's sanctum at 210
Dean Street, where I found him busily engaged in shaping data concerning the
Philippine Islands muddle." (At least one of his scrapbooks contained information
on Pacific Islands and Manila from the late 1890s.) The two men reminisced about
John Brown, and Dorsey showed off some of his collection. The inclusion of his
street address, and the idea that Bolivar might spontaneously drop by, suggests
that the reader was welcome to visit too. Bolivar's desire to "breath[e] the air" of
Dorsey's "sanctum" suggests that it is a place where African Americans might go
to feel rejuvenated.

Similarly, a column from the Philadelphia correspondent of a black New York
paper, *The Globe*, places the reader in the room, where a visitor might view the artwork, and then

> if his taste runs in another direction he might take one of the many
> scrap-books that are neatly and carefully arranged and he will find a biog-
> raphy, autograph or picture, one or all of any eminent man of African
> blood. These are all catalogued so that any one person may be found
> instantly.

The scrapbooks were shelved with other books, also available for perusal: "One
case is devoted exclusively to the works of colored authors. In an adjoining case
are the works of other writers bearing upon the African race." Dorsey's scrapbooks
included items about published books on African American topics.[63]

The journalists made clear that the scrapbooks and the rest of the collection
itself were valuable to black Philadelphians. One writer not only admired the collection itself but worried that items would be separated and its value as a repository consequently lost. Credit for making the collection was precious as well:

> Now what will become of this collection in the event of their present
> owner's death? Why, they will be squandered and gathered up by other
> people, and in the years yet to come other races will receive the honor of
> possessing this or that memento—the only one of its kind in the US. But

Figure 4.8 Drawing of William Dorsey's Museum, accompanying an unidentified newspaper article. (Dorsey biographical scrapbook, Thomas and William Dorsey Collection, Moorland Spingarn Collection, Howard University)

they will never think of acknowledging the fact that they procured them from a colored man's studio.

W. E. B. Du Bois drew on Dorsey's scrapbooks in his research for *The Philadelphia Negro*, though Dorsey received only a cursory credit. Reporters for black papers recognized that as alternative histories scrapbooks preserved information and perspectives on black life not available in books and that white institutions had little sympathy for this project.[64]

Dorsey's friend Joseph W. H. Cathcart's room full of scrapbooks in the Philadelphia office building where he worked and lived could be visited too. Cromwell's newspaper wrote admiringly of Cathcart's collection in 1877, suggesting that it "should be in the possession of some Negro American Historical Society."[65] As we have seen, most of the reporters who visited him were from white newspapers. Though they admired the sheer scale of his work, they did not mention how other people might view the scrapbooks; nor did they indicate whether he circulated his volumes. They did note, however, his habit of stamping his scrapbooks "GSBM," for "Great Scrap Book Maker." Other volumes bore titles with his name on them, like "Comic Sketches JWH Cathcart." The stamping of his name or the initials of his nickname on the spines suggests that the works left the premises and therefore needed identification. If reporters could visit and read his books, presumably many others came and used them as well. The articles' information about his location, while not as warmly inviting as the items in the black press on Dorsey's museum, hint that the newspaper readers could appear at Cathcart's office door as well.[66]

More than thirty years after Cathcart's death, and twenty years after Dorsey stopped making scrapbooks, L. S. Alexander Gumby sought to increase knowledge of black history. In 1926, he displayed his scrapbooks in his second-floor loft space in Harlem, which he later said he would have liked to call "Gumby's Scrapbook Studio" but which was known as Gumby's Bookstore or Gumby's Book Studio. He also collected rare books, artwork—and artists, his friend Bruce Nugent teased. He held poetry readings, art exhibits, and parties attended by many luminaries of the Harlem Renaissance, including a "stag reception" for Countee Cullen on his return from Paris in 1930 (where another collector, Arthur Schomburg, made a scrapbook of the guests' autographs). His nicknames included not only "the Great God Gumby" and "Count" but also "Mr. Scrapbook" (Figure 4.9).[67]

Unconsciously echoing Gertrude Bustill Mossell's suggestion decades earlier that black people create "an unwritten history," Gumby wrote that his collection "could well be called 'The Unwritten History.'" It was still needed because "there are so many startling historical events pertaining to, or relating to the American Negro that are not recorded in the Standard Histories, dictionaries, and school text-books, or if so, they are shaded so that they sound like a Ripley's 'Believe It or Not.'" Guests at Gumby's Book Studio were hungry for this history; his appreciative visitors constituted "the first unpremeditated interracial movement in

Figure 4.9 A gathering at L. S. Alexander Gumby's studio. Gumby is at right in a flowered jacket; scrapbooks are visible on the back bookcase. (From Gumby Scrapbook Box 65 scrapbook 35; , Columbia University Rare Book Collection)

Harlem," he wrote. The African American writer and literary critic Aubrey Bowser, writing in 1930 in New York's black *Amsterdam News,* called Gumby's studio "one of the sights of New York." Documentation was a necessity for creating works such as historical novels, he explained.

> Negro letters especially have suffered from the lack of adequate documentation. Much priceless information has been carelessly destroyed and much more is lying around in odd corners of the world, waiting to be found.... In recent years, several gleaners, notably Arthur Schomburg, have gathered large collections of books and prints about the Negro; but there are many scattered and fugitive things that cannot be found without a systematic and concentrated search.[68]

Bowser's grasp of the value and importance of coherent, usable newspaper clipping scrapbooks may have owed something not only to his own work on newspapers but to the scrapbook keeping of his father-in-law, black newspaper publisher T. Thomas Fortune. Fortune's scrapbook contained historical materials as well as his own writings. Gumby's specialty was "the gathering of these bits and putting them together.... He aims at producing a complete history of the Negro in scrapbook form."[69]

"If you visit Gumby's studio," Bowser wrote, invitingly suggesting that the reader might well do so, "you may be surprised when he pulls an enormous ledger-sized book from a shelf and informs you that it is devoted to you and your doings." Though most readers would not actually find their own doings chronicled by Gumby, the idea of his collection being so inclusive that they might be represented there and that Gumby might care enough about an ordinary black person's life to make a cellophane frame for clippings about him or her and save them in an enormous book was an enticement to visit—if only to be sure that the representation was suitable for public display. (His scrapbooks included some dedicated to erotica, not mentioned in the articles.) Gumby lost his studio when the wealthy friend who had bankrolled his collecting lost his money in the 1929 stock market crash, and Gumby soon after entered a hospital for what became four years of treatment for tuberculosis.

Perhaps because so many did find themselves and their doings included in his scrapbooks, either as individuals or as a community, his works attracted a large following. The four hundred members of the Harlem community who turned out for a fundraising ball to more securely store his scrapbooks and collections during his illness included not just the artists and writers who had gathered in his Studio but Cotton Club dancers and a dance orchestra who contributed their services, perhaps honoring Gumby's interest in theater and music, enshrined in multiple scrapbooks on entertainers. Despite the fundraising, the scrapbook collection was stored in a damp basement. By the time Gumby retrieved it, many volumes had to be reworked, and some of those described in the articles are no longer extant.[70]

In 1934, Gumby sought a place in Harlem to recreate a setting to display his books "in the proper atmosphere where people genuinely interested may come and browse among them." In such a place, his scrapbooks "could be made available to the people who wish to make use of them for research work." Instructions in the books themselves speak for Gumby's expectation that other people would use them. A pasted-down handmade envelope containing clippings of ads for runaway slaves, for example, bears the note, "Notice: Handle with care in removing and returning to packet. Don't force—go slow." The caution is also an invitation, welcoming readers to re-enact the search for hidden history and to participate in the collector's quest by reaching into an envelope and drawing forth more evidence, more stories.[71]

Gumby exhibited his scrapbooks in Philadelphia and Boston as well as New York for Negro History Week, a tradition that started in 1926. Because the growing interest in black history didn't extend to publication of enough books, scrapbooks and unwritten histories were still needed.[72]

Black readers of the white press materialized their oppositional reading in scrapbooks and made them available to others in their homes or passed them hand to hand. In this way, scrapbooks became part of counterpublic "training . . . for agitational activities," as we have seen. Readers who did not write novels, edit magazines or newspapers, or even join clubs or write letters to the editor engaged in that critique. Members of this counterpublic thus became creators of their own media.

Passing It On

With the scarcity of books on black history extending into the twentieth century, the black press encouraged children, especially, to make and share scrapbooks. In 1920, a girl reading W. E. B. Du Bois and Jessie Redmon Fauset's children's magazine *The Brownies' Book* joined the tradition of using scrapbooks to make a record of high-achieving African Americans, when she wrote in to say that she had a home-made scrapbook in which she kept "all the pictures I can find of interesting colored people and all the interesting things they do." Reading *The Brownies' Book* taught her that "there must be a lot of important colored people I didn't know about," and now she wanted their pictures for her scrapbook as well. At least one black newspaper ran a column titled "The Scrapbook" (Figure Intro.3), while others modeled the idea of collecting African American-related items with columns such as the *Indiana Freeman's* "Race Gleanings" (Figure 4.10).[73]

In the 1930s, the black weekly the *Chicago Defender* extended such work by giving African American children prizes for the scrapbooks they made for patients in black hospitals in Chicago and the South. The project recirculated the *Defender* into hundreds of scrapbooks and then to children and their parents in the South who might not have seen the paper, thus increasing its readership. Making scrapbooks from the *Defender* had multiple benefits. The Chicago children who took part in the contest learned to read it, southern black children were supplied with books with black faces in them (a rare commodity), and the process was celebrated in the newspaper, inspiring other children's clubs and their leaders to take up the project (Figures 4.11). The paper likewise celebrated the making of a "Negro history scrapbook to be made of news clippings that tell of interesting Negro accomplishments" for a high school library. Especially during the Depression, scrapbook making was an enticingly cheap activity for children. But advice and encouragement to make them also points to the continued need and desire for those unwritten histories.[74]

Even in the latter part of the twentieth century, scrapbook making continued to be linked with unwritten black history. In 1974, when Toni Morrison was working as an editor at Random House, she became involved in a project on black history and culture called *The Black Book*. This collagelike compilation of newspaper clippings, sheet music covers, bills of sale of enslaved people, photographs, patent applications, letters, and other memorabilia presents slices of U.S. black history from its beginning to the 1940s. Bill Cosby's introduction frames it as a scrapbook:

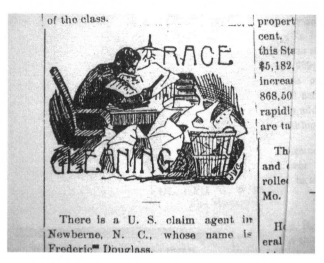

Figure 4.10 "Race Gleanings" column heading from the *Indiana Freeman* shows an editor participating in exchange work and also models the idea of clipping the press.

Figure 4.11 Children with their *Chicago Defender* scrapbooks, 4 May 1934. (Courtesy of the *Chicago Defender*)

Suppose a three-hundred-year-old black man had decided, oh, say when he was about ten, to keep a scrapbook—a record of what it was like for himself and his people in these United States. He would keep newspaper articles that interested him, old family photos, trading cards, advertisements, letters, handbills, dreambooks, and posters—all sorts of stuff.[75]

For Toni Morrison, working on this scrapbooklike book was highly generative and provided historical background for novels such as her own *Beloved*. In fact, *The Black Book*—like Cathcart's collection—includes a clipping on Margaret Garner, the escaped slave who killed her child rather than let her be returned to slavery. Carolyn Denard writes:

> In explaining her desire to do this kind of book, Morrison said that she was tired of histories of black life that focused only on leaders, leaving the everyday heroes to the lumps of statistics. She wanted to bring the lives of those who always got lost in the statistics to the forefront—to create a genuine black history book that simply recollected life as lived.

William H. Dorsey, Joseph W. H. Cathcart, Charles Turner, L. S. Alexander Gumby, and many anonymous scrapbook makers would have agreed with Morrison. That had been their project too.[76]

5

Strategic Scrapbooks

Activist Women's Clipping and Self-Creation

Women entering into public life in the nineteenth century sometimes acted in ways we now might assume would have undercut their authority. A report on an 1860 antislavery convention observed, "A large proportion of those present were ladies, who employed their spare time in industrious knitting, a pursuit which gave the ball a pleasant domestic air." Were women so busy that they had to bring their work along even to a public meeting? Were they so nervous at being in this large political setting that they needed to occupy their hands? No. Rather, knitting in public and political venues was a strategy: in a time when public life was a male domain, and women's entry into it left them liable to questions and accusations about their morals and worth, public knitting allowed women to pointedly perform their domestic duties and portray their allegiance to home. Connecting themselves to domestic values and activities while engaging in political writing, organizing, and especially public speaking was one strategy for having their ideas, words, and public presence taken seriously. Their scrapbooks documented this strategy and were one way they enacted it. In discussing the place of their scrapbooks within activist strategies, this chapter also looks at activists as speakers, readers, and writers.[1]

From the earliest years of the nineteenth-century women's rights movement, activists understood how important it was to address and influence public opinion. They read and clipped newspapers to follow their press coverage. For women who spoke to audiences, the clippings constituted a record of their activities and public response to it, which helped them work out how to counter the considerable disapproval of women lecturing. The scrapbooks women's rights activists made document both a movement, as seen through the press, and their individual makers' activities, growth, and changes. As nineteenth-century women became active in public life they constructed records of their activism using articles from newspapers that they did not control. Cutting and pasting coverage into scrapbooks moved women's rights issues beyond publications that preached to the already converted. Their scrapbooks document an extraordinary assertion of their selfhood and their claim to act in the public arena. Perhaps Gertrude Stein and

Virgil Thomson recognized the role of the scrapbook in telling the movement's story when they chose to begin their opera about Susan B. Anthony, *The Mother of Us All*, with Anthony pasting clippings into her scrapbook.[2]

The scrapbooks discussed in this chapter were made largely by middle-class women active in public writing and speaking for a variety of reforms. These activists were vulnerable to being criticized as "unwomanly." In creating their public personas, and staking out public space as writers and speakers, they had to present their womanly, domestic credentials to get the message across—such as by public knitting. In their homes, the scrapbooks bridged their public life as speakers and writers with their domestic lives and connections. Scrapbooks helped them craft and monitor public personas that highlighted domesticity. Even as women entered the lyceum circuit as public speakers after the Civil War, scrapbooks helped them strike a balance for themselves, bringing their public selves into the home to be integrated with domestic lives.

Scrapbooks also mark the changing relationship between women activists and the press. Like the black people who made scrapbooks on African American topics, women activists understood the press not as a simple record but as a set of voices and conversations to be read critically and culled by the scrapbook maker who ensured that the correct view, as she saw it, survived. They made their scrapbooks into tools to teach others to reinterpret and critique the press. The scrapbooks also preserved alternative histories and gave those histories ongoing life, as activists gathered and sorted information, reinterpreted it, and put it to new use in speeches and writings. Items that recirculated through newspaper exchanges and worked their way from the specialized suffrage press into the mainstream press were quoted or reprinted in the suffrage press, offering evidence that activists had made an impact. Activists thus used press notices to build a political and readerly community. Unlike the African American collectors, whose race pride extended to an understanding of black people as a political group and who sought to offer their communities the fruits of their collecting (for example at Dorsey's Museum or Gumby's Studio), women had much further to go to see themselves as a political group, subject to similar forces and constraints. Women's rights advocates who encouraged others to keep and use scrapbooks to monitor the press, and to create reference works of needed materials, helped to build women's consciousness of themselves as a class.

Newspaper clipping scrapbooks marked public activists' affiliation with the home and domesticity through trappings such as ornamented covers suitable for parlor display, or notes to their children or family, or by being bequeathed to the activists' families. Clara Barton, for example, had embarked on her work nursing Union soldiers and soliciting supplies for care of the wounded when, in 1864, she was excited and pleased to receive a "beautiful scrap-book designed for *my own* articles." Scrapbook keeping was not new to her; in her years as a teacher, she had kept scrapbooks made from old used copybooks or notebooks. This gift of the scrapbook celebrated her success in writing for Union soldiers, but the aesthetic refinement of the book was important to her as a bridge between the unconventional life she took up in that campaign and the domestic comforts and tokens she had left behind. It is "a beautiful article and I prize it much," she reiterates in her diary (Figure 5.1). Even the scrapbook of Susan B. Anthony, who never married, began with her father's suggestion when she was 35 that in a scrapbook "the many and amusing observations by the different papers...years hence, in your more solitary moments, you and maybe your children can look over."[3]

As documents of self-construction, the scrapbooks preserve evidence and testify to the activities and accomplishments of individuals working within larger movements. The African American scrapbook makers we have examined subsumed their individual or family experience into the larger picture of black life and history, as William Dorsey did when he surrounded his great grandmother's obituary with stories of other black centenarians, rather than make a scrapbook of family history. (Other women's rights activists took Frederick Douglass's approach and focused more tightly on their own life and work.) The scrapbooks of these women working for reform reveal them in the process of negotiating what it meant to take a place in public, and developing

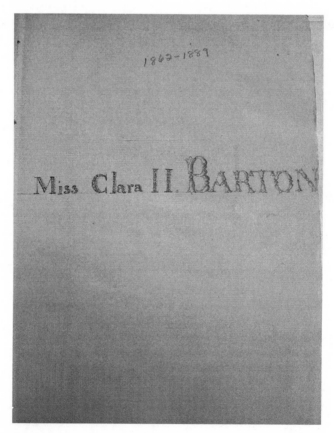

Figure 5.1 First page of Clara Barton's scrapbook for her "own articles." (Library of Congress)

strategies for using the press over the course of decades of women's rights struggles. Although the scrapbooks documenting their engagement in various movements preserve material about those movements, they often hew closely to individual involvement, as though to make the point that their individual development within the movement was worth attention, and stay within the interest range of their own household's readership. Keeping track of their multiplying identities might have seemed like more than enough to do, without documenting the entire movement. So, although Caroline Healey Dall preserved clippings about the 1855 women's rights convention in Boston, where she made her first speech, she clipped off parts of the articles that do not concern her own performance. Alice Moore Dunbar's (later Dunbar-Nelson) scrapbook on her involvement in a 1915 suffrage campaign includes almost exclusively the coverage of her own work on the campaign, with only a few items about the campaign's results to give it narrative closure. Matilda Joslyn Gage (1826–1898), a suffragist writer, speaker, and documenter of the suffrage movement, comments on this typical practice in one of her scrapbooks: "I find articles placed very irregularly & unsystematically in my scrapbooks, no less than three [scrapbooks] including this one having woman's rights articles, speeches, &c of <u>myself</u> and others and a fourth is in contemplation as neither of these three will hold my present accumulation of scraps." The narrative thread running through these scrapbooks is the writing, speaking, political involvement, and development of their makers.[4]

Like diaries, scrapbooks can be intended for self-reflection or for an audience. But scrapbooks are made by cutting and pasting mass-produced public materials, not by inscribing in the maker's own hand. Even scrapbooks that accumulate only the maker's own published writings mark the presence of those writings in the public space of the newspaper; they interpose layers of imagined readers, as they show how those writings—edited, framed by column heads, even if cut free from the newspapers' surroundings—appeared to others. The scrapbooks of women's rights activists are in constant negotiation with their sources. They document the lives of women writing for the press—often to support themselves—appearing in the press, and reading and commenting on the press, all through the medium of cut-and-pasted press clippings.

Although this chapter touches on scrapbooks made by such notable activists as suffragists Susan B. Anthony and Elizabeth Cady Stanton, and Frances Willard (leader of the largest nineteenth-century women's movement, the Women's Christian Temperance Union), most of the scrapbooks explored here are from less-prominent activists working around the country from the 1850s to the 1910s. Because scrapbooks are a decentralized medium—everyone can have one—stories about these less-well-known women's scrapbooks more clearly demonstrate that the strategies for using and responding to the press developed across a broad geographic and social spectrum and were taken up by women in various relationships to the movement. Additionally, two of the four compilers wrote about scrapbook making and use; they thus offer a richer understanding of how they and other women's rights activists made the scrapbooks tools in their political organizing work.

The first compiler is Caroline Healey Dall (1822–1912), a Boston abolitionist and women's rights pioneer who lectured, wrote, and kept a diary for seventy-five years, whose scrapbook was one stop along the way in her engagement with the press. Lillie Devereux Blake (1833–1913), a prolific New York–based writer who began speaking and writing for women's rights in 1869, worked to change legislation concerning women rather than focus more narrowly on getting the vote. Her columns in the suffrage press and sometimes in mainstream papers are part of her scrapbooks, and she wrote about using scrapbooks to teach about women's legal disadvantages in her novel *Fettered for Life*. Elizabeth Boynton Harbert (1845–1925), an Indiana-born women's rights activist in Illinois, was president of the chief Illinois women's suffrage organizations from 1876 to 1888 and wrote for suffrage publications, but she also reached a much larger readership through her column "The Woman's Kingdom," which ran from 1877 to 1884 in a Chicago mainstream daily. Her column built a community of women readers through the kinds of circuits of reprinting that, as we have seen, moved poetry and articles through the press in the nineteenth century, and she pointed out to her readers how scrapbooks fit into those circuits. Her own scrapbooks demonstrate how women speakers used scrapbooks to negotiate conflicting demands.

In a later generation, Alice Moore Dunbar, later Dunbar-Nelson (1875–1935), an African American writer, speaker, and teacher, created a scrapbook of her work on a 1915 Pennsylvania suffrage campaign. Her scrapbook reveals the suffrage campaigners' use of the newspaper in the more professionalized 1910s, and her own approaches to deploying her celebrity as Paul Laurence Dunbar's widow.

As they bridged public and domestic life, the scrapbooks reveal the work of impression management that women speaking in public undertook. In their scrapbooks activists created a coherent record of the great shifts in their individual lives, while they marked their own place in public through the press. Beyond their careers, their scrapbooks create alternative histories that point out women's accomplishments and the wrongs done to women. They talk back to the press and critique it, more often through pasting down their published responses than through the strategy of juxtaposing articles African American scrapbook makers developed. These women attempt to teach others to correctly read the press. The scrapbooks participate in and document the route of recirculation through which printed material for organizing—articles, notices of meetings, interviews, columns, and published letters—traveled through the country.

Crafting the Public Person

Women speaking in public were ridiculed and disapproved of in the midnineteenth and into the later nineteenth century, especially when they addressed mixed audiences for pay. Women who lectured on abolition, for example, sometimes met violent resistance through the midnineteenth century directed at both the abolitionist content of their talks and at their gender. "The appearances of the antislavery women on the platform were praised as angelic and excoriated as diabolical," notes Jean Fagan Yellin, "but in and through their public presence they dramatized the possibility of female freedom on a human level." Women speaking on women's rights met even stronger opposition and recognized public speaking as a vital, emblematic move out of second-class status. At best, public speaking by women was considered an affront to gentility. In 1869, Elizabeth Boynton (later Harbert) clipped for her scrapbook an item that criticized her own participation at a suffrage convention. The writer was "grieved to see the names of Mrs. Ames and our good Lizzie Boynton figuring so largely. Much as I am interested and greatly as I sympathize in the movement and desire its success, there are those who can do a nobler work for the cause than by public speaking." If women gave up claims to "nobility" simply by speaking, they would surely have difficulty persuading audiences to take their messages seriously.[5]

The opposition that women met as public speakers was very much on the minds of scrapbook makers as they documented their activist careers in their scrapbooks. Susan B. Anthony intended her thirty-three-volume scrapbook as a record for posterity. She had worked hard on the published multivolume *History of the Woman Suffrage Movement*. Her set of scrapbooks, which she arranged to place in the Library of Congress, was another way of telling her story and the story of the movement.

Significantly, Anthony begins Volume 1 of her scrapbook with an admonition from a church governing body instructing women not to speak, preach, or even teach: when "a woman assumes the place and tone of man as a public reformer ... her character becomes unnatural," it declared. That hand-copied, pasted-in sample of opposition is a volley to which the rest of the scrapbook responds. And yet the source of the clipping, as well as her use of it, imbeds this argument in a community of support for women's speaking. She copied it from the abolitionist newspaper *The Liberator*, which had published it to be held up for criticism. This clipping thus simultaneously documents the church's opposition *to* and her abolitionist community's support *for* women's speaking in public. Other clippings early in her scrapbook document opposition to women speaking for the temperance cause, and she frames the objections to her speaking for temperance as having prompted her to focus on women's rights. Perhaps in response to the church admonition not to speak or teach, Anthony—who had taught school for fifteen years before becoming a full-time activist—pasted in her teaching credentials. Teaching was a mode of public speaking generally permitted to women, so Anthony thus both refuted the objection to women speaking in public and illustrated the trajectory of her career as a public speaker. Her mode of pasting in the items forces the reader to engage physically with her argument: the objection to women's speaking in public is tipped in, pasted along a single edge, and the reader lifts the article as though turning a page, to disclose the teaching certificate pasted beneath it (Figures 5.2 and 5.3).[6]

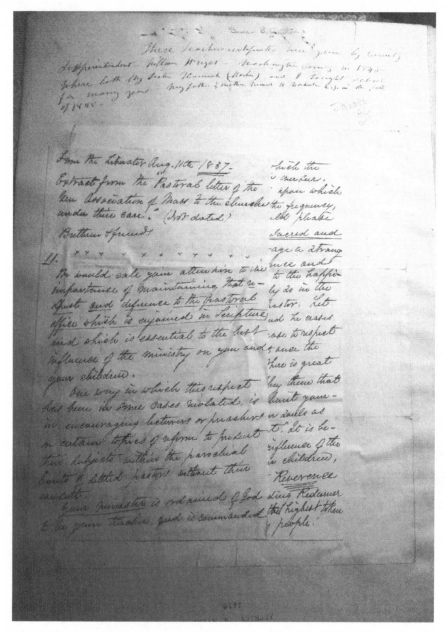

Figure 5.2 First page of Susan B. Anthony's scrapbook, with hand-copied article opposing women's speaking. (Library of Congress)

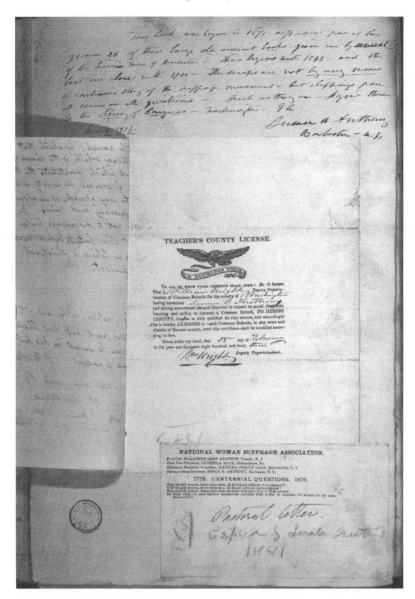

Figure 5.3 Teaching credentials of Susan B. Anthony and her sister, under layers that include the article criticizing women's public speaking. (Library of Congress)

Women's rights advocates often used the strategic argument that they sought power only to protect the home and family—and therefore performed domesticity and effaced their bodies, enacting justification for their presence on the platform within their performance. Women speakers had to assert allegiance to the domestic sphere, which would credential them as not "unnatural" women who could therefore be listened to, while paradoxically staking out public territory. Suffragists' demand for the vote and full citizenship pressed for power that was *not* based on a familial role. Speakers as well as attendees highlighted their domestic allegiance by publicly engaging in domestic activities such as knitting. "Mrs. Lucretia Mott, a Philadelphia Quaker, is meek in dress but not in spirit. She gets up and hammers away at woman's rights, politics and the Bible, with much vigor, then quietly resumes her knitting, to which she industriously applies herself when not speaking to the audience," a young woman attending her first women's rights meeting noted in her diary in 1853. Speakers adopted stratagems to screen or mute their bodies by remaining seated, not more assertively standing to speak. Some wore clothing such as the subdued gray Quaker costume that buttressed the seriousness of their message.[7]

Other women speakers took a different route, choosing to wear stylish garments made from rich fabrics, highlighting their femininity and social standing. Such choices registered awareness that their clothes would be commented on in the press; how they dressed was an element of their performance. Harbert, who knew from personal experience as a speaker that clothing choices were subject to press scrutiny and sneers, and who steered toward the stylish approach, even made a preemptive strike against such coverage in her column in a general newspaper, with an item, also preserved in her scrapbook, "How Women Suffragists Dress," detailing the highly suitable clothing worn by leadership at a "recent NY meeting." She takes notice of "Mrs. Lillie Devereux Blake, in brown silk of two shades ... [and] Mrs. E.C. Kay, the young colored lawyer, in handsome black silk."[8]

Although resistance to women speaking in public slackened, speaking—especially for pay—remained at the border of propriety into the beginning of the twentieth century. Mary Church Terrell (1863–1954) was active in African American women's clubs, women's suffrage, and later the NAACP. She was a member of the African American elite that was notoriously anxious about its gentility and noted in her autobiography that in 1895, when

> my husband consented to let me go on the lecture platform, some of his friends were so shocked and horrified that words simply failed them as they attempted to express their disapprobation and to show him what an irreparable mistake he was making. When a woman became deeply interested in civic affairs and started on a public career, they said, that was the beginning of a disastrous end. Under such circumstances a happy home was impossible.[9]

Women activists also had to showcase their competence as knowledgeable speakers, marshaling well-organized facts and evidence. Their scrapbooks embodied women's rights activists' platform strategies. Scrapbooks foreground both accomplishments and command of facts while asserting their domestic ties and womanliness. Formally and visually, the scrapbooks often show the women as highly organized workers, maintaining a file of their published work. Lillie Devereux Blake, for example, a prolific story writer for high-class publications such as *Harper's* and low-class ones such as the Beadle and Adams dime novel series and *Leslie's Illustrated Weekly*, made at least three separate scrapbooks for different uses. A blank book with numbered pages preserved a file of her writings on women's rights issues for mainstream dailies and syndicated via the American Press Association from 1876 to 1909. It included her letters to the editor. In a second scrapbook she preserved a file of her column "Our New York Letter," from the suffragist *Woman's Journal* from 1890 to 1904. Her scrapbooks thus separate writing for the suffrage press from writing for the mainstream press audience, and both of these types of women's rights writing from the popular story writing she did solely for money. They create an organized record of her writing. These scrapbooks of her own work are distinct from a third one she used to gather material to use in her talks and writing.[10]

The *type* of scrapbook used could display organization and seriousness as well. Elizabeth Boynton Harbert assembled different paper versions of herself in her scrapbooks. Some scrapbooks preserved records of her writing and speeches. The one she devoted to files of "The Woman's Kingdom," the weekly column she wrote for the *Chicago Inter Ocean* for twelve years, is a Mark Twain Self-Pasting Scrap Book. As we have seen, such scrapbooks embodied paradoxical qualities of association with Twain's authorship and creative persona, paired with associations of businesslike efficiency. The pre-glued columns enforced visual decorum, while the alphabetized indexing pages in the front of the book hinted at aspirations toward even greater orderliness.

Mark Twain Scrap Books were also selected by an anonymous women's rights supporter from the Rochester, New York, area, beginning about 1888, that collects more than fifty unsigned newspaper columns of "Woman's Word and Work" from an unnamed newspaper, and by the prominent professional orator Anna E. Dickinson (1842–1932), who began her lecturing career in 1860 and became a published novelist in 1868. Dickinson's begins with reviews and other material on her new venture as a playwright and actress in 1877, the year the Mark Twain Scrap Book was first manufactured. The technological innovation thus marks a shift in her own life, beyond lecturing and novel writing. Perhaps it was easier to assert herself in her new writing role under the aegis of Twain's name. (He had enjoyed moderate success as a playwright with his 1874 dramatization of portions of *The Gilded Age*.) Elizabeth Boynton Harbert's use of the Mark Twain Scrap Book for a collection entirely of her writing suggests a similar sense of lining herself up as a writer among other writers.[11]

But if the scrapbooks of women's rights speakers proclaimed order and professionalism both through content and through their formal qualities of organization, reinforced by the straight lines of pre-glued strips, scrapbooks also paralleled the speakers' demonstrating ties to domestic space and femininity. They brought the public world of the platform back home as scrapbooks that would fit into parlor decor. Like Clara Barton valuing a "beautiful" scrapbook for her public writings, Harbert's Mark Twain Scrap Book for her "Woman's Kingdom" columns softened its allegiance to the commercial world by way of a whimsical cover of a cherub with scissors and net (Figure 2.8), while Dickinson (who had made numerous scrapbooks using pastepot, brush, and blank books) chose the Mark Twain Scrap Book with a cherub knocking over a pastepot (Figure 2.6) on its cover. Some women linked their scrapbooks to parlor activities. Matilda Joslyn Gage includes among the notices of her speeches and clippings of her varied types of writing, an undated item reporting success in producing feminine fancy work: she won a two-dollar prize at a fair for a picture frame she festooned with flowers and vines.[12]

Maintaining genteel social status in the conservative South was especially difficult for—and incumbent upon—white women moving into any kind of public activity. Sallie Southall Cotten (1846–1929), a North Carolinian married to a Confederate veteran and planter, was a founder and leader of the women's club movement, and a supporter of women's education. She advocated that women serve on school boards, framing this activity as an extension of their responsibilities as mothers and a foot in the door of civic participation, but she did not endorse women's suffrage until the 1910s. Her private support for women's involvement in politics is hinted at by an early page in her scrapbook, from around 1885. The page contains a picture of the Washington Monument (much in the news when it was completed in 1884) next to an engraving of Belva Lockwood, a lawyer who was the first woman allowed to argue a case before the U.S. Supreme Court and who ran for president on the Equal Rights ticket in 1884 and 1888, financing her campaign with paid speeches. Cotten affixed a handwritten slip beneath Lockwood's portrait: "First female candidate for the position of Pres. United States." Cotten's juxtaposing a monument to a founding father with a pioneering woman in politics strongly suggests her support for Lockwood's enterprise. But rather than publicly endorse a role for women in politics, Cotten adhered to a moderate, deferential message.[13]

In Cotten's earliest public work, she was one of the "Lady Managers" for the 1893 World's Columbian Exposition. She addressed women to raise money for a North Carolina building there and eventually scaled back to a memorial to Virginia Dare, the first white child born to European colonists in Roanoke Colony, "the primal settlement of the Anglo-Saxon race in America," in what is now North Carolina. The goal of her organizing was far from transgressive and drew on the language of white supremacy as a warrant for white women's presence in public activities, but she softened even that extent of stepping into the public realm by holding meetings in hotel parlors, a genteel (and whites-only) space between public and private. She set up notices of meetings as formal invitations, such as one printed in italic type on a white card: "The Lady Managers for North Carolina of the Worlds Fair, invite the Ladies of Winston-Salem to meet them Tuesday afternoon, at 4 o'clock, in the Parlors of the Hotel ZIZENDORF, in order to consult with them."

These invitationlike notices, signed as "Mrs. Robt. Cotten," went into her scrap-book, along with articles about her later work, which took pains to distance Cotten from a demand for suffrage. She saved an undated article from this period that framed her speaking within acceptably feminine terms, and reasserted that such femininity ought to bar women from voting. It celebrated her as

> a beautiful and clever woman, whose interest in public matters and the movements that tend to elevate women, has not deprived her of her love of domesticity, or her confidence in the capacity of men as rulers ... she is the ideal advanced thinker, the clever woman, who believes in the influence that women can have in affairs of state, and still wear all the "ruffles" and "curls" that would not be proper at the ballot box.
>
> Mrs. Cotten has a beautifully modulated voice and her gentle, persua-sive utterances could win as many voters as she might ask in any assem-bly and save her the trouble of facing the clamoring multitude that surround the modern ballot box.[14]

A nearby article in her scrapbook asserts that Cotten "is an advocate of equal suffrage because she believes it to be right, not because she feels the need of it." Cotten wrote in the margin to correct the claim that she advocated suffrage. The scrapbook became a place to document her work for causes involving women, to mark the work's ties to domesticity, to assert the limits of her connection to political goals that may not have seemed feasible to work toward in North Carolina, and yet to hint at stronger ambitions.

If the scrapbooks of some nineteenth-century activists highlight the domestic connections of their public work, others bring public work back into the home specifically for the family. Elizabeth Boynton Harbert made two sets of scrap-books, one for her adoptive mother and others for herself; they play out her con-cern about the contradictory demands that women who engaged in public life had to meet. The scrapbooks were a site for trying out public personas on paper. Harbert had already been in the public eye: when barely twenty, she led a group of other young women in seeking admission to all-male Wabash College, and she wrote about it in the national publication *The Independent*. Harbert's earliest extant scrapbook clipped her 1868 series "A Hoosier Girl in Washington," written when she was twenty-three, the kind of travel correspondence that often gave journalists a start. The volume contains notices and reviews of the speeches on women's rights she began making shortly thereafter, and longer notices of wom-en's rights conventions she attended, with particular emphasis on her speeches there. But she made another scrapbook as a Christmas gift to her mother, in a decorative album with pages in alternating colors. Although it covers some of the same time period and contains some of the same material (copies of her writing), it includes more of her sentimental stories and fewer notices of her speeches—and some of these praise her femininity. One such item, "City News: Before

Suffrage, What?" for example, reports that her talk at a YMCA addressed crowded rooms and

> a most appreciative audience. The fair lecturer more than met the expec-
> tations and no one, even those entertaining views antagonistic to those
> expressed in the lecture, could fail to admire the calm, clear, dignified
> and elegant manner in which the subject was presented. Miss Boynton is
> one of the few women who can stand before an audience complete
> mistress of the situation, and at the same time lose none of her
> womanliness.[15]

The distinction between the version of her work that she offered her mother and the material she saved for herself is highlighted in a notice from the same period pasted into her own scrapbook but omitted from the one for her mother. It invites readers to "An Hour with the Strong Minded," reporting that Miss Boynton is "a zealous worker in the cause of removing the disability and subjection in which man's law has placed the feminine portion of our citizens." ("Strong minded" was a mocking term disciplining activist women for straying into masculine styles of expression.) It urges readers to hear this "young lecturess and modern 'Portia' pitch into the masculines generally, and tell them of all their faults and tyranny." Instead, the scrapbook for her mother includes notices of her marriage placed nonchronologically with notices about her speaking and writing. The end of the final page is filled out with newspaper notes on the birth of her first two children: "The happy home of Mr. and Mrs. Capt. Will. Harbert has been made more happy by the advent of a young defender of his country and a future advocate of women's rights." The paper version of her life she presented to her mother thus shapes a story of Harbert's accomplishments that includes a large sampling of her writing, leaning toward selections of her published sentimental Christmas stories complete with orphaned waifs, her "A Hoosier Girl in Washington" columns, a soupçon of her work speaking for suffrage, and a thorough collection of notices of marriage and motherhood.[16]

Harbert's scrapbooks exemplify the contradictory demands made of women on the lecture platform, demands she complained of in her 1871 novel *Out of Her Sphere*, where she noted that "many of our journalists even yet demand utter impossibilities of women, since to satisfy their requirements any woman desiring to enter the lyceum as a speaker should be *young, beautiful, well dressed, accom-plished,* a superior *housekeeper,* and the *mother* of *at least six children.*" Though she could critique such demands, like many other suffragists Harbert strategically presented women's involvement in government and politics, particularly in tem-perance work, as doing the housekeeping or mothering of the larger community. With this claim that motherhood and reform work were intertwined, it is not sur-prising that at least one scrapbook of clippings of her "Woman's Kingdom" col-umns was intended for her three children. She addressed them in a handwritten note in the scrapbook explaining why she stopped writing the column in 1884. "The Woman's Kingdom," was unusual in that it appeared regularly in a mainstream daily, the *Chicago Inter Ocean*, and went out to the rural Midwest in a weekly edition, reaching a far larger audience than she had when she wrote only in suffrage papers. Relinquishing it meant giving up an amplified podium speaking for women's rights that had helped create a women's print community.[17]

She writes in her scrapbook note, "Why I resigned Editorial Control of the Woman's Kingdom":

> Earnestly scrutinizing my motives I do not think that I have ever been allowed to make so true a sacrifice for the cause of woman as in the resigning my Editorship of the Kingdom. Entirely misunderstood by my best friends (outside of my precious home circle) as I expected to be in this matter, I am confident that they will some time recognize the moral conviction that made it impossible for me to work to circulate a journal that persisted in giving its editorial weight against Prohibition, and Woman Suffrage.
>
> I write this for you my dear children assuring you that the consciousness of having been true to one's own convictions of duty brings the greatest happiness of Earth. Since only by being true to ourselves can we be true to others.

If writing the column was part of "a mother's duty," then her children logically deserved an explanation for the shift she made in her job description. In her scrapbook note, her family becomes both the haven in a heartless world that the nineteenth-century middle-class man expected to find in the home and the final court of posterity whose judgment she must appeal to. The scrapbook was the medium of communication from her public speaking and writing to her family. It was a portfolio showing the children the accomplishments of her column, and it was the place to explain her choices about it.[18]

Press Coverage of Women on the Platform and Its Critique

Women speakers checked newspaper coverage as a gauge of how well the public was receiving their ideas, and they sought coverage for personal publicity; this need was stronger for those women who looked to the lecture platform to earn a living through lyceums and chautauquas, speaking on topics such as health and education, as well as women's rights. Speakers used scrapbooks as a tool to track newspaper reports of their talks, and to record their readers' reception of such reports. The scrapbook records reveal speakers tracking and writing back to papers to correct or criticize their own newspaper coverage, and critiquing the coverage of women's speeches more generally. Newspaper reportage gave women's rights workers complex feedback on their speaking, often telling more about journalistic hostility and condescension toward women speakers than about the audience's response. But since speakers needed the write-ups to draw the audience to the next meeting or speaking appearance, they saved them and learned to work with them. The scrapbooks reflect their public and private responses to such coverage. Women's rights activists taught one another to reinterpret, rebut, and not be discouraged by hostile press coverage.[19]

Anna E. Dickinson did not filter out unfavorable notices of her speaking in the extensive scrapbooks she kept of notices of her speeches. She was not shy about attacking her critics, whether in print, from the lecture platform, or even stepping out of role on stage, in costume, in her later acting career. In the privacy of her scrapbooks, too, she takes on her critics, occasionally annotating unfavorable reviews line by line. She comments on one hostile review of an 1871 talk in Oskaloosa, Iowa, for example, by heading it "This little country editor thinks he has done a big thing." The article begins by counting up the amount of money the "country editor" believes Dickinson made from her lecture, and she taunts in the margin that he "does not say how much he had for adv[ertising]"—pointing out that his newspaper itself benefited from her talk. The editor bestows the contradictory characterization a "Pennsylvania Dutch Quaker girl" and she responds in the margin "Oh my!" His attack focuses on her body, complaining of her "protruding chin" and saying she is "short and 'chunky'" and "may be sweet, but she looks somewhat sourish, has an arm and other muscular developments like a Roman gladiator. She wears short hair and dresses plainly." She responds: "Fighting weight 117 lbs.—Heavy gladiator." He implies that her gifts and performance are commonplace, writing, "Verily it is true that if Anna Dickinson was herself on last Friday night, Iowa has a thousand Annas." Her marginal response drips with the sarcasm she was known for: "Unhappy Iowa." Although Dickinson persistently read and collected negative reviews, even as a renowned speaker she was capable of being irritated enough by a notice in a very small town to bother talking back to it.[20]

Scrapbooks preserved their makers' published rebuttals of criticism as well. The Boston writer and women's rights pioneer Caroline Healey Dall exemplifies how scrapbook making connected public speaking, newspaper reading, and the newspaper reader's awareness of other readers. Her engagement with diaries and letters as well as scrapbooks illustrates something of the differences among these modes of life writing, and it allows fuller understanding of how Dall addressed and responded to the press as she embarked on her lecturing career. Her annotations in her scrapbook, too, unveil the otherwise hidden sources of aid she received.

Dall's scrapbook from the period when she began speaking in public shows her making her way into the public realm, using the public materials that reflect her new place in venues such as the lecture platform. She debuted at the September

1855 Woman's Rights Convention in Boston, speaking about Massachusetts laws. Newspaper remarks on her presence in the public realm do not mention that she is a novice; rather, she appears fully formed, with a natural place on the lecture platform. Her previous absence from general public notice at this time shows itself only in the varied spellings of her name in these clippings: Caroline Dale and Dahl, and Carolina Dall.

She showed her excitement about this talk through her thoroughness in clipping several pages worth of accounts of the convention from a number of newspapers, saving only the portion of each item that included some mention of her speech. Like many other women's rights scrapbooks, hers does not document the women's rights movement but rather her development within it. By the time she made this scrapbook, she had already written for twenty years in the diary that eventually spanned seventy-five years. The diary, too, records her excitement about the responses she received for her talk. After noting that her diary "pages...may never meet, any other eyes, than those of my children," and adding a sprinkling of self-deprecatory remarks, she records at length the praise she received after her speech and an impromptu debate afterward.

> My report...had a most unmerited success. E.P. Whipple said it was the ablest thing done in the Convention, some stupid person that it would have done Dan. Webster credit.! –!...[Even] conservative friends... sought me out, several of them, and spoke with warmth....Elizabeth Peabody said, "you don't know how much better you did than I thought you would." Several pressed my hand silently or said 'I am glad you belong to Boston.' Miss Hunt said, "How brave and beautiful you have been." Mrs. Severance, with her clear true face, "Noble words!"[21]

She wrote down even more such praise, perhaps as support for subsequent lectures. She was wise to keep such encouragement at hand, since her own family was profoundly discouraging. With this praise ringing in her ears, she thought seriously about lecturing for money, a more daring and transgressive act than just speaking in public, especially to mixed audiences, and got advice and further encouragement from the convention's chair, Paulina Wright Davis, editor of *The Una*. Davis shared her own experience as a lecturer and laid out her approach to impression management, writing of her need to control how her own lectures were discussed. Rather than call them lectures on scrofula, for instance, "I would prefer that they should be spoken of as lectures on Anatomy & Physiology or Science—as I always advertised scientific lectures, and was always more cordially welcomed among the scientific than among the reformers."[22]

Dall needed to earn money after her husband had a mental breakdown, lost his pulpit, and left for India, where he remained for most of his life, leaving her to raise their two children alone. Shortly before the Boston convention speech, she began turning down nonpaying writing requests, and after attending a lecture by her friend James Freeman Clarke (evidently heartened by its mediocrity) she speculated about how much he had been paid and wondered if she could lecture for money as well. Her diary reveals her well-off father's refusal to help her family with expenses, while her sister scolds her for wanting to lecture in public and her mother plants further doubts. But with her success at the convention behind her, she asks friends for help gaining and promoting lecture engagements. The public fruits of her work are saved in the scrapbook. Her diary shows a friend bringing her a one-paragraph notice of her first paid lecture in the *Boston Evening Traveller*: "It did not please me—I scribbled a little note wh[ich] I hope the Editor will print." Dall was disturbed because she believed that the *Traveller* editors had mischaracterized her position when they wrote, "In respect to the right and duties of the female sex, [Dall's] position was materially different from those of the so-called Woman's Rights Advocates." Dall may have been concerned that the mischaracterization could cost her lecture engagements.[23]

The scrapbook was where she saved both this one-paragraph objectionable notice and her eight-paragraph "little note" reply, addressing the slant as well as the content of the writing, and pulling apart its assumptions as carefully as a media studies scholar. Her reply takes the newspaper editors to task even for the wording of the notice's headline, which she assumes is meant as a slur. One paragraph from her note reads:

> "Lecture by a female." Female what? Parrot, popinjay, or monkey? This phrase does not hurt me on my own account, but I confess that I am weary of this popular coarseness. I suppose you will acknowledge, Messrs. Editors, that there are women who feel it their duty to address public audiences. If so, why add to the painful notoriety, which circumstances at present ensure them? If, after a brilliant political dinner, you were to see this caption—*Fine speech by a male*—what should you think? That your compositor had gone crazy, I am sure. Very truly yours. Caroline H. Dall.

Once her letter was published, she mailed out copies of the newspaper containing it, presumably sending them—though not the original notice—to other sources of lecturing engagements. She also pasted it into her scrapbook.[24]

In one sense, Dall simply interprets the *Traveller* article; but her scrapbook preserves a record of her awareness of others reading this article and the need to counteract a reading she believes will damage her. Dall imagines an uncritical reader who will not recognize the charged political implications of the *Traveller's* distressing editorial notice, and this concern sparks her letter. She averts the misreading and heightens the reader's attention to the editors' hostile intent by highlighting and critiquing their phrasing, while countering damaging statements (Figures 5.4 and 5.5).

Like her detailed diary record of praise for her speech, her preservation of the short notice and lengthy, thorough reply thus reminds her both of how

Figure 5.4 Notice of Caroline Healey Dall's 1856 lecture collected in her scrapbook, and her letter to the editors of the Traveller, objecting to the notice. (Massachusetts Historical Society)

necessary her efforts are and of her efficacy in the world. Far more than a souvenir announcement of her first paid lecture, it preserves and reinforces her recognition of the need to read over the shoulders of other readers, to be aware of how others will receive accounts of her performance, to speak back to those perceptions.

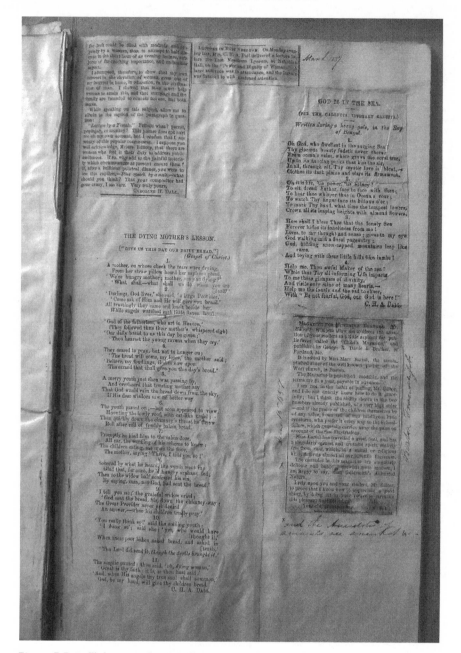

Figure 5.5 Dall's letter to the *Traveller*, continued. Page also shows handwritten corrections to another of her letters to a newspaper. (Massachusetts Historical Society)

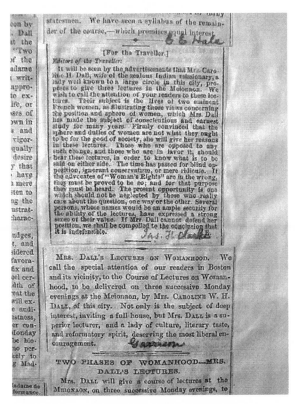

Figure 5.6 Unsigned notices of Dall lectures in her scrapbook, with authors' names written in by hand. (Massachusetts Historical Society)

Her scrapbook served as a kind of account book as well. After her experience with unfriendly coverage of her speeches, she managed press notices more strategically as she developed her lecturing business, and she kept track of these efforts in her scrapbook. The *Traveller*'s subsequent glowing unsigned notices were written by her friends, as her penciled annotations in her scrapbook reveal. They show that it is "Garrison" who calls her a "superior lecturer" or that T. S. King is the writer who regards her as "amply qualified by abilities, by faithful preparation, and enthusiasm for her subject, to do justice to the themes she will treat." The scrapbook becomes a set of blurbs to draw on, a private repository of truth, a reference for remembering who said what, and an account book of favors extended (Figure 5.6).

Activists whose anger at disparaging reception of their own speeches primed them to notice biases in the press went on to teach others how to read them. Elizabeth Boynton Harbert wrote and clipped an item in which Mary Livermore suggests that when newspapers lied about a suffrage gathering or covered it dismissively, this should be interpreted as a sign of "near triumph," because "its opposers do not dare to report it correctly." Harbert preserved this cue that activists ought not be discouraged or fault themselves for hostile coverage, but instead subject it to interrogation, examine its causes further, and perhaps reinterpret it as a form of tribute to their power.[25]

The feminist activist, speaker, and writer Lillie Devereux Blake extended and modeled the scrapbook as a mode of critique and a lesson in how to read the hostile press in her 1874 novel *Fettered for Life*. In one scene, a feminist doctor, Mrs. D'Arcy, shows her protégé Laura her extensive scrapbook that serves to critique the press's mode of writing about violence against women. She demonstrates that the scrapbook is not simply a private record; it can be shared and discussed. It is a pedagogical tool to teach Laura about political work, focusing on the press's power. Mrs. D'Arcy begins by pointing out the absurd contradictions in a list of blanket terms writers use to characterize *all* women, and then she moves to the press's power to besmirch women as a class.

> [T]he doctor opened her desk and took out her book of extracts. "Now here," she said, "are two expressions, in one of the most carefully-written journals of the city, which have especially annoyed me. In an article…occurs this expression: 'It is an understood thing, that for a certain sort of dirty job you must get a woman. Every man knows that the only animal that will strike an enemy when it is down is a woman!' When I read that, my blood boiled with indignation. This was penned by one of that sex whose members kill their wives and destroy young girls, and I thought of the men who had struck helpless women unable to rise; of the husbands who have kicked their wives to death when they were in a situation that made them peculiarly powerless, and especially liable to injury; of murdered girls whom fiends in the form of men have rendered senseless by brutal violence and then deliberately killed, that they might not witness against them."

A sharp critic of the press, the doctor is alert not only to events reported in the press but to *how* they are reported. Massing her clippings together in her scrapbook allows her to demonstrate patterns of misrepresentation. As she instructs Laura about the insulting language that ignores men's power and violence but blames women for their problems, she uses her scrapbook to illustrate issues of representation and documentation.[26]

Activists saw much in the press to critique, but they also needed the press to communicate their own messages and build community. Activists published women's rights periodicals such as the *Una*, briefly edited by Caroline Dall, and the longer-lasting *Revolution* and *Woman's Journal*, among others. Like other nineteenth-century newspapers that exchanged copies with one another and freely reprinted material, these newspapers passed along and reprinted items from each other's pages and exchanged with sympathetic papers such as the abolitionist *Liberator*. They thus created a stronger sense of common interests.

Women's Columns and Recirculation

Cutting and pasting articles into exchanges and scrapbooks moved women's rights ideas and information beyond publications that preached to the already converted. The journalist Elizabeth Boynton Harbert used a contemporary industrial metaphor to explain her understanding of the press's potential to spread the impact of the women's reform movement. Exchanges and recirculation made the press into "that Corliss engine of public sentiment," Harbert explained in a handbill announcing that her column "The Woman's Kingdom" would appear in the *Chicago Inter Ocean*, a Chicago Republican newspaper. Her column offered an unusual opportunity to move women's rights discussion to a large-circulation paper, where readers seeking news or other features would stumble upon it; it was also a vehicle to reach other papers with which the *Chicago Inter Ocean* exchanged articles. Just as the Corliss engine circulated steam and turned it into power, the press circulated articles and converted them into "public sentiment."[27]

"The Woman's Kingdom" created the sense that Harbert's readers were a community in a variety of ways. When she reported receiving "hundreds of letters" from readers on a subject, she concretized the "imagined community" of her column's readers, to use Benedict Anderson's concept of newspaper readers' awareness of one another as having significant interests in common. Anderson's theory of nationhood forged by newspaper reading elucidates Harbert's work in her newspaper column for Midwestern women. Her readers became a community of Midwestern women, many living on farms, with a regional identity who sought a larger role for women in a world struggle. By reading and responding to her column in the *Chicago Inter Ocean*'s weekly edition, they gained a community voice. Even readers who did not write letters to her themselves knew that letters from readers were always welcome and that other readers and writers expressed thoughts similar to their own. Harbert's column connected them not just to one another but to the women of exemplary accomplishments and to a literary world in the Midwest and beyond. Through the Corliss engine of recirculation, she clipped and passed along items from other papers and books, extending the sense of community and inviting her readers to see themselves as literate people keeping abreast of important work.

Her readers helped to keep that community going. Clara Berwick Colby, vice president of the Nebraska Woman Suffrage Association, wrote to Harbert that she had told the editors of the *Chicago Inter Ocean* that she was resubscribing specifically because of Harbert's column, and that she recommended it to other Nebraska women. The "Woman's Kingdom" noted other columns on women's rights issues appearing in general newspapers. Harbert's work inspired such columnists as Carrie Chapman (later Catt), whose "Woman's World" column in the Mason City, Iowa, *Republican* similarly "listed conspicuous accomplishments of women, . . . harvested notes of feminist interest from other publications," and advocated organizing for suffrage. Catt wrote to Harbert more than thirty years later, reflecting on the latter's effect on her:

When I was a young girl in Iowa, you were editor of the woman's column in the Interocean which came weekly to our home. I never failed to read those columns and I have always felt that your words at that time made a very great impression upon me in determining to work for woman suffrage.[28]

Women Reading News

Women newspaper readers were often derided for supposedly being interested only in fashion news and household hints. *Puck's* cartoon in Figure Intro.4 of a modern apartment where everything is delivered forecasts future media catering to segmented readership and niche markets; it also presents a common idea of women's reading. Only fashion and religious news unspool for the women of the house. With this background, we can see how radical Harbert's column and her success in publishing it in a mainstream daily was. From its first announcement "The Woman's Kingdom" implicitly critiqued other newspaper "women's columns": It was to be a "department not devoted to Fashion or Cookery, but . . . in lieu of 'what she wears' and 'what she eats,' will oftener contain account of 'what she says,' and 'what she does.'" The space Harbert had staked out within the largely male virtual space of the newspaper allowed her to encourage women to participate in the assumed-male space of newspaper reading.[29]

This critique of women's columns was central to Harbert's analysis of competition for women's time and her advocacy of reading, especially newspaper reading. Even farm women taken up with the boundless work demands of a farm could and should make time to read, she reiterated. This was all the more true for women with more control over their time. Harbert tells in her column of recommending a book to a friend to read to her children: "'Don't say read it to the children to me,' was the reply. 'I have not a minute to read the daily papers.' And then I looked at her six ruffles and unnumbered yards of knife pleating on her own dress and tucks and puffs ad infinitum on the child's dress." Harbert asserts that a woman who has time to iron pleats or to read about fashion would be better off reading the news of the country or the world.[30]

When a reader with two young children wrote to object that she had no time to read the newspaper, Harbert referred to her own household as a warrant for her domestic expertise and for her reordered priorities. "I for the first time lift the veil of the kingdom most sacred to every true woman, the sacred shrine of home" to advocate simplified housekeeping and the husband's cooperation: "thanks to the kindly thoughtfulness and unselfishness of the father, the piano has not been . . . closed nor the morning paper unread; although, pies have been almost unknown quantities and very many Mrs. Grundys [the voice of convention] have taken exception to the methods adopted."[31]

Harbert recirculated the work of other writers and speakers who advocated women's newspaper reading, especially for farm women. By way of supplying practical help on the topic, she excerpted a long passage from Julia McNair Wright's *The Complete Home* on how cash-poor farm families could obtain reading matter.

> I was at Cousin Ann's son's farm one day, and Reed was walking about with me showing me his territories.... [O]ne handsome young heifer he called "Books," and a big sheep "Maga," which he informed me was "short for magazines," and a family of black Spanish hens ran to the call of "Papers!" ... He told me that when he married, his mother gave him a pair of black Spanish fowls, and told him to let their produce *keep him in papers*. He accordingly called them "papers" for fun, and he found that the eggs and chickens would supply him handsomely with papers. When the supply exceeded the demand he would lay the surplus up to begin a fund for providing his children with reading.[32]

Harbert offered advice on budgeting resources for reading matter, while signaling to farm women that she understood their concerns. An "excellent array of papers" constituted the library of another farm family, in an account of a speech she reprinted from an agricultural fair. Harbert's reprinting from other sources for her column extended the chorus of voices advocating newspaper reading and backed her claims about it.[33]

Harbert asserted that women's newspaper reading did not mean selfishly pulling away from familial duties—unlike the paterfamilias-in-training in the *Harper's Young People* cartoon "He Knew His Part" (Figure 5.7), who withdraws from the family behind his newspaper—but rather enhanced family relationships. When women engaged with periodicals, just as when they worked for the community, including their work for women's rights, they simply extended their domestic duties, Harbert explained.

Scrapbooks were a way to cultivate and encourage newspaper reading. Clippings moved up in status from newspaper to book—or in Cousin Reed's (Read) barnyard hierarchy, from chickens to cows—emerging as homemade histories, valuable to entire communities, like the set of Civil War scrapbooks made by Mrs. G. S. Orth of Indiana, which Harbert praised in her column.

Harbert's columns circulated into the world, where others excerpted and quoted them; they also circulated privately into Harbert's and other people's scrapbooks. She enhanced the value of this private circulation by encouraging her readers to make scrapbooks from newspaper clippings. Women who had collected Harbert's columns wrote in to ask that the accounts of their scrapbook making be relayed to other readers; they then circulated gratitude back to Harbert. For example, Harbert published a letter from a reader who signs herself "One of Many":

Figure 5.7 "He knew his part," *Harper's Young People* cartoon commenting on expected gender division in newspaper reading. The girl suggests they play that they are married. She will bring the baby to show its father. He responds, "and I will say, 'Don't bother me now; I want to read the paper.'" 8 Feb. 1887, 244.

> I have for years treasured scraps that I liked, and I thought it might be of interest to you and your many readers to know that I have a book filled almost entirely with selections from "Woman's Kingdom." . . . I appreciate the effort you have put forth for the advancement of sister women, and I wish you to know it.[34]

Correcting the Record: Scrapbooks as Alternative Histories

The women's rights activists shared with African American scrapbook makers the idea of mining the newspaper for an alternative history and preserving that history in scrapbooks. The scrapbooks they created included information on women's accomplishments in the world, on women's rights activism, and on injustice and brutality toward women.

The "accomplishments" strain is perhaps best understood as a private version of compiling exemplary biographies of women, a longstanding proto-feminist practice, dating back to Christine de Pizan in the fifteenth century. It has been a mode of demonstrating women's fitness for various activities, understood as "sound evidence concerning women's nature and as reliable guides to feminine excellence," Alison Booth notes in her study of collective biographies of women.

Scrapbooks of this kind saved information about women's achievements not available in published books. One writer in a column in *The Ladies' Home Journal* noted that she had started making scrapbooks on illustrious "persons" for a visiting child, but she then notes that "one volume I have set apart for the scraps about woman, and the noble work she is doing in the world." Her scrapbook about women is a separate category from "statesmen, authors of prose and poetry, scientific men," etc. Her unstated reasons for separating them hover between notions of propriety based on separate spheres ideology, which suggests that men and women's work ought not be made the object of implicit comparison by juxtaposition, and the biographical-compilation model of singling women out to make them exemplary models. "The Woman's Kingdom" column, which some of Harbert's readers clipped for their scrapbooks, presented exemplary women and their activities as one mode of arguing for women's rights and of showing what was possible for women to do. (The published racial uplift collections discussed in Chapter 4 have overlapping inspirational motivations.)[35]

Harbert spelled out the need for such information on women, suggesting in the "Woman's Kingdom" that the scrapbook could fill in for the absence of information in books on women's lives and situations:

> What is the need of a scrap-book in these days of encyclopedias? do you ask. I would answer, attempt to prepare a paper upon the progress of the higher education of women; the admission of women to the professions; women's industries; and consult the four popular encyclopedias, and tell me how much information you will find.[36]

Harbert complained that information specifically on achievements and accomplishments of women is missing from reference books. Since newspapers focus on what is most current, they more reliably supply information on fast-moving advances. Her newspaper column, of course, provided such information. Some women's rights activists used scrapbooks precisely as Harbert suggested, to compile material for papers or speeches. As part of a strategy of chipping away at the wall around the vote by winning the vote for specific groups of women in particular elections, Anne Fitzhugh Miller, of the Political Equality Club in Geneva, New York, drew on her scrapbook collection of material on women taxpayers of Geneva to urge women taxpayers to assert their right to vote in a 1902 local election; she used her scrapbook compilation in testimony before a state senate committee urging an extension of the franchise. Miller converted newspaper reports into data that she could slice differently according to the occasion, and indexed them, to more readily find information by topic. Caroline Dall, too, understood Harbert's proposed use of scrapbooks. She filled her scrapbooks with both her own speeches and writings, and some of the statistics and other informational matter that went into them as well as her articles and accounts of her speeches. Margherita Arlina Hamm, a suffragist and pioneering woman war reporter, used scrapbooks both to compile information for her writings devoted to "women in the field of invention and discovery, to women in pharmacy and medicine, and to the Women's Christian Temperance Union" and to track the results. Scrapbooks were a modern tool for engaging and reusing information, and suffrage campaigners saw them as something like blogs, which could record the press's information and critique it.[37]

Even the categories that activists created for their alternative histories could be politically and conceptually innovative. To think of brutality toward women as a category, for example, requires that one hold the idea that women are a class or group subject to injustice, who occupy a particular position in law. Scrapbook collecting of items on that topic marks a developing consciousness of subjugation, and also that the scrapbook makers were subject to the same forces, rather than believing the common claim in such accounts that brutality was normal, or that some women had bad luck or deserved it. Temperance activists might focus on the attacker's drinking when they compiled similar materials as evidence of the destructiveness of drink and an argument to prohibit alcohol and wove the articles into speeches or into their own writings. Blake collected articles on men beating their wives and used them when she wrote and spoke. But for activists like Blake, such collections were evidence for the need to change laws and attitudes applying to women and to marriage.

In Blake's 1874 novel *Fettered for Life*, the feminist doctor's scrapbooks not only critique the press, as we saw earlier, but furnish a record of legal tolerance of men who mistreat their wives. Laura learns of the dismal legal situation of abused women from her older friend, the doctor:

"Then there is legal authority for a man's abuse and ill-treatment of his wife?"

"Certainly; here are a few instances of man's brutality and its reward, taken from various papers, and which I have preserved."

The doctor opened a drawer in a table and took from it a book containing slips. From these she read:

"John W. Smith, who beat his wife on the head with a crowbar, was lately sentenced to six months' imprisonment! The woman's life was at one time despaired of; but she did not die, and so he escaped any serious punishment."

"Thomas Fitzpatrick, who beat and kicked his wife to death a few days ago, at their residence in Van Brunt street, was yesterday indicted by the Grand Jury for murder in the first degree. He was arraigned, and his trial set down for the October term of the Court of Oyer and Terminer. The District-Attorney expressed a doubt whether the prisoner could be tried for anything but manslaughter, and he was admitted to bail in one thousand dollars."

"Now just contrast the amount of bail in this last case with that charged for offences against the property of other men."

Mrs. D'Arcy reads from her scrapbook examples of men charged heavy bail for crimes against property.

> "It is horrible injustice!" exclaimed Laura, her gray eyes glowing with excitement.
> "Horrible, indeed!" repeated Mrs. D'Arcy; "but it is no wonder that such atrocities are lightly punished, when we realize what is the general tone of our laws with regard to women."[38]

The exemplary, ideal scrapbook within the novel stores documentary evidence of the legal standing of women, laying out the narrative thread of an argument. It aggregates isolated stories of men brutalizing their wives and escaping appropriate punishment and converts them into data that can then be mined and used in new ways. The doctor presents the scrapbook as a teaching tool. Instructing Laura in its meaning introduces her to the concept that women are a class whose subjection is inscribed in law. Laura models and expresses the indignation a reader should feel in confronting this situation, while the doctor points out that political power is the solution.

Although the legal horrors seem entirely evident from Mrs. D'Arcy's strategy of juxtaposition, comparing assaults on women with assaults on property, not everyone knows how to read this material correctly:

> "What flagrant injustice!" cried Laura. "It seems amazing that men do not hasten at once to do away with such oppression."
> "They do not realize it, my dear," said Mrs. D'Arcy, mildly. "A change will take place in time, let us hope."

The doctor expresses faith that the problem with the law is that "men" do not recognize the injustice. Compiling data to make the point, and educating people to use it, is the logical solution, and the scrapbook is one way to pull together the information.[39]

Blake herself collected material like the doctor's to use in her speeches. She kept a scrapbook she entitled "Articles about Woman's Position and Interesting Items," pasted into an easy-to-carry daily diary overriding its intended use. It covers material before and after she wrote the novel. She collected items on Susan B. Anthony's 1873 attempt to vote, and on women's wages as tailors and hairdressers, for example, but also stories of "everyday heroism" and of brutality, evidently intended to be used as source material, either for fiction or for talks. At least one, an 1874 news account of two men kicking a woman to death, made its way into one of her suffrage speeches; it may have been a source for Fitzpatrick's case in the novel's clipping. The act of collecting these items on subjugation in scrapbooks suggests the makers had a use for it, possibly to teach others.[40]

When activists saved work on their own writing and speeches, they contributed to an alternative history of women's rights activism. Others activists collected such material on behalf of clubs or organizations, compiling it on suffrage and women's rights conventions, campaigns, and activities. They thus created alternative histories of their movements as a whole. Frances Willard, for example, called on every local, state, and national division of the Women's Christian Temperance Union to preserve the history of its activities. Not just favorable items were to be kept; they should have "scrapbooks of its history as written up by current journalists, for while they may abuse us one day they are sure to praise us the next, so that the general average is not far from fair. Literature, badges, banners, mottoes, programs, photographs, should all be kept." She noted by way of encouragement that her own large collection of scrapbooks would be part of this larger, valuable gathering. It included a scrapbook Willard's mother had made entirely of journalistic abuse her daughter had received, which Willard noted with satisfaction had grown in size in the previous year.[41]

Women's rights activists documenting the history of the suffrage movement were conscious of creating a record, as they focused on particular events or created institutional histories of groups in which they participated. Elizabeth Cady Stanton, for example, created a scrapbook of the 1848 Seneca Falls Woman's Rights Convention that contained newspaper clippings from supportive and hostile newspapers. Unlike Dall, who collected accounts chiefly of her own appearances at a convention, Stanton documented the event. Her record of the Seneca Falls convention was an organizing tool and contact list: she carefully included the name of each source paper, and often the name of its editor or publisher. For her daughter, Harriot Stanton Blatch, born eight years after the convention, this scrapbook became a more general repository for the history of the movement and her mother's involvement in it. As Blatch repurposed the now-outdated organizing tool with its long-dead contacts, she interpreted the focus of this scrapbook more broadly and supplemented it by pasting in later material related to her mother or to the convention, such as a commemorative list of all the signers of the convention's "Declaration of Sentiments" printed in 1908, six years after Stanton's death. In Blatch's hands, a useful tool reemerges as a souvenir and family document.[42]

Other scrapbook compilers focused on institutional history. So Elizabeth Smith Miller and her daughter Anne Fitzhugh Miller of Geneva, New York, assembled scrapbooks from 1897 and 1911 preserving the history of the local suffrage group they had organized, the Geneva Political Equality Club. In an address to her group, Anne Fitzhugh Miller praised the value of her club's history, compiled in scrapbooks, and called for every club to have a scrapbook. In the 1910s, the by then large and well-organized suffrage movement hired organizers and speakers and ran complex campaigns. Tracking press coverage became a broad-based, more professionalized enterprise, often aided by subscribing to clipping bureaus as well as hiring dedicated publicity agents. A wealthy supporter of the National

Women's Party, Alva Vanderbilt Belmont, paid clipping services, which created a nineteen-volume scrapbook on the organization for her for eight years, and other scrapbooks on related organizations. Scattershot professionalization did not guarantee that all materials would be gathered or organized in a permanent fashion, however, or that they would be preserved as documentation of the struggle. When former suffragists Katherine Sumney and Grace Richardson of Nebraska in the 1940s produced retrospective scrapbooks documenting their version of the movement they had devoted themselves to, they stored papers in an old flour can and passed the project back and forth over the course of years of working on it.[43]

Individual Accomplishments: Alice Moore Dunbar-Nelson

By the 1910s, women's public speaking was more routine, no longer meeting fierce opposition, and suffrage speaking was more professionalized. Rather than receiving pay from lecture bureaus and on the lyceum circuit (which highly accomplished speakers such as Anna Dickinson and Mary E. Livermore had done in the 1870s and 1880s), in the final decade of the push for the vote, able suffragists were hired by suffrage organizations to conduct campaigns. They targeted speakers at specific communities in the course of statewide campaigns to ratify women's suffrage amendments. Alice Moore Dunbar was one such speaker and organizer.

Like their nineteenth-century forerunners, suffragists in the 1910s documented their work in scrapbooks for the organization and cause, and as well to mark their individual accomplishments. Alice Moore Dunbar (later Dunbar-Nelson), more often known in the press as Mrs. Paul Laurence Dunbar, was an African American writer, teacher, and activist. She spent the summer and fall of 1915 working on a campaign to pass a women's suffrage resolution in Pennsylvania, ending in a November 2 ballot. Her scrapbook includes the months of her involvement, using press clippings—nearly all from the white press—handbills, and bits of advertising. It also documents African American participation in the suffrage campaign not otherwise visible in suffrage histories.[44]

The resulting story negotiates between at least two narrative layers. One contains public perceptions of Dunbar's persona and actions, which she managed through interviews, speeches, her choice of name, and selection of venues. The underlying layer—the unseen glue beneath the scrapbook pieces—is the information on her life carefully omitted from the public record.

Dunbar may have chosen to document her speaking tour in a scrapbook because she was well aware of how difficult it was to find documentation of the work of black speakers. In 1913 she had edited the five-hundred-page compendium *Masterpieces of Negro Eloquence: The Best Speeches Delivered by the Negro from the Days of Slavery to the Present Time*. Introducing it, she notes, "Much of the best is

lost; much of it is hidden away in forgotten places. We have not always appreciated our own work sufficiently to preserve it, and thus much valuable material is
wasted." Help in recovering the speeches that she did find came to her from the
African American journalist John E. Bruce (known as Bruce Grit), a scrapbook
compiler, and Arthur Schomburg, president and secretary of the Negro Society for
Historical Research. Both of them were collectors of books and newspapers on
African American life and history. And although her introduction to the anthology
complains that it "has been difficult to obtain good speeches from those who are
living because of their innate modesty, either in not desiring to appear in print, or
in having thought so little of their efforts as to have lost them," she, too, omitted
her own speeches from her scrapbook. Several news articles in the scrapbook
reported them in some detail, however.[45]

The multiple constituencies the suffrage movement engaged by 1915 included
the Negro Women's Equal Franchise League and the College Women's Equal
Suffrage League. Various groups of male voters were addressed by speakers who
would most likely to appeal to them. This segmented approach meant that very
different messages might be in circulation to particular groups. The scrapbook
Alice Dunbar made of her work on the Pennsylvania campaign, for which the
National American Woman Suffrage Association's speakers bureau endeavored to
"supply each locality with the speaker best suited to it," shows her speaking both
to black and mixed audiences. Her presence—probably salaried—in this campaign
demonstrates the movement's awareness that garnering votes from multiple constituencies was crucial to victory. Other speakers on the campaign therefore
included African American women's club activist Mary Church Terrell, radical
economist Scott Nearing, Pittsburgh Reform Rabbi J. Leonard Levy, and German
community worker Clara S. Laddey. Dunbar evidently took time off from teaching
and administrative work at Howard High School in Wilmington, Delaware, and
from giving talks on literature for her speeches to open air rallies and select social
clubs.[46]

Because names and the endorsements and implied endorsements they carried
were valuable, as Mrs. Paul Laurence Dunbar her name itself was an asset.
Although she and the poet had separated in 1902 after three years of marriage,
his death in 1906 made her his widow. Her second brief marriage, after Dunbar's
death, had been secret, and her marriage to Robert Nelson took place in 1916, and
so nearly all the clippings in her 1915 suffrage campaign scrapbook feature her as
Mrs. Paul Laurence Dunbar, drawing on his substantial fame in the black and
white communities. The campaign in the black community positioned other
names and associations strategically as well. A picture of Lincoln crowds the text
of one flyer, headed "Colored Citizens, Where Do You Stand?" Its caption reads,
"Abraham Lincoln, emancipator, said: 'I go for all sharing the privileges of the
government who assist in bearing its burdens; by no means excluding women.'"
Other events paired her speech with a performance by the violinist Joseph
Douglass, whose name, as the grandson of Frederick Douglass, was also an asset.

A speaker during at least one additional event referred to the elder Douglass's support for women's suffrage.[47]

As they had with nineteenth-century speakers, newspapers made Dunbar's physical appearance and demeanor the subject of interest and comment. She mobilized that interest strategically in modes that new technologies offered. The glamorous publicity photo repeated in ten clippings in the thirty-page scrapbook was evidently sent out to newspapers for reproduction. Taken approximately fifteen years before the campaign, when she lived with Dunbar, it shows a pensive, bare-shouldered, light-skinned, possibly racially ambiguous woman. The repurposed household budget book that she used for her scrapbook features a copy of it pasted on the cover. It is paired with stamps of a map shaded to show suffrage progress, with the slogan "Votes for Women: The map proves it a success," the kind of decorative paper ephemera that had become increasingly common in suffrage campaigns (Figure 5.8). She thus situated this photo of herself as a married woman in her twenties as emblematic of her participation in the campaign, in her forties.[48]

Dunbar's glamour shot reinforced and directed the angle of the newspapers' interest in her appearance, so that one weekly called her "a youthful looking person." One white newspaper proclaimed, as she arrived in Pennsylvania, that

Figure 5.8 Alice Dunbar-Nelson's scrapbook cover with her picture and ad, "Votes for Women: The map proves it a success." (University of Delaware Special Collections)

"her exceptional beauty has proved irresistible to would-be opponents and she has taken entire delegations of negro clergymen by storm." Another article praised her both for her appearance and the arguments tailored to the black men whose votes she sought:

> Tall and graceful, a voice beautifully modulated, and an easy flow of force-ful, logical arguments could not fail to move her audience. The burden of her arguments were to the point, how suffrage would help the colored people as a race, how the colored woman with a ballot could help her colored men, which direct benefit the men would derive from the increased colored vote. Much nodding of heads and murmurs of approval punctuated her telling arguments.

Her personal connection to Paul Laurence Dunbar was a rich piece of social capital for negotiating the speaker's platform and the press. Dunbar had been not only a beloved and revered poet but an icon of black achievement, who already had black schools, hospitals, libraries, and other African American institutions named after him. Alice Dunbar's marriage to him guaranteed the interest of the white newspa-pers that wrote about her and of the audiences that attended her speeches. Headlines and articles refer to her as "Widow of Negro Poet" and "the wife of the noted negro poet Paul Laurence Dunbar." Recitationists followed her on the platform to entertain by performing his poems. Her years of separation from him disappeared, so "she has taught school since the death of her husband," one reported.[49]

In one interview, after telling a reporter that her "eight years of marriage" to Dunbar were the happiest years of her life, she put him forward as "an ardent suf-fragist long before she was." He suddenly became an element in a conversion nar-rative when she applied his posthumous endorsement to the campaign.

> She said, that like many other women, she had always believed in suffrage but she did not quite like the idea of going to the polls to register her ballot. One day, while they were in Colorado, Mr. Dunbar drove around to a voting place, so that she could see just how the women voted, and this of course converted her.

Casting herself as a timid lady who must be persuaded that it is appropriate for women to go to the polls, she invited men to identify with Paul Laurence Dunbar's role not simply supporting women's suffrage but taking the lead as an encour-aging guide. She used her (real or invented) personal history for political ends and relied on public interest in the private life of the celebrated black poet to ensure attention to her story. It was important to her audience that, as one article reported, "their marriage was ideal. Each was suited to the other in intelligence, ideals and life work."[50]

At a speech a week before the ballot, she addressed the audience in a select black club with a resonant repeated metaphor she had used before, suggesting that the continuing denial of the vote to women was a form of abuse that men within the community could choose to rectify or perpetuate: "I appeal to you, men, not to slap your wives, sisters and mothers in the face on November 2, but vote 'yes' on this question." Her audience would probably not have known that Dunbar had physically abused her, and that she had left him in 1902 after he badly beat her. Acknowledging the unhappiness of her marriage to Dunbar, let alone the complex details of it, would have meant tarnishing his reputation and thus the value of his name, and thus her own reputation as well. In the absence of any accepted analysis, at the time, of violence against women as a political problem, her mention of an abusive marriage could also undermine the plea for women's equality by suggesting that her interest in women's rights stemmed from personal sorrow or bitterness. In the white press, it would have been immediately enfolded into virulent racial stereotypes and thus undermined the status of all black people by association, and especially that of the black men whose votes she sought. Although Paul Laurence Dunbar had literally slapped and kicked her, she could use his name to appeal to her audience—particularly the men, who of course were the only ones voting—to end the abuse that denial of the franchise constituted.[51]

Her scrapbook ends with a palm card addressed to voters: "The women of Pennsylvania have faith in you. They believe YOU believe in fair play. Here's your chance to prove it." The columns of vote tallies she pasted in show that although the suffrage amendment lost, it carried in Pittsburgh, where she had done much of her work. She pasted a poem by Florence Ripley Mastin, "An Older Woman to a Younger," dated the day after the unsuccessful ballot, into the inside front cover. Dedicated to suffragist Anna Howard Shaw, it is an exhortation to keep fighting, and await the spring of ultimate victory.[52]

As we have seen, nineteenth-century women's rights activists had to demonstrate loyalty to Victorian ideals of women's place in the home, even while disrupting it, in order to be taken seriously on the platform; their scrapbooks likewise perform their domestic allegiances. Although white suffragists responded to the argument that leaving home to vote would take them away from their domestic duties by minimizing the commitment required, pointing out that voting took no more time than going to church, as a suffragist of a later period and as an African American working woman Dunbar took a different tack. Speaking in African American spaces, she was explicit about black household economics and the disconnect between black women's work and the claim that women would be soiled by politics. Having deployed several sorts of capital to secure a place on the platform, Dunbar used it to make a point that was unspoken elsewhere.

> Our women are the least at home. Only one out of every 90 can remain in the home. She dare not stay at home and face want and suffering, and

I am talking about the married woman now...as a race we have no leisure class; all of us have to work some sort of a way. There are 42 races in this country and we are the only one where all the women work. We hear politics is awful. You shouldn't be in the mire. Well. Politics is the only dirt we don't get into at present.

Later, speaking to a mixed white and black crowd just before the election, she repeated but softened the point, noting that the eight million working women in the country couldn't afford to stay home if they wanted to, and asserted "we realize that women's place is in the home and that's why we want her to have equal suffrage with men."[53]

As she highlighted publicly neglected facts of women's personal and economic lives—particularly black women's lives—and selectively framed her own personal history, Dunbar made her political demands visible and increasingly popular, especially to African Americans.

*

The scrapbooks of women's rights activists were like those of other speakers whose scrapbooks were inextricably tied with the labor and background work of public lecturing. They were a repository for converting information into usable data, and they were the working materials of clergymen and other speakers. Women's rights scrapbooks were not unique but they played a special role in these women's project of publicly performing their domestic fitness, straddling or negotiating between home and podium.

The scrapbook-making doctor in Lillie Devereux Blake's novel concludes her talk with her young friend about her scrapbook thus:

> "The record of what our sex has suffered from the other is a long and bitter history that centuries of freedom and happiness can never make us forget."
>
> There was a moment of silence. "It is a cruel thing to remember," Laura said softly.
>
> "It is not well to think upon it," rejoined the doctor; "lest it make us unjust in our turn."

And yet of course the scrapbook record the doctor has made ensures that this history can be remembered. The scrapbook's own work of shaping memory entered into the archive and into our understanding of women's rights.

6

Scrapbook as Archive,
Scrapbooks in Archives

Few people have had Isabella Stewart Gardner's means and vision to create a private museum for her twenty-five hundred pieces of art on Boston's Fenway. A collector of Whistlers, Sargents, and old masters, she hung her art on the walls of her "palazzo" alongside architectural elements such as fountains, balconies from Italy, Roman sarcophagi, Japanese screens, and hundreds of other objects distributed around its rooms. She sought to produce the sense that the objects had arrived in her home in the course of centuries of tasteful collecting. The juxtapositions were to introduce the visitors to her way of seeing the artwork, "figuratively taking them by the hand in hopes that they too would revel in it as she had." Her 1924 bequest extended her vision into the dimension of time: her will stipulated that nothing was to be sold or added to the collection, nor moved within it—with a $3.7 million endowment to make that possible. The collection's permanence was enforced by the threat that the collection would be dismantled and sold to benefit Harvard if the museum's directors didn't adhere to her wishes. Eighty-five years later, Gardner's vision still stands much as she left it. Her museum is a site-specific installation, a work of art in itself. Through instruments of money and estate law, collectors such as Gardner ensured that their taste continued to be concretely represented on the walls of their institutions.[1]

Scrapbooks are like the Gardner Museum with its fixed exhibits. And like the Gardner, and other museums, scrapbooks display material in a deliberate arrangement. The scrapbook maker takes readers by the hand to lead them through a unique understanding of the clippings in the book. Museum visitors comprehend exhibits through their physical placement in relation to the exhibits, so that moving through the museum space is a structured performance, in which knowledge is ordered and paced. A scrapbook, too, embodies a script for moving through it, for turning pages in sequence, as Robin Bernstein has argued in relation to printed books. In a scrapbook, the order of the materials on the page remains the same and uses the language of juxtaposition. It is not possible to lay an item from the fourth page next to one on the tenth to see them together without destroying the pages or copying them. The scrapbook maker, unlike the newspaper clipper who places clippings between the leaves of a Bible or in a wallet, demands that the reader acknowledge the predetermined path through the clippings. Scrapbooks declare that they are something other than files of clippings; the framework and arrangement of materials they embody are works in themselves. Scrapbooks, and museums like the Gardner, as well as anthologies, materialize the collector's vision, and each reflects the desire to promulgate a particular understanding of or relationship to the material it presents.[2]

Like archives and libraries, scrapbooks preserve records and documents. Theorists who have written on archives, such as Michel Foucault, Jacques Derrida, and Caroline Steedman, generally use the term to refer to public records, kept by government or religious institutions, that yield information about people as their lives were touched or controlled by the state or other powerful entities. Foucault points to archives' function as controlling and delimiting knowledge, framing what it is possible for us to know. Archives, even in this sense, can make the lives of ordinary people visible to historians.[3]

But archives in the sense often used in the United States encompasses a far more miscellaneous group of collections: private historical societies such as the Massachusetts Historical Society, and historical societies with ties to the state, such as the Nebraska State Historical Society; library special collections such as Howard University's Moorland Spingarn Collection or the University of North Carolina's Southern Historical Collection; and collections called archives but including books and magazines usually more often found in a library, such as the Lesbian Herstory Archives. Such archives might contain official documents but also encompass personal papers and sets of records that their makers deliberately constructed to tell their own histories, or to be useful to themselves and others. Aware of the framing function of archives, African Americans and feminists are among those who have sought to create archives that include their history and experience. That is, they seek not only to have their materials enter into existing archives but to preserve their own systems for ordering knowledge, and to assert their own systems for controlling access.[4]

In this more inclusive sense of the term, scrapbooks are archives in themselves. Nineteenth- and twentieth-century scrapbook makers devotedly combed the press for any mention of feminist activity; for poetry that spoke to their situation, feelings, or political beliefs; for profiles of black centenarians; or for notices of their own speeches. Some endowed their scrapbooks with accoutrements or structures that announced their significance: like William Dorsey, they indexed their scrapbooks, or like Henry Ingersoll Bowditch, they wrote notes about their projects. Displacing the contents of substantial government records such as Congressional Records or Patent Office reports lent their works official weight and literal poundage. Their care in cutting and pasting into the best structures available to them, whether expensive blank books, cannily obtained government reports, or obsolete ledgers from the family business, attests to their desire to have their books endure and be treated with respect. Although the intimacy of a scrapbook made by an individual makes it unlikely that scrapbook makers would see themselves serving the unpredictable needs of future users as archives do, they do anticipate a later readership—whether it is the makers themselves or an intended public.

The vernacular, decentralized archives that scrapbook makers created in their homes are a far more democratic form than institutional archives, museums, or repositories. Few people can buy parts of old cloisters or collect rare books, but almost anyone can scissor the newspaper and make a scrapbook from clippings. Even people who occupied positions far from political power or social authority could do it, and sometimes thereby enhance their own cultural authority. So L. S. Alexander Gumby, a black gay man, demonstrated his collecting prowess with the scrapbooks he displayed in his studio in the 1920s, or Joseph W. H. Cathcart the Philadelphia janitor compiled his substantial array of scrapbooks about black life, which garnered column inches in white newspaper accounts about him. Women's rights activist Lillie Devereux Blake made scrapbooks that asserted the importance of her writings even as factional fighting within the suffrage movement substantially erased her from later histories. Scrapbooks are often a form of history writing from the ground up: an attempt to mark a place, and create a history even from positions of little power.

Although scrapbooks can be troves of many kinds of information, on which people hold differing viewpoints and labor long and hard their version of what constitutes knowledge and their structure and shaping to organize knowledge have often not made its way into bricks-and-mortar institutional archives. Because institutions have limited space and resources for cataloging and organizing, they are necessarily selective in what they acquire or accept as donations, with some institutions historically accepting only material donated by members or alumni, or only artifacts connected with a war or a prestigious family. By the later twentieth century, the collecting policies of many institutions changed to reflect greater interest in history from the ground up. Archives more often seek to include materials documenting the lives of ordinary people and members of subordinated groups, rather than the relics of great men. Yet the guidelines that were once used to decide what to accept or acquire have left an enduring mark on what is available for study today. Although government archives may hold material on marginalized people as they ran up against the law, for example, they won't contain the materials those people themselves saved and organized. The fact that a city's historical society did not *earlier* welcome or seek such material means that it may own little by local immigrants, African Americans, working class people, or members of activist social movements.

Many of today's institutions have set out to fill that gap. So even though they won't deaccession George Washington's false teeth or the Savannah Polo Club records, they might actively meet with Chinese American community groups to persuade them to deposit their papers, for example. Still, those gaps in the earlier record have affected both what institutions now hold and public perception of their holdings. They shape how meaning is made about people documented in the past, how meaning is made about the past, and how ideas are carried through into present-day governmental and other programs addressing specific groups of people who are either invisible or only newly visible in the archives. This is where the study of the scrapbooks of the nineteenth century becomes most relevant. Scrapbooks are the archives of marginalized groups and ideas made when such groups were largely kept out of bricks-and-mortar collections. As organizational structures, they reflect and embody the thinking of those groups.[5]

The Problem of the Scrapbook as Archive: Obstacles and Attributes

Scrapbooks have a basic formal problem getting through the archive door: they are, well, *scrappy*. Because they are disheveled—made up of scraps from ubiquitous newspapers, sometimes with pages stuck together, pasted on crumbling paper—they can seem too common and trivial to be worth saving, useful only for the newspaper items they contain, if that. Whatever order the scrapbook maker had in mind may not be discernible. Archivists may find their fixed arrangements to be obstacles for categorizing them according to their own institutional logic. But scrapbooks embody a crucial record of reading and understanding; they hold evidence of their makers' contact with printed materials and their choices. This record has too often been ignored. In architecture, pastiche might be celebrated as a grafting of valuable old materials onto new, and blending them, as at the Gardner Museum. Newspaper clipping scrapbooks, however, bear the visible, physical, gluey marks of that joining together.

As literary works, scrapbooks proclaim their noncanonical status as the poor relation of the published anthology. Even published anthologies have only recently been taken seriously as objects of literary study with their own history within writing, editing, and publishing. Published anthologies at least create the appearance of uniformity; scrapbooks with their mixed typefaces, columns of different widths, yellowing and browning paper, and messy, protruding unpasted clippings, lack even that visual unity. Scrapbooks announce that they have not traveled through publishing's gatekeeping process of being chosen as likely to interest others in their selectiveness and inclusiveness, not duplicating existing works, and having at least some claim to accuracy. Because scrapbooks lack the economic constraints of published books, they can include an almost infinite number of items and are equivalent to the products of twentieth- and twenty-first-century desktop publishing and print on demand that Paul Wright has called "booklike objects": artifacts with some of the physical attributes of books, but without the underpinnings of the labor of a team of screeners and editors that those attributes have commonly denoted. They instead reflect individual taste and desires. Many scrapbook makers sought to make their scrapbooks booklike, pasting in neat columns and snipping off newspaperly identifiers such as dates and sources. But as much as nineteenth-century writers asserted that a poem's presence in a scrapbook showed that it had appealed to the popular heart, no authority vetted a scrapbook to test this out, to ask just how popular Alice Cary's poems were, or whether a poem repeated themes the scrapbook had already completed, or even if it repeated the same poems two or three times. And so the institutions that hold them have understood scrapbooks as an inferior form of anthology—already a disparaged category.[6]

If they seem to be inferior literary productions, scrapbooks fare badly as historical documents, too. They can seem redundant and superfluous, because they duplicate the materials of the press and often make those materials less usable as a conventional record by stripping off dates and attribution information. In the Solomons Confederate scrapbook, accounts of the same events recur, separated by many pages, because the compiler likely received newspapers from sources months apart. It evoked from its library cataloguer the note "Unfortunately, the arrangement of clippings is not exactly chronological." It might be unfortunate for a historian who regards the scrapbook as a simple digest of the newspapers, but the Solomons scrapbook's recursiveness supplies readers with a vivid materialization of the press restrictions Georgians experienced during the war.[7]

Other difficulties for historians proliferate. Because the scrapbook compilers may have clipped away what wasn't important to them, retaining only the portion of an article in which their speech appears, for example, such scrapbooks reflect their makers' subjectivity but can seem inadequate as historical records. When a scrapbook maker saves brochures and broadsides as well as clippings, backs and middles are likely to be obscured by pasting. Again the selections are dependent on the scrapbook maker, rather than constituting a comprehensive assemblage.

For institutional repositories, scrapbooks can pose significant conservation problems. The physical elements involved may require conflicting treatments. The acidic leaves of some late-nineteenth-century blank books crumble. Some glues have darkened over time. Bindings fall apart, so that a library may separate scrapbook pages into smaller clusters, making the original extent of the project harder to experience. One archivist notes that "reformatting is often the preferred treatment option for scrapbooks"; in so commenting, he focuses attention on the "contents" of the scrapbook. If they are valuable as artifacts,

> a combination of filming and conservation may be the best option. The microfilm will document the scrapbook's original format and layout. After filming it can be disassembled, some parts that are neither unique nor intrinsically valuable, such as newspaper clippings, can be discarded. Other items such as photos, letters, and drawings, can be rehoused as part of an archival collection.

The archivist reveals his gatekeeping function, asserting institutional order. Although a curator who decides to move the paintings around at the Gardner

Museum would soon be in trouble as a result of the legal strictures of Isabella Stewart Gardner's will, an archivist disassembling a scrapbook meets no such consequences.[8]

But what constitutes disorder? And what constitutes uniqueness? The scrapbook is an archive itself, shaping and delimiting knowledge; even though the newspaper was mass produced, each clipping was chosen and cut out individually. In this respect a scrapbook parallels what book collectors call an association collection, a collection of books of interest to collectors, scholars, and librarians because of who once owned it. Every item in the scrapbook is like an association copy. Association copies need not be unique or even rare, but their ownership by a particular person enriches knowledge of both the owner and the text. Knowing who owned a book lets us trace the marks in the margin back to the hand that made them, and it makes inscriptions and marginal annotations meaningful. The mass-produced book becomes unique, touched by the associations of a specific reader. Entire association collections, though they demand more space, reveal to biographers and other scholars significant information on what a writer, thinker, or activist's mind was stocked with. Reading through the books once owned by Richard, Increase, Cotton, and Samuel Mather, and their families, colleagues, and correspondents, now locked in glass cases at the American Antiquarian Society, allows us to see what was available to a Puritan minister, and what the Mathers drew on to formulate their theology, so influential in Puritan New England. The National American Woman Suffrage Association's library, preserved intact at the Library of Congress and arranged by its original categories, shows how that group of activists conceptualized their struggle.

Aside from interest in the marginalia in such books, the items in these collections gain meaning both from their association to their owner and from their association to other works in the collection. (Interest in such connections is widespread enough to feed virtual association collections and to have been crowdsourced, via the "I See Dead People's Books" feature of the website LibraryThing, where volunteer contributors from all over the world can confirm that famous people once owned specific books.) Just as association collections turn mass-produced books into unique copies, scrapbooks convert widely distributed ephemeral newspaper items into unique items and groupings. The act of cutting clippings from the newspapers—and perhaps selecting only the portion of coverage of a suffrage convention that concerns one's own speech, or trimming away the name of the newspaper but writing in its date by hand—and placing it on the page constitutes an intimate act of writing with scissors that converts mass-produced print into manuscript. The scrapbook extends the association collection beyond ownership by notables to ownership by historically significant types of people: late-nineteenth-century African Americans, immigrants, suffragists, antisuffragists, farmers.

Like the site-specific installation of painting, sculpture, and other artifacts called the Isabella Stewart Gardner Museum, the scrapbook of items pasted into a ledger or other work is an integral construction, and the puzzlement that the choice and arrangement of clippings elicits is as much part of the scrapbook as any information contained in its surfaces. Such scrapbooks are enigmatic and sometimes frustrating works, and removing those qualities by isolating the clippings radically changes the scrapbook as surely as would ripping pages out. Frustrating reticence is built into the scrapbook, and this is its engaging hook. We make sense of the scrapbook through our necessarily biased perspectives of time and experience. When libraries, archives, or individuals attempt to bring "order" to it or destroy its integral order, they hide or destroy its puzzling quality, but they do not solve the puzzle.

Even those who seek to recover or cherish works produced by marginalized groups may focus on the thing saved and disregard the mode of saving. Dealers and librarians who disassemble scrapbooks focus on the significance of the items within—the glued and saved objects—and not on the structure or archive the scrapbook maker created for them. Libraries or archives that have seen scrapbooks as simply a group of clippings, and considered their order and layout unimportant, have often disassembled and photographed crumbling scrapbooks, with no record of whether the new work preserves the arrangement of the original.[9]

The present-day abundance of access presents its own threat to scrapbooks. As more newspapers are digitized, librarians mistakenly believe that the newspaper clipping content of scrapbooks is readily available online, not realizing how many newspapers are missing from the digital record and even from the existing paper record, other than in the form of scrapbooks. But tens of thousands of newspapers were published in the nineteenth century. Prestigious institutions' earlier failure to save periodicals produced by marginal groups is compounded when those same institutions are the sources of materials to digitize.

African American scrapbooks are sometimes the only place where anything from short-lived black newspapers with small press runs survived. The rescue of those fragments, along with the furiously passionate dedication that set someone to years of documenting lynchings, for example, or carefully gleaning nearly two hundred items on centenarians from the press over thirty years is undone by the decades of failure of institutions to solicit, or even accept, and catalog them and preserve them. The gap between the power of the scrapbook maker to clip the newspaper and make an archive of those clippings, and the difficulties of seeing that unique collection preserved within the powerful, three-dimensional archive that can offer preservation, access, and cataloging, is especially dramatic in the case of these black scrapbook maker/historians.[10]

When a scrapbook embodies two competing historical documents, the archivists' decision may run against understanding the scrapbook as an integral construction, and preserving its puzzling layering. A used 1840s ledger, repurposed as an 1870s scrapbook, for example, poses a problem. If an institution decides that the "real" work is the business record and not the scrapbook and determines that removing the clippings to be saved in a separate envelope is the best solution, the possibility of understanding generations in dialogue or engaged in coercive silencing or blocking out the past is lost.

Such a dialogue appears in a North Carolina ledger. Sallie Robertson of Caswell lost her brother fighting for the Confederacy in the Civil War and then became responsible for her younger sisters and invalid mother. When in the 1870s she cut out the recipes and household hint items from her local newspaper, often attributed to exchanges with Northern newspapers, and made a scrapbook of them by covering over a ledger that had once tracked her family's slaves and tobacco business, she implies a desire to be done with the antebellum past. At the very least, she did not cherish that underlying ledger, though she also did not let it go.[11]

Digitally photographing the scrapbook pages, as has been done, seems a reasonable compromise. It preserves a record of the scrapbook's enigmatic state, and of its work of covering over, while stripping the clippings from the ledger pages reveals what Robertson chose to obscure. Although color digital photography supplies greater detail than black and white microfilm, many scrapbooks can suffer under such treatment: layers and parts of the text disappear in the photograph, foldouts and envelopes can no longer be opened, paper napkins can no longer be touched or even identified, and tactile elements vanish.

Waste Paper or Valuable Artifacts?

Though scrapbooks were made to preserve fugitive traces of reading, by the late nineteenth century those who stumbled upon somebody else's scrapbooks pasted into old schoolbooks, ledgers, and agricultural reports might well have thought them just pieces of the detritus of everyday life, too ordinary to save. Scrapbooks went through the cycle that Michael Thompson identifies in *Rubbish Theory: The Creation and Destruction of Value*, parallel to the decorative machine-woven Stevengraph pictures that he takes as a case study. The inexpensive Stevengraphs embodied transient value when they originated as souvenirs from the 1879 York Exhibition; many people bought them and displayed them as attractive signs of modern technology, as souvenirs of attending the exhibition, and then as souvenirs of the settings shown in their pictures. By the midtwentieth century, Stevengraphs were no longer a novelty, but a sign of distastefully outmoded Victorian preferences. They were oppressively familiar and became rubbish that people threw out. It was only later, after many had been disposed of and they were no longer being made, that the remaining Stevengraphs became scarce and therefore potentially valuable. Their scarcity made them unfamiliar and thereby restored novelty and curiosity about them. During the middle period, owners of such artifacts who moved house faced a prompting to consider whether they really wanted to pack them up and keep them; those who lived in larger spaces with ample storage were inclined to leave them alone. Scrapbooks went through this same cycle. Because they are bulkier and scrappier, scrapbooks were even more likely to be discarded in a move.[12]

Furthermore (and beyond the toll taken by house fires), the fact that scrapbooks were made up of the same materials identified as waste paper weighed against them in the home or office. One physician lost two large scrapbooks on "scientific projects," ten years in the making, when they were accidentally sold by a janitor to a junk dealer, who in turn sold them for paper pulp before they could be traced. Dr. Emerson saw his scrapbooks as valuable information on chemistry and medicine, the fruit of his reading of papers from around the world; but the junk dealer who classified the scrapbooks as wastepaper had the last word. Such pulpings took place wholesale during patriotic wartime waste paper drives. In the 1940s, a few years after African American newspapers urged children to make scrapbooks of the black press, the same papers praised children for gathering paper to be reused or pulped for the war effort, and they celebrated the tonnage they accumulated—one of many sources of destruction of the thousands of scrapbooks earlier produced.[13]

Scrapbooks were a site where readers could transmute their cheap newspapers into higher-ranking books, and accord respect for the items they had selected. These self-made works, however, were always vulnerable to being returned again to the scrap heap, broken down into their component parts, or separated from the identity of their makers and thus no longer offer the knowledge generated by their status as association collections.

Scrapbooks initially had transient value: they were valued by their makers, or valued for straightforward use as the contents of their clippings. Those that carried earmarks of worth that asserted their importance—created by a president, or someone connected to the preserving institution, or ensconced in an orderly multivolume set pasted into blank books or professionally bound pages—might be saved, and so accorded higher status. Others were less likely to be accorded value and were moved into the category of rubbish.[14]

Many scrapbooks were thus destroyed or were not given to archives. In turn, archives have not always given much space to scrapbooks. Vanished scrapbooks may have been lost because their owners, far from positions of power, had no idea that documents from their lives could be useful and valuable to others. Many scrapbooks were made for the individual or the family, and even later generations would still have seen them as intimate, domestic items, not for the public. Some who inherited scrapbooks had reason to think the book would be more respected within the family than in a possibly hostile public venue.

Fragmented knowledge about lost scrapbooks is tantalizing. There is no information on what became of Sojourner Truth's two-volume scrapbook, which she called "The Book of Life," and which her collaborator, Frances Titus, drew on in revising the *Narrative of Sojourner Truth.* Although Truth couldn't read, she was well aware of writings about her and kept a scrapbook of such pieces read to her by others, and of autographs and letters written for her. Such a scrapbook could provide insight into how someone like Truth negotiated literacy and the newspaper. As far as I have been able to learn, however, it no longer exists. Perhaps it was dismantled for its salable autographs after Truth's death in 1883.[15]

Even the multiple classified scrapbooks that E. W. Gurley made and wrote about in his book *Scrapbooks and How to Make Them* have disappeared without a trace. By the time nineteenth-century scrapbooks become untethered from their connections to their purposes and contexts and entered the stream of flea markets, auctions, and eBay, even the vital information of the name of a scrapbook's maker or owner is often missing. Its value as an association collection is lost when that information is severed from the object.

Identity and the Archive

Repositories do more than simply store documents. Ideally, they preserve biographical and historical material about the people who made them—a crucial layer of knowledge about documents. The family of William H. Scott (1848–1910), an escaped slave who became a minister, bookstore owner, and member of the Niagara Movement, the forerunner of the NAACP, kept his papers, including his scrapbooks, together for decades. Scott's grandson, Henry T. Scott, bequeathed them to Randall Burkett, Emory University's curator of African American collections, whose students had begun studying Scott after his long obscurity. Burkett then donated them to Emory. The bequest carried with it the request that Scott's "story be brought to public attention." The family was surely the better guardian of Scott's legacy for decades after his death, at a time when white Southern institutions would not likely have honored such a request.[16]

For a scrapbook to be more fully understood, information needs to exist about its maker and his or her reason for creating it. If the scrapbook is separated from its maker's vision, the context is lost. Scott's identity is crucial to understanding his scrapbooks. Burkett notes that a casual review of Scott's scrapbook on the Spanish American War would suggest that he supported the war, when he was in fact a major figure in the Anti-Imperialist League, collecting and reading those clippings critically. If this biographical knowledge of its provenance had been severed from the scrapbook, his actual use of the clippings would not have been legible. Similarly, because the scrapbook Elizabeth Farnham May created from the clippings her mother saved during the Civil War, discussed in Chapter 3, is preserved within a collection of other May family materials, including genealogical information, at the Massachusetts Historical Society, it is possible to situate the scrapbook in familial chronology and to understand the timing of its creation in relation to her parents' deaths. Without the information supplied by this context, the book is an oddly sorted collection of poetry clippings, rather than a rich dialogue between mother and grieving daughter.[17]

Biographical information likewise reframes the scrapbook made by Frances A. Smith, Willa Cather's Aunt Franc, with which *Writing with Scissors* begins. Although it appears to be a collection of advice a farmwoman might collect, covering problems of farm life, because it is embedded in Cather's well-documented family history, with information on the chronology of her Aunt Franc's life, it is revealed to be a scrapbook made by an unmarried teacher, a graduate of Mt. Holyoke, engaged to George Cather, preparing to homestead in the west with him, and storing up wisdom for her future frontier life. Only with this information is the complex work this scrapbook accomplishes apparent: the scrapbook compiler addressed her future self, living in very different circumstances. Frances Smith, clipping newspapers, undertook to imagine and supply what the future Frances Smith Cather might need. Her scrapbook reveals what speculation must go into selecting for one's unknown future.[18]

The fact is that when scrapbooks arrive in an archive without provenance information, they have less to tell. The Huntington Library in Pasadena, California, a well-endowed repository with thorough records on many of its acquisitions, owns two anonymous scrapbooks on African American life and history, possibly bought in mixed lots at auction and acquired before the institution kept good records. As fascinating as they are, their use is limited by the lack of information on their makers. Moved to public space with the narrating voice long gone, scrapbooks become enigmatic as historical texts.

I have identified the maker of one of these Huntington scrapbooks via internal evidence: he was Charles Turner, an African American civil servant and Republican Party activist in St. Louis, Missouri, who saved records of his attendance at cakewalks and concerts, mixed in with news clippings about lynchings and the suppression of the black vote. Another six of his scrapbooks are at the Missouri Historical Society in St. Louis, halfway across the continent. Whatever his intent in creating this personal and political record, it is lost. Also lost is information on how parts of his endeavor were separated, who sold one volume to California, who placed its siblings in a repository in Missouri, and whether he created only these seven volumes.

Once a scrapbook is separated from its provenance information, it is usually too late to find out anything about who made it and why. Its usefulness to a researcher or reader—the legibility that derives from knowing the context of who made it and what else they made—is therefore drastically obscured. The Isabella Stewart Gardner Museum tells a fuller story if we explore it in relation to Gardner's interest in John Ruskin's and Bernard Berenson's theories of art, her experiences of personal loss, and her enjoyment of giving parties, and if we recognize that she has inserted a swathe of her own ball gown into the collection, symmetrically balancing a painting with similar colors on the opposite wall. In the same way, collections of clippings in scrapbooks need context and background to guide the future reader.

Scrapbooks in and out of the Family

Scrapbook makers who left no specific instructions about the disposition of their books may not have imagined that their books could be valuable to others. Much depended on their survivors' recognition that the scrapbook was worth saving, either because its contents seemed historical and perhaps valuable for impersonal reasons or because they saw their relative's life as important and interesting. For many scrapbooks, preservation relied on connections within families; members kept a dead relative's scrapbook and at some point found reason to place it in a repository. People's sense that a relative's scrapbook was worth saving and their access to a public repository is highly contingent on power and status. It also depends on whether heirs see danger or exposure in moving the private record of the scrapbook and other papers into the public eye. Stories of how scrapbooks came to be available in repositories, and in what form they survive, remind us how fragile access to the histories of social movements and the lives of women and men without status can be.

The papers of the writer and race and suffrage activist Alice Moore Dunbar-Nelson, whose suffrage scrapbook I discussed in Chapter 5, came into public view when Akasha (Gloria) Hull, then an English professor at the University of Delaware, met Dunbar-Nelson's niece Pauline A. Young through community connections in Wilmington. She discovered that Young had

> a trove of precious information—manuscript boxes of letters, diaries, and journals; scrapbooks on tables; two unpublished novels and drafts of published works in file folders, clippings, and pictures under beds and bookshelves. I looked at it and thought...of how this illustrated, once more, the distressing fact that much valuable/unique/irreplaceable material on women, and especially minority women writers is not bibliographied and/or publicized, is not easily accessible, and is moldering away in unusual places.

The movement into public view of private documents, even those of people who have been dead many years, can be a delicate matter. Young's and Hull's shared identity as black women helped Hull in negotiating this terrain, she notes, "but, even so, Ms. Young was understandably careful about her documents. She never told me exactly everything she had...and allowed me to see it a little at a time until gradually I gained her confidence." When Hull discovered in Dunbar-Nelson's diary that the writer had had "romantic liaisons with at least two of her [women] friends," the trust and rapport was crucial in convincing Young not to censor this element of her aunt's life.[19]

Young was a retired librarian and Delaware historian, aware of the value of her holdings. She added dates and identifications to many items and filled in information for Hull, as she worked through Dunbar-Nelson's writings. Young sold the collection to the University of Delaware before her 1991 death. Hull's work with the papers helped make their importance and value evident as the work of a writer in her own right, not just as the wife of a more famous man, and therefore desirable to a collection, while Young's annotations made the papers more useful to scholars. Dunbar-Nelson's scrapbook of her suffrage work continues to be surrounded by other papers, including a scrapbook collecting reviews of her first book, and the scrapbook made by her sister, Pauline Young's mother, celebrating Alice's accomplishments and her marriage to Paul Lawrence Dunbar. A collaboration like that of Hull and Young seems less likely to occur with scrapbooks already in the controlled, remote space of the archive rather than the home. Yet at some point, families are often no longer willing or able to keep piles of materials, and they may also want to make material more generally useful.

Writing about the shifts in feminist historiography and the "ever changing relations between the present and the past," Ellen Carol DuBois notes that although Harriot Stanton Blatch deposited the papers of her mother, Elizabeth Cady Stanton in the Library of Congress, where historians such as Mary Ritter Beard could read them in the 1930s, the papers of such major figures as Frances Willard and Charlotte Perkins Gilman were held back by "organizational and family protectors" until the 1960s, hiding their role in history from generations of historians.[20]

Some scrapbooks and other papers of suffragists held by families were actively solicited by a historian. Mary Earhart Dillon assembled an extensive collection of suffragist papers in the early 1940s to write a book about Willard, the suffragist and temperance leader. Suffragists and their descendants were eager to give Dillon their papers when they learned of her project, and that these papers would have a worthy repository at Northwestern University, where Dillon taught. People sent her trunks full of their own papers and papers they had been saving. But once Dillon completed her book, the Northwestern library said it had no space or money to process the collection, and she was asked to "remove it as soon as possible from the basement of the building" where her office had been. Dillon then offered the collection to other repositories. Finally she found Radcliffe College's Schlesinger Library, which in 1943, through Beard's project, began to create a world center for women's archives. The collection included some of Elizabeth Boynton Harbert's scrapbooks, which thus landed at the Schlesinger Library. Others of Harbert's scrapbooks made their way to the Huntington Museum and Library in Pasadena, California, because Harbert and her husband lived there during the last two decades of their lives. Her daughter, one of the children to whom Harbert wrote her scrapbook note explaining why she quit writing her column, donated or sold them to the Huntington Library after Harbert's death.[21]

It's not surprising that Lillie Devereux Blake, a speaker and writer who discussed scrapbooks in her novel *Fettered for Life*, kept scrapbooks. At least one was entitled "Articles about Woman's Position and Interesting Items," which she evidently mined as source material for her writing and speaking. This scrapbook was saved in the Sophia Smith collection at Smith College, Northampton, Massachusetts, while her others, mainly of her own writings, are halfway across the country, in Missouri, where her granddaughter, who was a volunteer at the historical society, donated her papers.

Archive as Publication in the Women's Movement

Most scrapbooks that survived with information about the maker intact found their way to an institution that would care for them by donation during the maker's lifetime. Others were held by heirs who either cared about them and wanted to place them in a repository or had the means, space, and inertia to leave them alone, whether they cared or not, until they attracted the attention of another generation. When a scrapbook has been preserved within a family, its context and continued value are evident. The family knows who made it, and the family's interest in its ancestors may be enough to keep it safe for many years, unless it slides from Thompson's category of transient value to rubbish and becomes too much trouble to save. But scrapbooks such as William Dorsey's or Lillie Devereux Blake's—made as alternative histories with the intention of teaching others or passing along an analysis or body of information—require a more public setting to fulfill their maker's intention.

Before the advent of cheap photo-reproduction, it was virtually impossible to make copies of scrapbooks. They therefore were conceived as unique objects, like illuminated manuscripts, dependent on a single place of deposit for a continued readership. When institutions such as library special collections, local historical societies, and other kinds of archives devoted to preservation of artifacts and to providing some form of access make decisions both about what they accept and what they set out to acquire, they act as gatekeepers, much as publishers do. A scrapbook's acceptance into an archive is essentially its publication. The scrapbook "published" in this way starts to have an unknown public, unknown potential for circulating; it has entered into the possibility that others will make different sorts of meanings from it. Like print publication, deposit in an archive can depend on the maker's contacts and connections, the signs the work bears of its worthiness and authoritativeness. The formal earmarks themselves differ: a manuscript full of handwritten corrections might repel a publisher, but if it is by a prominent writer it could attract an archive more than a clean copy would.

Some scrapbook makers and their families understood the value of placing a scrapbook in an archive. Perhaps they felt entitled to do so because of family prominence or because they used archives or were involved in them themselves. Henry Ingersoll Bowditch, whose brother Nathaniel belonged to and left an endowment to the Massachusetts Historical Society, presented his memorial volume about his son in September 1865, at the request of an MHS associate. Henry's nephew Charles Pickering Bowditch, too, became a member and was on the society council. Henry later submitted to the society "his own paper in defense of John Brown, along with an autograph letter of Brown to his wife and children," the society's records note. In 1923, his son, Vincent, went on to deposit the scrapbooks Henry had made on the case of the escaped slave George Latimer, and in 1930 Henry's great-grandson deposited what seem to have been the remaining contents of Henry's Memorial Cabinet, discussed in Chapter 3.[22]

The 1880s scrapbook Elizabeth Farnham May created from her mother's Civil War clippings entered the Massachusetts Historical Society as part of a collection of the papers of four generations of the May family. There is no record of her efforts to save the scrapbook, but it was donated a century after she made it by family members, including Henry F. May, a historian, after he used the papers for a book he wrote about himself and his father. Placing the collection in a public repository gave more scholars the chance to consider the family's place in Massachusetts history and to write about the family, an outcome in which he would have had a professional interest.[23]

Archival "publication" was pressed into use to supplement other forms of distribution, and to direct works to influential readers. Suffragists knew they needed to save the history of their own struggles. By the late nineteenth century, they saw that histories of their movement were not being issued. Publishers were uninterested in works on the "Woman Question" because they did not sell well, Mary Livermore noted in a letter to Elizabeth Boynton Harbert in the 1870s. If buyers wouldn't come to the books, suffragists attempted to bring the books to the readers. In the 1880s and 1890s, using their own money supplemented by a bequest, Susan B. Anthony and Elizabeth Cady Stanton issued their multivolume *History of Woman Suffrage*. They presented more than a thousand copies of the first volumes to libraries as one means of getting the word out. Not all libraries accepted the gift.[24]

With the struggle still in progress, the next generation of activists needed to know what came before, and suffragists wanted to be the ones creating the historical record. Anthony asked suffrage comrades for documents for a kind of scrapbook she wanted to place in libraries, especially in the Library of Congress. She wrote to Harbert in 1901:

> I am trying to gather up the reports of the Party Conventions—to <u>bind</u> in <u>books</u>—have you any old Congressional Documents. . . . I want to make as many volumes of them as I can to put into <u>Libraries</u>—the <u>Congressional</u> library at Washington is my first aim—I want to get everything pertaining to woman into that one—any way—have you any documents of any sort—of this kind—and will you let me have them—

Making material available in libraries was one mode of distribution, suffragists realized. But Anthony was not just after general distribution in libraries. She wanted this material to repose in the Library of Congress, the closest institution to a national archive that the United States had at that time. (The National Archives were not established until 1934.) Anthony's earlier suggestion that the Library of Congress devote an alcove "especially to books and works on the Woman Question" had already met with Congressional Librarian Herbert Putnam's refusal;

thus moving bound pamphlets into the library was another approach to making suffrage history and arguments visible in the archives. Anthony's emphasis on having the pamphlets bound "in <u>books</u>" testifies to the value she attributed to booklike permanence, even of one-of-a-kind compilations. The idea that these pamphlets are part of the nation's political history, not just a fringe movement, is a position that seems unremarkable now, but in 1901 this was a radical claim. Its current unremarkableness testifies to Anthony's success. The Library of Congress is a site of power, both as the nation's copyright depository and as a storehouse from which senators and representatives could page works. For a movement seeking to convince legislators, placing its pamphlets in the legislators' library was strategic.[25]

Depositing a thirty-three-volume scrapbook record of her own political work in the Library of Congress allowed Anthony to read her self-constructed works into the public record and the larger historical record. She donated her annotated scrapbooks to the Library of Congress in 1903, three years before she died. She understood that placing work in an archive was a form of publication and that the documents she organized in her scrapbooks could shape people's understanding of a movement still in progress. Her scrapbooks of newspaper clippings, programs, handbills, and memorabilia, reaching back to 1855, were part of this collection. She arranged for the Library of Congress to take the scrapbooks from the same motive that animated the project of compiling and publishing the *History of the Woman Suffrage Movement*. That massive document is itself a sort of scrapbook, full of newspaper reports gathered from attics, where they had been saved by assiduous newspaper clippers in the movement. Both the scrapbooks and the *History of the Woman Suffrage Movement* respond to the sense that the information is hard to come by, has slipped away, and doesn't exist in complete form anywhere. Scrapbooks, the *History,* and the pamphlet collection documented the struggle midstream and made sure the next generation of activists knew what had happened before.

The library of a government that was hostile to the suffragists' demands to be treated as full citizens hardly seems a congenial setting in which to leave scrapbooks and papers chronicling their struggle to making a fundamental change in that government. It meant giving over control of those papers about the struggle still in progress to an institution owned by the government and freely accessed by representatives who had helped block victory. The act of placing materials about the suffrage struggle in the Library of Congress set two facets of the library in tension: as a place owned by legislators and as holder of the nation's history.

Unlike the pamphlets and reports, scrapbooks and letters were unique objects, and giving up local control over them carried the risk that they might be discarded, dismembered, morselized back to individual clippings, or separated from their makers' vision. Twenty-five years earlier, Anthony, Stanton, and Matilda Joslyn Gage had been denied a place in the Philadelphia Centennial celebration to present their Declaration of the Rights of Women, a presentation which would have permitted reading women's rights into the national record. In placing their papers in the Library of Congress, suffragists claimed full citizenship and asserted they were entitled to a place in the nation's history and to be present in the physical space documenting that history. They asserted, too, their faith that their scrapbooks and papers, like their more expository pamphlets and reports of party conventions, could convert the legislators.

The journalist Ida Husted Harper (1851–1931) worked with the scrapbooks beginning in the 1890s in writing Anthony's three-volume biography; she would have become even more acutely aware of the value of scrapbooks as she collaborated on the fourth volume of *The History of Woman Suffrage* and wrote the fifth and sixth volumes. She followed in Anthony's steps by donating fourteen volumes of her scrapbooks, largely containing her own writings, to the Library of Congress in 1916, noting that although they were still convenient to her as a reference in her journalism she wanted them to "render more general service" through their availability at the nation's library. Suffragists' conflicting desires to place scrapbooks in appreciative and safe hands, and to "publish" their contents in the archive, may explain Amy Mecklenberg-Fanger's observation that scrapbook bequests among suffragists ran in something of a chain, with suffrage activist Harriet Taylor Upton's scrapbooks bequeathed to Carrie Chapman Catt, from whose estate they were donated to the Library of Congress in 1947, while May Wright Sewall's arrived at the Library of Congress via her literary executor Ida Husted Harper. Elizabeth Cady Stanton's papers, including now-disassembled scrapbooks, arrived at the Library of Congress both from Susan B. Anthony, with Anthony's 1903 gift, a year after Stanton's death, and from Stanton's daughter, Harriot Stanton Blatch, twenty-five years later. These scrapbooks and papers first were held by friends and comrades and only later moved to public space. Another chain of documentation appears in Anthony's saving Harper's columns in her scrapbooks, and Harper's saving obituaries and memorial writings on Stanton and Anthony.[26]

Matilda Joslyn Gage, who also collaborated with Stanton and Anthony on the *History of Woman Suffrage*, singled out her own scrapbooks for special treatment among her papers. Her 1885 will divided real estate, valuables, and books among her four children and bequeathed to her youngest daughter, Maud Gage Baum, "all of my woman suffrage papers, books and documents of whatever character except my scrap books, which latter I desire that she shall deposit in some permanent public library." Perhaps she shared Anthony's belief that their presence in a public library might help to convert people to women's rights causes. Four of her scrapbooks are in the Library of Congress, but one (on the Civil War, women's war activities, and women's rights speeches and activities) is separated from the others in the collection of her local library in Fayetteville, New York. Whether and where these records were saved in an accessible place had a great impact on how historians wrote about suffragists. Unless its documents were in public repositories, Ellen Carol DuBois notes, "the past of the women's rights movement could not become 'history'; it lacked a public dimension and the capacity to outlive the individuals who had participated in it."[27]

Other feminists desired to see their papers preserved because they understood their own importance as individuals who had made a mark on the world and deserved a place in the public record. They were aware that men of their class and social position had received such a place. Caroline Healey Dall started thinking about this problem early; she was concerned even at age twenty in 1842 about what would become of her papers. Her thinking might have been prompted by a visit to the American Antiquarian Society in Worcester, where she read letters deposited by people who were part of her upper-class Boston world. She thus saw that she might expect her papers—which already included her notes from Margaret Fuller's "conversaziones"—to be of interest to posterity. A few months after her visit to the AAS, the idea of preserving her own writings took root. She was

> arranging and writing a list of my Mss. and other private papers.... Who will care for these many papers—who will ever read—or at my request, take pains to preserve that I have written? ... If I were likely to die wealthy and could pay an institution for taking care of papers so precious to me—I would do it ... but as it is, as it is <u>like to be</u>, I must trust the common chance.

Dall's awareness that archival preservation was something one might buy one's way into was surely sparked by her formerly wealthy father's financial collapse not long before. Worrying at age twenty about the disposition of one's papers might seem premature, but it marks her turn toward the archives as an additional mode of publication for someone who was already a published writer, and her awareness that her unpublished writing like diaries and scrapbooks could thus be "published" too. Even published works could turn back into manuscript and depend on the archive for "publication." Her scrapbooks contain, among other things, copies of her publications, hand-corrected. The archives contain the version closer to the author's intentions than the mass-produced copies.[28]

Dall worried that her father's wealth was at the root of attention she received, and she was relieved when people continued to treat her well after he lost his fortune. But access to archival publication extended beyond personal friendship, and this note marks her awareness that her loss of position could well mean she would be cut off from such a place. Fifty years later, Dall did not trust to "common chance" but carefully arranged for her papers, including the scrapbooks that tell of her early speaking career, to go to the Massachusetts Historical Society. Helen Deese, who edited Dall's diaries, reports that even then the papers were "not unanimously embraced by the Society—one member objecting to the expense of storing what seemed to him worthless trivia." When the Massachusetts Historical Society did nonetheless house them, its resources made it possible for later generations to read and see all of her papers—diaries, scrapbooks, letters, bound volumes of periodicals she worked on and annotated—together as an articulated whole, with background information on Dall available.[29]

Black Collectors' Works in the Archive

African Americans rarely had the family connections that would have found their scrapbooks a place in the nineteenth-century archive of libraries and historical societies. Moving their materials into an archive, however, was an extension of the lifetime efforts of such collectors as William Dorsey, Joseph W. H. Cathcart, and L. S. Alexander Gumby to make their collections available and useful to readers. The archive and library were sites of publication, complicated by the limited resources of African American institutions on the one hand and of white institutions' history of unreliability and often hostility toward the project of saving black history on the other.

As we saw in Chapter 4, William Dorsey opened his home as Dorsey's Museum in the 1880s and 1890s, inviting visitors to see his collection of African-American-related artwork and rare books as well as his scrapbooks. He made his knowledge and collection useful by forming the American Negro Historical Society with other Philadelphia black collectors in 1897. He carried the title Custodian of Documents and donated much material; the collection was housed for a time in a black church. The society petered out and was nearly gone by the time of Dorsey's death in 1923.[30]

At his death, the scrapbooks went to his alma mater, the Institute for Colored Youth, now Cheyney University, probably donated by William's son Thomas. Born in 1837, the son of an escaped slave, William Dorsey had grown up with a powerful awareness of slavery, the oppression of black people, and the invisibility of black history. But many members of Thomas Dorsey's generation would have seen the work as "simply a messy hobby which consumed space and time, better devoted to other things," the historian Roger Lane, who has made extensive use of Dorsey's scrapbooks, suggests. The scrappiness of Dorsey's collection, in a hodgepodge of different-sized and repurposed books, made its vitality and significance hard to discern. Dorsey's scrapbooks were ignored until 1976, when they were found behind a wall in a massive office cleaning, according to one account; hidden in storage according to another; or reclaimed from the bottom of a janitor's closet according to a third. Even rediscovery during a period more interested in black history has resulted in limited access. Cheyney University obtained a federal grant in 1980 to microfilm and catalog the scrapbooks but ran out of grant money before finishing, though the specifically African American–focused volumes have been filmed.[31]

Black bibliophile Charles Blockson calls the disappearance of Dorsey's scrapbooks

a minor disappointment in the larger tragedy of many private collections of information with regard to African people. Often, because our institutions do not have the necessary funding to facilitate timely processing and upkeep, donated items languish for months and even years in storage. Some items deteriorate beyond reclamation. At other times, the people placed in charge of the items either do not have an idea of their significance or are simply not interested.

Dorsey's contemporary John Wesley Cromwell worked to donate his own scrapbooks to Wilberforce University and eventually deposited them at Howard University. Cromwell's newspaper *The People's Advocate* had published a profile of Joseph W. H. Cathcart, the Philadelphia prodigious scrapbook maker. Like suffragists, these activists formed a chain of bequests. Cromwell evidently inherited Cathcart's scrapbooks when Cathcart died in 1895, and he donated what remained of them to Howard University before giving them his own scrapbooks. Dorsey's collection included a scrapbook by Ira D. Cliff, a black musician, Civil War veteran, and Republican Party activist, evidently left to him when Cliff died in 1872. But Cathcart's scrapbooks, which he once proudly displayed in his bookcases, and which attracted the attention of Philadelphia reporters, are now part of a library with limited resources, and not evident even in its catalog. Processing, as Blockson notes, is an expensive undertaking and therefore unevenly distributed. In this respect Cathcart's and Cromwell's scrapbooks in Howard University's Moorland Spingarn collection are in sharp contrast to albums in a library with abundant resources such as Harvard's Theatre Collection, where the catalog yields a page-by-page description of certain albums seen as containing particularly valuable contents. This distribution of resources reproduces and continues earlier inequitable access to resources: it is very easy to delve into the subjectivity and theater attendance of white elites, while the homemade African American histories are far more difficult to access.[32]

Although scrapbook makers who left material to black institutions intended to keep them useful within the African American community, the overstrained budgets and chronic space shortages of such institutions have limited the public's access to them. The mission of some African American institutions, too, has also sometimes conflicted with archival preservation and on occasion meant losses of material. So when a black institution enabled "publication" of a unique scrapbook by providing a site for its use, that site might not offer the kind of protection that institutions with an archival mission furnish. The Schomburg Center for Research in Black Culture, for example, long functioned as both a neighborhood branch library and African American studies collection, and in earlier times it kept scrapbooks on open shelves; the result was that some disappeared.

By the midtwentieth century, some resource-rich white institutions began to see black history as valuable. L. S. Alexander Gumby's personal magnetism as a host and arts impresario sparked enthusiasm for his collection among a broad interracial array of writers and artists and other friends and acquaintances. His interviews in the press highlighted the distinctiveness and preciousness of his carefully framed scrapbook items—and framing was another mode of inciting interest in them. He had once displayed his scrapbooks and invited others to read them in his studio, where he held parties and readings. Moving them to an archive reshaped and extended that enterprise (minus the music and cocktails). Ultimately donating the collection to Columbia University in 1951, he explained his somewhat surprising selection of a white institution to house his scrapbooks as a place where the collection "would be safeguarded and where it would be of more extensive use than I could offer." As a gay man, his concerns about his collection extended beyond preserving black history to according protection to his theatrical and movie star scrapbooks, and even to the scrapbooks of gay erotica that he initially left to his friend Bruce Nugent, deposited with Columbia University after Nugent's death. His remarks on the attractiveness of the men on Columbia's then all-male campus—he wrote to Nugent that they were "like a harem," perhaps implying that many were gay—reinforces this rationale for seeing it as a congenial home for his materials. Moreover, he arranged for Columbia to hire him to curate them for a time, something black institutions would not have had the resources to do.[33]

Moving Forward: "Publication" Redistribution

The historian Carolyn Steedman, in her evocative meditation on historical research, *Dust: The Archive and Cultural History*, repeatedly returns to the figure of the researcher opening the faded red string tied around a bundle of archival papers—of census enumerations, of trial records, of parish registers—seeking to "save the lives" of the forgotten, anonymous dead. The scrapbook reader, too, undoes the string holding a fragile newspaper clipping scrapbook together, and...does what? Pages through racist verse, through fashion plates, through clippings on the stock market, through the lives of centenarians, through sermons, through short stories obscuring sermons, through poems about dead babies obscuring other poems, through items from columns headed "For Your Scrapbook" which someone has obediently clipped and pasted. Reading these may not reanimate the life of their maker, but it places us for a moment behind the maker's eyes, to glimpse what he or she saw in reading the newspapers about to be cut up to make the book. The scrapbook thus adds another ghostly figure alongside the researcher: the archivist/scrapbook maker who came before, with his or her own vision.

Scrapbooks are a democratic form of archives. Anyone can make a newspaper clipping scrapbook, and thousands of Americans did. Writing with scissors and cheap newspapers allowed many who did not write books or diaries to record something about their thinking. Preservation in a larger bricks-and-mortar archive has been less democratically distributed. A scrapbook's presence in a well-endowed archive multiplies into greater visibility. Initially well cataloged, information about it may now be even easier to find via repository catalogs that have migrated to the web and are available in the National Union Catalog of Manuscript Collections (NUCMC), which has come under the

WorldCat umbrella and is freely accessible online. The fact that scholars can receive endowed research fellowships at repositories such as the Massachusetts Historical Society, the American Antiquarian Society, the Huntington Library, and Winterthur Museum and Library—just to list those that have aided the research for this book—means the scrapbooks at such institutions are more likely to be researched and discussed in print. The makers of scrapbooks that ended up at such institutions effectively launched their scrapbooks off into the future in stouter vessels. They more successfully ensured that their dead sons would be remembered for posterity, that their version of their suffrage work would be visible, that their unique reading of the Civil War in newspapers could be accessed by others.

Nineteenth-century newspaper-clipping scrapbook makers used the cheapness and ephemerality of the newspaper to pass along their readings; those who thought they were making lasting creations were not always able to make their collections permanent. Present-day digital media share some of the same tensions. Social media such as Facebook entries and file-sharing sites, and even websites, seem vulnerable to disappearing overnight—and are superseded by the next round of shared links, Farmville triumphs, and news reports. At the same time, students, job seekers, and office seekers are warned that whatever they put on the web is permanent and findable, so they must not post anything compromising. Web material oscillates between archival permanence and ephemerality, sharing scrapbooks' oscillation between public and private (or the presumption of privacy) as well. Newspaper clipping scrapbooks, made of entirely public materials, passed into private space and became personal, sometimes intimate documents. As E. W. Gurley noted, his scrapbooks, "though written by authors unknown to me, and written for the public, are yet such true interpretations of my own feelings, that they show the secret history and aspirations of my soul." Many of these intimate documents then disappeared. Often enough for us to read some, others moved back into public view, through the "publication" of the archive.[34]

What took the place of nineteenth-century ways of reading and working with printed matter? Newer methods no longer leave the fixed, personal, idiosyncratic records that we have seen in scrapbooks. But commercial newspaper storage, clipping services, and eventually our present-day methods have sought to manage reading on a larger scale.

The Afterlife of the Nineteenth-Century Scrapbook

Managing Data and Information

> I regard the invention of the press clipping business as almost of as much importance as the appearance of the first newspaper. The thousands of papers to-day scatter the news, the press clipping bureau focuses it.
>
> —Henry Romeike, *press clipping bureau owner, 1896*[1]

Writing with Scissors has largely focused on the activity of scrapbook makers, the people who wrote mainstream and alternative histories and created expressive scrapbook anthologies using the abundance of public printed matter that the nineteenth-century press made available. But individuals scanning and clipping the papers they happened to receive, even when their work resulted in sets of hundreds of scrapbooks, ran up against significant limits. Their activity required that the clipper predict what would be wanted later, and it fell short of storing the wealth of newspapers extending back for decades; nor did individual scrapbook makers systematically scan hundreds of newspapers to find information on a subject. Their ability to read and manage the news in print was limited by their time, resources, and individual interests.

By the end of the nineteenth century, the strategies of newspaper scrapbook compilers were extended and expanded by commercial technologies for managing newsprint. Two such technologies—storage facilities for back numbers of newspapers by the hundreds, and clipping bureaus, which zeroed in on specified subjects—arose. In turn, these became the predecessors of present-day methods of slicing and managing information. As they illuminate forgotten beliefs and assumptions, both technologies reveal how scrapbook work and the understandings of information it developed allowed people to see newspapers as extractable sources of data. They mark the path from scrapbooks to our current age of digitized information.

Back Number Budd

Scrapbook-making advice and descriptions repeatedly emphasize that scrapbooks transform the press from the ephemeral to the preservable. As E. W. Gurley noted:

> Many beautiful, interesting, and useful thoughts come to us through the newspapers, that are never seen in books, where they can be referred to when wanted. When they are gone they are lost. If one should keep a regular file of one of our principal papers, as the *Tribune* or *Herald*, in a few years it would be found to be valuable.... But they cannot be bought.

Gurley asserts that scrapbooks were needed because it was impossible to keep such a file of newspapers. But one man *did* keep regular files of principal (and more obscure) papers, found them valuable, and made a living by offering them for sale.[2]

Robert M. Budd, an African American man known as Back Number Budd, had a career that weaves through the movement of print in the nineteenth and early twentieth century. His work shows how newspapers were transformed into data and displays developing technologies for storing and accessing newspaper contents beyond scrapbooks. It highlights, too, how peculiarly dependent on idiosyncratic individual initiative the work of storing and offering access was–whether in making scrapbooks, collecting periodicals, or, in this case, storing and reselling newspapers. The paradox that struck late-nineteenth-century newspaper creators, consumers, and scrapbook makers so forcefully–that newspapers could be historically and economically valuable yet were extremely cheap–was crucial to Budd's business. It allowed him to buy low and sell high.

Budd recognized the value of the newspaper both as data and as concrete, tangible evidence. Born in 1852 in Washington, he got his start as a child selling newspapers to the soldiers in camps near Washington during the Civil War. Several weeks after the Battle of Bull Run, soldiers offered him an extravagant $3 each for his remaining copies of newspaper describing the battles they had been in. "The boys were willing to pay almost anything for them for the sake of getting the news," he later explained. Realizing there was money in old newspapers, he set himself up in the business in New York, where he first combined a shoeshine and newspaper stand selling the day's papers with his back-number newspaper business in the 1870s. He crammed his 24 foot by 65 foot gaslit basement on Broadway and Thirty-Second Street, stockpiling millions of old papers, and by 1888 he had acquired a barnlike warehouse to store papers and lived adjacent to it, across the river from Manhattan in what is now Astoria, Queens. Newspaper reporters and lawyers—his two main categories of clients—came to both sites.[3]

The pairing of newspaper reporters seeking background information for their stories and lawyers seeking physical evidence exemplifies the crucial doubleness of the newspaper: Is it data, or is it sheets of paper? Reporters often paid to read his papers on the premises. They thus treated the newspaper as a vehicle for information and used his storehouse as a library or reading room, carrying away the information they needed in the form of notes to be reprocessed into new articles. When they bought Budd's papers, it was for the convenience of keeping or transferring the words at a later date. Lawyers who wanted documentation of dates of events or notices, however, needed the materiality of the news item on paper, physical evidence that it had been published on a specific date. Lawyers therefore not only bought the old papers but sometimes paid Budd to swear to a newspaper's authenticity. In other words, if one had failed to save the all-important item—the iconic precious clipping, the clipping proving that Judge John J. Parker was a racist, or the clipping related to a bequest that would have been worth a thousand dollars—Budd's vast storehouse of newspapers might supply it.

His storerooms seemed densely cluttered, but the appearance was deceptive. The papers were bundled and arranged chronologically on shelves, so that Budd could readily pull out a newspaper of a specific date. At first he acquired papers principally through paying hotel cleaning staff by the pound for old newspapers and magazines from hotel lobbies and their newsstands. Other papers came to him free, directly from publishers who put him on their subscription lists, evidently seeing value in keeping works in an offsite repository. He contracted with clubs to buy their daily newspaper files by the month, and he staked bets on elections with files of newspapers. His bookkeeping system for tracking his sales allowed him to audit his inventory, so that he was keenly aware of when he had only a single copy left. He reprinted papers, reproducing such notable issues as one covering George Washington's inauguration, to advertise his business. The collection suffered two major fires, one in 1895 and a more devastating one in 1922, though he was still in business in 1931.[4]

Because Budd's business both honored newspapers and served reporters, journalists found him a convenient and engaging subject to interview and write about. A few cast his conversation in improbable minstrel dialect, but most treated him respectfully, presumably because the reporters relied on his services. Periodicals even advertised that he collected their issues. The *New York World* claimed in its article about him that their paper was the one Budd's clients most often called for; while The *Amusement Bulletin* boasted that he was laying in copies of their weekly because he believed their illustrations would become valuable. Although his steadiest clients were lawyers and reporters, General Ulysses S. Grant bought a month's worth of papers in June 1886, perhaps for work on his memoir. By 1895, Budd occasionally scanned through and clipped his newspapers for his clients as well, making a commissioned scrapbook for Helen Gould on the death of her father, the financier and railroad magnate Jay Gould, in 1892, and another on the first wedding of Astor family heir Jack.[5]

Reporters marveled at his ability to charge so much for papers that had once been worth only a penny, and marveled also that he stuck to his rates (an issue surely on the mind of any reporter who had just tried to bargain with him). The relationship between value and price, worth and cost, was already complicated through advertising's subsidy of newspapers, so that the cover price did not reflect production cost (and possibly not even the cost of paper and ink). But the 1895 fire at his warehouse demonstrated how slippery cost and value are in relation to old newspapers: it revealed that insurance companies had been unwilling to consider his collection as anything but waste paper, and so he received no compensation for his loss. Census takers indicated similar unease about the value of old newspapers with their descriptions of his occupation. The 1900 census ambiguously designates him as a "paper dealer," and only in 1910 is he transformed into "proprietor, news store," while in 1920 his used newspapers perhaps seemed so hard to categorize that the census taker calls it a stationery business. Budd was, in essence, repurposing old newspapers not as insulation, basket lining, or fish wrapping but as a data source. Insurance companies and others, however, insisted on seeing only the wastepaper and not its transformation.[6]

Budd set uniform prices based on the age of the newspapers, with additional charges based on rarity. A reporter seeking a series of articles from a few months earlier and being unable to find them in a library, told of being directed to Budd's establishment, where Budd located them easily and then shocked him by charging "ten times their original price." Although the daily paper depended for its value on freshness and up-to-dateness and the readers' sense that they are reading at the same time as their neighbors and fellow citizens, Budd discovered that there was value in age. Unlike the scrapbook makers who redeemed news items from the larger whole of the newspaper according to their own calculations of what was valuable to them, Budd, like archivists or special collections librarians, understood that he could not predict what would later interest people. Value accrued to his copies of the newspapers as other people disposed of them or reused them for their paper and not their news, so that (as Michael Thompson's *Rubbish Theory* could tell us) his papers became rare. At least as important, his newspapers were organized and retrievable: he created a warehouse organized like a set of calendars, which permitted reaching back into bundles of the Boston *Daily Advertiser* or the *New York World*, to pull out the correct date. Budd's prices reflected the value added in creating a system to organize the papers so they could be located again, and in storing bulky, vulnerable materials. His journalist customers, like the insurance companies, found this concept difficult to grasp. Their articles marveling at the high prices paid for specific items frame those anecdotes with Budd as a shrewd go-between, creating riches from waste, almost by chance. The casual racism of some articles contributes to this framing, positioning Budd's enterprise as outside the bounds of legitimate business, while other articles reported on his marital troubles, as though he were a comic celebrity. When he boasted in an article about how much he had been paid for individual newspapers, other newspapers picked up the stories, perhaps because they burnished their sense that copies of their own works could be valuable. So the tidbit that the Kansas Historical Society had been willing to pay $10,000 for a file of the *Leavenworth Journal* was avidly reprinted by newspapers around the country.[7]

Budd archived the nation's history from a position that was both marginal—as a black shoeshine stand operator and later as a dealer in typical junkshop staples such as shoelaces and old dime novels—and central, a man presiding over an unparalleled storehouse and exchange center of the nation's documents. Newspaper reading rooms like the Merchants' Exchange or Stock Exchange Reading Room, which was located in the New York Stock Exchange and catered to the men involved in the Exchange, had offered a broad selection of the press from the United States and abroad. Such a collection was geared to news of the moment and it disposed of older papers. Using the Stock Exchange Reading Room required a substantial investment: by 1864, its dues were $25 per year. Some subscription or private membership libraries kept a select stock of newspapers. But unlike these exclusive repositories with gatekeepers screening their collections, Budd's collection was vastly inclusive: *The Amusement Bulletin* and the black *Pittsburgh Courier* were not likely to be in the stacks at select libraries. Budd supplemented and amplified the work of libraries. People could buy the evidence they needed rather than attack a restricted collection with surreptitious pocket knives. The collection was thus porous; its historic goods moved in and out. And they sometimes circled back: after his first fire he bought files of newspapers he had previously sold, to rebuild his collection (Figure 7.1).[8]

He also reprinted, to fill in for the problem of selling the last copy of an article in heavy demand. Budd made it possible for those who were not dedicated antiquarians, or who did not visit repositories such as the American Antiquarian Society, to see the nation's historical print productions by reprinting a 1789 *Ulster County Gazette* and *Gazette of the United States* with news of George Washington's inauguration. His reprint copies can be distinguished from originals by typefaces, by his ads on the back, or by a copyright notice he inserted. His *Gazette of the United States* adds, on the edge of the first page, "Gen. Geo. Washington's Inauguration, Our First President, 1789," with the possessive pronoun firmly asserting Budd's own equal ownership of the nation's past. His reprinting work registers an understanding that both the physical form of the item and the information it contained were valuable. People wanted the tangible connection to the past, even in facsimile form[9]

Budd's interest in physical evidence, in newspapers as concrete traces of events, which had started him in business as a boy in the Civil War, sprawled with unfortunate consequences into acquiring other historical memorabilia: he collected an example of every sort of cartridge used by both sides of the Civil War. His interests in physical objects and data collided dramatically when these cartridges exploded amid his newspapers during his 1895 fire, worsening the losses.[10]

The dwindling number of newspaper articles about him after the turn of the century suggests that newspaper reporters no longer relied so heavily on his

Figure 7.1 Back Number Budd in his shop: "If What You Want Was Published Within Past 98 Years, He Has It, Back Number Budd Says," *Amsterdam News*, 2 Sep 1931. (By permission of the *Amsterdam News*)

storehouse. Rather, they could find what they needed in their own newspapers' morgues or clipping files, and in growing libraries, or through the more specialized and directed production of clipping bureaus. Budd's warehouse aspired to encompass and make available the newspaper's information and its physical reality, which lent it special status as legal evidence. But those exploding shells make it impossible not to notice that materiality was also vulnerability, as it was for E. W. Gurley's barrels of newspapers eaten by mice, or the doctor's volumes of clippings on scientific subjects sold for scrap by a janitor, or the many newspapers and scrapbooks pulped in wartime scrap paper drives. Budd amassed grandly inclusive libraries of printed matter and developed a system to locate desired items, only to have them turn to ashes.[11]

Data Retrieval: Past and Present

Scrapbooks, newspaper collections, clipping services, library cataloging systems, filing systems, and even pigeonhole desks embody overlapping modes of thinking about information, how to concentrate it, and how to find it again. They are the foundations of more recent filtering of information via digital methods, namely Google, LexisNexis, blogging, personal sharable note-taking applications such as Evernote and Zotero, and the like. Each technology understands that pieces of information—whether in the form of articles, books, or snippets—are detachable, movable, and classifiable under multiple headings. Although the clipping scrapbook seems solidly grounded in the materiality of paper and paste, it leads toward the understanding that items can be detached from their original sources while retaining an association via identifiable style and typeface, even if the name and date of publication have been snipped away. In the scrapbook, items could be drastically recontextualized and moved into new meanings, while additional copies could be categorized in other directions.

Earlier projects hinted at the potential to understand the press as a source for sortable, extractable data. In the 1840s, the abolitionists Sarah and Angelina Grimké and Theodore Weld turned Southern newspapers into a source of data about Southern slavery. Working from undifferentiated advertisements for runaway slaves, rendered in the neutral language of commerce, the three interpreted this material through the Grimkés' knowledge from growing up in a South Carolina slaveholding family to write *American Slavery As It Is: Testimony of a Thousand Witnesses.* They used the slaveholders' press against itself. Ads for runaways casually mentioned scars and maimings caused by brutality as identifying marks. The Grimkés and Weld clipped and sorted the items into categories such as "tortures, by iron collars, chains, fetters, handcuffs, &c.," "brandings, maimings, gun-shot wounds, &c.," and "Mutilation of Teeth," creating information about the routine and accepted torture of enslaved people and elucidating its purposes. Reinterpreting runaway ads had been an abolitionist tactic for years. British abolitionists used the slaveholders' words against themselves in this mode as early as 1791, and William Lloyd Garrison's *Liberator* used it frequently in the 1830s. The Grimkés, however, because they used the press as a database, stretched beyond such anecdotal uses. In six months, they scanned, marked, and categorized an estimated twenty thousand newspapers. The sheer number of papers in the Grimké-Weld database refuted pro-slavery objections that they were listing atypical situations. The Grimkés' remarkable and dedicated feat of turning newspapers into a corpus that could be scanned and sorted for data extraction was routinized and commercialized in the clipping bureaus that took off in the 1890s.[12]

Clipping bureaus industrialized the work of segmenting and morselizing information that commonplace books hinted at and scrapbooks extended. Some clipping bureau owners got their start as exchange editors, people who knew intimately the value of information's mobility. Although clipping bureau promoters often noted that they created scrapbooks for clients, the real power and focus of the clipping bureau was that it detached clippings from their previous contexts and freed them to move into multiple new contexts.

Clipping Bureaus

Back Number Budd conceptualized newspapers as piles of printed paper that would become valuable over time, and that people would buy if the papers were properly sorted and stored so they could access an item from an already known date. The alternative was to search through files, paper by paper. It was up to the purchaser to decide whether to view the newspaper item as movable data or as concrete evidence, fused to the date-stamped materiality of the paper. The newspaper clipping services or bureaus, which coexisted with Budd and outlasted him, instead framed their task as organizing and sorting the information in the newspapers.[13]

Employees at clipping bureaus scanned and clipped items from current newspapers for material on topics specified by clients, who periodically received packets of clippings by mail or courier. Clipping bureaus rationalized the labor of reading and saving the newspaper. They divided the task into scanning according to keywords and subjects, marking with a pencil, cutting with scissors or knife, sorting the items, and mailing them. Though the newspaper might have been written and assembled by dividing the work among the city desk, the telegraph editor, the exchange editor, the advertising department, and other departments, and its pages might have reflected divisions into news, poetry, ship arrivals, the women's page, and so on, the clipping bureau atomized the newspaper according to the logic of the reader or client, reconceptualizing it as divisible into items within subject headings.

Each reader or scanner worked with a list of multiple clients and topics. An economy of scale joined with piecework wages to make it a profitable process for the bureau. George Bernard Shaw, visiting Hemstreet's New York clipping service in 1915, was drawn to "the scientific efficiency of this institution" and dazzled by "the long rows of workers with their glittering scissors flashing in the sunlight snipping away with a rapidity and an accuracy that made my brain whirl." At Romeike's Newspaper Clipping Bureau, by 1932, every client was assigned a number; sixty women scanned and marked the publications with the clients' numbers, and then "a whole paper is ... passed to a group of boys who slash deftly with razor knives, paste the clippings on dated slips. A second staff of girls sorts the clippings into pigeonholes keyed to the clients' numbers, for mailing." The

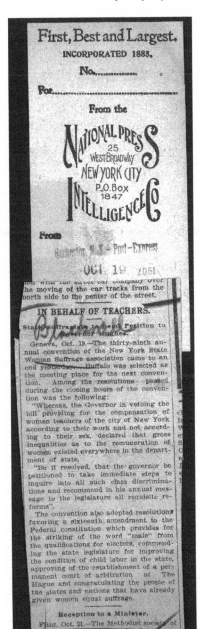

First, Best and Largest.

INCORPORATED 1885.

No................

Poe..

From the

NATIONAL PRESS
25
WEST BROADWAY
NEW YORK CITY
P.O. Box
1847
INTELLIGENCE CO

From

Rochester, N. Y.—Post-Express

OCT 19 2061

...with the street car company over
the moving of the car tracks from the
north side to the center of the street.

IN BEHALF OF TEACHERS.

State Suffragists to Send Petition to
Governor Hughes.

Geneva, Oct. 19.—The thirty-ninth annual convention of the New York State
Woman Suffrage association came to an
end yesterday.—Buffalo was selected as
the meeting place for the next convention. Among the resolutions passed
during the closing hours of the convention was the following:
"Whereas, the Governor in vetoing the
bill providing for the compensation of
women teachers of the city of New York
according to their work and not according to their sex, declared that gross
inequalities as to the remuneration of
women existed everywhere in the department of state,
"Be it resolved, that the governor be
petitioned to take immediate steps to
inquire into all such class discrimina-
tions and recommend in his annual message to the legislature all requisite reforms".
The convention also adopted resolutions
favoring a sixteenth amendment to the
Federal constitution which provides for
the striking of the word "male" from
the qualifications for electors, commending the state legislature for improving
the condition of child labor in the state,
approving of the establishment of a permanent court of arbitration at The
Hague and congratulating the people of
the states and nations that have already
given women equal suffrage.

Reception to a Minister.

Flint, Oct. 21.—The Methodist society of

Figure 7.2 Clipping service slip in the Elizabeth Smith Miller and Anne Fitzhugh Miller Scrapbooks; "Blackwell" as the account that ordered the topic. Newspaper title is minimized. (Library of Congress, Rare Book and Special Collection Division, NAWSA Miller Scrapbook Collection.)

dated slips, produced by yet another set of workers, were headed with the bureau's name and address and the newspaper source title. The slips featured the clipping bureau as the item's primary source, displacing not only the author—as newspaper exchanges had by crediting only the newspaper as source—but overriding the newspaper as well, much like today's student citing "Google" as the source of an article[14] (Figure 7.2).

Clipping bureaus began in the late 1870s and gained traction in the 1890s. Proprietors of the services were affiliated with the press: William F. G. Shanks, a writer, indexer, and former city editor of the *New York Tribune*, started the National Press Intelligence Company in New York in 1885, possibly inspired by the work of Henry Romeike, who began work in France and Germany and set up shop in New York as well by the mid-1880s. Robert Luce, an exchange editor on the *Boston Globe*, started their fast-growing competitor, the Luce Clipping Bureau. By 1899 there were at least a dozen and possibly as many as a hundred such agencies. Eventually, clipping bureaus spread across the country, reading local papers and patching together a national network via cooperating bureaus. Traces of the mechanisms of the network were erased to make it appear that every bureau had unlimited range. Frank Madison, who ran a press clipping bureau in Illinois beginning in the 1910s, told an interviewer,

> [W]e couldn't read all the papers in the United States. No one could. The[re]'d be one in Omaha reading all of Nebraska and that territory, and one in California, and one in Seattle, and New York, and so forth. And when we'd get an order that [required papers from other regions]..., we'd tell them to read their papers, and send them to us and then we'd tear off their slips and paste them on our own slips."[15]

Clipping bureaus were an outgrowth of the newspaper morgue, a repository of saved information to be reused in preparing obituaries on short notice, and subjects sure to be referred to again; and of the in-house newspaper exchange department. Newspapers sometimes hired the bureaus to clip their exchange papers. Specialized trade publications were particularly enthusiastic about the clipping bureaus' ability to glean from a larger array of papers, thus "systematizing" the exchange editor's work, as the editor of a business journal exulted. Another trade press editor celebrated the clipping bureau for ridding editors like him of the chore of clipping the exchange list: "Either the exchange list was turned over to the bureau to be read and clipped, or it was abolished entirely." The clipping bureau centralized the relationship between exchange papers and replaced it with a conduit or middleman, as though there were now a railroad trunk line rather than many regions connecting directly with one another via meandering local trains. As it reduced the need to read one another's papers and increased the spread of materials reaching subscribers and readers, it must also have diminished the experience of community among editors[16] (Figure 7.3).

Other values associated with the task of clipping the newspaper shifted, too, when clipping was outsourced from the hands of the decision-making editor and moved to the clipping bureau. The bureaus' readers did not call forth the praise for their exemplary breadth of knowledge that exchange edi-

Figure 7.3 Ad for Burrelle's clipping service, featuring its geographic range, and placing Burrelle at the center of it all, as the agency's representative "man who reads the newspapers"—obscuring the largely female reading staff (*The Clipping Collector*, 1896.)

tors had received (or bestowed on themselves); rather, the readers' facility for scanning and selecting was described more mechanically. The lower status of the mainly female corps of clipping bureau reader/markers accounted in part for this shift. Atomizing or rationalizing the work of clipping the paper, as on an assembly line, and defining some of the tasks as women's work deskilled and downgraded it and had the effect of allowing bureaus to keep wages low, as in factory work. The claim that women were more able to mechanically scan and not get caught up in reading the papers played on the earlier stereo-types that asserted that women did not read newspapers, Richard Popp notes (Figure 7.4).[17]

The reader/markers' ability to keep long lists of clients' interests in mind as they read and marked or clipped was declared uniquely feminine. A "girl" doing the work developed a special ability to "see certain names and subjects at a glance at the page of a newspaper. They are the names of the subjects she is paid to look up through hundreds of newspapers every day." These women became models of specialized reading, adapting themselves and their vision to the subjects called for. "'They stand right out,' said [one reader] laughingly, 'just as if they were printed in bold black type, and all the rest was small print. I couldn't help seeing

Figure 7.4 Picture from a trade card for Romeike's clipping service, showing workers, 1884 or later. (Courtesy of the American Antiquarian Society)

them if I wanted to.'" Like Charlie Chaplin working on an assembly line in *Modern Times*, tightening bolts and then unthinkingly continuing to tighten such boltlike objects as buttons, the ideal clipping bureau reader kept a single-minded focus on the interests of her employers' clients.[18]

In a fictional account of clipping bureaus, Francie Nolan, the heroine of *A Tree Grows in Brooklyn*, working at a bureau in 1916 and 1917, memorizes the two thousand headings on call and soon can "take in an item at a glance and note immediately whether it was something to mark." Although other commentators frame women's clipping bureau work as a mechanical skill, the fifteen-year-old Francie, who has left school and lied about her age to get the job, sees her work as an education: after reading for eight hours a day for a year she has her "own ideas about history and government and geography and writing and poetry" and so couldn't go back to school without jumping up to correct the teacher. But she lacks the exchange editor's power to decide what to reprint, and she is likewise removed from E. W. Gurley's domestic vision of the family passing around the paper to select according to their own interests and disassemble it into their own scrapbooks.[19]

The clipping bureau readers who tracked a name or a topic through the newspapers not only turned up many surprising contexts in which the clients had been written about but revealed the extent to which articles were reprinted via exchanges. Some customers were not so pleased to find themselves paying for stacks of the same item. Rupert Hughes was a prolific writer who, as an editor himself, understood the exchange system and might have wanted to keep track of reprints of his various works. Hughes claimed that a sonnet he had sold to a magazine for fourteen dollars cost him nearly a thousand dollars in unnecessary duplications:

> The press-clipping bureau clipped the clipping. The total charge for these was only a few dollars more than I got for the verses. In addition to this, the magazine editors also sent out a digest of the table of contents, in which my mere naked name was mentioned among the "also wrotes." This digest was sent to 20,000 newspapers. Every one reprinted it. The press-clippers caught every reprint and sent me a copy at the regular rate of five cents per clipping. Deducting the fourteen dollars I received for the sonnet, I have lost down to date exactly $986—a heavy fine to pay even for such a poem.[20]

Bureaus reassured disgruntled clients, however, that when they supplied multiples of the same notice from different papers they were not padding their bill but providing valuable evidence that the client's publicity had traveled widely into remote areas. Some writers early on recognized the utility of such a service; an 1888 query to *The Writer: A Magazine for Literary Workers*, before the term *clipping service* was familiar, asks for a bureau that makes a business of "finding the reprints or copies of any specified article in other papers than that in which it first appeared." As the public relations industry developed, it checked on such duplication as evidence of saturation of the concepts it promoted.[21]

Although the human readers who selected the articles were capable of judgments about the likely value of specific items, the governing algorithm was "clip all," an imperative given greater weight by piecework wages and billing the customer by the item. At least early in their existence, clipping services provided bundles of unsorted, unprioritized hits, explaining that it was more efficient to charge low rates but have the client winnow—"to pass careful judgment on each of the 20,000 clippings a day that are sent out would slow down the work so that prices would have to be much raised," noted one bureau owner in 1913.[22]

Clipping Service as Database

The noun *information* shifted its meaning in the nineteenth century from an abstract process, of "formation or moulding of the mind or character, instruction," a meaning surviving in the verb *to inform*, to instead almost exclusively meaning movable fragments of objective data, Geoffrey Nunberg has shown. The clipping services' idea that newspapers were a vehicle for data that could be isolated and re-sorted according to multiple criteria has shaped the interfaces of LexisNexis and other digital news sources. Such databases disassemble the newspaper via keyword searches and offer a pileup of hits to articles on those topics or via keywords from different sources, rather than slicing through what others were reading in the newspaper at that date, or offering Back Number Budd's stacks organized by newspaper title. Clipping bureaus thus laid the ground for the internet's fragmentation of the public convened around a day's reading of the newspaper. The bureaus' prices highlighted the value of information that had been processed and categorized: clippings cost approximately three cents each, while the entire newspaper itself cost one or two cents. The clipping bureau was a significant step toward digitized information. Both the clipping bureau and the internet extended the logic of scrapbooks. All three conceptualized the press as a collection of detachable, extractable, movable, reclassifiable information. We can learn about the differences between scrapbooks and clipping bureaus through errors, accidents, and surpluses. Newspaper clipping scrapbooks, no matter how sharply focused, nearly always contain off-topic surplus items pasted in because they were next to the relevant material in the paper, or because they interested the compiler while the pastepot and scrapbook were at hand. The clipping bureau's incidental errors, however, are false hits stemming from a mistaken, literal, or overly broad understanding of a keyword, as when an astronomical observatory interested in scanning the press as well as the skies received a news item about a racehorse named "Solar Eclipse." The deviations in the scrapbook stem from the materiality of the press and scrapbook, while errors made by the clipping service mark the movement from newspaper item to morselized data.[23]

Although the *Oxford English Dictionary*'s earliest citations for the term *keyword*, in the sense that is commonly employed for information searches, appear in the midtwentieth century, clipping services were using the term by 1913, linking it to their staff's need to move rapidly through the newspapers: "Our readers have not time to read anything through. They look for key-words, and finding one that is suggestive, must [mark the item and] jump on to the next item or article," noted Robert Luce, owner of the Luce Clipping Bureau.[24]

Luce explained the new conception of information in 1913:

> [A] newspaper or magazine is simply a collection of unrelated bits of information or discussion, all printed at the same revolution of the press only because men find money profit in throwing them together. The cord on which they are strung deserves no reverence. And when you take them off the cord, assort, and restring them, they are not beads to make a pretty necklace, but—if I do not too much force the metaphor—dried apples to be eaten.[25]

The scrapbook by contrast created a new necklace by restringing the "unrelated bits" on stronger cord, rather than turning them into nourishing morsels. This logic or understanding of information as beads or bits became more sharply apparent with the clipping bureau, which both extended and commercialized the individual practices of scrapbook making and made redistribution systems central to them. The bits of information are individually consumable—dried apples on the string once needed to produce them, but now entirely incidental and disposable, in Luce's metaphor.

Luce complained that scrapbooks were a poor way to organize information. But the fact that clipping bureaus often produced scrapbooks for their clients established a link between scrapbooks and clipping bureaus that helped turn-of-the-century Americans comprehend the usefulness of the bureaus. The extensive scrapbook collections bureaus made for clients (among them "sumptuously bound" scrapbooks for the czar or other famous people) were attractive topics for newspaper articles about the work of the bureaus. It made clipping service work intelligible by giving the clippings a familiar destination.[26]

The more significant clients of bureaus were enterprises targeting potential customers, whom they could then solicit individually for their business. Manufacturers could contract with clipping bureaus for notices of "projected bridges, factories needing machinery, churches and schools wanting furniture," overriding locality to pitch their goods nationally. Learning from a local Midwestern paper of a planned schoolhouse, manufacturers from Chicago, New York, and Boston could bid on roofs and ironwork, Frank Burrelle explained. The clipping service helped shift commerce from dependence on locality and personal contact to a regional or national market. Manufacturers could subscribe to receive birth announcements to send circulars for baby food, or order up news of accidents involving lost arms and legs, to peddle artificial limbs to the victims. Through press surveillance, sifted and classified by the clipping bureaus, death notices could be converted to commercial occasions to sell memorial cards and tombstones.[27]

Like scrapbooks, clipping services pulled something individual and idiosyncratic from the mass-produced press, but they systematized that work and turned it to commercial uses. Present-day internet spyware that tracks a user's browsing interests or keywords in a writer's email and then sends related ads alongside the email opening page, has its roots in the clipping bureaus' approach to sifting the press and reframing news as commercial opportunity. It speeds up and individualizes this earlier practice, though it may result in links as inappropriate as the news of a racehorse sent to the astronomy lab.

Newspapers bought the services of clipping bureaus as well and used this technology of systematically scanning the press with a comprehensiveness beyond the scope of exchange editors. They sometimes engaged in stunts that spotlighted the work of newsgathering: one newspaper reportedly commissioned a bureau to clip four thousand reports on the activities of every person named Smith appearing in newspapers the previous week—thereby presumably getting the story and the name of the paper around, and of course selling papers to everyone named Smith. This Smith collection carries the seeds of later innovations, like websites where people with the same name gather (such as the International Brotherhood of Seans or the Steve Collective), or films such as the *Grace Lee Project*, for which a filmmaker named Grace Lee interviewed many other women named Grace Lee to break down stereotypes about Asian American women. As a one-time stunt rather than a social network or an exploration of identity, however, the Smith collection publicizes a new technology: the capacity to sift the haystack of the press to assemble a package of needles to sell. Its added value derived from the capacity to reconceptualize the press, reclassify its articles, aggregate them, and mine the whole as a database.

Half a century after they completed their arduous six-month task of scanning newspapers, the Grimkés could have hired it out. Clients used clipping bureaus to compile evidence to buttress their arguments. One newspaper commissioned a clipping bureau to find notices of trolley accidents, to use "as ammunition in a fight against this method of transportation." Media reception itself became a topic, as clients used bureaus to show how the press approached a subject, and thus to analyze both media and the information available to readers. Anke te Heesen describes the efforts of Ernst Gehrcke, an opponent of Albert Einstein and the Theory of Relativity, who from the 1910s to the early 1920s used clipping services to demonstrate that the "theory and principle of relativity were...only used in the press as catchphrases 'that have the effect on the masses of making everyone believe that he has heard something familiar.'" Gehrcke's clippings, compiled into at least twenty-one scrapbooks, were meant to show a process of mass suggestion at work in hyping and convincing readers of the validity of what he believed was a spurious theory. The comprehensiveness of clipping bureau work meant it could also show that the press refused to cover a topic, as Upton Sinclair asserted when he employed two clipping bureaus to follow up on his 1906 article "The Condemned Meat Industry," in *Everybody's Magazine*, and found almost complete silence in the press about his exposé. Sinclair then turned the data into evidence fueling another exposé, *The Brass Check*, this time revealing how the newspapers were beholden to corporate interests.[28]

Understanding that the newspaper was a databank that could yield information about how an article or speech was received, or how widely it circulated, meant that the press could be tapped for political organizing. Though scrapbook-making suffragists had already combed the press for this purpose on a small scale, clipping bureaus were hired to extend the older form; the wealthy suffragist and strategist Alva Vanderbilt Belmont paid clipping bureaus to compile her suffrage scrapbooks in the early 1910s, as the suffragist cause turned into a full campaign and became more sophisticated in its attention to public relations. But the individual suffrage scrapbooks were no longer adequate to their needs. Whole offices within the suffrage campaign were set up to clip newspapers to follow coverage as a step toward placing more material in the mainstream press. In 1909, Ida Husted Harper reported that suffragists had opened a national press bureau in New York, which paid for the services of a clipping bureau to follow coverage around the country, but it also did its own clipping, daily examining "sixteen papers of New York City" and carefully filing three thousand clippings on women's suffrage in five months. Their press bureau systematized publicity and public relations to spur newspapers to print editorials and articles favorable to the movement. More generally, clipping bureaus became an accepted tool for measuring the saturation of public relations campaigns, and calibrating their methods.[29]

Seeing newspapers as data suggested other ways of working with them. The machinery of new sifting and scanning methods creaks into gear in what Burrelle's Press Clipping Bureau called "back number work," which entailed searching through the limited files of old newspapers that some bureaus kept on hand. Since the economy of scale at work in clipping the daily papers didn't apply to searching past dates, the price was far steeper—enough so that when a customer was willing to pay the high price for scanning back numbers, one clipping bureau offered a reduced rate to piggyback on the search through the New York *Herald, World,* and *Tribune* from 1891 to 1896, noting that "those persons who want items published in those papers during that period, can get them by placing orders at once, at a much lower rate than if search was being made for them alone." As awkward and expensive as this offered service was, it suggested new possibilities for using the newspapers. Scrapbook advice givers had often warned that valuable information would slip away if one failed to save it in a scrapbook: "Everyone who takes a newspaper containing various items connected with housekeeping, the toilette, etc., will often regret to have it torn up, on account of some little scrap in it which was of importance to them," noted one scrapbook advocate. Scrapbooks and searching through Back Number Budd's warehouse were no longer the only options for finding a clipping again, though the substitute was expensive.[30]

Devaluing the Book: A New Relationship to Information

Henry Romeike was deeply self-interested when he made the proclamation on the significance of clipping bureaus with which this chapter began. But he also recognized that the clipping bureau enabled a new relationship to information. It paralleled and coincided with new developments in conceptualizing and working with information, like the Library of Congress Subject Headings (LCSH), published in 1898. The LCSH standardized and regularized terms and relationships and could be applied to any documents—to clippings as easily as to books.[31]

The clipping bureau made it possible to sort the press by multiple topical headings or keywords, so that the same item could appear in various subscribers' packets for different reasons. The process could be expensive, especially if the search parameters were not carefully (or even clairvoyantly) defined. As we have seen, it was not readily undertaken retrospectively. But those who agreed with Elizabeth Boynton Harbert's complaint that encyclopedias and other reference books were inferior to newspapers as sources of current information recognized that the capacity of clipping bureaus to sort and redistribute the information marked a technological leap. Forecasting that the clipping bureau had utopian potential for redistributing knowledge, Margherita Arlina Hamm, a journalist and suffragist, focused in 1896 on the clipping bureau's ability to decentralize and reconcentrate information in multiple, widely dispersed locations:

> As it stands now we depend first upon the text-book, second the magazine article, and special publications in many languages, and even then we are liable to be weeks, months, and even years behind some new fact, exploration, invention, or discovery. With the international bureau and press album this will be changed, and the specialist in the smallest country town will be better situated for the prosecution of his studies than the president of the learned society which makes those studies its chief object.[32]

As the clipping bureau allowed articles to be fragmented into "facts," culled according to the "key-words" or subject headings defined by the subscribers and then dispersed rapidly and cheaply into the hands of subscribers via the network of the postal service, it sped up the movement of data and its reuse, reshaping, and reintegration into new information. Speed was crucial. Americans were living in an "up-to-date age" of fast-moving new media, Robert Luce noted: "The telegraph, the telephone, the locomotive and the newspaper press urge on the swiftest, keenest competition the world has ever seen. Knowledge must put on seven-league boots if it would keep pace." The newspaper's "information may be fragmentary or inexact, but it is the only absolutely new information to be generally had."[33]

Nineteenth-century scrapbook makers repackaged their clippings as books. They smoothed over the ephemerality and dailiness of clippings to hide them behind handsome bindings of agricultural reports or sermons or other works with earmarks of permanence, much as early-twenty-first-century e-readers approximate the shape and appearance of bound books. Clipping services, however, flaunted the fragmentation of the materials they offered. The book was losing out to the clipping as a carrier of knowledge, conceived as morselized or morselizable facts, detached discoveries, and reports on experiments rather than extended arguments or narratives, or complex discourses. Routed to the right hands and properly filed, clippings were understood to have greater value. Books suffered by comparison to newspaper clippings: "New information and new ideas do not get within the covers of books for months, sometimes for years, after they ought to have begun helping," Luce asserted. In the scientific world, especially, currency of information was more important than its appearance in the prestigious form of a book; by 1902 medical practitioners were urged to keep abreast of new developments via clipping bureaus. "Scraps and clippings are more numerous, more fugitive and more valuable than books," the editor of a newsletter for scientists explained to his readers in 1928. "A book that is lost can usually be replaced for a dollar or so, but an item you cut from an unknown newspaper or a note you jotted down a la [Alexander] Pope on the back of an envelope may be worth much more to you and is irrecoverable."[34]

Though books, too, could be conceptualized as snippets of useful information, few book owners were willing to activate the concept with a pair of scissors. Writing in 1937 of her lifelong habit, Carolyn Wells, an author and book collector, reported that many people expressed shock when she snipped a picture from a dictionary she owned to pass it along to a friend who lived at a distance from bookstores and libraries and needed such a picture. She distinguished between the kinds of rare books she collected and enjoyed for their special qualities as books and those she was willing to treat as disposable repositories of information, to be disassembled and redistributed as needed.[35]

With an understanding that the book was inferior, the practice of displacing the contents of an outmoded or undesirable book such as the agricultural reports or old textbooks with fugitive clippings faded. Clippings suffered when pinned down in books. Libraries began to shun scrapbooks in favor of vertical files and other methods for holding clippings for use. Breed's Patent Portfolio Scrap-Book, for example, offered an intermediate step: envelopes bound together in book like form into which "scraps can be dropped and methodically filed by subject" and then taken out again (Figure 7.5). The language of juxtaposition through which scrapbooks had made a permanent record of their makers'

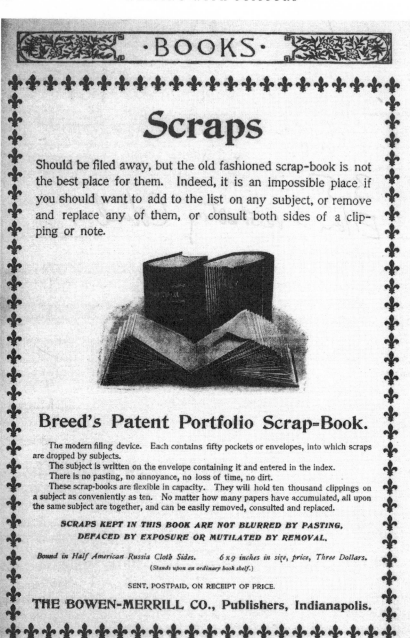
Figure 7.5   Ad for Breed's Portfolio Scrap-Book, *Scribner's*, Oct 1894, 11.

thoughts was less compelling, too limiting in the face of the ability to continually sort and re-sort many more clippings into new data sets and thus different juxtapositions and classifications—an ability especially attractive to institutional users.

Scrapbooks were a nascent technology forging a new way of thinking about materials and data. Classification schemes available to clipping bureau clients overlapped with and shifted from those that scrapbook makers kept in mind. Nineteenth-century scrapbook makers were sometimes already using transferrable descriptors, even if they weren't spelled out: "items about black centenarians," "articles about men who brutalized their wives," "articles about the Boston woman's rights convention that mention Caroline Dall." But scrapbook makers' organizing schemes also grew from engagement with the paper, or from catching patterns as they emerged. It would have been impossible to delegate the individual, idiosyncratic collections of nineteenth-century scrapbooks by writing orders to clip "poems that moved me after my son's death," "articles on crime that demonstrate injustice toward blacks in contrast to whites accused of the same crime," "obituaries about people I once knew," or "items that appealed to me."

The impersonal thoroughness of the clipping bureau made it a closer ancestor of the internet's searching and scanning capabilities than the scrapbook. Hamm's vision of democratized access to knowledge, with its specialists in the smallest country town receiving parcels of knowledge delivered to the door (albeit for a substantial fee) is familiar now because it sounds so much like late-twentieth-century excitement about the internet offering decentralized access to information resources. The importance of this connection, however, is not that clipping bureaus are a pale foreshadowing of the internet, the steampunk version of Google, complete with a corps of scissors-wielding women in neat shirtwaists carrying out keyword searches of the day's print productions and passing slips into pigeonholes. Rather, the clipping bureau—along with developments in classification such as the Library of Congress Subject Headings—extended the scrapbook and the newspaper exchange system's capacity to isolate items from one context and reclassify or reslice them and reframe them in another, to produce new knowledge. It thus affirmed a conceptual understanding of items as bare "facts," floating free of their contexts, with only a uniform clipping bureau slip identifying the newspaper source. Commentators on this shift in reading were as polarized as are recent writers on how the internet has affected reading. They greeted readers' growing use of fragments of the press as marking a precipitous decline in the ability to think, on the one hand, or as a great improvement in developing knowledge via enhanced access to information, on the other.

The clipping bureau thus augmented cut-and-paste writing. It allowed individual writers to pull articles, news, and standalone "facts" from a wider set of sources and gave them access to the exchange editors' resources. Like the commonplace book, it positioned other people's writing as a natural resource to be incorporated into one's own writing. Elbert Hubbard, a businessman, founder of the Roycrofters Press and workshop, and scrapbook and commonplace book compiler, praised the clipping bureau for gathering the raw materials: "It brings the warp and weft for you to weave and pattern, the nuggets for you to refine, the rough diamond for you to cut, polish and set." Hubbard unselfconsciously treats other people's work as unprocessed materials, and the clipping bureau subscriber as the real writer, although the article once written would enter the stream of the press and become another writer's nuggets and rough diamonds. If, as the *Hartford Post* editor wrote in 1886, with the exchange system and well-used scissors "five hundred brains" wrote the newspaper, by 1915 five hundred brains could easily write every article, if a writer adapted and reused the clipping service packet.[36]

The name of one clipping bureau proprietor even became a verb: *Romeiking* for a time referred to "compiling articles or writing books from press clippings." Will Clemens, who made a career of patching together and reselling assemblages of other people's writing, recognized his connection to press clipping bureau work clearly enough to own a bureau for a time (claiming, of course, that its intent was to help out his "uncle" by generating clippings for users of Mark Twain's Scrap Book). He evidently found the work of gathering and dispersing the clippings to other clients less remunerative and returned to creating and selling his own pastiches. At the same time, however, the clipping bureau made such reuse more visible to readers beyond the exchange editor's desk. This, along with changes in copyright laws, may have contributed to the twentieth century's greater premium on authorial originality and increased policing of the borders between invention and reuse.[37]

The habit of reading in snippets or reading on the run, which the press fostered and which the scrapbook was alternately supposed to remedy and accused of worsening, by the early twentieth century was tied to the need to stay abreast of developing knowledge. It was reframed as a potential virtue. As Margherita Hamm understood it, the clipping bureau could fulfill the promise of the 1883 "flat of the near future" seen in Figure Intro.4, with its specialized publications continuously unreeling into each family member's lap. It was not important that the household members were no longer gathered around the gluepot to divide the newspaper among themselves according to their individual interests, in E. W. Gurley's model. Rather, they could shut out or simply be unaware of one another's interests, receiving an already disassembled newspaper. In the terms of the cartoon, they could receive their papers through their own slots; in terms of the actual practice of the clipping bureaus, they would open the day's personally directed envelope from Burrell's or Luce's clipping agency, with its requested clippings. Every subscriber was his or her own segment of the readership.

The Place of the Scrapbook in Media History

Newspaper clipping scrapbooks dramatized the possibilities of writing with scissors: creating new works from old with ease and creating new value from those old works via renaming, reclassifying, and recombining materials. If we look past their bulky bindings and yellowing pages, we can see how innovative and path-breaking they were. From the middle to late nineteenth century, these scrapbooks were a cutting-edge technology allowing its adaptors to understand the press as a structure holding written items in a temporary arrangement. They allowed their users to think of media as separable into fragments of information and expression that could be recast and reassembled into new entities. Scrapbook makers detached the items as they wished and saved them in a new and permanent, though uniquely individual, configuration that announced its stability and value by assuming the prestigious form of a book.

The scrapbook's rootedness in newsprint and ink anchored it in the clippings' origins in the date-stamped press. The scissors offered the option of keeping or stripping away those obvious connections of newspaper title or article author but they enforced retaining visual ties to the original typography and layout, as the commonplace book had not. The exchange system and reprinting detached the clipping further from its origins and set articles roaming freely through the press, allowing them to be clipped repeatedly for more recirculation or to be pinned down in scrapbooks. Back Number Budd's business made it obvious that there were people avid to retrieve old articles, and that though some needed their material qualities others (like later digitizers) cared only for their contents. The clipping service retained the physical trace of the original form of the clipping, but its use of keywords to search the press furthered the process of morselization and made it easy to sort according to multiple and sometimes standardized categories.

Scrapbook makers recognized that the press could be cut apart and reassembled to create new knowledge. This understanding led to clipping services and the many forms of digitized data retrieval and distribution that followed. Scrapbook forms and uses, like later bookmarks or favorites web lists, created coherence from broadly miscellaneous materials as well as materials without attribution, even if the coherence or associations are clear only to the creator.

Like today's blogs, email, note-taking software, and news feeds, scrapbooks allowed users to transfer items from one medium into another. They could share their classifications with a circle of readers in the same stroke. As this basic concept has been picked up and developed in the media of the twentieth and twenty-first centuries, the earlier interest in permanent or semipermanent packaging has been largely replaced by an emphasis on searchability, speed of transmission, duplicability, and rapid transformation into new material.

In the twenty-first century we are familiar with the sense that we know something because Google can find it, or know where we are going because our GPS guides us, or know a telephone number because our phone has stored it—the sense, in short, that our digital devices are prosthetic or auxiliary brains. Nineteenth-century newspaper scrapbook makers would have recognized our diffused intellects in their feeling that the scrapbook record of their reading was a part of them, a second self. Scrapbooks were constantly renewed reference works, molded to the maker's needs, an analog to the maker's life. "Every day brings its contributions, and the leaves accumulate until the book is filled," as E. W. Gurley wrote.[38]

Capacious, expandable, fluid hypertext is in many ways superior to three-dimensional scrapbooks constrained by paper and glue. But scrapbook links do not expire. And so we have these thousands of records, evidence of seeking and reading and sharing, from another era's searches and links.

NOTES

Introduction

1. Scrapbook of Frances Amanda Smith Cather, George Cather Ray Collection (MS 113). Archives & Special Collections, U of Nebraska–Lincoln Libraries.
2. "Have a Scrap Book," *The Lynchburg Virginian*, 17 Feb 1883, 4, col A.
3. Michael Schudson, *Discovering the News: A Social History of American Newspapers* (New York: Basic, 1981), 17–18. The initial move from six-cent subscriber-supported papers to one-cent advertising-supported papers did not stem from recognizing the value of advertising. Rather, Benjamin Day, a printer, first issued the *New York Sun* as a small afternoon paper to advertise his shop's job printing; he "scissored out the news" from the morning papers to draw readers. The paper itself—sold by newsboys rather than by subscription—became wildly popular, went on to sell advertising, and attracted competitors on the same lines. ("A Pioneer in Journalism; The Busy Life of Benjamin Henry Day," *New York Times*, 22 Dec 1889, Web, 14 June 2011).
4. Benedict Anderson discusses the concept of the nation as an imagined community—with the readers' awareness that others are reading the same newspaper simultaneously as an important constitutive element—in *Imagined Communities: Reflections on the Origin and Spread of Nationalism* (New York: Verso, 1991). As we will see, this concept not only is complicated by reprinting, in the way that Meredith McGill notes, but is literally shredded by saving newspapers in scrapbooks. See McGill, *American Literature and the Culture of Reprinting, 1834–1853* (U Pennsylvania P, 2003). The Union News Company, created in 1864, stabilized newsstands as an ongoing, large-scale business allowing urban readers to be sure of finding those newspapers to which they did not subscribe. Thomas C. Leonard, *News for All: America's Coming of Age with the Press* (New York: Oxford UP, 1995), 159. David M. Henkin and Isabel Lehuu have both discussed the growing importance of the individually owned copy of the newspaper in the antebellum period: Henkin, *City Reading: Written Words and Public Spaces in Antebellum New York* (New York: Columbia UP, 1998); Lehuu, *Carnival on the Page: Popular Print Media in Antebellum America* (Chapel Hill: U North Carolina P, 2000). Such individual ownership was a prerequisite for cutting up newspapers for scrapbooks.
5. The number of dailies quadrupled between 1870 and 1900, increasing from 574 to 2,226, while Sunday editions swelled in size and readership. Individual papers reached more readers as well, with their average circulation rising from 2,600 to 15,000. Paul Starr, *The Creation of the Media* (New York: Basic, 2005), 252; Julia Colman, "Among the Scrap-books," *The Ladies' Repository*, Aug 1873, 89.

6. David Paul Nord discusses the nineteenth-century newspaper's increasing appetite for "facts" and its fondness for miscellany columns in his *Communities of Journalism: A History of American Newspapers and Their Readers* (U Illinois P, 2001); he estimates that the Chicago *Times*, a particularly miscellaneous publication, would have commonly contained a thousand "bits of news" in an eight-page edition (115). See Figure Intro.3, from the *San Jose Evening News*, 26 June 1908, 6; and the *Savannah Tribune*, an African American paper, 12 Aug 1912, 7. Similar headings appeared in earlier newspapers as well. "French Flat" in the cartoon's caption was a term for a middle-class apartment with all rooms on the same floor.

7. "Editor's Study," *Harper's New Monthly Magazine*, Sep 1892, 639. Anke te Heesen has written on clipping bureaus in Germany, in relation to clipping practices in visual arts, in "News, Paper, Scissors: Clippings in the Sciences and Arts Around 1920," in *Things That Talk: Object Lessons from Art and Science*, Lorraine Daston, ed. (Brooklyn, NY: Zone, 2007). Some of my thinking on changing conceptions of facts and information in the nineteenth century is indebted to Geoffrey Nunberg, ed., "Farewell to the Information Age," in *The Future of the Book* (Berkeley: U of California P, 1996), 103–38.

8. My estimate is based on the number of scrapbooks that have survived in nearly every public collection, evidence of scrapbooks in private hands, accounts of destruction of scrapbooks, and the assumption in every nineteenth-century article and story mentioning scrapbooks that readers already have detailed knowledge of what they are. On medical scrapbooks, see Katherine Ott, "Scrapbooks of Nineteenth Century Medical Practitioners," in Susan Tucker, Katherine Ott, and Patricia Buckler, eds., *The Scrapbook in American Life* (Philadelphia: Temple UP, 2006). Lincoln's scrapbook is at Abraham Lincoln Papers, Library of Congress, available online at http://lcweb2.loc.gov/cgi-bin/ampage?collId=rbc3&fileName=rbc0001_2004stern00001page.db&recNum=0. Accessed 25 July 2009.

9. For gendering and asserting hierarchies of scrapbooks, see Brander Matthews [Arthur Penn], *The Home Library*, (New York: Appleton, 1886) 44–47. Perhaps because Jefferson could afford to cut up the more expensive newspapers of his era, he was an early scrapbook maker. Although Amy Mecklenburg-Faenger suggests that the term *scrapbook* was always gendered female as a species of insult, I argue that since both men and women made newspaper clipping scrapbooks, the shift to seeing scrapbooks as a synonym for jumbled collection, and as female, came as news clipping services and later filing systems took over and industrialized the work of clipping newspapers. Systems replaced scrapbooks, so that by the 1920s, with some exceptions, the last scrapbooks left standing were memorabilia books and poetry scrapbooks, more closely associated with women and more vulnerable to derision. "Trifles, Abominations, and Literary Gossip: Gendered Rhetoric and Nineteenth-Century Scrapbooks," *Genders Online Journal*, 55 Spring 2012. Accessed 23 Apr 2012.

10. On using scrapbooks to supplement readers, see for example "Notes on Teaching Reading," Indiana State Teachers Association, *The Indiana School Journal*, 34, 7 July 1889. On students making scrapbooks, see N. W. Taylor Root, *School Amusements; or How to Make the School Interesting* (New York: A. S. Barnes, 1869), 207–8, 216–17.

11. "Preserver of Literary Derelicts," *Bangor Daily Whig and Courier*, 17 Oct 1894, originally published in the *Kansas City Star*. Will M. Clemens, "The Evolution of the Clipping," *The Clipping Collector*, Jan 1896, 1:1, 3; E. W. Gurley, *Scrap-books and How to Make Them: Containing Full Instructions for Making a Complete and Systematic Set of Useful Books* (New York: Authors' Publishing, 1880), 5–6.

12. The stories in the Baxter scrapbook and their relationship to the ideology of moral uplift are further discussed in my "Less Work for 'Mother': Rural Readers, Farm Papers, and the Makeover of "The Revolt of "Mother,""" *Legacy: A Journal of American Women Writers*, 2009, 26:1.

13. From James Tate, "The Horseshoe," *Selected Poems* (Wesleyan UP, 1991) 184. Nearly every present-day reader who has worked with scrapbooks points to their enigmatic qualities. Todd Gernes comments, "Although these traces and historical imprints seem evident, even familiar, like teeth marks on a beloved baby book, interpreting them is another matter." "Recasting the Culture of Ephemera," *Popular Literacy: Studies in Cultural Practices and Poetics,* ed. John Trimbur (Pittsburgh: U Pittsburgh P, 2001) 111.

14. Damon Darlin reported in 2006 that scrapbook devotees spent an estimated $3 billion in 2005 on special paper, fabrics, and other goods for their scrapbooking. "Trend: Goodbye, Glue. Hello, Digital. The Once-Humble Hobby of Scrapbooking Has Moved On," *New York Times,* 7 June 2006, http://tech2.nytimes.com/mem/technology/techreview.html?res=9801E3D81431F934A35755C0A9609C8B63, accessed 12 Jan 2011. Liz Rohan notes the rise of commercially produced objects to aid memory in the nineteenth century in "I Remember Mamma: Material Rhetoric, Mnemonic Activity, and One Woman's Turn-of-the-Twentieth-Century Quilt," *Rhetoric Review* 23 2004, 368–87.

15. Amy Matilda Cassey, *Original & selected poetry &c.*, Library Company of Philadelphia. For a discussion of this album in relation to connections between African American women, see Erica R. Armstrong, "A Mental and Moral Feast: Reading, Writing, and Sentimentality in Black Philadelphia," *Journal of Women's History,* 16:1, Spring 2004, 78–102. The album can be seen at http://www.librarycompany.org/Cassey/index.htm. Such albums are also like another popular nineteenth-century genre, the friendship quilt, to which friends and family members each contributed a square, typically for someone moving away.

16. Earle Havens in his study of commonplace books notes that works called commonplace books and scrapbooks overlapped, especially by the nineteenth century, though he sees the shift as one of compilers pasting printed matter into commonplace books. *Commonplace Books: A History of Manuscripts and Printed Books from Antiquity to the Twentieth Century* (New Haven: Beinecke Rare Book and Manuscript Library, 2001).

17. C. Vann Woodward discusses some of Chesnut's clippings in Mary Boykin Miller Chesnut and C. Vann Woodward, *Mary Chesnut's Civil War* (New Haven: Yale UP, 1993).

18. David M. Henkin, *City Reading,* 130–31. Amos Webber, an African American activist workingman living in Philadelphia and Worcester, Massachusetts, wrote a diary from 1854 to 1903, which often copied or summarized newspaper accounts; some clippings are stuffed in as well. Nick Salvatore, *We All Got History: The Memory Book of Amos Webber* (New York: Times Books, 1996) xvi, 237. Liz Rohan discusses another hybrid of diary and scrapbook in "I Remember Mamma."

19. For an extensive discussion of trade card scrapbooks, see my *Adman in the Parlor: Magazines and the Gendering of Consumer Culture, 1880s–1910s* (New York: Oxford UP, 1996). William Davies King's *Collections of Nothing* discusses the affective dimension of collecting and arranging commercial memorabilia in the twentieth century in ways that are provocative for thinking about this kind of scrapbook as well (Chicago: U Chicago P, 2008). For some of the uses to which scrapbook makers put pre-snapshot photos, see Elizabeth Siegel, *Playing with Pictures: The Art of Victorian Photocollage* (Chicago: Art Institute of Chicago, 2009); and Beverly Gordon, "Scrapbook Houses for

Paper Dolls: Creative Expression, Aesthetic Elaboration, and Bonding in the Female World," in Tucker et al., *The Scrapbook in American Life*, 116–34. Sally Newman has explored the elusiveness of analyzing college girls' scrapbooks with images of cross-dressing in "Sites of Desire," *Australian Feminist Studies*, 25:64, 2010, 147–62.

20. For further discussion and a visual sampling of memorabilia scrapbooks, see Jessica Helfand, *Scrapbooks: An American History* (New Haven: Yale UP, 2008). Baby books, another kind of memorabilia book, are a type of scrapbook documenting motherhood. They are more often structured by printed pages directing the maker to focus on specific elements of the infant's development. (For more on them, see Janet Golden and Lynn Weiner, "Reading Baby Books: Medicine, Marketing, Money and the Lives of American Infants," *Journal of Social History*, 44:3, 2011, 667–87.) For more on school and college scrapbooks, see Susan Tucker, "Reading and Re-reading: The Scrapbooks of Girls Growing into Women, 1900–1940," in *Defining Print Culture for Youth: The Cultural Work of Children's Literature*, Anne Lundin and Wayne Wiegand, eds. (Westport, CT: Greenwood P, 2003). The African American Amherst student was William Tecumseh Sherman Jackson, class of 1892. Information from Karen Sánchez-Eppler, personal communication, May 2012.

21. Alice Austen Scrapbook, 2004– m40. Box 1. Schlesinger Library, Radcliffe Institute, Harvard U. A hint of Austen's interest in the playful cross-dressing evident in her photographs appears in a cartoon suggesting that if women can't wear trousers in a tennis doubles game where men and women compete against one another, the men should wear dresses and big hats ("Lawn Tennis"). Her photographs were made using glass plate negatives in the demanding dry plate process, which entailed carrying heavy equipment and developing the photos in a running stream.

22. Helfand, as a visual artist, objects to the aesthetic choices of current scrapbookers, in contrast to the older memorabilia books she has collected. The more significant contrasts for this volume, however, are the differences in purpose and audience between past and present scrapbooks. Nineteenth-century clipping scrapbooks characteristically drew public materials from the larger world, making them available for personal, domestic, or professional use, and sometimes sent them back into circulation for organizational or political use. Current scrapbooks more often draw mainly on materials produced by or referencing the family and become a representation of that family to other families, or to other scrapbook makers. Helfand, *Scrapbooks* 166. Analyzing late-twentieth-century scrapbooks as a form of life writing, or "genre of self," Tamar Katriel and Thomas Farrell find them prizing and valorizing family life. "Scrapbooks as Cultural Texts: An American Art of Memory," *Text and Performance Q.* 11:1 Jan 1991, 2. Others focusing on scrapbooks as memory aids compare them to atlases, creating "personal topographies." See also Clare Farago, "'Scraps as it were': Binding Memories," *Journal of Victorian Culture* 10:1 Spring 2005, 114–22.

23. Diana Taylor, *The Archive and the Repertoire: Performing Cultural Memory in the Americas* (Durham, NC: Duke UP, 2003), 20. Patrizia Di Bello also takes up the issue of the gesture of cutting, which in collage work "cuts and repairs, fragments and makes whole again." *Women's Albums and Photography in Victorian England: Ladies, Mothers and Flirts* (Aldershot, UK: Ashgate, 2007) 3.

24. Walter Benjamin, "Attested Auditor of Books" in *The Work of Art in the Age of Its Technological Reproducibility, and Other Writings on Media* (Harvard UP, 2008) 170.

Chapter 1

1. Ann Blair's work on Renaissance commonplacing brilliantly conveys how relative the sense of being overwhelmed by print is. See Ann M. Blair, *Too Much to Know: Managing Scholarly Information Before the Modern Age* (New Haven: Yale UP, 2010).

2. Blair's *Too Much to Know* lays out the "four S's of text management" in use in early modern compilations: storing, sorting, selecting, and summarizing. All but the last are crucial to scrapbooks. She notes as well that cutting up texts into slips for the reader to sort took place even with manuscripts. The move from copying to cutting is not new with nineteenth-century scrapbooks, but it became more widespread with cheaper print. Thoreau and Emerson: see Meredith McGill, "Common Places: Poetry, Illocality, and Temporal Dislocation in Thoreau's *A Week on the Concord and Merrimack Rivers*," *American Literary History*, 19:2, Summer 2007, 357–74. Although Cary Nelson sees poetry scrapbooks as simply a variety of commonplace book, it is my observation that the very different labor and opportunities that clipping creates result in works far removed from commonplace books. Nelson, "The Temporality of Commonplaces: A Response to Meredith McGill," *American Literary History* 19:2, 2007, 375–80. Kate Sanborn, *Memories and Anecdotes* (New York: Putnam's, 1915), 4. The verse is by John Byrom, from "A Hint to a Young Person, For His Better Improvement by Reading or Conversation," *Miscellaneous Poems* (Manchester: J. Harrop, 1773). The commonplace book of a Princeton student who copied it between 1834 and 1837, Samuel Humes Porter, is online at http://paw.princeton.edu/issues/2008/05/14/pages/6669/index. xml, where the annotators have misattributed the verse to Lord Byron, demonstrating the tendency of commonplace passages to be reattributed. Accessed 1 Sep 2009. Catherine La Courreye Blecki and Karin A. Wulf have shown how a commonplace book's circulation through its compiler's community constituted a form of publication. *Milcah Martha Moore's Book: A Commonplace Book from Revolutionary America* (Pennsylvania State UP, 1997).

3. Earlier examples include David Evans Macdonnel's much-reprinted *A Dictionary of Quotations in Most Frequent Use, Taken from the Greek, Latin, French, Spanish, and Italian Languages, Translated into English, with Illustrations Historical and Idiomatic* (London: G. G. and J. Robinson, 1798). This was more likely intended as a pony for translating quotations and tags encountered in reading.

4. John Todd, "Introduction," *Index Rerum; or, Index of Subjects; Intended as a Manual to Aid the Student and the Professional Man in Preparing Himself for Usefulness, with an Introduction, Illustrating its Utility and Method of Use*, 2nd ed. (Northampton, Mass.: Bridgman and Childs, 1833, 1835), 5; and John Todd, "Address Before the Society of Inquiry, Sabbath Evening, August 25, 1833" (Amherst, Mass.: JS&C Adams, printers, 1833), 11.

Todd developed his system from John Locke's proposed indexed commonplace book, or perhaps he had seen a commercially produced version, *A Common Place Book. Upon the Plan Recommended and Practiced by John Locke, Esq.* (Boston: Cummings and Hilliard, 1821). Locke's plan appears in John Locke, *A New Method of a Common-Place Book*, in *The Works of John Locke*, vol. 2 (1686, London: C and J Rivington, 1824). Todd's, however, proposed to index its owner's library, without inserting passages from the reading. The dozen copies of Todd's *Index Rerum* seen for this study were all blank, abandoned, or repurposed after brief use. John McVey's website "Ongoing Gathering of John Todd's Index Rerum" shows many examples of abandoned and repurposed *Index Rerums* and compares Todd's with other forms of indexing reading. Accessed 18 Nov 2008.

The *Index Rerum* assumed continued access to the books one referenced, in stable form: the same editions, so that the page numbering would hold true; it assumed a unified, organically growing self, so that the lines that struck the reader at age twenty would be the passage still needed at age forty; it assumed that items would be categorized intelligibly enough to be found again and that alphabetical tags were the best categorizing or memory-cuing method; and of course it assumed that the reader would be organized enough to keep the *Index Rerum* at hand, and be diligent enough to take the notes in the first place. Thomas Augst notes that Locke's index was a method "for storing and retrieving knowledge already deemed to have objective, intrinsic value." Augst, *The Clerk's Tale: Young Men and Moral Life in Nineteenth-Century America.* (Chicago: U Chicago P, 2003) 35. But the value of material gathered in scrapbooks seemed more dubious: it did not carry the status of having been published in a book.

5. The 1870 census, which for the first time asked separately about reading and writing, found that about 25 percent more people could read than could write. "Introduction," *Nineteenth-Century Women Learn to Write*, ed. Catherine Hobbs (Charlottesville: U Virginia P, 1995) 11.

6. For more such advice, see Jacob Abbott, *Mary Gay; or, Work with Girls* (New York: Hurd, 1865), 184. Despite the title, the book suggests that boys and girls both make scrapbooks. An older girl working with young children selects items for them to paste in and reads them aloud, telling them, "When you grow a little older and can read well, it will be all the more amusing to you when you sit down to look over your books to have stories in them to read and some riddles to guess, as well as pictures to see." Horace L. Traubel reported that Whitman handed visitors copies of "The Midnight Visitor," a translation of a poem by Henri Murger. "Walt Whitman and Murger," *Poet Lore*, 6, 1894, 484.

7. Niklas Luhmann, *The Reality of the Mass Media*, Kathleen Cross, transl. (Palo Alto, Calif.: Stanford UP, 2000).

8. The parody of Thomas Hood's "Song of a Shirt" unsurprisingly was clipped and made the rounds of the newspapers, in six- and seven-stanza versions. John Brown, "Song of the Editor," *The Liberator*, 28 Feb 1845, 36, credited "From the St. Louis Reveille." It was clipped without the author's name in a scrapbook begun by Issacher Cozzens and probably continued by Deborah Cozzens Barnard; manuscript collection, New York Historical Society. Items are 1832–1884.

9. Meredith McGill, *American Literature and the Culture of Reprinting, 1834–1853* (U Pennsylvania P, 2003). A. F. Hill, *Secrets of the Sanctum: An Inside View of an Editor's Life* (Philadelphia: Claxton, Remsen and Haffelfinger, 1875), 65.

10. An 1843 count of newspapers mailed found each paper receiving an average of 364 exchange newspapers during one month, with city newspapers more active in both sending and receiving. Richard B. Kielbowicz, *News in the Mail: The Press, Post Office, and Public Information, 1700–1860s* (New York: Greenwood P, 1989), 149. By the 1870s, some editors were said to send out from a thousand to sixteen hundred exchange papers to other editors across the country, and more internationally. Rufus Anderson, *Foreign Missions: Their Relations and Claims* (Boston: Congregational Publishing Society, 1874), 316.

11. Unattributed, undated verse, in Rose Sevenoaks scrapbook, circa 1880s, Bancroft Library, U of California, Berkeley, F856 S4.

12. John H. Holmes, an owner of the *Boston Herald*, quoted in "The Columbian Reading Union," *Catholic World*, Sep 1897, 864. News was also sent into wide circulation via readyprint or patent insides or outsides of country weeklies, which often purchased sheets already printed with national or regional news on one side; the editors supplied only local news. Material on either side of the sheet might already have made the rounds of exchanges. Joan Shelley Rubin, *Songs of Ourselves: The Uses of Poetry in America* (Cambridge: Belknap P of Harvard UP, 2007) 297–300.

13. "Scissors Swingers: Annual Meeting of the Wisconsin Editorial Association," *Milwaukee Daily Sentinel*, 5 Oct 1881, 3. H. T. Peck, "College Journalism," *The Journalist: A Pictorial Souvenir*, New York, 1887, 39. Thomas Weaver, of the *Hartford Post*, in "The Editorial

Shears," *Texas Siftings*, 27 Feb 1886, 5:43, 5. *Texas Sifting's* editor asked other editors for their "opinion as to the value of the scissors" in editing. "The Exchange Editor and His Varied Duties," *San Antonio Sunday Light*, 18 Sep 1904, 10.

14. "The Editorial Three," credited to the *Western Journalist*, in *Macon Telegraph*, 25 Oct 1889, 4.

15. The paste proclaims, "I'm so very important you see,/That no editor's table/Has ever been able/To prosper at all without me." "The Editorial Three."

16. Jeannette Gilder, *Taken by Siege* (1886, New York: Scribner's, 1897), 7. As the editor of the *Critic*, an early promoter of literary celebrity, and the sister of Richard Watson Gilder, the editor of *The Century*, Gilder was particularly aware of how reputations were built. Robert Luce, "What Is News?" *The Clipping Collector*, May 1896, 1:5, 52; reprinted from *Newspaperdom*. Rufus Anderson, *Foreign Missions*, 316.

17. Lillie Devereux Blake, *Fettered for Life or Lord and Master: A Story of To-day* (1874, New York: Feminist P, 1996) 259. Fanny Fern [Sara Payson Willis Parton], *Ruth Hall* (1854, New Brunswick: Rutgers UP, 1986) 130, 158–59.

18. James Cephas Derby, *Fifty Years Among Authors, Books and Publishers* (New York: Carleton, 1884), 208.

19. Thanks to the members of the SHARP-L listserv for information on these uses of newspapers.

20. The treasured clipping typically inspires strong feeling and serves as a stand-in for the bestower's good advice, as in the story of a grandmother whose runaway grandson carries with him an item she had clipped for him "about a boy's duty to his mother and father." After he rereads it often enough, it prompts him to return. "Her Clipping Bureau," *Youth's Companion* 9 Feb 1911, 74. E. W. Gurley, *Scrap-books and How to Make Them* (New York: Authors' Publishing, 1880), 56, 15.

21. Mary Clemmer [Ames], *The Poetical Works of Alice and Phoebe Cary with a Memorial of Their Lives by Mary Clemmer* (New York: Hurd and Houghton), 45. A reviewer who disliked the Cary sisters' work and complained that too much poetry was published, picked up on just this claim, grumbling, "how can we forgive you for sending your whole scrap-book to the printer!" "Books and Authors: Alice and Phoebe Cary," *Christian Union*, 10 Sep 1873, 8:11, 207. "An Unenviable Position," *The Green Mountain Gem: A Monthly Journal of Literature, Science and Art*, Aug 1845, 3:8, 192. "Gossip of Authors and Books," *Current Literature*, July 1892, 10:3, 439. Critics complained that deserving American poets had never received book publication and therefore had "no habitation but the corner of a newspaper, or the scrapbook of a friend." "Melaia and Other Poems" (review), *Southern Literary Messenger*, Mar 1844, 168. In a similar positioning of the scrapbook as a counterweight to high culture, Georgia poet Frank L. Stanton in 1892 was said to have his verses "copied far and wide.... People cull his verses for their scrapbooks and women carry them around in their pocketbooks." Thirty years later, in a nostalgic look back at scrapbook making from the modernist 1920s, the same poet was praised as "'preeminently the scrap-book poet.' It is a wreath of laurel not to be despised." Being saved in a scrapbook distinguished his work from modernist poetry, which the writer believed lacked the ability to inspire or comfort and was therefore not likely to be saved. "Scrap Books," *Youth's Companion*, 12 May 1927, 101:19, 334. See Rubin, *Songs of Ourselves*, for more on the tensions between scrapbook and modernist poetry. Another popular newspaper poet, James Whitcomb Riley, won acclaim directly from a reader, who wrote of his poetry in Riley's own style: "When Charlie and I have read all the lines through/We clip from the paper, with blessings on you." "To J.W. Riley," *Indianapolis Herald*, 16 Oct 1880, quoted in Angela Sorby, *Schoolroom Poets: Childhood,*

Performance, and the Place of American Poetry, 1865–1917 (Durham: U New Hampshire P, 2005) 108.

22. This situation was significantly different from the world of mainly anonymous magazine publication that Edgar Allan Poe maneuvered within in the 1830s and 1840s. Poe benefited from decentralized publishing and a less-extensive exchange system by reselling his works to regional publications. He headed off unpaid use of his writing by inserting anticopying devices into works such as "Autography," which required reproduction of facsimile autographs. A publication seeking to reprint Poe's story would have to rent the original woodcuts from the *Southern Literary Messenger*, which Poe edited. McGill, *American Literature and the Culture of Reprinting*, 183.

23. Thanks to Paul Bergel for sharing his knowledge of the economics of rock band tours with me. Personal communication, 18 Apr 2009. R. C. MacDonald, "A Word to Exchange Editors," *The Writer*, June 1898, 9:6, 85.

24. Bill Nye, in "The Editorial Shears," *Texas Siftings*, 27 Feb 1886, 5:43, 5.

25. Ella Wheeler Wilcox to Editor, *Wisconsin State Journal*, Oct 1902; "The Letters of Ella Wheeler Wilcox" website, http://www.ellawheelerwilcox.org/letters/L1902101.htm. Accessed 27 Apr 2012. Angela Sorby notes that James Whitcomb Riley wrote advertising poems early in his career, and that later, "he simply used his poetry as a self-reflexive advertisement for James Whitcomb Riley." *Schoolroom Poets* 106. Such advertisements became even more valuable when they recirculated for free.

26. Loren Glass, "Trademark Twain," *American Literary History*, 13 no. 4, Winter 2001, 671–93, at 679. Mark Twain, "Letter from Carson City: Concerning Notaries," *Territorial Enterprise* (Virginia City), 9 Feb 1864; on Twain Quotes, http://www.twainquotes. com/18640209bt.html (accessed 8 May 2008). The story appears in Scrapbook 3 in the Bancroft Library's Moffett Collection (CU-MARK), 3.102. Other characters build up the dimensionality of Mark as a writer, with one addressing him as "Quill-driver." Mark Twain, "Letter from Carson City," *Territorial Enterprise* (Virginia City) 3 Feb 1863; on Twain Quotes, http://www.twainquotes.com/18630203t.html (accessed 27 Apr 2009). Twain also struck back at the exchange and recirculation system by using it against itself early in his career, in his "A Bloody Massacre Near Carson" (*Territorial Enterprise*, 28 Oct 1863), which graphically detailed a sensational family massacre—a father's bloody killing and scalping of his wife, and murder and mutilation of seven of his nine children. The man who brings the news to town explains that the murderer had been driven mad by the loss of his money—blamed on "the newspapers of San Francisco," which hid the wrongdoing of a water company and thus ruined unsuspecting stockholders. The story was riddled with glaring discrepancies of people's names and geography that would have been evident to locals, but not to those reading it in other newspapers at a distance, which reprinted it. The locals were not amused at the trick, however, and objected to the bad light such a horrifying event put the community in, while the San Francisco papers seem to have ignored the embedded dig at them. (For more on this, see Richard Lillard, "Contemporary Reaction to 'The Empire City Massacre,'" *American Literature*, Nov 1944, 198–203, and Ron Powers, *Mark Twain: A Life* (New York: Free Press, 2006), 126–27.)

27. Michael Foucault, "What Is an Author?" in *The Foucault Reader*, ed. Paul Rabinow (New York: Pantheon, 1984), 101–20. For more on this point, see Barbara Hochman, *Getting at the Author: Reimagining Books and Reading in the Age of American Realism* (Amherst: U Mass. P, 2001).

28. Benedict Anderson, in *Imagined Communities: Reflections on the Origin and Spread of Nationalism*, develops the concept of membership in an imagined community of readers (New York: Verso, 1991).

29. John Murray Forbes to William Curtis Noyes, 28 July 1862, and 12 Aug 1862, in Sarah Forbes Hughes, ed. *Letters and Recollections of John Murray Forbes*, vol. 1 (Boston: Houghton Mifflin, 1900), 324–27 and 28–29. On sock puppetry, see for example the case of *New Republic* blogger Lee Siegel writing as "Sprezzatura" to praise Siegel and attack his critics ("Sock Puppet Bites Man," *New York Times*, Late Edition, 13 Sep 2006, A22). John H. Holmes, an owner of the *Boston Herald*, quoted in "The Columbian Reading Union," *Catholic World*, Sep 1897 p. 864.

30. Henry Ingersoll Bowditch, "Waifs," Nathaniel Bowditch Memorial Collection, 1851–1886, Massachusetts Historical Society. Drew Gilpin Faust, *This Republic of Suffering: Death and the American Civil War* (New York: Random House, 2008), 6–31. Alice Fahs finds that such poems "imagined the soldier as an emotive and sympathetic figure, but they also, by implication, imagined the listener/reader on the home front as similarly emotive and sympathetic." *The Imagined Civil War: Popular Literature of North and South 1861–1865* (Chapel Hill: U N Carolina P, 2001), 101.

31. Other titles included "Rest," "Requiescam," "In the Hospital," and "Dying in Hospital."

32. The family was well connected. Three Woolsey cousins had been or were later to become presidents of Yale, and literary affiliations abounded: Mary Woolsey Howland's cousin Sarah Chauncey Woolsey later became a popular children's writer under the name Susan Coolidge; Charles Dana, editor of the *New York Tribune*, visited; another friend was a European correspondent for the *Tribune*. For more detail on the reprinting and circulation of "Mortally Wounded" and another Howland poem, see my "Anonymity, Authorship and Recirculation: A Civil War Episode," *Book History*, 9, 2006, 159–78.

33. George Whitfield Pepper, *Personal Recollections of Sherman's Campaigns in Georgia and the Carolinas* (Zanesville, Ohio: Hugh Dunne, 1866), 191–92. Charles Carleton Coffin, *Freedom Triumphant: The Fourth Period, or The War of the Rebellion From September, 1864, to Its Close* (New York: Harper, 1890), 225–26. Monday, late May 1864, in Georgeanna Woolsey Bacon, and Eliza Woolsey Howland, *My Heart Toward Home*, 353.

34. The "found under the pillow" introductory lines that became a virtual title by 1865 also echo the name of another battle site: Fort Pillow, where African American soldiers were massacred in 1864 when the fort was captured by Confederates who refused to take black soldiers prisoner and shot, burned, or buried them alive instead. This nearly subliminal connection may have been the attraction for the *Christian Recorder*, an African American religious paper, to reprint the poem. "Rest," *The Christian Recorder*, 6 Jan 1866, n.p. The *Recorder* interestingly credits the poem to the *Living Age*, rather than *The Liberator*, which had also included the "The following lines were found under the pillow…" ascription (15 Dec 1865, 35:50, 200). The anonymity function granted the poem a new life recently in Geraldine Brooks's novel *March*. In her research, Brooks found the poem copied out with the "lines found under a pillow" ascription in an 1886 letter from Louisa May Alcott to her aunt, discussing her own diminished strength, and her difficulties "learning *not to do*." Since Alcott quotes "the little poem found under a dead soldier's pillow in the hospital," Brooks reasonably assumed Alcott had found it under the pillow of a soldier she had nursed twenty years earlier. Brooks has her character Mr. March find one of the middle verses under a dead soldier's pillow at a turning point in her novel. Mr. March learns a lesson in patience from it: "How could an unlearned youth…write with such wisdom and resignation." Geraldine Brooks, *March* (New York: Viking, 2005), 265–66. The letter is from Alcott to her Aunt Bond (Louisa Greenwood Bond), written 16 Oct 1886; manuscripts division, Library of Congress. Personal communication with Brooks, 10 July 2007.

35. This possibility of popular endorsement for a version of authorship is more evident in the nineteenth-century context of decentralized recirculation; as print media

consolidated, anonymity, too, lost some of its power. Rapid dissemination via email, websites, and blogs has reopened forms of popular endorsement of authorship, while groups such as snopes.com, which vets email rumors, and mechanisms such as wikis provide for both popular claims of authorship and swift policing of those claims.

36. Emily Huffington Miller, "Jamie's Bounty Land," *The Ladies' Repository: a Monthly Periodical, Devoted to Literature, Arts, and Religion*, 26, 9 Sep 1866, 547–50. The poem serves something of the same function in postwar accounts of hospitals as well.

37. In James Henry Brownlee's anthology *The Patriotic Speaker: Consisting of Heroic Pathetic and Humorous Pieces That Inspire Patriotism*, for example, the poem is introduced, "this beautiful poem was found under the pillow of a wounded soldier at Fort Royal, 1864." "Mrs. Robert Howland" appears as a tag at the end of the poem (New York: Hinds, Noble Eldredge, 1896, 175).

38. Russell Conwell's "Acres of Diamonds" speech and Booker T. Washington's anecdote enjoining listeners to "cast down your bucket where you are" are parallel celebrations of the value of recontextualizing or reinterpreting one's own place to see new value in it.

39. Charles H. Turner, "Our New Lieutenant," *Frank Leslie's Popular Monthly*, Apr 1895, 39:4, 17. Grant Richardson, "The Fighting Editor," *Frank Leslie's Popular Monthly*, Feb 1901, 61:4, 381–91.

40. Though similar, *gleaning* differs significantly from cultural theorist Michel de Certeau's concept of readers creating their own meanings from texts as *poaching* on authors, moving "across the lands belonging to someone else" and despoiling them, or moving into a text as temporary renters. Scrapbook makers' recontextualizing wrenches works into new contexts. They may, like de Certeau's readers, engage in a guerrilla action against the writer, who appears to have laid down the "meaning" of a text; Michel de Certeau, *The Practice of Everyday Life* (Berkeley: U of California Press, 1984, 174). But as Eva Hemmungs Wirtén notes, gleaning has a long history of social approval, bound-aried by elaborate rules (*Terms of Use: Negotiating the Jungle of the Intellectual Commons*, Toronto: U of Toronto P, 2008, 19–23).

41. Agnes Varda, *The Gleaners and I (Les Glaneurs et Une Glaneuse)*, film, 2000.

42. "When you reap the harvest of your land, you are not to finish to the corners of your fields in harvesting, the full-gathering of your harvest you are not to gather; your vineyard you are not to glean, the break-off of your vineyard you are not to gather—rather, for the afflicted and for the sojourner you are to leave them" (Lev. 19:9–10).

43. For more on present-day practices of textual poaching, see Henry Jenkins, *Textual Poachers: TV Fans and Participatory Culture* (New York: Routledge, 1992), and his *Convergence Culture: Where Old and New Media Collide* (New York: NY UP, 2008). E. W. Gurley, *Scrap-books*, 13.

44. "Frederick Dean's Will," *Indiana (Pennsylvania) Progress*, 2 May 1878, 2. Actual clipping scrapbooks of financial news exist.

45. Scrapbook of Frances Amanda Smith Cather, George Cather Ray Collection (MS 113). Archives and Special Collections, University of Nebraska–Lincoln Libraries.

46. Sometimes scrapbooks do assume the reader will need instruction. One scrapbook of poetry, stories, and household hints, inscribed in 1872 as a gift after being partially filled, contains the occasional "good" written on a poem, and the autobiographical note on the poem "Adieu to my Scholars" by M. I. Witherell, "Remember I read this to close school at Leicester—always thought a good deal of it." "Senate Documents" scrapbook; author's collection. E. W. Gurley, *Scrap-books*, 24.

47. See, for example, Amos R. Wells, *The Junior Manual: A Handbook of Methods for Junior Christian Endeavor Workers* (Boston: United Society of Christian Endeavor,

1895). "The Ministering Children's League," *St. Nicholas Magazine*, Feb 1887, 14:4, 291.

48. See Elizabeth Stuart Phelps, "The Madonna of the Tubs," *Harper's Magazine*, 72(427), Dec 1885, 94–115, for an example of this trope. Louisa May Alcott, "Little Pyramus and Thisbe, or A Hole in the Wall," *St. Nicholas*, Sep and Oct 1883.

49. The commonplace book was written into a copy of *A Common Place Book. Upon the Plan Recommended and Practiced by John Locke, Esq.* (Boston: Cummings and Hilliard, Boston Bookstore, 1821), 10. According to inscriptions in it, it was first owned by Ann Greenough Gray Whitney, in 1832, and then her daughter, Carrie B. Whitney, 1854. Collection of the Boston Atheneum. *Thaddeus of Warsaw* scrapbook clipping against novel reading 65–66, praising newspapers, 147, collection of the author. Daniel Cohen analyzes a multigenerational 1860s friendship album taken up and reworked (and mocked) by a group of girls in the 1930s—another form of reuse. "Rewriting *The Token of Love*: Sentimentalists, Sophisticates, and the Transformation of American Girlhood, 1862–1940," *Journal of the History of Childhood and Youth* 4:2, Spring 2011, 223–56.

50. "[]s for Using Books." In Baxter scrapbook, collection of the author.

51. Margaret Lynn, *A Step-Daughter of the Prairie* (New York: Macmillan, 1914), 215.

52. My discussion of government reports is indebted to Oz Frankel's *States of Inquiry: Social Investigations and Print Culture in Nineteenth Century Britain and the United States* (Baltimore: Johns Hopkins UP, 2006) particularly 33, 83, 101. The reports were even criticized as being "a mere scrapbook," with items inferior to those in periodicals. This criticism came from an agricultural magazine, however, which had reason to consider the free publication a rival. "Home Department," *Southern Planter*, 17, 1 Jan 1857, 11. Such reading perhaps trained those who relished it, among whom was Samuel S. McClure, who became publisher of an innovative, heavily illustrated, reporting-based magazine that he conceived of as appealing to Midwesterners. In his impoverished Indiana childhood, he recounts, "We had no books at home but a bound volume of 'Agricultural Reports,' sent us by our congressman, and this I read over and over." Samuel S. McClure, *My Autobiography* (New York: Frederick A. Stokes, 1914), 41. The book was ghost-written by Willa Cather.

53. E. W. Gurley, *Scrap-books*, 35–36. North Carolina Agricultural Experiment Station, *Report*, no. 19, Raleigh, 1896, lxvii. Will Hamilton, "The Making of Scrap-Books," *The Clipping Collector: A Monthly Magazine Devoted to the Collecting of Newspaper Clippings for Pleasure or Profit*, Apr 1896, 4:1, 40. [Rounsevelle Wildman] "As Talked in the Sanctum by the Editor," *Overland Monthly and Out West Magazine*, July 1896, 4–6.

54. Anthony's handwritten note in the front of the first volume of her scrapbook, donating the collection of 26 large volumes made from ledgers "given me by several of the business men of Rochester" to the Library of Congress, 1 Jan 1903, visible in Figure 5.3. Susan B. Anthony, Anthony Coll, Rare Bk. Coll., Library of Congress.

55. Horlbeck Family Book, #3672-z, Southern Historical Collection, Library of the University of North Carolina at Chapel Hill. Information on the Robertson scrapbook, pasted over the business records of Dr. George Robertson of Yanceyville Township Caswell County, North Carolina, by his daughter, Sallie Robertson, is via personal communication with Karen Avants, 20 Nov 2008. The scrapbook is in the Caswell County Historical Association Collection, Richmond-Miles Museum, Yanceyville, North Carolina.

56. I discuss the contents of the Baxter scrapbook, which leads off with Mary E. Wilkins Freeman's "The Revolt of 'Mother,'" in "Less Work for 'Mother': Rural Readers, Farm Papers, and the Makeover of 'The Revolt of "Mother"'," *Legacy: A Journal of American Women Writers*, 2009, 26:1.

Chapter 2

1. Mark Twain's complicated Memory Builder Game was patented in 1885 and several models put on the market in 1891, without success. The board and instructions are reproduced on the Twainquotes website, accessed 4 Aug 2008. Daniel Slote, a New York stationery manufacturer, had been Clemens's cabinmate on the 1867 voyage that was the basis of *The Innocents Abroad*. Clemens later discovered Slote swindling him on yet another failed investment, the Kaolatype for printing illustrations, and sued. Slote died in 1882, but the scrapbooks continued to be manufactured. Ron Powers, *Mark Twain: A Life* (New York: Simon and Schuster, 2005).

2. Samuel L. Clemens to Orion Clemens, 11 Aug 1872, New Saybrook, Conn. (UCCL 00791). In Mark Twain Project Online (Berkeley: U Calif. P 2007). Kevin MacDonnell, "Collecting Mark Twain: A History and Three New Paths: Some New Paths in Twain-Collecting," *Firsts Magazine*, 1998, http://www.abaa.org/books/abaa/news_fly?code=53.

3. The letter appeared in many places, including the "Literary Chit Chat" column of the *New York Herald*, 11 Dec 1876, 8.

4. Like other forms of book advertising, an ad in a small-circulation literary review such as the *Dial* may have done less to boost sales and more to position the scrapbook as something to talk about, something that could be found in a literate household. The *Dial* was part of a new, Western literary scene. Published by a book distributer and stationer, the magazine was not connected to the earlier New England Transcendentalist publication of the same name.

5. Robert Underwood Johnson, *Remembered Yesterdays* (Boston: Little, Brown, 1923), 323. [Robert Underwood Johnson], "Culture and Progress: A New Book by Mark Twain," *Scribner's Monthly*, 13, 6 Apr 1877, 874–75. "News and Notes.; Select List for Book Clubs and the Smaller Libraries. New Journals," *The Literary World*, 24 May 1879, 10:2, 174.

6. "Messrs. Slote, Woodman, & Co." *Harper's Weekly* 2 Jun 1877, 434.

7. The record at the Harry Ransom Center at the U of Texas at Austin, as of November 2002, for example, recorded "14 Mark Twain Scrap Books," within the Samuel Clemens collection, and indicated that they included clippings and autographs. It appears that Frank C. Willson, a collector of Mark Twain memorabilia, housed such materials in a set of Mark Twain Scrap Books, so that the name in the record refers to both the "title" of the scrapbook and the contents, but not the compiler, though the catalog lists Mark Twain as "added author" on another Mark Twain Scrap Book. In these scrapbooks, a collector felt both licensed and invited in to play with the books. Willson evidently set out to buy many Mark Twain Patent Scrap Books, and to either save them intact or reuse them. He ripped out the clippings from earlier users in several instances to displace them with Twainiana.

8. Margaret Lynn, *A Stepdaughter of the Prairie* (New York: Macmillan, 1923), 223, 230.

9. "A Novel Scrap Book," *Chicago Inter Ocean*, 8 July 1881; Vol. X:90, 1. Shot July 2, Garfield died September 19, 1881. Garfield's interest in having a scrapbook made about his shooting seems fitting, since according to Brander Matthews, "President Garfield had most extensive scrap-books, and the effectiveness of many of his speeches in Congress and on the stump was due to his adroit handling of facts and figures treasured up for him in these garners of unconsidered trifles." Brander Matthews, *The Home Library* [Arthur Penn] (New York: Appleton, 1886), 80.

10. The scrapbook is initially given the same format as a novel title in the same sentence. Mary Abbott Rand, "The Christmas Grab-Bag," *Holly and Mistletoe* (New

York: Thomas Y. Crowell, 1881), 10. The book was reprinted in 1890 by the sticky-fingered Belford, Clarke & Co.

11. Rand, "The Christmas Grab-Bag," 12. The Larcom and Longfellow poems might have been familiar to children reading the story through their appearance in school readers, among other sources. An 1896 source finds "The Rainy Day" in *Appleton's* Fourth Reader and McGuffey's Fifth, with Larcom's poem in *Harper's New Reader* and the Canadian *Ontario Reader*. Rand McNally, *The Rand-McNally List of Selections in School Readers*, (New York: Rand, McNally, 1896).

12. "Holly and Mistletoe," *Literary World*, 8 Oct 1881, 350.

13. Hannah P. James, "Yearly Report on the Reading of the Young," *Papers and Proceedings of the General Meeting, American Library Association, Lake George, NY* (Boston: Rockwell and Churchill, 1885), 95.

14. This idea is from Peter Stallybrass, who develops the point that blanks and forms are limits and incitement, in "Printing and the Manuscript Revolution," in *Explorations in Communication History*, ed. Barbie Zelizer (New York: Routledge, 2008), 111–18, and with James N. Green in *Benjamin Franklin, Writer and Printer* (New Castle, Del.: Oak Knoll P, 2006), 88–89. Forms press us to notice the complementarity of printing and writing, Stallybrass and Green note. Print did not displace manuscript but rather incited more writing. Robin Bernstein has explored ways in which books are "scriptive things": objects that embody scripts for use, in *Racial Innocence: Performing American Childhood from Slavery to Civil Rights* (New York: NYU P, 2011).

15. One of the many varieties of Mark Twain's Scrap Book marketed allowed space for writing, but the extant ones examined for this study were not of this type. At least one scrapbook maker got around this restriction by pasting entire collaged sheets onto the pages of a Mark Twain scrapbook.

16. Julia Colman, "Among the Scrap-books," *The Ladies' Repository*, Aug 1873, 89.

17. For more on the developing ideas of brand spokesfigures as companions and characters who could be appropriated into other play and narratives, see Susan Strasser, *Satisfaction Guaranteed: The Making of the American Mass Market* (New York: Pantheon,1989); and my *Adman in the Parlor: Magazines and the Gendering of Consumer Culture* (New York: Oxford UP, 1996). For more on the author as companion, see Barbara Hochman, *Getting at the Author: Reimagining Books and Reading in the Age of American Realism* (Amherst: U Mass. P, 2001).

18. Other companies eventually produced scrapbooks with gummed pages. The Ideal Scrap Book, produced by the Ideal Specialty Company, Chicago, in 1901, for example, offered pages with gummed dots, but it could not call them Mark Twain scrapbooks.

19. Siva Vaidhyanathan lays out Clemens's shifts in detail in *Copyrights and Copywrongs: The Rise of Intellectual Property and How It Threatens Creativity* (New York: NYU P, 2001), 35–80.

20. Emphasis added. "Copyright vs. Trademark vs. Patent" LawMart, accessed 20 July 2011, http://www.lawmart.com/searches/difference.htm.

21. *A Connecticut Yankee in King Arthur's Court*, in Mark Twain, *Historical Romances* (New York: Library of America, 1994), 267. Yale Law School, *Two Centuries' Growth of American Law, 1701–1901* (New York: Scribner's, 1901), 430–31.

22. The American Book Company published *Sketches Old and New* in 1875, with Twain's cooperation. In 1880 Belford, Clark printed a collection called *Sketches by Mark Twain* using substantially the same material, in a similar binding. The American Book Company had shortened the title to *Sketches* on the front cover, so Belford's cover looked very similar (Twainquotes website). Belford, Clarke had previously pirated *Tom Sawyer* in a Canadian edition, which they distributed in the U.S., undercutting Twain's profits. They

reprinted his contributions to *The Atlantic* in *Belford's Magazine* after he had refused them permission and then printed *A Tramp Abroad* from advance press sheets, under-selling the edition that would have brought Twain royalties. Barbara Schmidt, "A Closer Look at the Lives of True Williams and Alexander Belford," at Twainquotes website, accessed 11 May 2009. *Samuel L. Clemens vs. Belford, Clarke & Company*, US Circuit Court, N. D. Ill. *Chicago Legal News* January 20, 1883; Twainquotes. Rudyard Kipling lost a similar suit in 1903.

23. Claims of how many scrapbooks were produced and how much they brought varied considerably. An 1881 letter from Clemens to his nephew Charles Webster, who was handling his business affairs, said that he had been getting $1,800 to $2,000 a year for them but thought he was owed three times that much (to Charles Webster, July 9, 1881. Samuel Charles Webster, ed., *Mark Twain, Business Man*. Boston: Little, Brown, 1946, 161). An 1884 letter from Clemens said the profit had dwindled from an initial $12,000 for its first six months to $800 for a more recent six months (though profits were to be divided with Slote and his partner, and this may be the overall amount; Twain to Charles Webster, n.d. 1884, Webster, *Mark Twain, Business Man*, 273). An 1885 article extolling his financial successes claimed 100,000 sold every year for eight years (Charles H. Clark, "Authors at Home V: Mark Twain at Nook Farm," *Critic*, 17 Jan 1885, 55); another makes the even more suspect claim that Clemens earned more from it than from any other single book ("Mark Twain's Most Profitable Book," Mark Twain in His Times website). Twain claimed in his autobiography that Slote "made a good deal of money out of it. But by and by, just when I was about to begin to receive a share of the money myself, his firm failed"; Twain, *Autobiography*, 230.

24. Mark Twain, *Adventures of Huckleberry Finn* (New York: Oxford UP, 1999), 95.

25. Jean Lee Cole, "Newly Recovered Works by Onoto Watanna (Winnifred Eaton): A Prospectus and Checklist," *Legacy* 21:2, 2004, 229–34. Peter C. Walther, "Horatio Alger and His Scrapbook," *Newsboy*, June 2006, 5–7. Matthews, *Home Library*, 87.

26. Webster, *Mark Twain, Business Man*, 92. The scrapbook is Scrapbook 7 of the Moffett collection, in Mark Twain Collection, Bancroft Library, U Cal. Berkeley. Twain is known as the first author to turn in a typed book manuscript, for *Life on the Mississippi*. Lisa Gitelman observes that typewriting was a mode of separating the act of writing from authorship. *Scripts, Grooves, and Writing Machines: Representing Technology in the Edison Era* (Palo Alto, Calif.: Stanford UP, 1999). Twain's remote storage of his newspaper writing allowed him to reconstitute it at a distant geographic and temporal point.

27. Matthews, *Home Library*, 80; and "Strange News of the Day," *Current Literature*, Apr 1901, 30:4, 385. Charles F. Adams, "The Young Collector: Great Scrap-Book Makers," *Harper's Young People*, 23 Oct 1888, 894. Deshler Welch, "Profitable Scrap-Book Making," *The Writer*, 27, 8 Aug 1915, 113–15. Alcott herself published a series of books with the overall title *Aunt Jo's Scrap-Bag*, metaphorizing stories as reused cloth—another kind of material to be reworked with scissors in hand. Louisa May Alcott, *Little Women, Little Men, Jo's Boys*. (1868–69, New York: Library of America, 2005) 371.

28. Mark Twain, *Following the Equator: A Journey Around the World* (New York: Harper and Bros., 1899), 155–56. The scrapbooks are in the Mark Twain papers at the U of Calif., Berkeley.

29. Powers, *Mark Twain: A Life*, 302. William Dean Howells, *My Mark Twain: Reminiscences and Criticisms*, Marilyn Austin Baldwin, ed. (Baton Rouge: LSU P, 1967), 145–46.

30. A 1907 lecture notice, for example, invited members of a union lodge to "hear Mr. Will M. Clemens tell us all about his famous uncle, Mark Twain, the greatest American nov-

elist" (Broadside, Horace Greeley Council, No. 798, National Union, New York, 1907, Special Collections, U of Va.). *The Canadian Magazine*, reviewing his snippet biography of Kipling, assured readers that "the writer of this volume is a brother of Mark Twain, and consequently is able to give some insight into the relationship existing between Kipling and Clemens the greater" ("Books and Authors," *The Canadian Magazine,* June 1899, 13:2, 193.). Twain referred to Will Clemens as a "troublesome cuss" and "mere maggot," in a letter to the businessman who helped him with business and legal difficulties. SLC to Henry Huttleston Rogers, 13 June 1900, *Mark Twain's Correspondence with Henry Huttleston Rogers* (Berkeley: U Calif. P, 1969), 447. "Charlatan and a cheat" is in a note by his secretary Isabel Lyon to Mr. Howe, 17 Jan 1937, Berg Collection, NYPL. "Born fraud" appears in a handwritten note on letter from Wm. Clemens to Samuel Clemens, 19 Sep 1907, Mark Twain Papers, U. of Calif., Berkeley.

31. The list of Will M. Clemens's productions includes *Sixty and Six: Chips from Literary Workshops* (New York: New Amsterdam Book, 1897); *Famous Funny Fellows* (Cleveland: William W. Williams, 1882); *A Manual for Writers and Others,* also titled *Mistakes of Authors: A Manual for Writers and Others. Being a Treatise on Bulls, Blunders, Mistakes, Errors, Literary Anachronisms and Misfits* (information from advertisement in Florence Nightingale Craddock, *The Soldier's Revenge,* London, The Abbey P, 1900, 17); and *The Depew Story Book* (New York, Thompson & Thomas, 1898, 1902). Quotes are from "The Literary Show: Minor Mention," *Town Topics,* 20 Apr 1899, 41:16, 15. "Mr. Kipling's Side," *New York Times,* 6 May 1899, BR303; "Kipling Loses His Suit," *The American Lawyer* Feb 1903, 51. Samuel L. Clemens to William M. Clemens, London, 6 June 1900, Berg Collection, NYPL.

32. Will Clemens to Mark Twain, 10 July 1900. A handwritten note on the envelope comments "a threat." CU-MARK (U of Cal., Mark Twain Collection, Berkeley, UCLC 32962). In Mark Twain et al. *Mark Twain's Correspondence.*

33. Will[iam] M. Clemens to Samuel Clemens, 7 Jan 1881. A handwritten note on the envelope comments "shucks!" CU-MARK (U of Calif., Mark Twain Collection, Berkeley, UCLC 40668). Thanks to Sarah Payne and Don Solomon at the National Humanities Center for clarifying the meaning of "bless your heart." See also the Urban Dictionary, accessed 11 May 2009. Will M. Clemens, *Famous Funny Fellows: Brief Biographical Sketches of American Humorists* (William W. Williams, 1882). Will M. Clemens, *Mark Twain: His Life and Work* (San Francisco: Will M. Clemens Co., 1892, and Chicago: F. Tennyson Neely, 1894), 11, 172.

34. The claim that Twain was Clemens's cousin or uncle and helped Clemens start the bureau in 1888 became standard. Robert Stein repeats it in "Your Name In Print," *Los Angeles Times,* 15 Aug 1948, F18. The story took on fanciful details and assumptions about how the nineteenth-century press operated as it traveled through time: "Twain was trying to sell the idea of a scrapbook for press clippings. He told his cousin, Will Clemens, about the idea, and Clemens later opened one of the nation's first newspaper clipping bureaus. That service primarily went to newspaper editors who were eager to know what the competition was doing." "Twain's Idea of Clippings Is Alive, Well," *Memphis Press Scimitar,* 23 Feb 1982, n.p. See also Rob Morse, "News That's Fit to Clip," *San Francisco Chronicle,* 25 Mar 2001.

35. Mark Twain, *Punch, Brothers, Punch and Other Sketches* (New York: Slote, Woodman, 1878). Harry Ransom Center, U of Texas, Austin.

36. Isaac H. Bromley [Winkelried Wolfgang Brown], "The Horse-Car Poetry: Its True History," *Scribner's Monthly,* Apr 1876, 910–12. The first round of unadorned verse, "Horse-Car Poetry," in the third person instead of the imperative ("The conductor when he receives a fare/Must punch...") and "boys" instead of Mark Twain's "brothers," appeared in the *New York Tribune,* 27 Sep 1875, 35:10, 5.

37. Annie Dillard, cited on website "The Tattered Coat," accessed 29 Apr 2008.

38. Joseph Bucklin Bishop, *Notes and Anecdotes of Many Years* (New York: Scribner's, 1925), 78–80. "Editor's Drawer," *Harper's Monthly*, Feb 1876, 471–72. Bromley mentions in passing that the thudding hoof beats and rattle of the horsecar drive it into people's head, but the poem got its reputation as an ear worm only after Twain's story appeared.

39. Bromley, "The Horse-Car Poetry," 910.

40. "A Literary Nightmare," *Atlantic Monthly*, Feb 1876, 167–69; "A Literary Nightmare: Mark Twain's Sad Experience with Horse Car Poetry," *Trenton State Gazette*; 27 Jan 1876, 30:23, 1; "Mark Twain. His Sad Experience with Horse-Car Poetry—Punch, Brothers, Punch with Care!" *San Francisco Bulletin*, 29 Jan 1876, 41:98, supplement 2. "A Literary Nightmare" *Macon Weekly Telegraph*, 17 Oct 1876, 70:9, 3, among others. All of these credit the *Atlantic Monthly*.

41. "Personal," *Harper's Bazar*; 26 Aug 1876, 9:35, 547. *The Lake Superior Review and Weekly Tribune* repeats the story and notes, "The last words of Charlotte Cushman will not be awarded an important place in sentimental history" (11 Aug 1876, 7:15, 2). A biographer reports that in her dying weeks she was amused by Twain's story and softens the inappropriateness of the utterances by surrounding them with more elevated poetry read to her in her dying days. Joseph Leach, *Bright Particular Star: The Life and Times of Charlotte Cushman* (New Haven: Yale UP, 1970), 395.

42. William M. Clemens [Rodney Blake], "The True Story of 'Punch Brothers Punch,'" *The Book-Lover Magazine*, Summer 1901, 8, 369–70; "Punch, Brothers! Punch," in *The Biblio*, 2:1, 1922.

43. Comic poet Carolyn Wells linked the Twain story to the irresistible rhythm of "a horrid old advertisement" that interferes with her reading other parts of the newspaper, with its insistent "silly words . . . 'A tissue-paper pattern/Of a tucked shirt-waist.'" It replaces the "worn-out nuisance" of the "trip slips/For a five- or ten-cent fare." In 1904 she could assume that her readers still recalled the joke of Twain's story. Carolyn Wells, "An Irritator." *Folly for the Wise* (Indianapolis: Bobbs-Merrill, 1904), 112–13.

44. Other writers used the verb before Twain without becoming visible to the *OED*. A Texas reference antedates him by ten years, in an item that uses scrapbook pasting as a sign of acclaim. It praises and welcomes a contributor, Miss M. E. Moore, "Some of the poems . . . were admired and scrap-booked by our readers before they had received critical endorsement." "Miss M. E. Moore," *Galveston News*, 4 Oct 1869, 28:16, 2.The *North Star* referred to in the *OED* is a British publication.

Chapter 3

1. Alice Fahs, "Northern and Southern Worlds of Print," in Scott Casper et al., *Perspectives in American Book History* (Amherst: U Massachusetts P, 2001), 216. Oliver Wendell Holmes, "Bread and the Newspaper," *Atlantic Monthly* Sep 1861, 348.

2. Jane E. N. Woolsey to Georgeanna Woolsey and Eliza Woolsey Howland, Letter, 19 July 1861. In Georgeanna Woolsey Bacon and Eliza Woolsey Howland, *My Heart Toward Home: Letters of a Family During the Civil War* (Roseville, Minn.: Edinborough P, 2001), 63. My idea of the text public is indebted to Benedict Anderson's idea of the imagined community and Michael Warner's idea of the text public, itself drawn from Jürgen Habermas.

3. Robert "Back Number" Budd, an African American newsboy, went on to take a more central position in recirculation of newspapers with his business of selling old newspapers at a premium, to be discussed in Chapter 7. "New York Letter," *Literary World*, 5 Mar 1898, 73.

4. Eliza Richards examines the significance of newspapers in Civil War poetry in "Correspondent Lines: Poetry and Journalism in the US Civil War," *ESQ* 2008, 54.1–4, 144–69.

5. Mary S. Robinson, *A Household Story of the American Conflict: The Brother Soldiers*, and *A Household Story of the American Conflict: Forward with the Flag* (New York: N. Tibbals 1871). Both volumes are copyright 1867; the preface to the first is dated 1866 and to the second 1867.

6. Edward Everett Hale, *Memories of a Hundred Years* (New York: Macmillan, 1904), 218–19: "The Man Without a Country," *Atlantic Monthly*, Dec. 1863.

7. Hale explains that he intended the story to aid the defeat of Confederate sympathizer Clement Vallandigham, who had said he "did not want to belong to a country that did what Lincoln and the Government were doing." Hale, *Memories*, 217. Linda Kerber notes that Vallandigham objected to suppression of civil liberties ("Toward a History of Statelessness in America," *American Quarterly*, 2005, 57:3, 727–49).

8. Ella Gertrude Clanton Thomas, *Secret Eye: The Journal of Ella Gertrude Clanton Thomas, 1848–1889*, Virginia Ingraham Burr, ed. (Chapel Hill: UNC P, 1990), 236.

9. Jochen Wierich notes that the post–Civil War creation date of this painting marks it as a history painting, addressing a historical moment. Wierich points to the tensions in the mother's attention to baby and newspaper and suggests that "the correlation between maternal, infantine, and national body remains unresolved because the artist herself could not reconcile these demands with her professional aspirations," 42. The painting was largely ignored in its time, and it does not seem to have been reproduced for sale as a lithograph. "'War Spirit at Home': Lilly Martin Spencer, Domestic Painting, and Artistic Hierarchy," *Winterthur Portfolio*, 37:1, Spring 2002, 23–42.

10. E. W. Gurley, *Scrap-books and How to Make Them: Containing Full Instructions for Making a Complete and Systematic Set of Useful Books* (New York: Authors' Publishing, 1880), 7. The narrator of Gurley's first-person short story "The Story of Our Mess" speaks of being still in the army after Lee's surrender at Appomattox in 1865. The story won the first prize of the New York *Weekly Tribune*'s contest for best war story in 1887. *The Story of Our Mess and Other Stories of the War* (New York: John W. Lovell, 1887). Elkanah Walter Gurley (1834–1908), born in Ohio, was a schoolteacher, principal, and editor before the war, in Pepin County, Wisconsin, on the Minnesota border (Franklyn Curtiss-Wedge, compiler, *History of Buffalo and Pepin Counties Wisconsin*, Winona, Minn., H. C. Cooper, Jr., 1919; State Historical Society of Wisconsin Library and Ada Tyng Griswold, *Annotated Catalogue of Newspaper Files in the Library of the State Historical Society of Wisconsin*, Madison, State Historical Society, 1911, 416). After intensifying his sense of loyalty to the cause through living for a time in the Unionist Colony in Greeley, Colorado, Gurley moved to the section of western North Carolina that had not seceded, where he wheedled copies of the state agricultural reports to paste his collections into. Gurley later moved to Hendersonville, North Carolina, according to a family genealogy, courtesy of John Beatty; personal communication, Apr 2008.

11. Charles Pickering Bowditch (1842–1921), scrapbooks, Massachusetts Historical Society.

12. Letter from Ellen Tucker Emerson to Ralph Waldo Emerson, 17 May 1861, in *The Letters of Ellen Tucker Emerson*, Vol. 1. Edith W Gregg, ed. (Kent, Ohio: Kent State UP, 1982), 251. Immediately following the war Edith married the son of John Murray Forbes, president of the New England Loyal Publication Society, who had encouraged publication of pro-Union works in the press she clipped.

13. David Curtis, "The Evolution of the Scrap-book," *The Clipping Collector: A Monthly Magazine Devoted to the Collecting of Newspaper Clippings for Pleasure or Profit*, Feb 1896, 15.

14. Ella Thomas, *Secret Eye*, July 1863, 218.

15. "Army Correspondence of the Savannah Republican: Books and Letters found in the Federal Camps, Memphis, April 25 [1862]," M. J. Solomons Scrapbook, 1861–1863, Duke U. Special Collections Library, Manuscripts 2nd 78:G c.1 Box 1, 201. No date, no publication information; headed "We copy and adopt as our own the annexed which we clip from the Macon Georgia. *Confederate*. Like our friend of the *Confederate* we are anxious to purchase clean *white* cotton and linen rags in small or large quantities." Davidson County (N.C.) physician's account book, 1835–1839, Duke U. Special Collections Library: F:50. Alice Fahs notes that there were only fifteen paper mills in the South in 1861, which could meet less than half of the needs of the Southern newspapers. *The Imagined Civil War: Popular Literature of the North and South, 1861–1865* (Chapel Hill: UNC P, 2001), 21. J. T. H., "Blankets for Soldiers," *Memphis Daily Appeal*, 29 Aug 1861, 4.

16. A broadside advertising Richmond's Confederate Reading Room in 1863 offers a day's access for fifty cents (Richmond: s.n., 1863, American Antiquarian Society, BDSDS). Broken access to papers is suggested by noticing what is missing: although Solomons often clipped articles about donations to help soldiers or to raise money for warships, she omitted an item from the *Macon Telegraph* listing contributors to help wounded soldiers that names both Mrs. M. J. Solomons and Mrs. J. M. Solomons among the "generous ladies of Savannah." If not herself, these were at the very least relatives in the close-knit Solomons family with its many repeated names, evidence that not all papers were available. "Letter to the Editor," *Macon Telegraph*, 23 July 1862, 764, 4.

17. The M. J. Solomons family donated the scrapbook to Duke University, but there is no other information about who in the family made it. Moses J. Solomons, age thirty-two, is listed in the 1860 census in the same household as Henrietta E. Solomons, presumably his third wife, aged twenty-three (he married Frances Joseph in 1851, and his second wife, Henrietta Joseph Solomons, died in 1856; he married Henrietta S. Emanuel of Georgetown, S.C., later that year). (Barnett A. Elzas, *Jewish Marriage Notices from the Newspaper Press of Charleston, S. C. (1775–1906)* (New York: Bloch, 1917.) Both M. J. Solomons and Henrietta E. Solomons survived the war, as did a fourteen-year-old, Leah, also in the household. M. J. Solomons died in 1901. Moses J. Solomons was a thirty-three-year-old druggist when the war began; his brother, Joseph M. Solomons, who was also a druggist, and at least one other brother, Judah, fought for the Confederacy. M. J. Solomons was active as a druggist through the war at least until 1863, as evidenced by an ad offering "imported leeches" for sale by M. J. Solomons of Bay Street in Savannah in the *Savannah Republican*, 29 Oct 1863, 2, while A. A. Solomons, probably his brother Abraham, continued in the grocery business, as evinced by other ads. Solomons clipped scrapbook items from multiple newspapers, including *The Richmond Dispatch* and the Richmond *Daily Examiner*; the *Daily Courier* of Bowling Green, Kentucky; and the *Charleston Mercury*, though publication information is often missing. M. J. Solomons Scrapbook, 1861–1863, Special Collections Library, Manuscripts 2nd 78:G c.1 Box 1, Duke University.

18. Alice Fahs offers an illuminating discussion of the genre of dying soldier poems, noting that poems in the voice of the dying soldier allowed the reader on the home front a role as well; *Imagined Civil War*, 99–103.

19. Solomons did not, for example, paste items in categories, or hold clippings until additional items on Beauregard accumulated before pasting them in together. And she

exhibited control over her pasting by generally keeping clippings from continuing to the next page.

20. "Rock Me to Sleep" was set to at least two tunes and sung in army camps as well as in the home. Wigfall worked after the war to bring the bodies of South Carolinians back for burial and to erect a monument to a prewar hero, South Carolina's antebellum proslavery politician John C. Calhoun, known as the Father of Secession. Scrapbook of Elizabeth Mary Lesesne Blamyer Wigfall, Blamyer, Mss 0104, Wigfall, Deas family collection, 1824–1975, Special Collections, College of Charleston.

21. Scrapbook OS Box XXV, "US Civil War," Massachusetts Historical Society. It is also possible that he displayed them in some fashion before folding them up and packing them away.

22. Charles French, Civil War Scrapbooks, OS Box XXXVII, Massachusetts Historical Society. John George Metcalf, "The Irrepressible Conflict," in Civil War Collection, 1861–1868, American Antiquarian Society. Metcalf was from Mendon, Mass. Elizabeth Boynton Harbert, "The Family Scrapbook" in column, "Woman's Kingdom," *Chicago Inter Ocean*, 10 Jan 1880. Harbert's scrapbooks are discussed in detail in Chapter 5.

23. Cathcart's scrapbooks are in the Cromwell family papers, Series K, Moorland Spingarn Collection, Howard U. The clipping is attributed to *The American and Gazette*, possibly Philadelphia's *North American and US Gazette*. No page, no date.

24. "Critical Notices," *The North American Review*, Jan 1862, 266–67. *The Record* of Richmond, Va., attempted a Southern version of *The Rebellion Record* and began in June 1863 to supply the South with a digest of Confederate news as well as material from the European and British press, calling itself a scrap-book "ready-made." *The Record*, 9 July 1863, 29.

25. Lincoln-Douglas debates scrapbook site, American Memory, Library of Congress http://www.loc.gov/exhibits/treasures/trm124.html, accessed 1 May 2012. Jeffery Alan Smith, *War and Press Freedom: The Problem of Prerogative Power* (New York: Oxford UP, 1999), 101–21.

26. The wallpaper newspaper was among the treasures of newspaper collecting that Back Number Budd displayed to visitors to his newspaper warehouse in the 1890s. "Budd Is Digging in the Ruins," *New York Tribune*, 16 June 1895, 17. The newspaper was a hybrid: the announcement of victory turned into a taunt when Union soldiers printed off a copy a day later, noting "This is the last wall paper edition, and it is, excepting this note, from the types just as we found them. It will be valuable hereafter as a curiosity." As the soldiers interpreted the newspaper's contents as ironic nonnews, they immediately converted it to a souvenir of media. It is not known whether Budd had a rare original, or one of the abundant reproductions.

27. William Mumford Baker [George F. Harrington], *Inside: A Chronicle of Secession*. In *Harper's Weekly*, 20 Jan–7 July 1866; reprinted, New York: Harper & Bros., 1866, 183. Baker (1825–1883), a Presbyterian minister, lived in Austin, Texas, during the war (Appleton's *Cyclopedia of American Biography*, James Grant Wilson and John Fiske, eds., New York: Appleton, 1887–1889).

28. Daniel Robinson Hundley, *Diary*, in *Prison Echoes of the Great Rebellion* (New York: S.W. Green, 1874), 21 Oct 1864, 168.

29. "Selected Articles: Life in the Land of Chivalry: Three Months in Prison for Hating Slavery," from the *Cincinnati Gazette*, in *The Liberator*, 12 Apr 1861. John Hill Aughey, *The Iron Furnace: or, Slavery and Secession* (Philadelphia, W. S. & A. Martien, 1863), 56. The passage was republished in his novelized version of these events: *Tupelo* (Lincoln, Neb.: State Journal, 1888), 52. The couplet appears in Elizur Wright, Jr.'s "The Fugitive

Slave to the Christian," *The Liberty Minstrel*, George Washington Clark, ed., New York: Leavitt & Alden, 1845, 34–36.

30. Scrapbook of Ann Gray, approximately 1861 1864, Massachusetts Historical Society.

31. "A Southern Scene from Life," M. J. Solomons Scrapbook, 19; and n.p., 27 Nov 1861. Davidson County (N.C.) physician's account book, 1835–1839, Duke University, Special Collections Library, F:50, 3. When the poem appeared in the North, as "specimen of rebel verse," the title was altered to "A Southern Scene." It was credited to the *Richmond Dispatch*. *Philadelphia Inquirer*, 21 Jan 1862, 2. Nathaniel Paine in Massachusetts collected it from another Northern paper in his "Poetry of the Rebellion" scrapbook. Vol. 1[–2]. American Antiquarian Society.

32. "Speech of a Patriotic Negro," no publication, n.d., M. J. Solomons Scrapbook. For more on "bobolition" speeches and broadsides, see John Wood Sweet, *Bodies Politic: Negotiating Race in the American North*, 1730–1830 (Baltimore: John Hopkins UP, 2003), esp. 380–81.

33. "Would be Glad to Get Back," *Norfolk Day Book*, M. J. Solomons Scrapbook, 24.

34. "For Abraham Lincoln. On reading the Emancipation Proclamation," Written for the Commonwealth, Oct 1862. M. J. Solomons Scrapbook, 293.

35. "Abolition Villainy" [Correspondence of the *Savannah Republican*] Richhope, McInosh County, Ga., 9 Oct 1862. M. J. Solomons Scrapbook, 412. Cavalry, Letter to Editor, *Savannah Republican* dated Camp Gignilliat, near Darien, Ga., 10 Nov [1862], M. J. Solomons Scrapbook, 423.

36. One element of Lost Cause ideology is missing from the Solomons scrapbook: the idea that slavery civilized black people by Christianizing them. The Solomons family were Jewish, so this would not have been a central issue for this scrapbook maker, although she did collect some poems with specifically Christian references.

37. [Meeting of German Jews] Savannah, 13 Sep 1862, Solomons scrapbook, 406. M. J. Solomons's father, Israel, was born in Amsterdam. Solomons included at least two clippings asserting that Jews are loyal citizens of the Confederacy, and one rabbi's prayer for the South.

38. Katherine Ott discusses how nineteenth-century physicians used scrapbooks in "Domesticated Science in the Scrapbooks of Medical Practitioners," in Katherine Ott, Susan Tucker, and Patricia Buckler, eds., *Scrapbooks in American Life* (Philadelphia: Temple UP, 2006).

39. Drew Faust discusses other ways Bowditch expressed his grief in *This Republic of Suffering: Death and the American Civil War* (New York: Knopf, 2008), 167–70.

40. James R. Randall, "At Fort Pillow," n.p., n.d. R. Y. (Richard Yeadon) Dwight, 1837–1919 Scrapbook, 1860–1866 (34/644 OvrSz), South Carolina Historical Society. "Documents: The Fort Pillow Massacre," *Rebellion Record*, Vol. 8 (New York: Van Nostrand, 1864), 2. Cathcart's brief editorial is undated and unattributed. Joseph W. H. Cathcart scrapbook, "Slavery Volume 4," Cromwell family papers, Series K, 24 S6, Moorland Spingarn Collection, Howard University. The poem was later collected in W. L. Fagan, ed. *Southern War Songs: Camp-fire, Patriotic and Sentimental* (New York: M. T. Richardson, 1890) 137–40.

41. "A Compliment to South Carolina," n.p., n.d. R. Y. (Richard Yeadon) Dwight, 1837–1919 Scrapbook.

42. James Randall, "The Lone Sentry," R. Y. (Richard Yeadon) Dwight, 1837–1919 Scrapbook.

43. For more on entrainment and the emotional work of imagining oneself into a wartime community, see Barbara Ehrenreich, *Blood Rites: Origins and History of the Passions of War* (New York: Holt, 1997), 184, 198–200. Alice Cary, *The Poetical Works of Alice and*

Phoebe Cary with a Memorial of Their Lives by Mary Clemmer (New York: Hurd and Houghton), 45.

44. As a conventional term for poem, "song" could denote either poetry or song lyrics. Information on this scrapbook is in "The Great Scrapbook Maker: A Colored Janitor's Unique Library" (Philadelphia) *Times*, 24 Feb 1882, n.p., Cathcart folder, William H. Dorsey Collection, Cheyney U.; but this Cathcart scrapbook does not appear to be in the collection at Howard U. Nathaniel Paine, "Poetry of the Rebellion. The poetry comprised in the following pages consists of cuttings from the various newspapers of the day, in relation to the rebellion of the Southern states." Vol. 1[–2]. American Antiquarian Society.

45. Henry Ingersoll Bowditch, "Waifs," Nathaniel Bowditch memorial collection, Massachusetts Historical Society.

46. "Bohemian," Correspondent Richmond Dispatch [William Shepperson], ed. *War Songs of the South.* (Richmond, Va.: West and Johnson, 1862) 4. Alice Fahs, *Imagined Civil War,* 29.

47. Mary Louise Kete's *Sentimental Collaborations: Mourning and Middle-Class Identity in Nineteenth Century America* (Durham: Duke UP, 2000) discusses how circulation of mourning poetry drew a community together. Mike Chasar sees twentieth-century poetry scrapbooks as a mode for creating a unified self and suggests some of their other uses in "Material Concerns: Incidental Poetry, Popular Culture, and Ordinary Readers in Modern America," in *The Oxford Handbook of Modern and Contemporary American Poetry,* ed. Cary Nelson (New York: Oxford UP, 2012), 301–30.

48. Ann Greenough Gray Whitney's book was written into a copy of *A Common Place Book. Upon the Plan Recommended and Practiced by John Locke, Esq.* (Boston: Cummings and Hilliard, 1821), 10. According to inscriptions, it was first owned by Whitney, in 1832, and then by her daughter, Carrie B. Whitney, 1854. (Ann Greenough Grey Whitney, 1800–1873, commonplace books, 1826–1859. Collection of the Boston Athenaeum.)

49. Jeffrey Steele, Mary Louise Kete, and others have assumed mourning was primarily a feminine activity for nineteenth-century Americans. Rev. Chandler Robbins, "A Discourse Delivered at Boston on the Death of Children," in Pickering Dodge, "A Tribute to the Memory of the Infant Dead," Salem, 1841; collection of the American Antiquarian Society. I am indebted here to Karen Sánchez-Eppler's discussion of memorial photographs, which she sees as keeping and cherishing loss. *Dependent States: The Child's Part in Nineteenth Century American Culture* (U Chicago P, 2005), 109. In Dodge's gift to the mother of their dead son, the poems serve as tokens of shared pain, shared experience that mother or father can enter and inhabit. Though the speaker of the poem moves through the world as a man, sitting in his study chair, walking the crowded street, and praying with the boy's mother, he offers an intimate and specifically domestic experience of grief. Whitney collected it, too, possibly after her first child's death.

50. Dodge worked with gatherings of folded sheets, one inside the other, which required planning and either knowledge of bookbinding or advance consultation with a binder. The album was given to the American Antiquarian Society from the hands of a daughter born after George's death. Max Cavitch has suggested that grieving parents were unwilling to be consoled by existing verse, and so they besieged poets such as Lydia Sigourney for elegies for their children. Personal collections like Dodge's and Bowditch's, however, demonstrate the importance of sharing grief, and of memorializing grief itself, as much as the specific child. *American Elegy: The Poetry of Mourning from the Puritans to Whitman* (Minneapolis: U Minn. P, 2007), 146.

51. Kirsten Silva Gruesz's essay "Feeling for the Fireside: Longfellow, Lynch, and the Topography of Poetic Power," in *Sentimental Men: Masculinity and the Politics of Affect in*

American Culture, Mary Chapman and Glenn Handler, eds. (Berkeley: U of California P 1999), 53. Paula Bernat Bennett makes a related point in *Poets in the Public Sphere: The Emancipatory Project of American Woman's Poetry, 1800–1900* (Princeton: Princeton UP, 2003) 22.

52. Mary Louise Kete, *Sentimental Collaborations*.

53. "Driving Home the Cows" was clipped from *The Evening Transcript*, which reprinted it from *Harper's*. Two other poems in this section celebrate the return of husbands to wives; one, "When the Boys Come Home," by John Hay, exults in general terms about the "happy time coming" at the boys' arrival, with no mention of parents, while another, "The Joy-Gun," by Lte. Richard Beale, celebrates the Emancipation.

54. Henry I. Bowditch, "Nathaniel Bowditch Memorial Scrapbook" and "Brief Memoranda of Our Martyr Soldiers who fell during the Great Rebellion of the 19th century," Nathaniel Bowditch Memorial Collection, 1851–1886, Massachusetts Historical Society.

55. Faith Barrett and Cristanne Miller have also focused on the meaning popular Civil War poetry held for its readers. See Introduction, *Words for the Hour: A New Anthology of Civil War Poetry* (Boston: U Mass. P, 2005).

56. Herman Melville, "Donelson," in *Battle-pieces and Aspects of the War* (New York: Harper, 1866). The close relationship between the emotion and the experience of reading the poetry in its newspaper setting may be one explanation for Lawrence Buell's finding that collections of Civil War poetry, especially those by individual poets, did not sell well. "American Civil War Poetry and the Meaning of Literary Commodification: Whitman, Melville, and Others." Steven Fink and Susan S. Williams, eds., *Reciprocal Influences: Literary Production, Distribution, and Consumption in America* (Columbus: Ohio State UP, 1999).

57. For Bowditch's antipathy to the Courier, see Vincent Bowditch, *The Life and Correspondence of Henry Bowditch*, vol. 2 (Boston: Houghton Mifflin, 1902), 50.

58. Her name is also spelled Lacoste. Living in Savannah, Georgia, Solomons might have known La Coste. M. J. Solomons, "Scrapbook, 1861–1863." "The Picket Guard" or "All quiet along the Potomac" is another poem claimed during the war by both sides, and widely reprinted and collected in northern and southern scrapbooks. It first appeared in 1861 in *Harper's Weekly*, written by Ethel Beers.

59. Emily Virginia Mason, ed. *The Southern Poems of the War* (Baltimore: J. Murphy, 1867), 192. "Somebody's Darling," *Littell's Living Age*; 23 Feb 1867; 92:1186; 450.

60. Finch's poem is in Cathcart's scrapbook, stamped on spine: "To Readers and Anxious Inquirers. Vol. 3. 1872-73-74-75-76. J.W.H. Cathcart." Scrapbook 24-S32, Cromwell family papers, Series K, Moorland Spingarn Collection, Howard U. Finch's poem was collected in 1874 by thirteen-year-old Benjamin A. R. Ottolengui of Charleston, S.C., who took over the scrapbook of his mother, Helen Rosalie Rodrigues Ottolengui, who had died in 1866. The scrapbook is inscribed: "This is 'Mamma's' scrapbook and was given to me by 'Mother' [his stepmother] and 'Papa' on the 25th of September 1874. B.A.R. Ottolengui." Items in it include published writings by the mother. The Ottolenguis were related to the Solomons family. (Special Collections, Manuscripts; Mss 1053, Addlestone Library, College of Charleston, S.C.)

61. Cited in Joan Shelley Rubin, *Songs of Ourselves: The Uses of Poetry in America* (Cambridge: Harvard UP, 2007), 108. Marie La Coste, "Somebody's Darling," William Holmes McGuffey, ed., *The New McGuffey Fourth Reader* (American Book Co., 1901), 121–22. Rand McNally, *The Rand-McNally List of Selections in School Readers* (Chicago: Rand McNally, 1896). Louise L. Stevenson surveyed reading textbooks for their inclusion of

Civil War material in her *The Victorian Homefront: American Thought and Culture, 1860–1880* (Cornell UP, 2001), 92–93.

62. Sallie A. Brock, for example, parallels her Ruth-like "gleaning" of poetry with the work of Southern women gathering the bones of Confederate soldiers for reburial. *The Southern Amaranth* (New York: Wilcox & Rockwell, 1869), v–vi. Although Max Cavitch suggests that this gathering of poems "contributes to the process whereby it is forgotten that they were once far more present to the living…through manuscript circulation and periodical reprinting," as we have seen, poems continued to be reprinted in the press and even written out by hand after they had been anthologized. *American Elegy,* 30–32. "Southern Poetry: A Sketch," *The Southern Review,* Jan 1879, 24. Lizzie Cary Daniel, *Confederate Scrap-Book* (Richmond, VA: J. H. Hill Print. Co., 1893). The New York Public Library's copy, for example, is inscribed "Presented to the New York Public Library, New York, by the Confederate Memorial Literary Society, Richmond, Virginia." David Blight has discussed the work of Southern groups such as the Southern Historical Society in promoting a view of the Civil War sympathetic to the Confederacy, in *Race and Reunion: The Civil War in American Memory* (Cambridge: Belknap P of Harvard UP, 2001).

63. Elizabeth Farnham May (1832–1878) scrapbook, 1862–1895, May family papers, Massachusetts Historical Society.

64. Juliana Paisley Gilmer Diary in Addison Gorgas Brenizer Papers, #2719, Southern Historical Collection, U NC, Chapel Hill. Brenizer was Gilmer's son-in-law. The first dated item in the scrapbook is a July 15, 1862, obituary for two-year-old Willie Walkup Miller, son of Dr. J. M. and Eugenia A. Miller.

65. Karen Sánchez-Eppler, *Dependent States,* 109.

66. Juliana Paisley Gilmer Diary.

67. *Bret Harte's Writings: Poems* (Boston: Houghton Mifflin, 1870) 17–19. E. W. Gurley, *Scrap-books and How to Make Them,* 56.

Chapter 4

1. The item, copied from the *New York Tribune,* argued against allowing slavery in the Nebraska Territory. "Black Heroes," *Frederick Douglass' Paper,* 10 Mar 1854, 3.

2. The journalist Mrs. N. F. Mossell [Gertrude Bustill Mossell] called for "unwritten histories" in "Our Women's Department," *New York Freeman,* 31 July 1886, 1, col. C. When scrapbooks are contextualized, the language of juxtaposition may reveal other relationships between clippings. Carla L. Peterson's analyzes an isolated scrapbook page from an unknown maker, which contained the obituary of her ancestor Philip Augustus White, from the black newspaper *The New York Age.* Her research allowed her to see the relationship to White's life of each of the four poems grouped with the obituary. For Peterson, the scrapbook is a still-resonant metaphor for recovering black history. Peterson, *Black Gotham* (New Haven: Yale University Press, 2011) 2–4, 213–14.

3. Dorsey's scrapbooks stop around 1903, with the last materials pasted in around 1905. The historian Roger Lane, whose rich study of late-nineteenth-century black Philadelphia mines Dorsey's scrapbooks, speculates that he lost his vision around that time. Roger Lane, *William Dorsey's Philadelphia and Ours: On the Past and Future of the Black City in America* (New York: Oxford UP, 1991) 333–34.

4. Carl Caestle et al., *Literacy in the United States: Readers and Reading Since 1880* (New Haven: Yale UP 1993). For more on the problems black papers faced staying afloat, see Barbara McCaskill, "Savannah's *Colored Tribune,* the Reverend E.K. Love, and the Sacred Rebellion of Uplift," in *Post-bellum, Pre-Harlem: African American Literature and Culture,*

1877–1919, Barbara McCaskill and Caroline Gebhard, eds. (New York: NYU P, 2006); and Eric Gardner, *Unexpected Places: Relocating Nineteenth-Century African American Literature* (Jackson: UP Mississippi, 2010). For more on black literary societies' encouragement to read newspapers, see Elizabeth McHenry, *Forgotten Readers* (Durham: Duke UP, 2002). Such encouragement appears as well in novels such as Frances E. W. Harper's *Iola Leroy*.

5. "A Word to Mothers. The Family Newspaper," *The Christian Recorder*, 23 July 1864.

6. Eric Gardner finds the theme of encouraging literacy in other *Christian Recorder* articles in his remarkable "Remembered (Black) Readers: Subscribers to the *Christian Recorder*, 1864–1865," which focuses on the *Recorder* as a periodical read by black readers. *American Literary History*, 23:2, 2011, 229–59.

7. The story previously appeared in "The Family Newspaper," *Advocate and Family Guardian*, 16 Apr 1864, 92, credited to *The Methodist*.

8. Marielle Rosello, *Declining the Stereotype: Ethnicity and Representation in French Cultures* (Hanover, N.H.: UP of New England, 1998).

9. W. E. B. Du Bois, *The Souls of Black Folk*, in *Writings* (1903, New York: Library of America, 1987), 438. Michael Warner has developed the concept of the press's anonymous sociability in *Publics and Counterpublics* (Cambridge: Zone Books, 2005). Nancy Fraser develops the idea of the counterpublic in "Rethinking the Public Sphere: A Contribution to the Critique of Actually Existing Democracy," in *Habermas and the Public Sphere*, Craig Calhoun, ed. (Cambridge: MIT P, 1993).

10. Frederick Douglass, *My Bondage and My Freedom*, 164.

11. Frederick Douglass, *Narrative of the Life of Frederick Douglass, an American Slave. Written by Himself* (Boston: Anti-slavery Office, 1845). Electronic Edition: Documenting the American South, 45. *My Bondage and My Freedom* (New York: Miller, Orton & Mulligan, 1855), 154. The same sentence appears in his *The Life and Times of Frederick Douglass* (Hartford, Conn.: Park, 1881), 74.

12. Mrs. N. F. Mossell, "Our Women's Department," *New York Freeman*, 31 July 1886.

13. Dorsey was elected assessor of Philadelphia's Eighth Ward in 1902. A list of the 260 microfilmed Dorsey scrapbooks is at www.cheyney.edu/library/William-H-Dorsey-Scrapbook-Collection.cfm. Accessed 3 May 2012. They are available at Cheyney University Archives and Special Collections. I am grateful to the staff at Cheyney University Archives for their help, and to Roger Lane for his great generosity in sharing information and research materials with me.

14. "Old Katy Jackson," *Press*, 10 Nov 1866, Dorsey, "Colored Centenarians," 1.

15. The clippings that follow Katy Jackson's obituary proceed roughly chronologically from 1873, with a handful from the 1860s and early 1870s that he probably also saved up. There are forty named newspapers. Dorsey usually wrote in the name of the newspaper, but some attributions are absent or illegible. Subsequent notes here for Dorsey's "Colored Centenarians" will show the title for those articles having one, the name of the newspaper source if available, and the page number in the scrapbook. They are pasted into the *Eighteenth Annual Report of the Commissioners of the Sinking Funds, Philadelphia*.

16. Although white-authored obituaries and elegiac materials on Northern antebellum black Americans downplay the facts of their subjects' enslavement, even in these as well as in the rarer black-authored memorial works their deceased subjects paradoxically achieve a voice, Lois Brown has noted ("Memorial Narratives of African Women in Antebellum New England," *Legacy*, 20:1&2, 30 Apr 2003, 38). Other black scrapbook makers saved occasional items about black centenarians, in their own projects of making meaning of newspaper items about black life, and sometimes, as with Henry

Louis Gates, Jr.'s grandfather, born 1879, who made scrapbooks for decades of his Maryland town's newspaper, they focused on the obituaries of black people (Gates, Jr., "Personal History: Family Matters," *The New Yorker*, 1 Dec 2008, 34–35).

17. Life expectancy for whites born between 1850 and 1900 ranged from 39.5 to 51.8, while for blacks it jumped from 23 to 41.8, making the life span of the centenarians all the more extraordinary. Michael Haines, "Fertility and Mortality in the United States," 4 Feb 2010, eh.net/encyclopedia/article/haines.demography. Janice Hume notes in her research on American obituaries that those of black people in white newspapers are very rare, and in the nineteenth century obituaries were predominantly of men. Exceptions to these rules come when the death itself is remarkable or the person has achieved extraordinary age (*Obituaries in American Culture*, UP Mississippi, 2000). An anonymous Boston African American scrapbook maker collected Sojourner Truth's New Year's greeting and pasted it next to Truth's obituary from 1883, which gave her age as 106; 26 Dec 1880 article, reprinted from *The Chicago Inter Ocean*, Obituary, *The Herald*, 27 Nov 1883, both in large, unattributed scrapbook, in box of miscellaneous scrapbooks, Museum of African American History, Boston.

18. Beth McCoy has termed such invocation of white testimony "white paratextual custodianship." "Race and the (Para)Textual Condition," *PMLA* Jan 2006, 21:1, 161. "He Lived 109 Years," n.p., 9 May 1893, Dorsey, "Colored Centenarians," 42; untitled, *Philadelphia Ledger*, 31 July 1878, Dorsey "Colored Centenarians," 14, *Times,* 22 June 1883, Dorsey, "Colored Centenarians," 28.

19. "Oldest Old Maid Living," *Evening Express,* 28 Feb 1877, Dorsey, "Colored Centenarians," 19; "100 Years Old 'Granny' Jefferson remembers Washington," Dorsey, "Colored Centenarians," 47.

20. Robert Purvis, *Philadelphia Press*, 14 May 1873. Quoted in Philip S. Foner, "Black Participation in the Centennial of 1876," *Phylon*, Winter 1978, 39:4, 284. Gary B. Nash, *First City: Philadelphia and the Forging of Historical Memory* (Philadelphia: U Pennsylvania P, 2006), 284.

21. African Americans continued to assert their connections to the nation's founding. Pauline Hopkins, in a 1905 speech at the centenary of William Lloyd Garrison's birth, declared, "at Bunker Hill my ancestors on my maternal side poured out their blood. I am a daughter of the Revolution, you do not acknowledge black daughters of the Revolution, but we are going to take that right." Lois Brown: *Pauline Elizabeth Hopkins: Black Daughter of the Revolution* (Chapel Hill: UNC P), 9.

22. "Decease of an Aged Colored Woman," *Boston Daily Advertiser*, 3 Oct 1860, Dorsey, "Colored Centenarians," 4.

23. "An Old Woman's Age" *Press* (Philadelphia) n.p., 23 June 1891, Dorsey, "Colored Centenarians," 34. Linda Frost, *Never One Nation: Freaks, Savages, and Whiteness in U.S. Popular Culture, 1850–1877* (Minneapolis: U of Minnesota P, 2005). Similarly, "Aunt" Julia Tunison, of Preakness, New York, was "proud of her scars…because they were the result of a desire to see the Father of His Country, Gen. George Washington, review the troops at Newburgh. Knowing that it would be useless to seek the permission of her mistress, she ran away and took the consequences." Born 1780, she remained enslaved until 1801. "Dying at 115 Years," *New York Recorder*, 11 Feb 1894, Dorsey, "Colored Centenarians," 43.

24. See for example James M. Guthrie, *Camp-fires of the Afro-American; or, The Colored Man as a Patriot* (Philadelphia, Afro-American Pub. Co., 1899), which Dorsey saved two notices of in another scrapbook.

25. Snow: "The Oldest Man in America," *Public Record*, 14 Aug 1875, and "A Negro Who Was Grown before the Revolutionary War Began," *Public Record*, 18 Nov 1875, Dorsey,

"Colored Centenarians," 2. James: "The Oldest Man in the World," *Christian Recorder*, 8 Sep 1887, from the *New York World*, Dorsey, "Colored Centenarians," 33. "Aunt Phillis," *The Press*, 25 Jan 1872, Dorsey, "Colored Centenarians," 11. Ferris: "Death of a Negress Who Lived in the Time of the Revolution," *The Press*, 18 July 1869 [?]. Article copied from "a Nashville paper." Dorsey, "Colored Centenarians," 7. Active contributions to the nation's wars continued into the War of 1812; Samuel Robinson, born a slave in Teaneck, New Jersey, helped erect forts against the British in 1812, "Born a Slave 107 Years Ago," 12 Jan 1892, Dorsey, "Colored Centenarians," 38. Philip Sheppard, 107 in 1877, saw Washington and served in the War of 1812. "Death of a Centenarian," *Ledger*, 9 Apr 1877, Dorsey, "Colored Centenarians," 20. When Ben Greer married at age 113, the report noted that he had been a "servant" in the War of 1812 under General Jackson ("Married at One Hundred and Thirteen," *The Day*, 25 Apr 1876, Dorsey, "Colored Centenarians," 8), while Daniel Webster had driven a baggage wagon for the Continental Army in that war ("Death of a Centenarian," *The Press*, 27 Dec 1881, Dorsey, "Colored Centenarians," 28).

26. David W. Blight, *Race and Reunion: The Civil War in American Memory* (Cambridge, Mass.: Belknap Press of Harvard UP, 2001), 333. William J. Simmons and Henry McNeal Turner, *Men of Mark: Eminent, Progressive and Rising* (1887); and Henry F. Kletzing and William Henry Crogman, *Progress of a Race: Or, the Remarkable Advancement of the Afro-American Negro from the Bondage of Slavery, Ignorance and Poverty, to the Freedom of Citizenship, Intelligence, Affluence, Honor and Trust* (Atlanta: J. L. Nichols, 1897).

27. "A Centenarian at the Polls," n.p. 5 Nov 1891, Dorsey, "Colored Centenarians," 37. "Death of a Centenarian," *Ledger*, 9 Apr 9, 1877, Dorsey, "Colored Centenarians," 20.

28. "Over a Century Old," *Item*, 8 Nov 1887, Dorsey, "Colored Centenarians," 13.

29. "Death of a Negress Who Lived at the Time of the Revolution."

30. "Eighty-one Years a Preacher," *Globe-Democrat*, Oct 1897; "A Negro Centenarian: Capt. Andy Montgomery's Long Life and Experience," *Globe Democrat*, 7 Nov 1897; "Want to Pension the Ex-Slaves," n.p., n.d. General Scrapbook 99 [Charles Turner], unpaginated. Huntington Museum and Library, Pasadena, Calif.

31. All the articles are unsigned; most are from white papers, although some may have had black authors, since white papers such as Philadelphia's *Press*, *Inquirer*, *Item*, *Times*, and *Bulletin* employed black reporters to cover the black community in the late nineteenth century. Roger Lane, *William Dorsey's Philadelphia and Ours*, 184.

32. "A Maryland Slave," *Press*, 10 Mar 1880, Dorsey, "Colored Centenarians," 24; "The Oldest Citizen," *Inquirer*, 10 June 1880, Dorsey, "Colored Centenarians," 25–26.

33. Gertrude Bustill Mossell wrote for the white Philadelphia *Press*, *Times*, and *Inquirer* as well as numerous black publications such as the *New York Freeman*. Roger Lane, *William Dorsey's Philadelphia and Ours*, 184.

34. "Decease of an Aged Colored Woman."

35. "May Be the Oldest Man," 20 Dec 1893, Dorsey, "Colored Centenarians," 45. "He was 102 Years Old: 'Prof.' Henry Richardson Yielded to the 'Hot Wave.'" 7 Aug 1892, Dorsey, "Colored Centenarians," 40. "An Old Woman's Age: She Claims to Have Been Born 109 Years Ago," Philadelphia *Press*, 23 June 1891, Dorsey, "Colored Centenarians," 34. "One Hundred Years Old: Reminiscences of a Colored Woman," Philadelphia *Evening Bulletin*, 3 Apr 1877, Dorsey, "Colored Centenarians," 3. Untitled, *Public Ledger*, 11 Aug 1875, 6. "Age 104," *Kansas City Times*, 10 Jan 1893, Dorsey, "Colored Centenarians," 41.

36. For more on the Grimké-Weld project, see my "Nineteenth-Century Abolitionists and the Databases They Created," *Legacy: A Journal of American Women Writers*, 27:2, 2010.

37. Wells's crusade began with her May 21, 1892, editorial in the Memphis *Free Speech*, which she co-owned. The editorial about eight men lynched countered the white claim that lynchings were spontaneous eruptions of irrepressible outrage at black rape of white women by pointing out the complicity of law enforcement officials, the familiar repetitious ritual of the lynching ("The same programme of hanging, then shooting bullets into the lifeless bodies was carried out to the letter") and asserted that "Nobody in this section of the country believes the old thread bare lie that Negro men rape white women. If Southern men are not careful, they will over-reach themselves and public sentiment will have a reaction; a conclusion will be reached which will be very damaging to the moral reputation of white women." (Ida B. Wells, *Southern Horrors and Other Writings; The Anti-Lynching Campaign of Ida B. Wells, 1892–1900*, Boston: Bedford/St. Martin's, 1997, 52.) For more on the honoring of Wells by black clubwomen, see P. Gabrielle Foreman, *Activist Sentiments: Reading Black Women in the Nineteenth Century* (Urbana: U of Ill. P, 2009), 1–2. Mossell noted it in her *The Work of the Afro-American Women* 2nd ed. (Philadelphia: Geo. Ferguson, 1908), 34.

38. Wells established that there was no special need for rapid punishment outside the legal system, as most of the lynchings took place in areas with functioning legal systems; that rape was not the only supposed crime for which black people were lynched; and that women and children were among the lynching victims. She showed that the accusation of crime was sometimes leveled against successful black businessmen or competitors of whites, sometimes as a cover for looting or destroying black businesses. Finally, her scouring of newspapers revealed that the accused rapists were often in consensual relationships with white women. Gail Bederman, *Manliness and Civilization: A Cultural History of Gender and Race in the US, 1880–1917* (Chicago: U Chicago P 1995), 63–64.Quotations from newspaper clippings became part of Wells's autobiography, too—instead of retelling events, she stops and includes either excerpts or entire articles about her travels. The extracts testify to her success in getting her crusade noticed in the white press. Ida B. Wells Barnett, *Crusade for Justice: The Autobiography of Ida B. Wells*, Alfreda M. Duster, ed. (Chicago: U Chicago P, 1970).

39. Unidentified clippings, 1899. Unidentified clippings on Key West, Florida, execution of Johnson, 1899. In Dorsey scrapbook 1, Thomas and William Dorsey Collection, NUCMC Number: DCLV96-A409, Howard University, Moorland-Spingarn Research Center.

40. *Raleigh News and Observer*, 21 May 1922, 21; *Greensboro Daily News*, 28 June 1922. In Charles N. Hunter papers, 1818–1931, Manuscripts 2nd 56:C, Special Collections Library, Duke University. Further information on Hunter's life and career is in John H. Haley, *Charles N. Hunter and Race Relations in North Carolina* (Chapel Hill: UNC P, 1987).

41. Clippings circa 1899, Dorsey scrapbook 1, Thomas and William Dorsey Collection.

42. Charles Turner [maker unknown], "Scrapbook of newspaper clippings, etc. relating to the Negro in Society and Politics." GS 99, Huntington Museum and Library.

43. Program, Columbia, S.C., n.p., 5 Dec no year. N.p., Chicago, 25 Mar 1892. Unidentified scrapbook, loose pages, remains of a spine. Museum of African American History, Boston.

44. Mary Church Terrell, *A Colored Woman in a White World* (Washington, D.C.: Ransdell, 1940) 226. The article she wrote from her clippings, "Lynching from a Negro's Point of View," appeared in 1904 in the *North American Review*.

45. Shirley Graham, "People in Books," typed ms., 3. Appeared in *Chicago Sun*, 10 Nov 1946; Schlesinger Library, Radcliffe Institute for Advanced Study, Harvard University, Shirley Graham Du Bois Papers.

46. "Raid Home of Scottsboro Mother; Literature Is Seized, Mrs. Montgomery Is Threatened," *Chicago Defender,* 16 Mar 1935, 4. The *Labor Defender* was a Communist-leaning magazine, not connected with the *Chicago Defender*.

47. Walter Francis White, *A Man Called White: The Autobiography of Walter White* (New York: Viking P, 1948), 107, 108.

48. Stephen J. Whitfield, *A Death in the Delta* (Baltimore: John Hopkins UP, 1991), 91.

49. " 'Let the South Alone in Handling Negro Question,' Says William Randolph Hearst: Important subject is discussed in letter to Mississippi Legislature," *SF Examiner,* 13 Mar 1904. Anonymous, General Scrapbook 113, 1890–1906. Unpaginated. Huntington Museum and Library, Pasadena, Calif. This scrapbook is pasted onto unused covers for sermons.

50. Elizabeth McHenry has noted similar work in antebellum and postbellum black literary societies, which inculcated active literacy; black readers were not merely to learn how to read but "to understand the public uses to which literature could be put." Elizabeth McHenry, *Forgotten Readers* (Durham: Duke UP, 2002), 103. Nancy Fraser, "Rethinking the Public Sphere," 124. In her essay "In Our Glory: Photography and Black Life," bell hooks discusses the importance of black image production and display on walls in African American Southern homes through the 1960s, as a mode of positioning subjects "according to individual desire" in resistance to apartheid and dehumanization. Scrapbooks could function similarly, articulating a "collective will to participate in a noninstitutionalized curatorial process," though working with texts rather than images (181). In *Picturing Texts,* Lester Faigley, Diana George, Anna Palchik, and Cynthia Selfe, eds. (New York: Norton, 2003) 175–83.

51. Hunter, Cromwell, and Dorsey all have such letters in their scrapbooks.

52. Adelaide M. Cromwell and Anthony Cromwell Hill, *Unveiled Voices, Unvarnished Memories: The Cromwell Family in Slavery and Segregation, 1692–1972* (U of Missouri P, 2007), 3, 106.

53. Clipping dateline is 7 Aug no year, n.p. Annotation on clipping: "Sunday Sun, May 30, 1897," p. 45. Series K, S-21, scrapbook titled "Miscellaneous Scraps," Cromwell family papers, Moorland Spingarn Collection, Howard University.

54. The Washington daily *Times* founded 1894 is unrelated to the present *Washington Times.* Two Washington, D.C., black papers were called the *Record*; one, founded in 1898 or 1899 was edited by Alex L. Manly and another, founded in 1901, was edited by Cromwell. Adelaide M. Cromwell and Anthony Cromwell Hill, *Unveiled Voices,* 106. Date of 1898 is from *American Newspaper Directory* 32nd ed. (New York: Geo. P. Rowell, 1900), 108. Healy is the subject of a recent study, James M. O'Toole, *Passing for White: Race, Religion, and the Healy Family, 1820–1920* (Amherst: U Mass. P, 2003).

55. Robert Adger to William H. Dorsey (Dear Bill); 20 Oct 1896, in Dorsey biographical scrapbook, Thomas and William Dorsey Collection, Moorland Spingarn Collection, Howard U.

56. "A Remarkable Literary Curiosity," (Philadelphia) *Sunday Dispatch,* 20 Mar 1881, n.p. This reporter appreciatively suggested that Cathcart's scrapbook collection was larger than any scrapbook collection made and admired his methodical attention to it. Other black men around this time concurred with the judgment that saving items from the newspaper was worthwhile, as seen in Douglass's 1854 exhortation to black men to save a notable clipping in their scrapbooks. The newspaper-infused diary entries of Amos Webber, also living in Philadelphia, date from 1854, though Nick Salvatore surmises that he began writing them in 1858. Nick Salvatore, *We All Got History: The Memory Book of Amos Webber* (New York: Times Books, 1996) 33–35.

57. The 1860 census lists Joseph Cathcart, a mulatto janitor in the 8th ward, thirty-seven years old, born in Pennsylvania; in 1870 a mulatto janitor of the same name, 8th ward, 22nd District, appears as a forty-three-year-old, born in New Jersey. "A Remarkable Literary Curiosity," (Philadelphia) *Sunday Dispatch*, 20 Mar 1881, n.p. "The Great Scrapbook Maker: A Colored Janitor's Unique Library," (Philadelphia) *Times*, 24 Feb 1882, n.p. Cathcart folder, William H. Dorsey Collection, Cheyney University. The same article was reprinted in the *St. Louis Globe-Democrat*, 7 Mar 1882; the *St. Albans Daily Messenger* (Vermont), which dropped the final paragraph; and (without credit) as "A Unique Library," in the *New Haven Register*.

58. "Paste and Scissors: Valuable Library of History and Biography from Newspaper Clippings," *The Philadelphia Inquirer*, 26 Feb 1884, vol. 110, 2. Another noted that "in his room is a large bookcase filled with neatly-bound volumes, each with the character of its contents stamped in gold upon the back, with the name of the compiler." "The Great Scrapbook Maker: A Colored Janitor's Unique Library."

59. "Paste and Scissors."

60. This 8" by 10" volume seems to have been pasted onto sheets of a periodical, possibly a Masonic newspaper, and bound later. John M. Sherry, *The Press*, 30 Mar 1886.

61. See my "Nineteenth-Century Abolitionists and the Databases."

62. "Bystander," "By the Way: Open secrets about the people we meet and what they are doing." *Daily News*, 28 May 1887 [or 1884]. In Dorsey biographical scrapbook. Albion Tourgee wrote a signed column entitled "A Bystander's Notes" in the *Chicago Inter Ocean* from about 1888 on, but this does not seem to be related. Unattributed clipping, probably from a black newspaper, before 1897, in Dorsey biographical scrapbook. This writer noted that the need for forming a historical society was "suggested by Mrs. N.F. Mossell."

63. Bonnie Tibbie, "Philadelphia letter," *The Globe*, 10 Sep 1881, n.p. In Dorsey biographical scrapbook.

64. Unattributed clipping, probably from a black newspaper, before 1897, in Dorsey biographical scrapbook.

65. "A Rare Collection," *People's Advocate*, in Dorsey Scrapbook 9: 51; Cheyney University.

66. "Negro Americana Begun at Howard University," press release, 2 Jan 1915, notes that John W. Cromwell, secretary of the American Negro Academy and author of "The Negro in American History," several years ago placed at the disposal of the University "the Cathcart Clippings" covering the period of the Civil War and Reconstruction; Kelly Miller papers, 71-1 Folder 15. Moorland Spingarn Research Center, Howard University.

67. L. S. Alexander Gumby, "The Adventures of My Scrapbooks," *Columbia Library Columns*, 2:1, Nov 1952, 21. Richard Nugent, *Gay Rebel of the Harlem Renaissance: Selections from the Work of Richard Bruce Nugent* (Duke UP, 2002), 224. John W. Douglas, "Unique Passion for Collecting Books about Negroes," *Baltimore Afro-American*, 7 June 1930, 11; "Book Studio Group Honors Cullen, Poet," *New York Amsterdam News* 17 Sep 1930, 10. Laura E. Helton has written of the social life of Gumby's scrapbooks—the community around Gumby convened in his scrapbook studio, while they and others mailed him clippings. "On the Politics of Collecting: Archival Publics and African American Documentary Practice, 1920–1960," paper, "To the Source" symposium, Rutgers University, March 2011.

68. Jo Kadleck, "Black History Remains Alive in Alexander Gumby's Popular Scrapbooks," *Columbia News*, 18 Feb 2002, http://www.columbia.edu/cu/news/02/02/alexander-Gumby.html. L. S. Alexander Gumby, "The Adventures of My Scrapbooks," 22. Aubrey Bowser, "Book Review: A Negro Documentarian," *New York Amsterdam News*, 13 Aug 1930, 20.

69. T. Thomas Fortune Scrapbook, 1889–1904, Schomburg Center. The scrapbook was probably at least partly made by his wife, as one clipping, which was presumably removed and then repasted, bears the handwritten note, "NY Herald, Sunday July 9, 1893. Mrs. Fortune takes this out of her scrapbook and says she must have it back." "Afro Americans to Become White...says T. Thomas Fortune." Fortune's scrapbook-making connections extend to the earlier generation as well: he worked in the print-shop of Cromwell's newspaper, *The People's Advocate* as a young man.

70. "The Arts Ball: Harlemites Dance to Aid L.S. Gumby," *New York Amsterdam News*, 25 Nov 1931.

71. "The Road Back: Alexander Gumby Plans Comeback with New Art Studio," *New York Amsterdam News*, 8 Dec 1934, 9.

72. L. S. Alexander Gumby, "The Adventures of My Scrapbooks," 22.

73. Ada Simpson, letter, "The Jury," letters column, *The Brownies' Book*, Apr 1920, 111. Another black publication encouraged readers to make scrapbooks of black poetry in the 1920s: The *Baltimore Afro-American*'s "Poem a Week" column offered readers "Poems by colored authors for your scrap-book," and asked them to send in other poems that they liked. 20 Jan 1922, 12.

74. "Make Scrapbooks for Hospital Shut-ins," *Chicago Defender*, 5 May 1934: A3, col. 1; and "Scrapbooks for Shut-ins," *Chicago Defender*, 19 May 1934, 15. "Prescott, Ark," *Chicago Defender*, 7 Mar 1936, 18.

75. Bill Cosby, "Introduction," Middleton A. Harris, *The Black Book* (New York: Random House, 1974), n.p. Morrison was the in-house editor; her name does not appear in the book, though her parents are thanked in the acknowledgments for lending materials.

76. Carolyn C. Denard, "Toni Morrison," *Black Women in America*, Darlene Clark Hine, ed., 2nd ed., (New York: Oxford UP, 2005) 815–19.

Chapter 5

1. "Report on the Second Day of the Anti-Slavery Convention," n.p., [1860]. In scrapbook "John Brown's Insurrection at Harper's Ferry," Joseph W. H. Cathcart. Cromwell family papers, Series K, 24 S6, Moorland Spingarn Collection, Howard University.

2. Anthony's companion in the opera, who protests that she "never liked to look at a newspaper," knits. Music by Virgil Thomson, text by Gertrude Stein, *The Mother of Us All: An Opera* (New York: Schirmer, 1947) 24.

3. Clara Barton, *Diary of Clara Barton*, Apr 1864, in William Eleazar Barton, *The Life of Clara Barton: Founder of the American Red Cross*, vol. 1 (Boston: Houghton, Mifflin, 1922), 270. Elizabeth Brown Pryor, *Clara Barton: Professional Angel* (Philadelphia: U Penn. P, 1988), 27. Ida Husted Harper, *The Life and Work of Susan B. Anthony* (Indianapolis: Bowen-Merrill, 1898), 125.

4. Matilda Joslyn Gage, Woman Suffrage Scrap Books, 1850–1898, Library of Congress.

5. Some women had "broken the sound barrier in their efforts to abolish slavery and in support of other reforms," notes Karlyn Kohrs Campbell, "Anna E. Dickinson," *Women Public Speakers in the United States, 1800–1925: A Bio-critical Sourcebook*, Karlyn Kohrs Campbell, ed. (Westport, Conn.: Greenwood, 1993), 156. Ronald Zboray and Mary Saracino Zboray report disapproving comments on women speaking in public among 1840s abolitionist women in New England. "Political News and Female Readership in Antebellum Boston and Its Region," *Journalism History*, 22 (Spring 1996), 2–14. Jean Fagan Yellin, *Women and Sisters: The Antislavery Feminists in American Culture* (New Haven: Yale UP, 1989), 52, cited in Linda Lumsden, *Rampant Women: Suffragists and the Right of Assembly* (Knoxville: U Tenn P, 1997), xxiii. MM, "A woman's letter from

California," Oakland 9 Dec 1869, no publication. Huntington Library general scrapbook collection, 97, Elizabeth Boynton Harbert, vol. 3.

6. From *The Liberator*, 11 Aug 1837, "Extract from the Pastoral letter of the General Association of Massachusetts to the churches under their care." The letter was written by conservative pro-Southern clergy in response to the success of Angelina and Sarah Grimké's abolitionist lectures to New England women. Though the real political point of the letter was its opposition to abolitionist lectures in church, the authors framed it as an objection to women's speaking, the point that Anthony seized on. See Gerda Lerner, *The Grimké Sisters from South Carolina: Pioneers for Woman's Rights* (New York: Oxford UP, 1998), 143–44. Anthony placed this material retrospectively. She took up the actual work of making scrapbooks in 1855, at her father's suggestion, in reaction to write-ups of her talks in the press. Harper, *The Life and Work*, 125. Harbert pointed out that women's teaching was acceptable, but not their preaching, in her 1870 novel *Out of Her Sphere* and in her newspaper columns; other women's rights speakers made the point as well.

7. Frances Ellen Burr, letter to Susan B. Anthony, 17 Sep 1885, quoting her diary entry of 7 Oct 1853. In *The History of Woman Suffrage*, Vol. III, 1876–1885, Elizabeth Cady Stanton, Susan B. Anthony, and Matilda Joslyn Gage, eds. (Rochester: Susan B. Anthony, 1886), 168.

8. Elizabeth Boynton Harbert papers, Huntington. Scrapbook 1.

9. Mary Eliza Church Terrell, *A Colored Woman in a White World* (Washington, D.C.: Ransdell, 1940), 158.

10. If Blake made a scrapbook of her popular stories, I have not located it.

11. "Woman's Word and Work" scrapbook, Seneca Falls Historical Society. Anna E. Dickinson papers, Library of Congress, scrapbooks 2 and 3.

12. Matilda Joslyn Gage, *Woman Suffrage Scrap Books, 1850–1898*.

13. For more on Sallie Cotten and women's rights work in North Carolina, see Donald G. Mathews and Jane Sherron De Hart, *Sex, Gender, and the Politics of ERA: A State and the Nation* (New York: Oxford UP, 1992), 3–6; and Anastatia Sims, *The Power of Femininity in the New South: Women's Organizations and Politics in North Carolina, 1880–1930* (Columbia: U South Car P, 1997).The items are undated, but surrounding material is from 1884 and 1885. In Scrapbook, folder 14g, p. 118, Sallie Southall Cotten Papers (#2613), Southern Historical Collection, U of NC, Chapel Hill.

14. "South's Women," *Atlanta Constitution*, n.d. In Scrapbook, folder 14g, p. 118, Sallie Southall Cotten Papers (#2613), Southern Historical Collection, U of NC Chapel Hill.

15. Lizzie M. Boynton, "Hoosier Girls and Wabash College," *The Independent*, 20:1035, 1 Oct 1868 2. "City News," n.p., n.d. Huntington Library general scrapbook collection, 97, Elizabeth Boynton Harbert, vol. 2.

16. P. A. Hamilton, "An Hour with the Strong Minded," in unknown paper, reporting that Boynton plans to lecture 1 Feb 1870; Huntington Library general scrapbook collection, 97, Elizabeth Boynton Harbert, vol. 3. For more on Harbert, see Steven M. Buechler, "Elizabeth Boynton Harbert and the Woman Suffrage Movement, 1870–1896," *Signs*, 1987, 13:3, 78–97.

17. Elizabeth Boynton Harbert, *Out of Her Sphere* (Des Moines: Mills, 1871).

18. Elizabeth Morrison Boynton Harbert Papers (Series II of the Mary Earhart Dillon Collection). Schlesinger Library, Radcliffe College, Harvard U.

19. Lisa Tetrault has written on the significance of women's earning through lecturing on the lyceum circuit of the 1870s and 1880s. Stanton, for example, lectured for twelve years, presenting such popular lectures as "Our Girls," and more explicitly suffrage lectures. "The Incorporation of American Feminism: Suffragists and the Postbellum Lyceum," *Journal of American History* 96:4 2010, 1027-1056.

20. J. Matthew Gallman compared a sample of Dickinson's scrapbook coverage of one of her tours against a selection of newspaper coverage of the period and found a similar ratio of favorable-to-unfavorable notices as appeared in the press. *America's Joan of Arc: The Life of Anna Elizabeth Dickinson* (Oxford UP, 2006), 214.

21. Caroline Healey Dall, Wednesday, 19 Sep 1855. *Daughter of Boston: The Extraordinary Diary of a Nineteenth-Century Woman, Caroline Healey Dall*, Helen Deese, ed. (Boston: Beacon, 2005), 231; "Conventions and Women's Meetings Held by Mrs. Caroline Healey Dall." In *Massachusetts in the Woman Suffrage Movement: A General, Political, Legal and Legislative History from 1774 to 1881* (Boston: Roberts Bros. 1881), 22.

22. Paulina Wright Davis to Caroline Dall, 24 Sep 1855. Dall-Healey family papers, Massachusetts Historical Society.

23. Her journal reports, "Mr. Clarke talked a little pleasantly about Italy.... If Mr. Clarke received 10$—as he surely must for that lecture, there is no reason why I should not receive as much for a better one." Caroline Wells Healey Dall Journal, 21 Nov 1854; 28 Jan 1856. Dall-Healey family papers, Massachusetts Historical Society.

24. Caroline Wells Healey Dall, letter to the *Daily Evening Traveller* (Boston), 30 Jan 1856. In Dall scrapbook, Dall-Healey family papers, Massachusetts Historical Society.

25. Lizzie Morrison Boynton (LMB), "Women's Rights Convention," Correspondence of the *Cincinnati Gazette*, May 15, no year. Elizabeth Boynton Harbert scrapbooks, Vol. 3. Huntington Library general scrapbook collection, 97.

26. Lillie Devereux Blake, *Fettered for Life, or Lord and Master a Story of To-Day* (1874, New York: Feminist P, 1996), 256–57.

27. In 1894, the *Chicago Inter Ocean* published Ida B. Wells's reports from her antilynching tour of England.

28. Jacqueline Van Voris, *Carrie Chapman Catt: A Public Life* (New York: Feminist P, 1987), 11. Catt, Carrie Chapman. Letter to Elizabeth Boynton Harbert, 13 Jan 1921. Elizabeth Boynton Harbert papers, Series II of the Mary Earhart Dillon Collection, 1870–1939, scrapbook, n.p. Schlesinger Library, Radcliffe Institute, Harvard University.

29. Elizabeth Harbert, "Our Young Women. A Department Not Devoted to Fashion or Cookery, But to Women as They Are," *Chicago Inter Ocean*, 6 Jan. 1877, 6.

30. Elizabeth Harbert, "Three Books," in "Woman's Kingdom," *Chicago Inter Ocean*, 12 May 1877, 6.

31. Elizabeth Harbert, "Letters to Young Mothers," in "Woman's Kingdom," *Chicago Inter Ocean*, n.d., n.p. in Huntington Library general scrapbook collection, 97, Elizabeth Boynton Harbert, vol. 1.

32. Julia McNair Wright, *The Complete Home: An Encyclopaedia of Domestic Life and Affairs* (Philadelphia: J. C. McCurdy & Co., 1879), 194, quoted in "Woman's Kingdom," *Chicago Inter Ocean*, 8:152, 27 Sep 1879, 9.

33. Matilda Fletcher, "The Poor Rich Man and the Rich Poor Man," in Woman's Kingdom, *Chicago Inter Ocean*, 2 Nov 1878. Scrapbook, Elizabeth Morrison Boynton Harbert Papers, Schlesinger Library.

34. A scrapbook in the Catharine Gouger (Waugh) McCulloch papers, kept by McCulloch's cousin, contains clippings from Harbert's column, "Woman's Kingdom," in the 1870s. Catharine Waugh McCulloch Papers, 1877–1983; Subseries D, 250. MC 378. Schlesinger Library, Radcliffe Institute, Harvard University. "Woman's Kingdom. The New Amendment—The Resolution to be Submitted to the Republican Convention," *Chicago Inter Ocean*, 9:46, 17 May 1880, 9.

35. Alison Booth, *How to Make It as a Woman: Collective Biographical History from Victoria to the Present* (Chicago: U Chicago P, 2004), 3. S.E.D., letter, in "Just Among Ourselves" column, Aunt Patience, ed. *The Ladies' Home Journal*, 7:5, Apr 1891; 27.

36. Elizabeth Boynton Harbert, "Woman's Kingdom: The Family Scrap-Book," *Chicago Inter Ocean*, 3 Jan 1880, 9.
37. Amy Mecklenberg-Fanger, who reads Miller's use of her scrapbook through the lens of rhetoric and composition studies, frames her use of them as "inventional"—a springboard for the speeches. "Scissors, Paste and Social Change: The Rhetoric of Scrapbooks of Women's Organizations, 1875–1930," dissertation, Ohio State U, 2007, 122–24. Margherita Arlina Hamm, "Scraps and Scrap-Books," *The Clipping Collector*, 1:4, Apr 1896, 42.
38. Lillie Devereux Blake, *Fettered for Life*, 140–41.
39. Ibid., 142.
40. "Murder in South Norwalk," 22 July 1874, n.p. In Lillie Devereux Blake scrapbook, Sophia Smith Collection, Smith College. Talk reported in "Good Templer's Column," *Iowa State Reporter*, 7 Nov 1877, 6.
41. Frances Willard, "President's Annual Address Before Eighteenth National and First World's WCTU Convention, Boston, Mass., 1891." In Minutes of the Eighteenth Annual Meeting (Chicago: Woman's Temperance Publication Association, 1891), 225.
42. Elizabeth Cady Stanton Papers, Manuscript Division, Library of Congress, Washington, D.C.
43. The Millers' scrapbooks are online via the Library of Congress's American Memory site, http://memory.loc.gov/ammem/collections/suffrage/millerscrapbooks/index.html. Accessed 30 Apr 2012. Elizabeth Miller was the daughter of the abolitionist Gerrit Smith and a cousin of Elizabeth Cady Stanton. See the Nebraska Woman Suffrage Association, Grace Richardson scrapbooks, Nebraska State Historical Society, Lincoln.
44. Rosalyn Terborg-Penn's history of black women's involvement in the women's suffrage struggle, for example, does not mention this campaign. Terborg-Penn, *African American Women in the Struggle for the Vote, 1850–1920* (Indiana UP, 1998).
45. Alice Moore Dunbar, *Masterpieces of Negro Eloquence: The Best Speeches Delivered by the Negro from the Days of Slavery to the Present Time* (n.p.: Robert R. Nelson, 1914).
46. These names appeared on the list of projected speakers for this campaign, laid out in 1914. Jennie Bradley Roessing, "The Equal Suffrage Campaign in Pennsylvania," *Women in Public Life*, Jane Addams et al. (American Academy of Political and Social Science, 1914), 157. Dunbar worked closely with the Negro Women's Equal Franchise Federation (also called the Lucy Stone Woman's Suffrage League), the Equal Franchise Federation of Western Pennsylvania, the Women's Political Union, and the Woman Suffrage Party.
47. Dunbar secretly married Henry Arthur Callis, a fellow teacher, in 1910 and later divorced.
48. Gloria T. Hull identifies this photo as one taken when she was living with Paul Laurence Dunbar in Washington, so before 1902. *Give Us Each Day: The Diary of Alice Dunbar-Nelson*, Gloria T. Hull, ed. (New York: Norton, 1986), 288.
49. "Women Here Slow to Get Vote, Thinks Widow of Negro Poet," *Ledger*, 7 Aug 1915. *Lansdowne News*, 30 July 1915. Dorothy Deane, "Mrs. Dunbar Made Strong Argument for Equal Suffrage," *Williamsport Sun*, 14 Aug 1915. All in Alice Dunbar-Nelson scrapbook 1, Ms. Box 113, Special Collections, U of Delaware.
50. Dorothy Deane, "Mrs. Dunbar."
51. "Women's Clubs," *Pittsburgh Dispatch*, 24 Oct 1915, in Alice Dunbar-Nelson scrapbook 1; in a speech in Williamsport, Pennsylvania, reported in August, Dunbar spoke to a black audience in what the reporter described as "a heart to heart with the men of her race," saying to men opposing suffrage "in the first place, you are slapping your women in the face, and at the same time you are kicking yourselves, because you need the ballot of the colored woman to help you in your fight for your own rights." Dorothy

Deane, "Mrs. Dunbar." An account of the Dunbar marriage appears in Eleanor Alexander, *Lyrics of Sunshine and Shadow: The Courtship and Marriage of Paul Lawrence Dunbar and Alice Ruth Moore* (New York: NYU P, 2001). Others in their social circle were aware of the physical abuse (165–66, 169).

52. "An Older Woman to a Younger," dated 3 Nov 1915, in Alice Dunbar-Nelson scrapbook 1.

53. "Women Ask for a 'Square Deal,'" *York Daily*, 2 Nov 1915, in Alice Dunbar-Nelson scrapbook 1.

Chapter 6

1. Cynthia Saltzman, *Old Masters, New World: America's Raid on Europe's Great Pictures* (New York: Penguin, 2008), 90. Another collector, Albert Barnes, left his art collection in Merion, Pennsylvania, with similar stipulations about moving its Renoirs, Matisses, or anything else, or adding explanatory tags. He wished to preserve his own much-criticized juxtapositions of objects to teach his ideas about art. Despite Barnes's stipulations, the Barnes Foundation collection has been moved from its original home to a new one near Philadelphia's Museum of Fine Arts, although Barnes's juxtapositions have been preserved.

2. Barbara Kirshenblatt-Gimblett developed the point that movement through a museum is a structured performance, in her talk "From Memory Palace to Performance Space: The Development of the Museum as Art Practice," Barker Center for the Humanities, 29 Oct 2003. Robin Bernstein introduces the concept of "scriptive things," or elements of material culture that, "like a play script, broadly [structure] a performance while simultaneously allowing for resistance and unleashing original, live variations that may not be individually predictable." Bernstein, "Dances with Things: Material Culture and the Performance of Race," *Social Text*, 27:4, Winter 2009, 68–69, developed further in *Racial Innocence: Performing American Childhood from Slavery to Civil Rights* (New York: NYU P, 2011). Claire Farago characterizes memorabilia scrapbooks as "paper museums," noting that they are "neither simple things not quite museums, but meta-objects." "'Scraps as it were': Binding Memories," *Journal of Victorian Culture*, 10:1, Spring 2005, 114–22.

3. For more on this point, see Thomas Osborne, "The Ordinariness of the Archive," *History of the Human Sciences*, 12:51, 1999, 61.

4. I use the term *archive* to cover these various types of collections, which include the library manuscript collections, rare book collections, and special collections where scrapbooks are located. Because scrapbooks are located in all these venues, I draw on all of them as points of comparison.

5. The problem of filling gaps in earlier collecting within immigrant and other underrepresented communities was discussed at the panel "Currents in Collecting: Documenting Underrepresented Communities," Schlesinger Library conference on the History of Women in America, 2 Oct 2003.

6. See, for example, Leah Price, *The Anthology and the Rise of the Novel: From Richardson to George Eliot* (Cambridge: Cambridge UP, 2000). Paul Wright, "Everyman His Own Gutenberg," paper presented at conference of the Society for the History of Authorship, Reading, and Publishing, Mainz, Germany, July 2000. Wikibooks, rapidly patched together from supposedly public-domain material on websites and marketed as print-on-demand titles via Amazon, do little more than transform a web search into booklike object. See Max Read, "'Celebrities with Big Dicks' and Other Tales from the Weird World of Wikipedia Books" *The Gawker*, 17 Apr 2012. Homemade scrapbook anthology making persisted at least into the twentieth century and can offer important insights

into how people used poetry in their lives, as Cary Nelson has shown in *Revolutionary Memory: Recovering the Poetry of the American Left* (New York: Routledge, 2003). Notable poetry scrapbook makers include Amelia Earhart. See Sammie L. Morris, "What Archives Reveal: The Hidden Poems of Amelia Earhart," *Provenance* 23 2005, 21–38.

7. Catalog card 4, Solomons, M. J. scrapbook, Duke University Library, Special Collections.

8. Robert DeCandido, "Scrapbooks, the Smiling Villains," Feature "Out of the Question," *Conservation Administration News*, no. 53, Apr 1993; online at http://www.well.com/~bronxbob/resume/54_7-93.html, accessed 26 Aug 2009.

9. The clippings in the scrapbook of Hiram Revels, a Reconstruction-era black senator, at the Schomburg Library, for example, have been removed and remounted on archival paper, in a manner said to preserve their arrangement, although clippings are now only on right-hand pages. But archivists have begun to recognize scrapbooks as a form with its own integrity. Conservators at Emory University working on African American scrapbooks, for example, seek to restore loosened items to their previous place, studying "the glue stains on the back to see if any empty page in the book carries a matching ghostly outline" as a map of its former position. Eve M. Kahn, "Saving Scrapbooks from the Scrapheap," *New York Times* 4 Aug. 2011.

10. In one emblematic story of black achievement, injustice, and archival loss, both the scrapbook and the black newspaper it contained have disappeared. A man interviewed by E. Patrick Johnson in 2005 tells of his mother, whose poem "Happy Work Song" won a hundred dollar prize and was used as lyrics for a song. The song, renamed "Whistle While You Work," earned other people considerably more money. "Ed" recalls the evidence of his mother's childhood scrapbook, with a clipping about the prize from a black newspaper around 1930—a newspaper he can no longer find. *Sweet Tea: Black Gay Men of the South* (Chapel Hill: UNC P, 2008) 29.

11. Robertson Scrapbook in the Caswell County Historical Association Collection, Richmond-Miles Museum, Yanceyville, N.C. Information on the Robertson family from Karen Avants, personal correspondence, 20 Nov 2008.

12. Michael Thompson, *Rubbish Theory: The Creation and Destruction of Value* (New York: Oxford UP, 1979), 13–33.

13. "A Lost Scrap-Book," *Clipping Collector*, 1:1, Jan 1896, 21. See items in black newspapers honoring children for gathering scrap paper and urging their readers to participate, such as "Save Your Paper," *Atlanta Daily World*, 17 Jan 1942, 4; "Afro Aids Scrap Paper Drive," *Baltimore Afro-American*, 29 Jan 1944, 7; and "Aid in Scrap Paper Drive," *New Journal and Guide* (Norfolk, Va.), 22 Jan 1944, B5.

14. Thomas Osborne in "The Ordinariness of the Archive" suggests that those mundane materials that enter the archive are accorded higher status and power.

15. The two scrapbooks that composed "The Book of Life" are no longer extant. Suzanne Pullon Fitch and Roseann M. Mandziuk, *Sojourner Truth as Orator: Wit, Story, and Song* (Westport, Conn.: Greenwood, 1997), 37.

16. "William H. Scott Exhibition Opens January 23 at Emory," news release, 21 Jan 2009, http://www.emory.edu/home/news/releases/2009/01/william-h-scott-exhibition-opens-jan-23.html accessed 4 Mar 2009.

17. Personal communication with Randall Burkett, 4 Mar 2009.

18. Scrapbook of Frances Amanda Smith Cather, George Cather Ray Collection (MS 113). Archives and Special Collections, U Nebraska–Lincoln Libraries.

19. Akasha (Gloria) Hull, "Researching Alice Dunbar-Nelson: A Personal and Literary Perspective," *Lesbian Subjects: A Feminist Studies Reader*, ed. Martha Vicinus

(Bloomington: Indiana UP, 1996), 16. Gloria T. Hull changed her name to Akasha Gloria Hull in 1992.

20. Ellen Carol DuBois, "Making Women's History: Activist Historians of Women's Rights, 1880–1940," *Radical History Review*, 49, 1991, 78.

21. Mary Earhart Dillon Collection, 1863–1955; finding aid, Schlesinger Library, Radcliffe Institute, Harvard U; and Ellen Carol DuBois, "Making Women's History," 79. A note in the finding aid to the Mary Earhart Dillon collection at Schlesinger reports that Dillon unsuccessfully offered the collection to the Newberry Library in Chicago, the New York Public Library, the Library of Congress, and possibly to Syracuse University. Janice E. Ruth of the Library of Congress Manuscript Division finds no record that she made this offer but notes that Dillon could have made the offer to another division or by phone. Personal correspondence, 29 Sep 2009.

22. Robert C. Winthrop et al., "September Meeting. Death of George Livermore," *Proceedings of the Massachusetts Historical Society*, 8, 1864, 459. Thomas W. Higginson et al., "June Meeting, 1887. John Brown of Osawatomie; Attucks Memorial," *Proceedings of the MHS* 3, Second Series (1886–87), 319–39. "March Meeting. Gifts to the Society; Persecution and Prosecution; Darien Bibliography," *Proceedings of the MHS* 63, Third Series (1929–30), 135.

23. Henry F. May, personal communication, 23 Sep 2009. May's book is *Coming to Terms: A Study in Memory and History* (Berkeley: U Cal. P, 1987).

24. Letter from Mary Livermore to Harbert. On letterhead from the Office of *The Woman's Journal*, no. 3, Tremont Place, Boston. The form provides the date 187_, but the rest is not written in; page 1 is missing. Alma Lutz, *Susan B. Anthony: Rebel, Crusader, Humanitarian* (Boston: Beacon P, 1959), 288–89, 393. The timely legacy also aided the books' publication.

25. Susan B. Anthony to Harbert, 12 Aug 1901. Elizabeth Boynton Harbert Series II of the Mary Earhart Dillon Collection, 1870–1939; folder A-68. Schlesinger Library, Radcliffe Institute, Harvard U.

26. Ida Husted Harper, note of presentation, quoted in "A Wondrous Woman's Book," *The Relief Society Magazine*, June 1916, 212. After the Nineteenth Amendment passed, barring restrictions on voting on account of gender, Harper donated an additional scrapbook to the New York Public Library in 1930, and her children made up two additional scrapbooks of her Indiana writings and placed them in the Vigo County Public Library, where they were eventually microfilmed and the originals discarded. Inventory, Ida Husted Harper Scrapbooks, 1878–1893, Accession Number: 20071009A, Vigo County Public Library, Terre Haute, Ind. http://www.vigo.lib.in.us/archives/inventories/women/harper_scrapbooks.php, accessed 21 Sep 2009. Amy Mecklenberg-Fanger, "Scissors, Paste and Social Change: The Rhetoric of Scrapbooks of Women's Organizations, 1875–1930," Dissertation, Ohio SU, 2007, 81.

27. "Last Will of Matilda J. Gage," recorded 1 Apr 1901, Surrogate's Court of the County of Onondaga, Syracuse, N.Y.; http://www.rootsweb.ancestry.com/~nyononda/COURT/W10P72.HTM, accessed 12 Sep 2009. Many of the remaining papers were given to the Schlesinger library at Radcliffe in 1956 by her granddaughter, Matilda Jewell Gage. Ellen Carol DuBois, "Making Women's History,79.

28. Helen R. Deese, ed., *Daughter of Boston: The Extraordinary Diary of a Nineteenth Century Woman: Caroline Healey Dall*, Boston: Beacon P, 2006; 7 Aug 1842, 53.

29. Helen R. Deese, ed., *Daughter of Boston*, x.

30. Leon Gardner, one of the last remaining members, donated some of its materials to the Historical Society of Pennsylvania, but others were lost.

31. Dorsey's scrapbooks stop around 1903, with the last materials pasted in around 1905. See Roger Lane, *William Dorsey's Philadelphia and Ours*, 334, 338. Behind a wall: Charles

L. Blockson, "Bibliophiles and Collectors of African Americana," http://www.broward. org/library/bienes/lii13001.htm, accessed 1 May 2012, from Damn Rare": The Memoirs of an *African-American Bibliophile*, by Charles L. Blockson, Tracy, Calif.: Quantum Leap, 1998. Hidden in storage: Roger Lane, *William Dorsey's Philadelphia*, 338. Reclaimed from janitor's closet: Sulayman Clark, former archivist at Cheyney University, http:// sulaymanclark.com/parents.html, accessed 8 June 2009.

32. Charles L. Blockson, "Bibliophiles and Collectors of African Americana." Letter from T. G. Steward, Wilberforce University, responding to J. W. Cromwell, 2 Sep 1915. Adelaide M. Cromwell and Anthony Cromwell Hill, *Unveiled Voices, Unvarnished Memories: The Cromwell Family in Slavery And Segregation, 1692–1972* (U Miss. P, 2007), 315–16. "Negro Americana Begun at Howard University," press release, 2 Jan 1915, notes that John W. Cromwell, secretary of the American Negro Academy and author of "The Negro in American History," several years ago placed at the disposal of the university "The Cathcart Clippings," covering the period of the Civil War and Reconstruction; Kelly Miller papers 71-1 Folder 15. Moorland Spingarn Research Center, Howard U. William Dorsey Collection, Cheyney U, Box 2 miscellaneous.

33. Quoted in Thomas H. Wirth, "Introduction," *Gay Rebel of the Harlem Renaissance: Selections from the Work of Richard Bruce Nugent*, Thomas H. Wirth, ed. (Durham: Duke UP, 2002), 29. Gumby's donation preceded most of the 1950s antigay witch hunts on campuses. Gumby may also have wished to distinguish his collection from that of his friend Arthur Schomburg, who had earlier deposited his immense collection, including his clippings, with the New York Public Library, which gave his name to the branch that ultimately became the Schomburg Center for Research in Black Culture.

34. Gurley, *Scrap-books and How to Make Them* (New York: Authors' Publishing, 1880) 17.

Chapter 7

1. "About Clipping Bureaus," *Clipping Collector*, 1:2, Feb 1896, 22–23.
2. E. W. Gurley, *Scrap-books and How to Make Them* (New York: Authors' Publishing, 1880), 14: 9–10.
3. "New York Letter," *Literary World*, 5 Mar 1898, 73. Budd may have first set up in Washington and Philadelphia before establishing himself in New York. Charles Grutzner, Jr., "If What You Want Was Published Within Past 98 Years, He Has It, Back-Number Budd Says," *New York Amsterdam News*, 2 Sep 1931, 9. According to earlier accounts, he first sold newspapers at his bootblacking stand and then branched into old papers. Some sources refer to Budd as Robert N. Budd. He claimed to have copyrighted the name "Back Number Budd" and signed his checks with that name.
4. "Odd But Profitable Business: How Back-Number Budd Is Getting Rich Out of His Newspaper Files," *Macon Weekly Telegraph*, 27 Dec 1888, 8; reprinted from *The New York World*. John S. Grey, "Back Number Budd," *Printers' Ink: A Journal for Advertisers*, 15 June 1898, 35–36. Wendell Phillips Dodge, "Budd, 'The Back-Number King,'" *Chicago Defender*, 7 Feb 1914, 6, reprinted from *Technical World Magazine*; "A Flood of Congratulations for Mr. Morton," *New York Tribune*, 10 Nov 1888, 2.
5. One patronizing account had him saying, "Paper am a great ting to stand de fire and water," as he spread out newspapers to dry after his first fire. "Budd Is Digging in the Ruins," *New York Tribune*, 16 June 1895, 17. [Miscellany column], *Amusement Bulletin*, 12 Oct 1889, 10. "'Back Number Budd': The Prosperous Business of an Enterprising Colored Man; Over a Million Copies of Old Newspapers Collected on an Original Capital of $8—Relics of Old New York," *Idaho Statesman*, 23:2, 29 July 1986, 4. Reprinted from the *New York World*.

6. "'Back Number' Budd's Great Loss: He Will Not Give Up His Business However," *New York Tribune*, 26 Apr 1895, 5.

7. "New York Letter," *Literary World*, 5 Mar 1898, 73. "A Valuable File," *The Hyde Park Herald*, 8 July 1887, n.p.

8. Charles Grutzner, Jr., "If What You Want," 9. Fowler, William Worthington, *Ten Years in Wall Street; or, Revelations of Inside Life and Experience on 'change*. (Hartford: Worthington, Dustin, 1870), 73.

9. WorldCat record, "Gazette of the United States, facsimile, 1789 May 2," http://www.worldcat.org/oclc/122625410&referer=brief_results, accessed 1 May 2012.

10. "'Back Number' Budd's Great Loss."

11. "A Lost Scrap-Book," *The Clipping Collector*, 1:2, Feb 1896, 21.

12. For more on the Grimké-Weld project, see Ellen Gruber Garvey, "Nineteenth-Century Abolitionists and the Databases They Created," *Legacy: A Journal of American Women Writers*, 27:2, 2010, 257–66. For British abolitionist use of newspaper ads, see Adam Hochschild, *Bury the Chains: Prophets and Rebels in the Fight to Free an Empire's Slaves* (Boston: Houghton Mifflin, 2005), 197.

13. For a substantial fee, Budd was willing to search through a year's papers for a desired article. He reported charging a hundred dollars for such a search ("Back Number Budd's Loss," *The American Stationer*, 9 May 1895, 857).

14. G. Bernard Shaw, *My Expensive Scrapbook* (New York: Hemstreet Press Clipping Bureau, printed by the Roycrofters, 1915), 7. "The Press: Clipping Business," *Time*, 30 May 1932. Frederick W. Johanect, "Influence of the Press Clipping Bureau," *The American Globe: Independent Magazine*, 9:3, Jan 1912, 93.

15. For more on Shanks, see *The National Cyclopaedia of American Biography* (J. T. White, 1893), 259–60. Romeike began work in London in 1881, set up shop in New York in 1884, and eventually occupied offices in the Judge Building, owned by the humor magazine of that name. Robert Luce, who later became a senator, started the bureau with his brother Linn. They were not related to Henry Luce. ("Let's Talk It Over," *National Magazine*, Aug 1916, 852–53.) "Clipping Bureaus," *Printer's Ink*, 9 Aug 1899, 28; A.G.L., "An American Idea," *Los Angeles Times*, 25 June 1899; 5. Frank H. Madison memoir, University of Illinois at Springfield, Norris L. Brookens Library Archives/Special Collections, http://www.uis.edu/archives/memoirs/MADISONF.pdf, 18, accessed 1 May 2012.

16. F. E. Seward, "From the Trade Paper Standpoint," *Clipping Collector*, 1:1, Jan 1896, 14. Geo. H. Reinnegel, "Clippings for Trade Papers," *Clipping Collector*, 1:2, Feb 1896, 17.

17. In 1889 services charged their clients about 4 cents per clipping; in 1902, 3–5 cents per clipping sometimes in addition to a subscription charge; in 1917, by which time charges to clients may have risen, the "girls" were paid a quarter of a cent per clipping. Agencies later responded to complaints of too many false hits by switching to an hourly wage. Information on price charged from W. A. Bardwell, "Report on Scrapbooks," *Library Journal*, May–June 1889, 195; information on wages from lawsuit, "Henry Romeike, Inc. v. Albert Romeike & Co.," *New York Supplement*, 179 App. Div. 712, New York Supreme Court, Appellate Div., 9 Nov 1917, 237. Richard K. Popp, "Reading as an Extractive Industry: Information Abundance and the Invention of the Press Clipping Bureau" (paper presented at the annual meeting of the Society for the History of Authorship, Reading, and Publishing, Washington, D.C., 16 July 2011).

18. "Training the Eye," *The Clipping Collector*, 1:2, Feb 1896, 23.

19. Francie's one moment of taking a clipping for herself is a violation of the rules. In 1917 she learns from reading the "extra" that has landed on her desk that war has been

declared and seeks to memorize the historic moment by fusing personal, sensory memories of her body reading at the desk with the tangible commemoration of the page of the newspaper, placed in an envelope with other items in her purse. She steps out of her role as hired eyes and must ignore the "clients who might be mentioned on page one or two." Betty Smith, *A Tree Grows in Brooklyn* (1943, New York: HarperPerennial Classics, 1998) 369, 419, 412.

20. "Bankruptcy via the Press-Clipping Bureau," *Everybody's Magazine*, 1 July 1903, 9: 126.

21. "Queries," *The Writer*, 2:7, July 1888, 173–74. In a reflection of the ingrown relationship between clipping bureaus and publications, the letter may have been planted, since Robert Luce, owner of the Press Clipping Bureau and the Authors' Clipping Bureau, was also part owner of *The Writer*, as a letter from the Authors' Clipping Bureau on *Writer* stationery reveals. Letter to Jack Crawford from the Authors' Clipping Bureau, 27 Oct 1893. Buffalo Bill Historical Center, Cody, Wyoming.

22. Robert Luce, "The Clipping Bureau and the Library," *Special Libraries*, 4; Sep–Oct 1913, 154.

23. Geoffrey Nunberg, "Farewell to the Information Age," in Geoffrey Nunberg, ed., *The Future of the Book* (Berkeley: U California P, 1996), 112. R. E. Delury, "News and Comments," *Journal of the Royal Astronomical Society of Canada*, vol. 22, 1928, 355.

24. Robert Luce, "The Clipping Bureau and the Library," 154. The term "key-word" was in earlier use in biblical explication, creating ciphers, teaching reading, and—closest to its use at the clipping service—indexing.

25. Robert Luce, "The Clipping Bureau and the Library," 155.

26. A.G.L., "An American Idea," *Los Angeles Times*, 25 June 1899, 5.

27. "Facts about Newspaper Clippings: Great Demand for Articles from the New-York Times," *New York Times*, 27 Aug 1895, 5; "Modern Methods," *Clipping Collector*, May 1896, 57. Frank Burrelle, "Business from Press Clippings," *Printers' Ink*, 10 June 1896, 5; "The Clipping Business," *Clipping Collector*, June 1896, 66.

28. *Clipping Collector*, Mar 1896, 38. Anke te Heesen, "News, Paper, Scissors: Clippings in the Sciences and Arts Around 1920," *Things That Talk: Object Lessons from Art and Science*, ed. Lorraine Daston (New York: Zone Books, 2007) 307–8. Upton Sinclair, *The Brass Check: A Study of American Journalism* (Pasadena, Calif.: published by the author, 1919), 35–36.

29. Ida Husted Harper, ed., *History of Woman Suffrage*, vol. 5 (New York: National American Woman Suffrage Association, 1922), 287. See, for example, a report on mobilizing public opinion on the New York State Health Department, Edward A. Moree, "Public Health and Politics," *Annals of the American Academy of Political and Social Science*, 64, Mar 1916, 134–45.

30. Henry T. Williams and Sophia Johnson [Daisy Eyebright], *Household Hints and Recipes* (Boston: Peoples Publishing, 1884), 132.

31. "About Clipping Bureaus," 22–23.

32. "Back Numbers," *The Clipping Collector*, 1:4, Apr 1896, 49. Although the New York *Tribune* was one of the rare newspapers that published an index, starting in 1876, Burrelle's client either did not know of it or found it inadequate to his or her purposes. The *Herald* also had an index compiled by employee Robert Bligh, probably only for in-house use, which is now in the collection of the NYPL. Margherita Arlina Hamm, "Scraps and Scrap-Books," *Clipping Collector*, 1:4, Apr 1896, 43.

33. Robert Luce, "The Clipping Bureau and the Library," 153.

34. Charles R. Hambly, *The Practice Builder: A Treatise on the Conduct and Enlargement of a Dental Practice*, 12th ed. (Bradford, Pa.: American Dental Publishing, 1902), 288. Edwin

E. Slosson, "How to Keep Scraps," *The Science News-Letter*, 14:381, 28 July 1928, 53–54.

35. Carolyn Wells, *The Rest of My Life* (Philadelphia: Lippincott, 1937), 239–40.

36. Elbert Hubbard, *A Little Journey to the Atlas Press Clipping Bureau* (Aurora, N.Y.: Roycrofters, 1915), 9. Thomas Weaver, of the *Hartford Post*, in "The Editorial Shears," *Texas Siftings*, 5:43, 27 Feb 1886, 5. Walter Benjamin's similar characterization of the scholar disassembling a book into a box of index cards, sorting them into a new order, and writing another book from them (discussed in the Introduction) unlike Hubbard, at least assigns equal value to the books at each end of the process.

37. "Henry Romeike," *Who's Who in America,* ed. John William Leonard (Marquis Who's Who, 1901), 966.

38. E. W. Gurley, *Scrap-books*, 5–6.

INDEX

Made in the USA
Columbia, SC
15 May 2017